WITHOUT
STOPPING

45

Ecco Press Books by Paul Bowles

The Delicate Prey (Stories)

A Distant Episode (Stories)

Jean Genet in Tangier by Mohamed Choukri
(Translation)

Points in Time (Fiction)

Their Heads Are Green and Their Hands Are Blue
(Essays)

Up Above the World (Novel)

Without Stopping (Autobiography)

About Paul Bowles

An Invisible Spectator by Christopher Sawyer-Lauçanno
(Biography)

WITHOUT
STOPPING

An Autobiography by
Paul Bowles

THE ECCO PRESS
NEW YORK

First published by The Ecco Press in 1985
26 West 17th Street, New York, N.Y. 10011
Published simultaneously in Canada by
Penguin Books Canada Ltd.
2801 John Street
Markham, Ontario, Canada L3R 1B4

PRINTED IN THE UNITED STATES OF AMERICA

Library of Congress Cataloging in Publication Data

Bowles, Paul, 1910-
Without Stopping.

Reprint. Originally published; New York; Putnam, 1972.
Includes index.
1. Bowles, Paul, 1910—   —Biography. 2. Authors,
American—20th century—Biography. I. Title.
PS3552. 0874Z5   1985   818'.5409   B   85-10271
ISBN 0-88001-267-6

WITHOUT
STOPPING

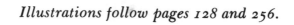

Illustrations follow pages 128 and 256.

I

Kneeling on a chair and clutching the gilded top rung of its back, I stared at the objects on the shelves of the cabinet. To the left of the gold clock was an old pewter tankard. When I had looked at it for a while, I said the word "mug" aloud. It looked like my own silver mug at home, from which I drank my milk. "Mug," I said again, and the word sounded so strange that I continued to say it, again and again, until I found myself losing touch with its meaning. This astonished me; it also gave me a vague feeling of unease. How could "mug" not mean mug?

The room was very quiet. I was alone in that part of the house. Suddenly the gold clock chimed four times. As soon as the last stroke was stilled, I realized that something important was happening. I was four years old, the clock had struck four, and "mug" meant mug. Therefore I was I, I was there, and it was that precise moment and no other. A satisfying new experience, to be able to say all this with certainty.

This was Uncle Edward's house in Exeter, next door to the Unitarian church, where he was the minister. For me the place already had a legendary aspect, since both Mother and Uncle Fred had spent their secondary school years there, he at Phillips Exeter and she at Robinson Female Seminary. Mysteriously, whenever she mentioned the name of her school, she laughed, yet if she spoke of Phillips Academy, it was almost with reverence. "I've already entered you," she told me, and this was disturbing insofar as I gave it any thought.

Now Mother was in the hospital just outside the town; when

Daddy arrived from New York, he took me aside and with more than his usual asperity said: "Your mother is a very sick woman, and it's all because of you, young man. Remember that."

I was bewildered and resentful. How could I have had anything to do with her illness? But already I took for granted his constant and unalloyed criticism. His mere presence meant misery; it was one of the inalterables of existence.

I went with Aunt Jen to visit Mother, carrying along two cookies that I had been allowed to shape and bake. They were grimy and inedible, but she laughed and ate them. Later, when we were back in New York, I asked her why it was my fault that she had been sick.

"Oh, my dear! Daddy didn't mean that. You see, you had a very hard time coming into this world. Most babies come in right side up, but you somehow came upside down. And you weighed eight and a half pounds." This did not explain very much, but it reduced my sense of guilt.

The following year there occurred a phenomenon similar to the one involving the mug, but this time I was forewarned and savored the sensation voluptuously, letting myself float in total awareness of the moment. It was at the Happy Hollow Farm. I sat on the swing under one of the giant maples, bathing in the smells and sounds of a summer afternoon in Massachusetts. And I let myself fall backward to hang with my head down, almost touching the grass, and stayed that way. Then a clock in the house struck four. It began all over again. I am I, it is now, and I am here. The swing moved a little, and I saw the green depths of maple leaves and, farther out, the unbelievably blue sky.

The Happy Hollow Farm was a 165-acre tract of forested hillsides. A meadow perhaps half a mile wide ran through the middle of the land, and there was a cold, deep-running brook that one could hear gurgling in the marsh grass and rushes before one saw it. The house dated from the end of the eighteenth century; it was the classical square, two-story clapboard building, white, with green blinds. It stood back from the road on a rise, partially hidden by four enormous maples. There was an ell at the north end of the house, which contained the kitchen and pantries and the hired man's room. Beyond that came the exciting part of the farm, a series of dark and rustic sheds that extended all the way back to the springhouse. The place smelled of the freshly cut wood that was stacked there, of mildewed burlap, apples, damp earth, and of a whole mysterious gamut of time-encrusted things. Whenever I was found exploring the dim recesses of the sheds, I was told to go outdoors. There in the sunlight I would pretend to be occupied. I could tell by the cadence of the voices coming from inside the house when it was safe to wander back into the sheds.

At the Happy Hollow Farm lived Grampa and Gramma Winnewisser with their two sons. Grampa had bought the property as a kind of retirement project after an accident with a runaway horse had made it difficult for him to walk. Up until that time he had owned the only "department" store in Bellows Falls, Vermont.

Grampa's first name was August. He was a moody and violent man, subject to sudden surges of temper, when his voice shook the house with bellowed imprecations in German and English. He had no sympathy with anything that required organization, like religions, societies, and governments. According to him, any group claiming to have a common purpose or belief existed only for the mystification and exploitation of its members. Notably exempt from his condemnation were the Freemasons, whom he held in respect, perhaps because he was one himself. I remember his calling my three small cousins and me in from play in order to ask us if we thought there was a god. I, who was under the impression that God was one of the things adults had invented in order to manage children more easily, carefully refrained from answering. But the three little cousins, having been told by their respective mothers that God was real, replied in the affirmative. This was Grampa's signal to explode. "Pah! There's no god. It's a lot of nonsense. Don't you believe it."

He was going on in this vein when my Aunt Ulla came in. With the clumsiness typical of the adult who consistently underestimates the intelligence of small children, she remonstrated with him, saying: "Oh, Father! Not in front of the children, please!"

He's right, I thought, even more firmly convinced. It *is* a lie. They don't believe it. Why should we believe it?

Right or wrong, he was a frightening man. His nose had been disfigured by an inexplicable operation he had suffered as a youth at the hands of his father. He had shattered the bones at the bridge of the nose with a hammer. It was not the strangely shaped and discolored nose which made him frightening, however, so much as the fact that he himself had performed the same operation on both his sons, so that they both had broken noses like his. This bothered me very much, particularly because my mother often spent twenty minutes or a half hour at a time rubbing my nose firmly between her thumb and forefinger. Young bones and cartilage, she told me, were malleable, and you had to be very careful what shape they took. I wondered privately if I were slated to be the next victim of the hammer.

Throughout his life Grampa's interest lay in the prices of consumer goods. He knew the exact price of each grade of every object you could name, wholesale and retail, and how much it had varied from the prices of former years. Since he had spent his active life studying price lists, he continued to do it after he sold the store.

On the rare occasions when his sister Fanny came to visit, Grampa seemed really happy. Retreating into the privacy of their own language, which no one else understood, the two would sit until nearly dawn drinking beer and eating rye bread garnished with Limburger cheese and onions. At these times Grampa seemed to have become another, totally different man, transformed by the mysterious language and its accompanying gestures into an urbane stranger.

The choice of names for his three daughters was solely his: he called them Emma, Rena, and Ulla. (They all married men with sissy names, he once remarked, continuing with snide inflection: Guy! Claude! Harold!) But he had a favorite among his sons-in-law, and that was my Uncle Harold Danser, a clever young businessman and, one might almost guess it, the son of a department-store owner himself. Neither Uncle Guy nor my father was remotely interested in business; both of them failed wholly to appreciate Grampa's talent for figures. In fact, my father considered him slightly unbalanced, and dismissed the thought of him with a contemptuous shrug, which was easy inasmuch as he arranged his life in such a way as practically never to come into contact with him.

Gramma was the principal counterbalance to the latent emotional violence that often seemed about to engulf her family. I used to look at her and think: What a nice mother she would make. In her presence the world seemed acceptable. Difficulties never made her cynical or despairing, as they did the other members of the family. I had the impression that they, secretly craving disaster, were constantly on the lookout for signs of it. Gramma was strong, calm, and sunny, with no religious convictions, but Grampa's murky blasphemies offended her taste. "Why do you shout?" she would ask if he began one of his anti-Christian tirades. "Why can't you just say it?"

Even the sound of Gramma's voice comforted me. When I heard it, I felt that nothing bad could happen. But the frustration caused by Grampa's tyranny had made her subject to severe headaches. When one of these struck, the house was paralyzed. If her daughters were visiting the farm when she was brought low by such an attack, they would sit all day beside her bed, commiserating with her. Grampa was cruel, they said, to have shut her away like this in the country. But Gramma was not sorry for herself. It was not torture for her to live on the farm; it was merely hard work, and she was used to that. Like most New Englanders of her generation, she was very much aware of "nature" and was happy in proximity to it. When she died, much later, her children all whispered to one another that it was the fact of having been forced to live on the farm that had killed her.

My father had hoped to be a concert violinist, but expectedly his parents, considering this a highly impractical ambition, vetoed it with energy, whereupon he retaliated by having a nervous breakdown. His older brother was already studying dentistry, a fact doubtless instrumental in persuading him, once he was over his tantrum, to follow suit. He married at thirty, and I was born a little more than two years later, his only offspring. Until I was five, he was busy building up his practice; after that he always seemed to have too many patients.

The winters of these early years are largely hidden in the mists that obscure infantile memories. We lived in an old brownstone house of the classical model, that had been painted gray, and it had a formidable flight of steps leading from the sidewalk up to the front door. The first floor housed my father's laboratory. I remember the entrance hall as dark and uninviting; there was a smell of gas burners and hot metal in the air. The laboratory was forbidden territory, and its doors were always shut. A long flight of stairs led up to the office and reception room. Still another stairway had to be climbed before we were home, in the four-room apartment on the top floor.

I spent my days playing by myself in the house, except for the occasional hour when I was turned out into the backyard. It was a large flat plot of grass shut in by a very high wooden fence. There was no way of seeing anything beyond the yard. However, on one side there were nine windows, looking out on me like nine eyes, and from any one of them could come a sudden shout of disapproval. If I stood still and watched the clock that was always placed in the window so I would know when the hour was up, I heard taps on a third-story window and saw my mother making gestures exhorting me to move around and play. But if I began to gallop around the yard, my father would call from the second story: "Calm down, young man!" Or his receptionist would wave and cry: "Your Daddy says to stop making that noise!"

In that house I had a toy chest. By Daddy's edict, everything had to be already in the chest when he came upstairs at six in the evening. Whatever remained outside would be confiscated and I never would see it again. I began the packing-up process at five o'clock; by quarter to six I always had it done and the lid shut. After that I could read until dinner if I liked, since books could be returned to the bookcase quickly. Writing and drawing, however, which were my favorite form of play, could not be resumed until the following day. My mother always claimed that I had taught myself to read, and very likely I did, since I can't remember a period when the printed word did not make its corresponding sound in my head as I looked at it. I still have a little notebook with stories about animals, invented by me and printed in pencil, each one carefully dated at the end, and the year is 1915, which means that I was four years old when I wrote them. My Grandmother Bowles visited us. I overheard her telling my mother, exactly as though I weren't present, that precocity should not be encouraged; she foresaw disaster unless I were somehow brought into contact with other children, so that I could "grow in other directions." I did not know what she meant, but I immediately determined not to accept other directions. "I warn you, Rena, you'll rue the day," she said, and I looked across at her and thought: she's trying to break in.

Among the games I kept stacked in the toy chest was one which consisted of several dozen cards, each bearing the likeness of a person one might conceivably have met on the streets of a big city in America in the 1890's. It ought to have been called Civil Status: if you drew a minister or a doctor you took three counters, if a lawyer or a banker, two, if a barber, one, while if your card turned out to bear the picture of a wife beater or an assassin, you were required to pay in three. All this seemed logical enough. But there were other neutral cards which, involving neither payment nor collection, struck me as superfluous and thus suspect. Why had they been included in the deck? They did not look neutral at all; they looked malignant (as indeed did all of the characters, the honored ones only slightly less than the others). These questionable people included an alderman, a druggist, and a tall formidable creature, wearing eyeglasses and dressed in a black cloak, labeled "Strong-minded Woman." I would study the picture of her as she advanced frowning along a street under trees. To me she was the most evil-looking of the whole lot.

"Mother, what's a strong-minded woman?"

"Well, your Grandmother Bowles is a strong-minded woman."

"Why is it bad?"

"Bad? It's not bad at all. It's very good."

"But why doesn't she pay anything, then? And why does she look so awful? Look at her!"

I was glad whenever it was Mother who drew the card.

Ostensibly to distinguish my father's parents from Grampa and Gramma, I was taught to call them Daddypapa and Daddymama. As if they had not been forever separated by the atmospheres of their respective houses! The farm was fully inhabited; the family left no emptinesses. But going into the Bowles house was like stepping inside a forest. There in the dimness and silence Daddymama and Daddypapa were sitting reading their books, he in his den upstairs and she in her study downstairs. The kitchen was cut off from the rest of the house, and I would go there and talk with old Mary, who had been doddering around the kitchen for many years, and her niece Lucy. They paid attention to everything I said, and they never offered suggestions for my improvement. But inevitably I would be sent for. Daddymama, sitting beside the fireplace, would remove her pince-nez and smile at me with an expression both benevolent and disapproving. I knew she loved me; I also understood perfectly that she was not disapproving of me myself, but of my mother in me. This seemed natural: since Mother was not of her family, she would feel hostility toward her. What I resented was the fact that Mother was afraid of Daddymama, dreaded being with her, and occasionally became so ill in her presence that she had to go to bed. But these things were natural phenomena, like the sequence of the seasons, and certainly did not preoccupy me. I could see that the world of grown-ups was one of distrust and intrigue, and I felt fortunate to be a child, so as not to have to take part in it.

Just before the War of 1914 Daddymama had gone to Paris and returned with very impressive clothes. I remember her pleasure in pointing out what she called the "exquisite workmanship" to the ladies who visited her. When I asked Mother the inevitable question: "Why don't you go to Paris and get things, too?" she merely laughed. I pressed her for an answer, and she said: "Mercy, I don't want Paris clothes! Besides, it'll be a long time before your father'll be able to send me to Paris. Daddymama was very fortunate to have gone when she did."

Daddypapa and Daddymama were like everyone else who lived on West Church Street in Elmira, save for the fact that neither of them had any religious affiliations. Daddypapa said that religion was a very good thing for those who wanted it. For Daddymama it was a private matter; she read Theosophical texts. Undoubtedly her thinking was influenced by her sister Mary and her brother Charles, who were both immersed in what they called the occult sciences.

Aunt Mary lived in Watkins Glen in a big old house known as Holden Hall, and Uncle Charles had a large property at Glenora, nine miles up the shore of Seneca Lake. Thus the three were able to see one another often and compare notes on their respective readings and meditations. Uncle Charles was an exponent of yoga, and at some point he convinced Daddypapa that proper breathing enabled one to inhale prana along with the air. This was surprising inasmuch as Daddypapa was not given to esoteric interpretations; however, he immediately decided that what I needed was more prana. (He even went so far as to suggest that prana could take the place of food when one was hungry.) I was obliged to learn to breathe by stopping and unstopping my nostrils with my fingers. This struck me as arbitrary and wholly absurd, like all the other things invented by the family in order to make my life more unpleasant.

Very early I understood that I would always be kept from doing what I enjoyed and forced to do that which I did not. The Bowles family took it for granted that pleasure was destructive, whereas engaging in an unappealing activity aided in character formation. Thus I became an expert in the practice of deceit, at least insofar as general mien and facial expressions were concerned. I could not make myself lie, inasmuch as for me the word and its literal meaning had supreme importance, but I could feign enthusiasm for what I disliked and, even more essential, hide whatever enjoyment I felt. Obviously this did not always give the desired results, but it often helped to deflect attention from me, and this was already a great victory. For attention meant "discipline"; each person was eager to try out his own favorite system on me and study the results. Once Daddymama had a woman come and talk with me for two hours. She was a nice woman; I felt at ease with her and conversed as freely as any other child of six. At the end, without waiting for me to go out of the room, she turned to Daddymama and said: "He has a very old soul, almost too old. You can only wait and see." It seems there never was a time when the Bowles family were not wont to sit discussing my defects. "It's not natural," was the commonest introductory phrase. "It's not natural for a child that age to spend all his time reading." "It's not natural for a child to want to be alone." I even heard Daddymama remark one day to Mother: "It's not natural for a child of his age to have such thick lips." (This I resented more deeply than her customary criticisms, since I knew I had my mother's mouth. If I was a monster, then Mother also was a monster, and why didn't Daddymama tell her so outright, instead of using me as the weapon?)

Daddymama had a crooked, sardonic smile, by which she made it clear that she accepted what one said, but with certain strict reservations whose terms she kept to herself. Mother said: "Your grandmother Bowles is the most *suspicious* woman I've ever seen. And your father is just like her. Don't ever let yourself get to be like them. It's terrible! It poisons everything."

Of my four grandparents, Daddypapa was the one who most interested me. He had mystery; with his bushy white mustache and his eyeglasses that clipped to the bridge of his nose, he sat alone in his den all day reading. Occasionally he reached for his penknife and cut an article from a magazine or newspaper. He had a filing cabinet full of clippings, most of them about the "Amerind," which was what he called the natives of the Western Hemisphere. The den was stuffed with books: bookshelves covered the walls up to the ceiling, fully a third of the volumes in French. At some point in his life Daddypapa had decided to learn French so as to be able to read Hugo and Dumas and Balzac in the original. Later, when he was in his seventies, he took up Spanish and continued to study and read that language for the rest of his life. He was a fanatical cat fancier and had decorated his big desk with framed photographs, not of people, but of cats he had known.

I would enter the den, he would greet me genially in French and motion to me to sit by his desk, and on the desk I would see a whole collection of pictures and objects which he had brought out of the cupboards and drawers, with the intention of showing them to me the next time I came into the room.

Daddypapa had fought in the Civil War, but he refused to call it that; for him it was either "the war" or "the War of the Rebellion." He was proud of having been in every state of the Union. "There were some years when I never slept twice in the same town," he told me. The perfect life, I thought; I too would collect mysterious Indian objects on my way and tales from each part of the country.

We never stayed long in Elmira but continued after a few days to Glenora, on Seneca Lake, where Daddypapa had three separate properties, each with a house ready to live in. It never occurred to me to wonder why he should keep three houses in the same community; I suppose originally he meant to have one for each of his sons and one for himself. About the end of the First World War Uncle Shirley took his family to Los Angeles, and Daddypapa sold Red Rough, which left Horseshoe Cabin and the Boat House.

Seneca is a long, narrow glacial lake. High shale cliffs edge its southern end. The Boat House had three levels: the boat shed, where the slips for the boats were; the kitchen and servant's room; and finally the living quarters at the top, full of Navajo rugs and blankets and with big Chinese lanterns hanging from the crossbeams. The west wall of each story had been left unbuilt, and the rough shale stuck out into the rooms. Two more flights of stairs had to be climbed before you came to terra firma, and then you were in the woods. It was a dark wood, but one free of undergrowth because its hemlocks had been shedding their needles for many years. A thick blanket of them padded the ground everywhere. Overnight strange things could push up through the blanket: puffballs, Dutchman's-pipes, fungi like slabs of orange flesh, colonies of spotted toadstools, and best of all the deadly *Amanita,* which I was taught early to distinguish. I would seek out an *Amanita* and stand staring down at it in fascination and terror. There at my feet grew death itself, only waiting for the decisive contact.

At night there were skunks and owls abroad, and the unceasing song of the katydids almost covered the patterned murmur of the waves against the cliffs. It was good to wake up in the night and hear that music all around me in the air, while the embers in the fireplace slowly settled and died.

Two boats were moored down in the shed: a large open motor launch and a cabin cruiser with accommodations for eight. This was the *Aloha*, which Uncle Charles had bought in New York and piloted through the Hudson River and the Erie Canal to Geneva, at the foot of the lake. The *Aloha* had a toilet that flushed and a galley with sink and stove, so that real meals, not just picnic fare, could be served aboard. Being good New Englanders, the family felt that it should be taken out only when there were guests to entertain, and accordingly used the open motorboat for everyday rides and picnics. Daddypapa never went on picnics. He called them "pleasure exertions" and was content to sit reading all day and eat alone at the Boat House. On the beach outside the boat shed there were two rowboats and a canoe, kept under tarpaulin. Eventually I was allowed to go out alone in the flat-bottomed rowboat and finally in the canoe.

One of my pastimes was the invention of lists of place-names; I considered them stations on an imaginary railway, for which I would then draw a map and prepare a timetable. In Glenora the idea occurred to me to carry the fantasy partially into reality: I printed the proper names on small slips of paper and deposited them, each one held down by a slab of shale, at what seemed the proper spot for each, along the paths in the woods. As I had expected, as soon as my father caught sight of them, he came to me and demanded that I go immediately and retrieve every piece of paper. Daddypapa then suggested that they be allowed to remain until the following day. Pulling at his mustache and looking amused, he added that the name I had given the edge of the creek (dry these several weeks owing to a much-discussed drought) was Notninrivo.

Surprisingly, my father chuckled and turned to me. "So you called the creek Notninrivo, eh? That's pretty good."

"What's that?" said Mother.

"Nothing in the river," he explained.

This was their own invention, crass and ridiculous. "That's not what it means," I objected.

Now Daddy's face became hostile. "What do you mean, that's not what it means? What does it mean, then?"

I hung my head. It seemed impossible to explain that Notninrivo was merely the name of the preceding station spelled backward. "You wouldn't understand," I said.

"Will you listen to the conceited little rotter?" he cried, beside himself. "Let's get to the bottom of this! He says the word means something else. I want to know what!"

He seized me and shook me. I hung my head still more.

"For heaven's sake, Claude, let the child alone," said Daddy-mama. "He hasn't done anything wrong."

"It's all affectation!" he snapped. "It's just a bid for attention." Even as he said the words, I was aware of the awful irony in the situation. He went on shaking me. "Come on, what does it mean?"

I shook my head. I wanted to say: "I'll never tell you."

Instead, I waited a moment and finally said: "Nothing."

He let go of me, disgusted, having proved his point. Shortly afterward I ran up into the woods and gathered all the station signs, starting with the one at the end of the bridge over the creek for Notninrivo and another one by a rotten tree stump a little farther along the path, this one for the town of O'Virninton. I had to destroy them in secret, for fear my father might discover the meaning of Notninrivo, which he must definitely never know. I carried the scraps of paper to a hidden cove down the shore and burned them. Then I ground the ashes into the wet shingle and piled several flat rocks on top of the spot.

When I was a baby, Max Eastman and his sister Crystal stayed at Glenora each summer. Mother had always had enormous admiration for Max. "Handsome as a prince and bright as a whip," she said of him. "And knows it," added Daddy sourly. For more than twenty years the Eastmans stayed away from Glenora. (In 1937 Max came back for a short stay, and I saw him then. At that time I was a Stalinist sympathizer, which, considering the fact that he was the most vocal Trotskyist of the period, made an exchange of opinion inevitable. We got onto the subject of Kautsky, Kamenev, and Zinoviev. It was obvious that I knew nothing save what I had read in party publications. Daddy sat listening, an expression of mingled amusement and disdain on his face. Presently he turned to Max and said: "Listen to that, will you? You'd think he'd been brought up in the slums of a factory town." Max laughed. "No, I wouldn't, Claude. I'd think he was the son of a Long Island dentist.")

Daddymama had a friend named Dorothy Baldwin who often came to Glenora. Dorothy used bay rum as perfume, insisting that she preferred the scent to anything on the market. "She was always unstable," said Daddymama, "but now she's simply degenerated into an out-and-out radical." "I feel sorry for the poor girl," Mother declared. "She's disappointed in life, that's all." Dorothy didn't seem disappointed to me; she seemed very sure of herself. One afternoon she asked me if I wanted to take a walk with her. I liked her, and we started out.

We had not gone far up the road before she turned into the waist-high vegetation and began flailing her way through it. "The path is farther on," I told her. She grinned at me. "We're going to make our own path," she said. "It's no fun to follow somebody else's." We helped each other get free of brambles every few minutes and made very little progress. At one point I plunged ahead of her and was suddenly attacked by wasps. We got out the way we had gone in. When we returned to the Boat House, I discovered eleven stings.

After Dorothy had left, the family turned to me as one person and expressed the hope that I had learned something from the escapade. Then they formulated the lesson: it was safer to stay on paths, literally and figuratively. The moralizing had its effect on me, albeit in the opposite direction from the one they intended. I knew that Dorothy and I had accepted implicitly the dangers of the walk and that it was not her fault that the wasps had stung me. Vaguely I understood that laws were made to keep you from doing what you wanted to do. Furthermore, I understood that for my family the prohibition itself was the supreme good, because it entailed the sublimation of personal desire. Their attempt to impose this concept was only one of numerous strategies for bolstering their power over me. They had an idea of how they wanted me to be; but insofar as I resembled it, I should remain subjugated to them, or so it seemed to me then. So, secretly I rejected every suggestion while pretending to accept it.

Mother had a thick green book, stuffed with clippings and notes, which she generally kept with her, even when she sat crocheting, and which she consulted several times a day. It was called *Child Psychology;* for some reason I could not fathom, she did not want me to look at it, and so it was not put out with the other books. The author was a Dr. Riker, a man for whose opinions Daddy had only contempt. There were passionate arguments between them over the value and application of the doctor's ideas, for their theories on child rearing were antithetical. Mother believed in showing infinite patience; Daddy was for unremitting firmness. This he called common sense. "It stands to reason," he maintained. "A kid will always go as far as you let him." Both of them, however, overlooked the fact that at the age of five I had never yet even spoken to another child or seen children playing together. My idea of the world was still that of a place inhabited exclusively by adults.

II

In the early years of the century a certain Dr. Fletcher announced that it was absolutely necessary to chew each mouthful of food forty times, regardless of its consistency. This action, he claimed, made it possible to form a bolus. The practice was known as Fletcherization. My father explained it to me in detail many times, beginning when I was five, and I was obliged to use the method at table. I chewed diligently, but sometimes swallowed without meaning to, before I had counted to forty.

"Fletcherize, young man!" he shouted, and at the same instant I felt the sting of a large linen table napkin as he flicked it across my face. Often it caught me in the eye, which, being painful, was even more humiliating. "Keep chewing. Keep chewing. You haven't made your bolus yet." By this time I was so confused that I no longer knew whether I was chewing or swallowing.

"What'd I tell you? I told you *not* to swallow!"

"I couldn't help it." Sometimes I still had the bolus in my mouth, for I learned to hold it under my tongue while the involuntary spasm of swallowing took place, and then I would open my mouth to prove that I hadn't really disobeyed. This was always considered an "impertinence" and was followed by fresh recriminations.

I would beg Mother to let me eat in the kitchen early, so as not to have to undergo the ordeal of sitting at table. This she never allowed unless I was sick. To fall ill was thus a great temptation; half my early maladies were pretexts for lying in bed and eating alone. One night when I did have a high fever, Daddy stood at the foot of my bed with his hands in his pockets. He said to Mother: "You know, I think he likes to be sick."

"Yes," I thought, "I do. And the best part is, I *am* sick, and you can't forbid it." I regularly settled into protracted illnesses with a shiver of voluptuousness at the prospect of the stretches of privacy that lay ahead.

In the summer of 1916, when I was five, my parents moved into the house on De Grauw Avenue. After the Glenora season was over, they took me back to the Happy Hollow Farm and left me there. When they were all installed, Grampa went down to New York to spend a week with them in the new house. He returned and described it to me, making his eyes round with admiration. "Wait till you see it. It's a very fine house," he said. I believed him, but I did not look forward to living in it, because Mother and Daddy would be there.

Nevertheless, the house impressed me. Everything glistened with newness. The floors were so shiny and slippery that after a few falls I pretended the open areas were deep water; my task was to get from rug to rug without stepping into the water.

The house was on "the Hill," which was then a forested ridge above the town of Jamaica, Long Island. Here the newly laid streets came to sudden ends in the woods. At the beginning the land around the house was all unspoiled, so that we heard many birds singing in the early mornings. Then Judge Twombley built a house on the east. Two or three years later men came and cut down the trees across the street. Mother decided that she no longer enjoyed living there. The destruction of the trees was her bitterest complaint. There were further disadvantages, such as the fact that the house was one of those two-family structures that look like one-family houses, the other part being occupied by the young architect who had designed it. The young architect had a wife with whom Mother seldom agreed. Another drawback to the place was the elevation on which it had been built; thirty-five steps had to be climbed in order to get up to it from the street below. However, at the beginning there were robins and dogwood all around—even thrushes and violets—and it was certainly pleasanter for me than the dark apartment with its empty yard below.

We had a housekeeper named Hannah, a wonderfully calm Finnish woman who wore her eyeglasses on a chain that wound into a little reel pinned beside her collar. Hannah's husband was an official of the Socialist Party, and she became increasingly involved with his work and eventually left us, although for several years she occasionally came and stayed with me at night when my parents went out. Helping Hannah was Anna, also a Finn, but one who had just arrived in the United States. I did not particularly like her, but that was because I heard only adverse criticism of her. She was young and brash, she sang as she worked, and she made unnecessary noises with pails and mops.

"Aunt Adelaide's" was a magic phrase; it meant not only the person but the place. She was Daddy's sister, a librarian working with Annie Carroll Moore, who was the head of the Children's Section at the Fifth Avenue Public Library. Seeing Aunt Adelaide meant being recognized as a person who really existed, rather than being treated as a captured animal of uncertain reactions. That was pleasant and relaxing; besides, she lived in a Japanese apartment in Greenwich Village, full of strange objects and wonderful smells. Sometimes Miss Moore was in the apartment among the screens and lanterns and flickering candlelight; her presence gave the occasion an unmistakable air of celebration, low-keyed and mysterious, the very essence of festivity in its conscious exclusion of the outside world. During those early years the visits to Aunt Adelaide's provided the high points of life in the city.

"Your father's a devil," Gramma used to tell me. "He's impossible," Mother's sisters assured her again and again. At mealtimes his irascibility reached its peak. He insisted on knowing the ingredients and the preparation of each dish, and whenever he had time, he stood in the kitchen and supervised the cooking. If the food turned out to be not exactly as he wanted it, he had a temper fit, slammed down his napkin, and rushed to the bathroom to take one of his digestive remedies. A temper fit made him ill until at least the next day; it usually gave whoever else was at the table indigestion as well. His rages came like a bolt of lightning, even as the food went down his throat, and were the more inexplicable since Mother had studied cooking at Simmons in Boston and was an expert. Throughout my childhood she herself baked all the bread we ate. Any other bread was "synthetic," and Daddy would not touch it.

The new house made it possible for me to be alone much of the time, since I had the third floor all to myself. I could go upstairs and shut my door, leaving the sounds of wrangling behind. Quickly I began to invent more timetables. I established the routes by walking along and naming the rocks and bushes as I went, without, however, tagging them as I had done at Glenora. For there were other children around, and my intuitions warned me that everything must be hidden from them; they were potential enemies. I printed the lists of place-names in notebooks when I got home: Shirkingsville, 645th Street, Clifton Junction, Snakespiderville, Hiss, El Apepal, Norpath Kay.

Soon I invented a planet with landmasses and seas. The continents were Ferncawland, Lanton, Zaganokworld, and Araplaina. I drew maps of each and gave them mountain ranges, rivers, cities, and railways. All this was interrupted by my entry into school. In the autumn of 1917 they cut off my hair and took me to see the principal of the Model School. He made me read aloud to him for what seemed a long time. Then he had me assigned to the second grade, for, as he said, although I could print very fast, I didn't yet know how to write in script, and my arithmetic was nonexistent. It was fortunate that Dr. McLaughlin did not start me higher, since I was already the youngest in the class, a situation which could only make things more difficult for me.

School was no good. It took me one day to discover that the world of children was a world of unremitting warfare. But since I had suspected this all along, it did not come as a shock. I accepted the group beatings as part of the pattern and stealthily launched punitive attacks on loners who had got separated from the pack. This usually resulted in a permanent personal hatred for me on the part of the victim, inasmuch as I sharpened stones beforehand in order to draw blood. For a boy to participate in a mass attack against me was legitimate, but for me to ambush him later from behind was apparently unforgivable.

"Now he knows what it's like," Daddy once said to Mother, a satisfied grin on his face, when I had come in dirty and bruised. "This is what he needs to bring him down to earth."

In such instances I could only look at him, but since I firmly believed that I *had* to win in the struggle between us or I should be hopelessly lost, it seemed to me that it was merely a question of holding out.

One evening from up in my room I heard music downstairs. They had bought a phonograph and were playing Tchaikowsky's Fourth. This is the first time that I recall hearing music of any sort. At the beginning I was not allowed to touch either machine or records, but after a few months had gone by, I was playing it much more than they were. Soon I began buying my own records. The first one was "At the Jazz Band Ball," played by the Original Dixieland Jazz Band. When Daddy heard it, he berated Mother. "Why do you let him buy trash like that?"

"He plays the other music, too," she said.

"I don't want any more of that stuff brought into this house. Do you hear me, young man?"

As always, I let my face rather than my words express my emotion. "Of course," I said curtly. After that I bought military bands playing Latin-American pieces.

Daddy continued to buy records. He had Dr. Karl Muck directing the Boston Symphony. ("A Hun. I don't know why they leave him there.") He had Galli-Curci singing Rossini and Bellini. ("Homely as a hedge fence," said Mother.) He had Josef Hofmann playing "Venezia e Napoli." ("So conceited he doesn't even suspect there's anyone else in the world." Daddy had been to a Hofmann recital.)

My teacher Miss Crane and I did not like each other. I began by refusing to sing. No threats could make me open my mouth. I was marked "Deficient in Class Singing" regularly on my monthly report card, not to mention being given the lowest possible mark for Effort. In Proficiency and Deportment I always got top grades; fortunately my stubbornness was put down to a lack of effort rather than to purposeful sabotage. To avenge myself I hit on an idea which would prove to Miss Crane that I was capable of doing my work correctly, yet which at the same time would anger her. I wrote everything perfectly, only backwards. My papers were consistently marked with a zero. Finally Miss Crane made me stay after school. "What does this mean?" she demanded; her voice was trembling with rage. "What do you mean by this?"

"By what?"

She shook the papers in the air.

"There are no mistakes," I told her smugly.

"I'm going to call your mother," she said. "In my day they'd have known what to do with a little boy like you, I can tell you that." She shoved the sheaf of papers into a manila envelope and locked them away in a drawer.

The feud ended when Mother spoke with me seriously about it, simulating anxiety as to what Daddy would say if he were to hear about my behavior. "I don't know what's got into you," she complained. I did not know, either, but I felt a vague menace on all sides.

Later things went more smoothly. Once I had left Miss Crane behind I had a clean slate or imagined I did. In fact, Miss Crane went all over the school, warning my future teachers about me.

The day the war ended, no classes were held. They told us to go home and get combs. Back in school we were coached in the melody of "Marching Through Georgia." When we knew it fairly well, we were given toilet paper to put over the combs and instructed to sing the syllable "ta." There was a great amount of confusion, which every child did his utmost to augment and prolong, but finally we found ourselves marching down the street, always to "Georgia," with people smiling and waving flags at us. None of it made any sense, but I enjoyed it because no one noticed whether I was singing or not.

I was seven, and my second teeth were growing in crooked. "Your father's going to take you to the city tomorrow to see Dr. Waugh," Mother told me. So began the semiweekly visits to the corner of Fifth Avenue and Forty-seventh Street, where the orthodontist had his offices. Since my case involved broadening of both the upper and lower jaw, the visits continued until exactly ten years later, when the last bands were removed, and the enamel on certain of the teeth was found to have been pitted, possibly as a result of the treatment.

"Orthodontia's made great strides," Daddy told me. "If your mother or I'd had crooked teeth, they'd have yanked them out."

"It was like the Dark Ages," Mother said, shuddering.

"I just want you to know how lucky you are, that's all," he warned me.

Lucky had nothing to do with the way it felt to have a wide platinum band cemented around every tooth, each one with an interior and exterior screw attached to it, and four gold arches being held in place by the screws. Tuesdays and Fridays I went and had the screws tightened a little. The pain this caused lasted two or three days, generally until just before the next tightening, so that there were very few days in the year when I could eat without wincing. All this metal in my mouth made it necessary for me to take precautions not to let blows catch me in the face. When they did, it was disastrous. The only bright spot in the tooth straightening was the fact of missing school two afternoons a week in order to go to Dr. Waugh's. The next year, when I was eight, I began going alone to the appointments. This delighted me, because everyone was scandalized by the idea of allowing so small a child absolute freedom to go around New York City by himself.

"But don't you just worry yourself sick?" insisted Aunt Ulla. "I'd be a nervous wreck every time, until he got back."

"Oh, I get a little uneasy sometimes, of course," said Mother.

Aunt Ulla turned to me. "Your mother's got bats in the belfry."

"But what could happen to me?" I demanded. "Why should anything happen to me?"

Mother was quite right; nothing ever did. And I saw more and learned more going by myself than I ever would have if a grownup had been along. About once a month I stopped by the Public Library to see Miss Moore. She always had time to talk for a few minutes, and she generally gave me a book to add to my growing collection. Often she had the authors dedicate them to me beforehand. Hugh Lofting wrote a whole page in the front of *The Story of Doctor Dolittle* and embellished it with drawings, as did Henrik Willem van Loon in *A Short History of Discovery*, who drew me a portrait of himself smoking a pipe. She had Carl Sandburg inscribe his *Rootabaga Stories* for me, too.

The winter when I was in the third grade there occurred an epidemic of Spanish influenza. We all caught it, including Aunt Adelaide, but whereas Daddy, Mother, and I got well, Aunt Adelaide's case was complicated by pneumonia and pleurisy, so that she died. The news was given me by Mother in such a way that the very memory of Aunt Adelaide became an obscenity, and I could not mention her name for a good seven years. Mother said: "Your Aunt Adelaide has gone away. You'll never see her again." To my involuntary: "Where? Why not?" she gave no answer but turned and walked out of the room. I understood that Aunt Adelaide was dead and felt a blind rage which, needing an object, fastened itself upon Mother for being the bearer of the news and, above all, for giving it to me in such a dishonest fashion.

Aunt Emma came to visit, all pale and trembly. About her the others said: "Emma's the temperamental one in the family." This was because she spent her time painting landscapes in oil and playing the piano; anyone "artistic" was always temperamental by definition. She took to bed, where she remained for a month with every sort of ailment. When she was better, we used to eat breakfast in her room. One Sunday morning early I heard loud laughter coming from what was called "the yellow bedroom." I ran in and saw Daddy in his pajamas, in bed with Aunt Emma, who was squealing and shrieking, while Mother leaned over the footboard, holding her side from having laughed too much. As I came in, he sprang up, crying: "Let's get to those buckwheat cakes." Then he went out of the room.

In a few minutes Mother called to me. "I want to speak to you. You mustn't tell anyone you saw Daddy in bed with Aunt Emma."

"I won't, but why?"

"They might think it was terrible."

"What do they care? It's none of their business, is it?"

"That's right. Of course it's none of their business. So don't tell anyone."

I wrote a rhyme and made a little book of it for Aunt Emma. Each page had half a stanza printed in its own color of wax crayon. The rhyme, which for some reason I could not fathom, made her laugh, ran:

> Poor Aunt Emma, sick in bed
> With an ice-cap on her head.
> Poor Aunt Emma, sick in bed!
> She's very sick, but she's not dead.

"Why'd you laugh?" I asked her.

"Because I liked the poem. You love your old aunt, don't you?"

"Of course." This embarrassed me, and I went out of the room.

I was brought up to consider burglars an ever-present menace. The house was always completely locked. Even Hannah and Anna did not have keys but had to be let in when they came to work in the morning. Strangely enough, I was allowed to have my own key to the front door, and I kept it in an ostrich-skin key-tainer. One afternoon I got home from school, shut the front door behind me, and immediately suspected that I was alone in the house. The silence was overpowering. I went to the kitchen; it was all shining and empty. Reluctantly I crept from one room to another, not even daring to call out anyone's name and finding no one, anywhere. I went into the living room and sat on the couch, my mind boiling with awful possibilities. Perhaps already a burglar had got in and was hiding in some corner. I decided I must look into every closet, under every bed, even, unfortunately, in the garret behind the trunks, because if I went on sitting and worrying about it, I should become much too afraid. I went through my parents' bedroom thoroughly, beating my hands against their clothes hanging in the closet to be certain no one was hiding there in the dark. Then I went into the guest room. There was an enormous old four-poster bed in there. I bent down to look under it and felt my heart explode. Someone lay under there, all bunched up. I was unable to stand up and run; I could only stare.

Suddenly the thing under there snorted and began to wriggle. Mother's head came toward me, and she crawled forth, flushed and laughing. "Hannah and Anna had to go out, so I thought I'd see what would happen if I disappeared, too," she said. "You wouldn't like it much, would you?"

She tried to joke with me about it; I could see that she found the episode amusing. I walked out of the room, clenching my fists, climbed upstairs to my own quarters, and shut the door. Fear naturally turns to anger; the anger did not go away for several days.

On the whole Mother and I got on well, principally, I suppose, because she would listen to whatever I read her and give me a considered opinion, even of a list of invented place-names on a timetable. From the time when I had been two she had always read to me at bedtime for a half hour; this continued until I was seven. Then we alternated reading to each other. I remember wanting to stay in Hawthorne's *Tanglewood Tales* and the combination of repugnance and fascination I felt at hearing the stories of Poe. I could not read them aloud; I had to undergo them. Mother's pleasant, low voice and thus, by extension, her personality took on the most sinister overtones as she read the terrible phrases. If I looked at her, I did not wholly recognize her, and that frightened me even more. It was in this period that I began to call out in my sleep and to enact lengthy meaningless rituals, eyes open but unconscious, while Mother and Daddy stood watching, afraid to speak or touch me. The following day I would have no recall of the nocturnal drama. On one occasion I went to bed in my own room and woke up a minute later to find myself lying in the big bed of the guest room, Daddy bending over me shaking his forefinger in front of my nose, repeating: "You stay in bed, young man."

The winter I reached the age of eight, it was decided that I should start taking music lessons. This involved buying a piano, and since Mother would have only a grand, it also meant rearranging furniture. After prolonged and embittered discussion the piano was purchased, and I was taken to Miss Chase. Tuesdays I had theory, solfeggio, and ear training, Fridays piano technique.

The piano lessons were conducted in private, and so I did not mind them. I enjoyed practicing: it guaranteed privacy for the time that I sat there. No one thought of disturbing me when I was working at the piano, as long as I was either playing the pieces I had learned or running up and down my scales. I discovered, however, that if I improvised even for a minute, Mother would appear in the doorway and say: "Is that your work? It doesn't sound like it to me." So I learned to finish my practicing first, before I allowed myself the luxury of being free to experiment. Fortunately the theory, solfeggio, and ear-training lessons were obligatory, for it was thanks to them that I learned musical notation and thus was able to write down my own musical ideas. Had they been optional, I should carefully have avoided them, since there were other pupils present, and for me it could only be boring to listen to their attempts and errors, just as it could only be embarrassing to have them hear my own.

In the same way as I learned to complete my practicing before I amused myself at the piano, I always finished my homework immediately and only then turned to the various daily chores I had set myself: I issued a daily newspaper of which I made one copy of four pages in pencil and crayon, I made daily entries in the diaries of several imaginary characters, I continued to add to the books of information on my fictitious world, and I obsessively drew houses (front elevation, no perspective), complete with lists of their prices and purchasers, for a gigantic real estate development. The newspaper featured a daily report on an improbable sea trip being made by correspondents; "Today we landed at Cape Catoche. Guess where we will be tomorrow?" I had a huge loose-leaf atlas, so heavy that I could barely lift it. I would carry it to the center of the room and open it out on the floor to sit, lost, looking down at its maps. New loose sheets arrived every little while; the book had to be unscrewed and the maps inserted in their proper place.

I filled in the diaries each day, the entries being in the third-person present tense, like newspaper headlines. "Viper comes to house begging chickens. Adele turns him out." Many of the characters had diseases and lost weight at an alarming rate. At some point in each diary I would get too intensely involved in the developments and begin to fill in several pages at a time. Once that started, it was impossible to go back to day-by-day entries. The speed of events grew, and soon the book would be full. There were two volumes about a woman named Bluey Laber Dozlen, who sails from an unidentified European country to Wen Kroy, where she immediately finds a huge sum of money and buys herself a self-steering automobile. During her first year she has many illnesses and recoveries, several marriages and divorces, and becomes a spy. During the second year she learns how to play bridge and smoke opium. Everyone else catches influenza and pneumonia and dies, but Bluey, blessed with excellent health, manages to survive and is last seen hiding out in Hong Kong from a vengeful housemaid she was once foolish enough to dismiss.

I also made (and sold to visiting members of the family when I could) monthly calendars which I embellished with designs in crayon. The calendars were accurate and legible enough, but the vertical and horizontal lines which formed the squares for the days were always curved instead of being straight. Naturally, everyone called my attention to this defect. I explained that I had tried again and again to draw straight lines, but they always came out crooked. Daddypapa suggested I use a ruler. I did not consider that a solution to the problem at all; it would be almost like getting another person to help me. Besides, I had practiced a good deal making curved lines that were parallel, and I rather liked them that way. My calendars continued to look as though they had been designed for the side of a globe.

At this time I began to write a protracted work called *Le Carré, An Opera in Nine Chapters.* It was, of course, not an opera at all, but a story with a few lyrics inserted. For these I composed melodies; I assumed the songs gave me the right to call it opera. The plot concerned two men who agree to exchange wives. To accomplish this, each man must so lower himself in his wife's esteem that she divorces him. When the exchange has been effected, however, the women are discontented with the new arrangement and sabotage it in order to get their original husbands back. In the second chapter there was a soprano aria whose text went:

Oh, lala,
Oh daba,
Oh honeymoon!
Say, oh say when . . .
But she got no further
For there was her ex-husband
Glaring at her like a starving pussycat.

I read *Le Carré* again and again to people who came to the house and discovered to my chagrin that the enthusiasm they showed for it came solely from the fact that they found it hilarious. When I was absolutely certain of this, I put the notebook away, and if anyone asked to hear it, I said it was lost.

Late one night there was a loud explosive cracking sound in the living room. In the morning it was discovered that the sounding board of the piano had buckled and split. Daddy flew into a rage against Wanamaker's and returned the instrument, insisting that no piano manufactured since the war could possibly be worth owning, because the wood was all unseasoned. Thus my music lessons came to a sudden stop. I did not mind too much, but Mother was unhappy about it for many months.

For relaxation Daddy had always played tennis. He looked very dapper in his white flannels. Much as Mother disliked having to play, she usually ended by giving in to his wishes, even though she knew a wrangle was inevitable. "I'm nearsighted!" she protested. "If my life depended on it, I couldn't see that ball."

"Nearsighted! You're blind as a bat."

Daddy had keen eyesight, but one morning he woke up blind in his left eye. A hemorrhage, his ophthalmologist told him. Although the damage was irreversible, he had several tests made. At breakfast one day he and Mother discussed them. I was busy pretending to look preoccupied, while following every word. Soon my curiosity overwhelmed me. "Why do they stick a needle into you?" I asked Mother.

"They have to take a sample of the blood . . ." she began, as Daddy gulped his coffee and slammed down his cup, roaring: "No!" And in answer to Mother's uncomprehending look he began in a singsong falsetto: "*My* father blablablabla blablabla . . ."

"I see," she said.

I felt slighted that he should imagine me capable of such abject behavior and could only conclude that he must have been like that when he himself was eight. This incident lowered my opinion of him considerably.

The doctors decided that Daddy had been working too hard. They ordered him to cut down on his schedule and to play golf three times a week. The suddenness of his partial blindness weighed upon him, and he brooded about his health, so that his hypochondria became more pronounced. The Hillcrest Golf Club was a few blocks from the house. A new routine began, in which all three of us marched off regularly to the club. Mother and I usually waited under the trees near the fifth hole. Sometimes, if he played alone, he insisted that we go along with him and help the caddy look for lost balls. One day he decided that I was going to caddy for him. It must have been obvious that I could not carry the bag properly, since when it was set down the top of it came level with my shoulder. Its regular bumping along the ground made Daddy so irritable that he could play only nine holes. "You make a fine caddy, I don't think," he said disgustedly when we got back to the locker room.

After they joined the club, Mother and Daddy made many new friends, and they began to go out nights to play cards. But now they did not think it necessary to have Hannah come and stay with me, so I had to be alone. Sometimes the card games were held in our house, and then there was a great racket throughout the house until two or three in the morning. Prohibition was brand-new, and people got drunk self-consciously; to show that one had been drinking was an elegant form of bravado.

Daddypapa came occasionally to visit us. He had a pleasant but embarrassing habit of going into the dining room before dinner and hiding money under my napkin. I could not understand why he never gave it to me in private so that Mother and Daddy would not know about it. I assumed that he liked me better than he liked them, because he constantly found fault with the way they lived. Each time he picked up a copy of *Vanity Fair* in the living room he snorted, riffled the pages noisily, and then slapped it down very hard on the table, remarking that it was not good to leave the magazine where I could get hold of it. But since I took its wrapper off when the postman brought it each month, I had already looked through it for as long as I wanted. While Daddy-papa was staying with us, Mother often reminded me that he belonged to another generation and thus could be expected to disapprove of what went on in our house. He had never been a drinking man, so that when the Eighteenth Amendment became law, he made a point of expressing his condemnation of those who disobeyed it, and he did not invariably hold his tongue when cocktails were served by Daddy before dinner.

"It's a great mistake," he said testily.

"Father, be reasonable," Daddy would remonstrate. "The law's unenforceable in the first place. Can't you see that?"

"Only because people like you choose to disregard it. It's the law of the nation. That should be enough."

Gramma spent time with us nearly every winter. We seemed always to be going out together in the snow; on her feet she wore what she called arctics. During the long cold walks I took with Gramma, I discovered in her an inexhaustible lode of spleen against Daddy. I had only to listen and say: "Why?" from time to time, and out it came, including details which I could not believe, young though I was, until they had been either confirmed or explained to me by Mother.

"Your mother's afraid of him, so she always stands up for him. But I know what he had in his mind. Your father wanted to kill you."

I was startled. "Kill me?" I repeated. The thing seemed only too possible. You could never be certain of what anyone really had in his mind. Children were treacherous and grown-ups inscrutable.

"When you were only six weeks old, he did it. He came home

one terrible night when the wind was roaring and the snow was coming down—a real blizzard—and marched straight into your room, opened the window up wide, walked over to your crib and yanked you out from under your warm blankets, stripped you naked, and carried you over to the window where the snow was sailing in. And that devil just left you there in a wicker basket on the windowsill for the snow to fall on. And if I hadn't heard you crying a little later, you'd have been dead inside the hour. 'I know what you want,' I told him. 'You shan't do it. You'll harm this baby over my dead body.' "

The idea of this dramatic confrontation excited me. "What'd he say?" I wanted to know.

"He was just jealous of the attention your mother was giving you. *He* was the baby. He felt she wasn't paying enough mind to him, that's all. So he thought: 'I'll let him catch his death of cold, and then I'll have her all to myself.' I know how his mind works. He's a devil, a devil! Like the old tomcat that comes back and eats his own kittens. He's got your poor mother where he wants her, right under his thumb."

Gramma enjoyed telling how just after I was born, she had gone to a clairvoyant, in order to make general inquiries about what my life was going to be like. The woman had claimed she saw piles of papers everywhere, and that was all. "She certainly got *that* one right," Gramma told me. "I've never seen so many papers as you've collected. I don't wonder your mother gets nervous. The mere sight of so many would drive me crazy. Couldn't you get rid of some of them? The old ones?"

I had to put that suggestion down immediately. "No, no! I have to have them all. I don't want to throw any away."

"Your poor mother!"

"She doesn't ever see them. They're all piled together in the closet. I like to look at them."

"But they're just your own scribbles. Why do you want to look at them?"

I realized that she did not share my interest in my own literary achievements; there was nothing to say.

In January, 1921, Daddy fell ill with pneumonia. The house was transformed into a hospital, with nurses coming and going,

and Dr. Brush calling by several times each day. Mother decided
to get me out of the way by sending me to Springfield to stay with
the Winnewissers. I went to Grand Central Station by myself and
took the New York, New Haven and Hartford, still stunned by
my unbelievably good fortune. The idea of an indeterminate
stretch of freedom ahead was intoxicating. I saw that life is po-
tentially pleasant, and gained great respect for the unforeseen.

I had scarcely been at Springfield for two weeks when both
Grampa and Gramma were stricken with pneumonia. Aunt
Emma came down from Northampton to help, and once again I
was sent away from the sickbed scene, this time to Northampton
to stay with Uncle Guy. He and Aunt Emma had separate apartments in the same building. Uncle Guy was a novelty: he wore
Japanese kimonos and spent a good deal of time keeping incense
burning in a variety of bronze dragons and Buddhas. I was delighted with the apartment and imagined it as the setting for a
murder mystery. As if to reinforce this impression there were a
few Sax Rohmer novels on the table beside my bed. Nights I
made the acquaintance of Dr. Fu Manchu.

So far I had been only three times in my life to see a moving
picture. Uncle Guy in all innocence took me every afternoon to a
barnlike building called the Academy of Music, where they
showed two different films each day. I saw Mary Miles Minter
and Charlie Chaplin and Viola Dana and William S. Hart, all
with a sharp and delightful awareness of the degree of disapproval Mother and Daddy would feel if only they knew what was
going on. Uncle Guy promised me he'd never tell them; he
treated me in a very special way which made me feel he was "on
my side," and he did not try to control my activities. I had never
before known such freedom; it was inevitable that I should consider Uncle Guy a friend. But then he decided to give a big
party. It would be in Aunt Emma's apartment; he had been
planning it for several days. When Saturday evening came, he
told me I was to eat early and go to bed. This was unwelcome
news indeed. During the evening I found some pretext for don-
ning my bathrobe and wandering through the corridors to the
other apartment. I could hear the dance music being played on
the piano, and a great racket of voices and laughter, before I got

to the door. When I opened it, I had a brief glimpse of the studio. It was crowded with pretty young men dancing together. At that second a rough hand clutched at my shoulder, spun me around, and propelled me through the doorway. I glanced up and saw Uncle Guy's face transfigured by rage. With his other hand he seized the back of my neck and squeezed it painfully as he pushed me down the corridor toward his own apartment. "I told you not to come, and you disobeyed," he said between his teeth. "Now I'm going to lock you in."

Once I was back in my room I sat on the bed consumed by fury and frustration. Uncle Guy had proved the same as all the others. Above me on the wall hung a large framed photograph of a pretty girl with an inviting smile. I stood up on the bed and rammed my fist into the picture as hard as I could, smashing the glass and cutting my knuckles. That was for Uncle Guy. Then I went to sleep with a sore hand. The next morning when I worked up the courage to admit to Uncle Guy that I had broken his picture, instead of being angry about it, he smiled, which was upsetting. I said I would pay him for whatever it cost, and he agreed. No part of the episode was mentioned again by either of us, including the roomful of young men, which did not strike me as having anything unusual about it until at least ten years later when I recalled it. And until this moment of writing it, I have never mentioned it to anyone.

Uncle Guy had a mysterious, fat friend whom we used to visit. His name was Mr. Bistany, and he was even busier with his incense than Uncle Guy, so much so that the air in his apartment was almost unbreathable. The floors and couches and walls were covered with soft Turkish rugs, which he kept changing. He was a Syrian who kept an "Oriental" shop specializing in imported goods. Each time we went to see him he insisted on presenting me with a gift, but since Uncle Guy objected vociferously, I was placed in an embarrassing position. Uncle Guy would snatch the object away from me and put it down, whereupon Mr. Bistany would immediately hand it to me again. Toward the end of my stay in Northampton we no longer went to see Mr. Bistany.

When a letter came from Mother telling me I must return to New York in a fortnight, I sat down and wrote her a pleading missive, begging to be allowed to stay a little longer. Naturally, this had no effect. The fateful day came, and I was put on a train and sent home, feeling very sorry for myself.

I had not been back very long before Miss Naul called on Mother to suggest that I be sent ahead into Miss Miller's class. In other words, I was going from the fifth grade into the sixth. The process was called skipping. Because being sent ahead was a sign of official approval, any boy who received the honor risked ostracism by his classmates.

At the end of that term Miss Miller recommended that the sixth-grade class rise and applaud my achievement. I had got the highest marks of anyone in spite of my tardy entrance. It was a moment of nightmare, and I wondered then if Miss Miller realized what she was subjecting me to by calling attention to my defects. (For the qualities adults think of as virtues in a child are generally considered by other children to be sheer sycophancy.) The question surely would come: Why was he skipped? And the answer, illogical and brutal, but not without its element of truth, was bound to be: Because he thinks he's smart.

"Tell me about when I was born."

"You've heard about it a thousand times," Mother would say.

This was true, but somehow I felt there was more to the momentous event than I had so far extracted. I hoped that by constantly eliciting more details I would eventually get the whole picture.

The delivery took place in the Mary Immaculate Hospital. (For many years I remained under the impression that the word "immaculate" modified "hospital" and was a kind of cheap advertising, like the word "painless" which bad dentists of that era used on their signs.) "It was the most convenient and the best equipped," Mother explained. "But if I'd had any idea of what was going to happen I'd have given it a wide berth."

This was always thrilling, since I knew what was to follow. It had been a forceps delivery; my head refused to emerge. "When I came out from under the ether, there you were, with a big cut on the side of your head." But the best was yet to come. At dusk on that same afternoon it seems that two nuns wandered into the room and announced that I must be taken out and baptized.

Mother refused, and they tried to lift me up by force, assuring her that I might not survive the night. That had nothing to do with them, she said; she would take the responsibility for my soul. They continued to clutch at me. "If you take that child out of the room, I'll follow you on my hands and knees screaming," she told them, and they went away.

When this tale was recounted, I always had the impression that Mother had scored an important moral victory, at the same time protecting me from what would have entailed a mysterious and obscene operation. She would hunch her shoulders and shudder. "Agh! Dirty creatures, with their old crosses dangling! They give me the shivers. Of course, some of them *are* very fine women, I make no doubt. But those black capes!"

"Nothing's so much fun as games you play with your own mind," Mother said one day. "You think you're running your mind, but then you find out that unless you're careful, your mind is running you. For instance, I'll bet you can't tell me exactly what motions you make to take off your topcoat. What do you move first? I've thought about it over and over, and I can't for the life of me tell you. Or this. Did you ever try to make your mind a blank and hold it that way? You mustn't imagine anything or remember anything or think of anything, not even think: 'I'm not thinking.' Just a total blank. You try it. It's hard. You may get it for a second, and then something flashes across your mind, and you lose it. I do it sometimes when I'm just resting in the afternoon, and I've got so I can hold on to it for quite a while. I just go into the blank place and shut the door."

None of this was lost on me. I said nothing, but I too began to practice secretly, and eventually managed to attain a blank state, although I was inclined to hold my breath along with it, which automatically limited its duration. Whatever powers of self-discipline I have now were given their original impetus at that time.

Early mornings in spring and summer had a particular magic. I could not go out, of course, nor could I get dressed and go downstairs before I was called, but I could go to the windows and look out and smell the air and hear the birds singing. That also was forbidden, but I was never caught at it. What did bring me to grief was my habit of sitting up in bed these early mornings, drawing houses to add to my collection of real estate. One cool July day I had got out of bed, tiptoed over to the door, locked it, and gone back to bed to work. Suddenly I heard Daddy bounding up the stairs. Long before I could get to the door he had tried it and immediately had begun to pound on it. I went and turned the key. His eyes were very narrow.

"What do you mean by locking that door, young man? What were you doing?"

"Nothing."

"Answer my question. Why was that door locked?"

"Because I was doing something I didn't want you to see."

"Oh, you were, were you? And what were you doing?"

"Drawing houses."

"And so you locked the door?" He did not seem to believe me.

"I didn't think you'd like me to be drawing houses before breakfast."

"I see. Well, just for that, I'm going to give you the whaling of your young life."

He seized me, threw me over his knees, facedown on the bedspread in my pajamas, and began to pummel my bottom. I lay there waiting for him to stop. When the tempo and volume of the blows had lessened, he said: "Have you had enough?" I did not answer, and so he continued in a desultory fashion for a moment, before he asked me again: "Had enough?"

I could never say yes.

I kept silent. "Speak up!" he told me.

I twisted my head to one side and managed to get out the words: "Whatever you say." Then he really pounded me.

When he was tired, he stopped and let me roll over on the bed. "Now I want all the notebooks you write in. Come on, hurry up." I got them out and laid them on the bed, and he went downstairs with them. Mother told me later in the day that I was to be deprived of them for two months, the shortest sentence she had been able to wangle for me. I was considerably relieved, having expected them to be destroyed once and for all. I also felt stronger, because I knew that no matter what physical violence was done to me, I would not have to cry; it was something I had not realized until that day. Decades later, looking through Mother's diaries, I found a reference to the incident. The entry for the day began: "Claude spanked Paul. Result: spent a miserable day with a sick headache."

This was the only time my father beat me. It began a new stage in the development of hostilities between us. I vowed to devote my life to his destruction, even though it meant my own—an infantile conceit, but one which continued to preoccupy me for many years.

III

When I was in the seventh grade, Daddy decided to buy a house of his own. The architect was the same man who had designed the other house, and it was in the same neighborhood, so that moving was not difficult. However, the added number of rooms necessitated buying more furniture and rugs. Trucks from Lord and Taylor's and Altman's and Wanamaker's arrived repeatedly, bringing things on approval. Relatives shipped antiques to us from New Hampshire and Vermont, including a lot of coin silver "from the time of the Revolution," Mother said delightedly.

There were fewer places now to explore. Houses went up everywhere at an alarming rate, and the woods were disappearing almost before my eyes. I resented the brutal changes, but then I decided that I was too old to think about such things and devoted myself even more intensively to my work. That year I was very busy writing a series of long melodramatic stories. They had titles like "Their Just Deserts" and "The Cry in the Fog." I took one of them to school and left it on Mrs. Woodson's desk. Apparently she was impressed, for she asked if I had others, and when I said I had, she suggested that I read them in installments to the class. I think she imagined that after a few days the material would be exhausted, for at the outset she had me reading during school hours. When two or three weeks had gone by and I showed no signs of running down (since once I had used up what was in hand I wrote feverishly every night in order to have the next day's installment ready), she decided that the sessions should be held directly after dismissal at three o'clock, attendance being optional. What should have astonished me, although I took it for granted, was that with two or three exceptions the entire class regularly stayed.

The readings would have continued indefinitely if I had not incurred Mrs. Woodson's displeasure: an offensive remark I had made about one of the girls in the class was reported to her. That afternoon instead of the reading, there was a lengthy inquisition. This began with everyone present; then the girls were excused, and only the boys remained; finally there were only she and I facing each other in a senseless confrontation. I could see that her indignation was largely feigned and that what really interested her was finding out exactly how much sexual information I had and where I had got it. (Very likely I had less than anyone in the class, inasmuch as I still remained under the impression that the sexes were anatomically identical, and did not discover otherwise until I studied biology in high school.) But I, being adept at seeming to know more than I did, led the poor woman on, so that she could not bring herself to cut the interview short. It was past five o'clock, and still she continued to talk.

"What I still can't understand is why, *why*, did you have to pick on the sweetest, daintiest, brightest girl in all the class? Can you tell me that?"

I suppose the answer was: precisely because she was all of those things. But I could not have said it even if I had been capable of formulating it, and so I shook my head. I had no idea why.

"How do you think your mother would feel if she were to hear about this?"

"She wouldn't like it much," I admitted. "But I don't think she'd mind as much as you do."

I ventured this opinion fortified by the memory of Mother's reaction when I reported Mrs. Woodson's statement that Unitarians were neither Christians nor Jews but fell somewhere between the two. ("Just remember she's an ignorant, narrow-minded woman," said Mother.)

"I don't see why you're disappointed," I told Mrs. Woodson. "What did you expect?"

She rose to her feet, white with anger. After a moment she said: "I expected something better. You may go."

It was dark when I got home. Mother was out, but Gramma was staying with us that month. She was concerned about my lateness. I told her the whole story. "But what did you say about the girl?" she wanted to know.

"I said she had a mustache between her legs."

Gramma's mouth opened. "Why, Paul! I'm surprised!"

"Why? Is that so terrible?"

"Well, it's certainly not very nice, is it?"

"No, but it's not so bad."

The matter rested there. But there were no more readings.

About this time Mother began to go out more often. She joined numerous clubs, among them one called the Delphian Society, and she subscribed to the Theatre Guild. I heard about Aeschylus and *The Brothers Karamazov*. At that time we had a housekeeper from Vermont and a black girl named Ida, so that I got fed regularly whether Mother was there or not.

Next door on the west lived Dr. Linville, who was president of the American Teachers' Union and an avowed Socialist. He had just lost his wife, and his four children were being cared for by a Polish housekeeper with two small babies of her own. "I wouldn't be in her shoes! I wonder the woman remains sane," Mother said. "The children are pretty well ungovernable by now, I make no doubt. No one's ever told them anything. They have no responses. Phlegmatic."

"Bovine!" corrected Daddy, to be funny.

Mother nodded her head seriously. "Typical Scandinavians. Slow."

The oldest of the three boys was already on unfriendly terms with me, as a result of an episode a year or so earlier when I had unintentionally cut his head in a rock fight. He still pretended to think it deliberate on my part, and we had constant scuffles. This enmity was fanned by his older sister, who indignantly told me that he still bore the scar made by my rock. It was true, and the sight of it gave me uneasy memories of the quantity of blood that had come out of his head at the time. To assuage my feelings of guilt I kept trying to be friendly with him, but we always ended up fighting. There was an illogical and babyish quality about him that both infuriated and excited me, and I determined finally to arrange his fate and watch him undergo it.

I extracted permission from my parents to use the third floor as a clubhouse once a week. Immediately I got out my printing press and made up some stationery headed THE CRYSTAL DOG CLUB. Using the paper, I wrote out eight or ten announcements of a meeting the next Friday night and gave them to two brothers who lived down the street, suggesting they hand them out to the other boys in our age group, making certain they communicated the information that there would be all the ice cream anyone could hold. I had the two brothers come around first, and we set up the clubroom the way we wanted it. It was understood that with the exception of us three founders, everyone must undergo initiation before he would be accepted as a member.

Friday night found everything happening according to plan. As I'd expected, the Linville boy demurred when I casually suggested his name as the first one to be blindfolded. His objections were taken by the others to denote lack of courage and fraternal feeling; he found no sympathy. He was trying to get out of it, so they all insisted that he be the first. From then on it was not necessary for me to say anything. He was already blubbering a little when the blindfold was applied. That was perfect.

The third floor had been left largely unfinished; there was no railing around the stairwell. My idea was to convince the boy that he was hanging out the window, when actually he was only dangling over the edge of the stairwell, and then, with proper psychological preparations, let him drop. The brothers fastened the rope around his waist, and I went and opened the window. He got very panicky when he heard the outdoor sounds, and they had to tie his hands behind him. When I was satisfied that he was well trussed, we lifted him off his feet. He was heavier than any of us, but we swung him around a bit and got him to the edge of the stairwell. (Fortunately Mother and Daddy had a party going on two floors below, and their friends were making much more noise than we were. They would sit that way for hours in a circle on the floor, with nothing in the center but dice and money.) As soon as we let him over the edge, the rope ran through our hands hot and fast, and we had to let go. Down he went in a heap to the bottom of the stairwell. For a second there was silence, and then he began such a howling and roaring that even the grown-ups heard it and came running. Both Daddy and Mother went over him carefully and found no serious damage— only scrapes and bruises. Nevertheless, he continued to scream.

"Just shock, nothing more," Daddy said and took him home to the Polish housekeeper. The rest of us were then briefly reprimanded as we ate our ice cream, and the club was thereupon disbanded by order of Dr. Bowles. We decided that nobody else would have behaved in such an abject manner. Shortly after that the Linville boy went away to school.

For a year the Kirschbaums had been building an ornate house on the corner of the street below. Everyone knew that Mr. Kirschbaum was a successful bootlegger; one of his daughters who was in my class often bragged of the amount of money he made at his work. Her brother Buddy was inclined to talk about his father's cars and how well he could drive them, but we had never seen him try. Buddy was completely unpleasant; nobody liked him. One day when it was snowing, he came up to me as I shoveled off the sidewalk and began to list the unpleasant things he could do to me if he felt like it. I finished shoveling and went into the house, where I expressed to Gramma my opinion of Buddy.

"I'll give you a dollar if you'll go out and beat him up," Gramma told me.

My immediate answer was: "I can't. He's bigger than I am. Besides, I don't know how to fight."

"Neither does he," she said. "Go on. I want to see it from here. And I'll give you a dollar."

My experience of hand-to-hand combat was limited to purely defensive ploys. I had never fought willingly and much less with the idea of "winning"; it was a question only of sustaining minimum damages. Gramma wanted something else from me, and I did not know how to do it. However, the dollar bill was uppermost in my mind. I went outside. When I saw Buddy, I merely walked straight toward him, and when I was about three feet from him, I leaped at him, knocking him over. Then we rolled in the snow for a while. Suddenly I was able to get both hands around his neck; by choking him, I managed to roll him over and sit astride him. Then I continued to choke him. I was afraid that unless I continued to press with all my might, he would be able to throw me off. When I finally banged his head on the ground and let go, he did not even move. I got up and went into the house, feeling resentful and ashamed. Not looking at Gramma, I said: "I think maybe he's sick."

"Don't be silly. He's all right." She pulled the curtain farther aside so I could see Buddy stumbling off through the snow. He and I never noticed one another again.

It was about now that I resumed taking music lessons. At the end of a bitter and prolonged struggle with Daddy, Mother had surrendered, and an old Chickering piano had arrived, sent by Daddymama from Elmira. "The mere sight of it makes me sick to my stomach," Mother complained. According to Daddy, the Coldstream Country Club, which he had recently joined, had taken the money that would have bought a new piano; this was exactly as it should be, since I could practice on the old one, whereas he needed the club for his health. He was quite right: the piano had an excellent tone, and very likely it was the frequent playing of golf that kept him from a second nervous breakdown. He was, after all, under extreme tension: he had to continue to practice dentistry with the sight of only one eye. Moreover, he had to practice it exactly as though he had perfect vision since if anyone guessed there were something amiss, he would risk losing his practice. Above all, he was haunted by the possibility that the good eye might also be afflicted by a sudden lesion. He even worried about losing his driver's license. "I shudder to think what would happen if your father's other eye should go," said Mother. "We have to make allowances for his temper. He's under a terrific strain."

Daddy's closest friend was Walter Benjamin, whom he had known as a boy in Elmira. Ben had left his wife and was living with a very attractive woman named Molly, whose husband would not give her a divorce, but who was willing to keep her lodged and smartly dressed in return for the pleasure of having dinner with her once a month. I found all this very interesting, particularly the fact that Mother felt called upon to defend Molly's position when she discussed her with her friends or even with Gramma. Gramma saw no reason why Daddy should stop by to see "that woman" two or three times a week on his way from the office and then telephone to say he would be late for dinner. "I wouldn't stand for it another day," she would tell Mother as we sat waiting for him to come so that dinner could be served. "Oh, it's not like that at all!" Mother would object. "Lord, *I* don't mind! He has to have some relaxation, you know." But Gramma only sniffed. Later she would say: "Did you smell him when he came in? He *reeked* of her perfume." Molly had a passion for ambergris; she sprayed her furniture and even her guests with Ambre Antique. It was impossible to come away from her apartment without smelling of it.

Ben owned a house on the beach at Napeague; it was the only habitation within a radius of several miles. Sometimes we would spend a week there, take Ben's boat, and go lobstering off Block Island. The fun of this was to haul up an occasional case of whiskey or champagne which friends with bigger boats left attached to the floating markers in place of the lobster pots. There was a good deal of boisterous fun for the grown-ups at Napeague. For me there were sandy paths through the wilderness of beach plum and scrub oak. The excitement inherent in exploring an unknown terrain was big enough to keep me fully occupied.

About this time I bought a book of poems translated from the Chinese by Arthur Waley. Poetry had never interested me; in school I had been made to memorize a bit of verse by Bryant or Whittier or Longfellow, and then as soon as possible, I had forgotten it. Waley's compact little pellets, however, suggested the existence of a whole series of other purposes for which the poetic process could be used. I began to look at the real world around me with the idea of defining it in as few words as possible. In the middle of doing my homework I would stop and tackle the problem of the foghorns I could hear blowing on Long Island Sound or the poplars rustling outside my windows. When I had kept the imaginary diaries and printed the daily newspaper, I had thought of myself as a registering consciousness and no more. My nonexistence was a *sine qua non* for the validity of the invented cosmos. Now with the poetic definitions it was very much the same psychic mechanism at work. I received and recorded them; others were people and had "lives." Perhaps two years later I found an even more satisfactory way of not existing as myself and thus being able to go on functioning; this was a fantasy in which the entire unrolling of events as I experienced them was the invention of a vast telekinetic sending station. Whatever I saw or heard was simultaneously being experienced by millions of enthralled viewers. They did not see me or know that I existed, but they saw through my eyes. This method enabled me to view, rather than participate in, my own existence. (Much later I read Gide, and understood his feeling perfectly when he wrote in his journal: *"Il me semble toujours m'appauvrir en me dessinant. J'accepte volontiers de n'avoir pas d'existence bien définie si les êtres que je crée et extrais de moi en ont une."*)

The year when I was twelve several things occurred to jar me out of my fantasies. First I had to have a tumor removed from my lower jaw. It was a bloody, two-hour operation, and it took me a while to get over it. Then one day when Mother and I were crossing Fifth Avenue, a double-decker bus came coasting down Murray Hill and hit her. It happened in front of Maillard's; from there she was taken to the old Waldorf-Astoria at Thirty-fourth Street, and for several weeks after that I visited her at the hospital. In the summer I went back to Exeter and Uncle Edward showed me around the campus. I could not summon any spark of enthusiasm at the prospect of spending the next four years in such a place. I suspected that attending classes there would be like being in a church, and I said as much to Mother. "Well, you're going to Exeter," she said. "I want to get you away from home."

However, I did not get away from home. Unexpectedly my father launched a violent anti-Exeter campaign on the ground that the school was a snob factory. Mother did her best, but there was no budging him.

While I was staying with Uncle Edward I wrote a long story called "Hadeized," in which the characters disappeared the moment they swallowed alcohol. (The touch of liquor "hadeized" them, and they were instantly transported to hell.) Uncle Edward found this amusing, but all the same gave me Emerson's *Essays* in red morocco, saying that he thought I was old enough for them now. The flattering approach worked: I read them with pleasure during the following months.

One day in class, some girls behind me were whispering. One of them said: "I can't. I have to go to a circumcision." I heard sniggers and no more. That night there were guests for dinner; candlelight, damask, the most easily breakable Limoges, and the heaviest silver were the necessary trappings of the ritual of hospitality. Tradition demanded also that unless directly addressed, I refrain from speaking during these gastronomical observances. But in the middle of the meal I was suddenly curious, and turned to Mother to say: "What's a circumcision?"

"I'll tell you later," she answered tonelessly, as if she were reading the words from a newspaper. Perhaps to forestall further inquiry, she called me before dessert into another room and said: "You wanted to know about circumcision? Well, when a baby is born, they take the little penis and cut a piece off the end of it."

I was thunderstruck; the idea was so unexpected and grisly. "But what for?" I cried.

"Some people think it's cleaner." That was all. But the information was of a perverse enough nature to go on preoccupying my mind. Eventually I got a needle and experimented on myself. The pain was not so intense as I expected, nor was the experiment really interesting. Still I could not imagine how civilized people could agree to practice such a barbarous act on helpless babies.

In school I began to take notes in a code I had invented, so that pupils with a roving eye would not be able to copy them. It was an extremely simple code: for a given consonant I substituted the next consonant following it in the alphabet; I did the same with the vowels. *Y* counted as a vowel, and became *A*, as *Z* became *B*. After a few months I could write almost as fast in my code as I could in English. The difficulty lay in reading it back, a much slower process. The rumor spread that I took all my notes in a foreign language. *(Hiuhsequja Vitv Nupfea.)*

The Model School was run for the benefit of several hundred teachers in training who occupied the upper floors of the building. They used to invade our classrooms fifty at a time, carrying campstools and notebooks. Occasionally one of the student teachers would be given a class to conduct in the absence of the regular teacher. This was always the signal for the unleashing of anarchy. I remember in one such burst of excitement I threw a safety razor at a substitute teacher named Miss Aaronov and hit her in the breast. Expectedly, she sent me to the principal's office, where I waited around for a while. Since he did not come in, I went home. Fortunately I never saw Miss Aaronov again.

Our house on Terrace Avenue was burglarized twice that year. The first robbery occurred while we were away over the weekend. I was impressed by the general dismay and the rushing around when we got home and found the house turned upside down. All my gold cuff links were gone, as well as a watch I particularly treasured, left me by Aunt Adelaide. Mother spent the evening pondering the fact that several drawers full of dinner silver were open, yet nothing was missing. "Now, something obviously scared them away," she kept saying. "But what could it have been?"

Then one night I had a dream, and I dreamed that I was standing downstairs in the dining room, looking toward the windows. I went over and pulled back the first curtains, and the second curtains, and saw that one of the windows had been broken and was open and the screen outside cut and unhooked. I stared, seeing the picture with an abnormal clarity and at the same time with a feeling of foreboding. (It comes at the moment when a dream ceases to be a neutral experience and declares itself a nightmare.) I realized that someone had seen me discover the broken window and very likely was watching me even as I stood there. I could go one of two ways in order to escape: to the left around the room and out through the butler's-pantry door, or straight ahead, through heavy curtains, and into the hall. But even as I looked at the curtains, I saw part of a hand slip between them. Then the lights went out, I was being strangled, and that awakened me.

The next morning early I was in a great hurry to get downstairs. The memory of the dream was so vivid and unpleasant in my head that I wanted to erase it by seeing the reality of the intact window and window screen. The trouble was that when I pulled back the curtains and looked at the window, the glass was broken and the screening cut, both just as I had seen them and in precisely the same places. It was a jolt, because I did not "believe in" such phenomena. Still, I could not deny that I had had the dream. Then I was assailed by a suspicion which gave me cold shivers: perhaps I had actually *been* in the dining room during the night, walking in my sleep, and had stood there staring at the window. In that case, when I turned, I must have been looking at a real hand holding the curtain. But after the suffocating and screaming I had waked myself, and was lying in my bed gasping and with my heart hammering, the same as after any nightmare. Naturally I ran upstairs and told my parents about it, but they were far more interested in the fact that the house had been broken into than in the manner of my discovering it. For me it was an unsettling experience and one that temporarily shook my stubborn faith in a rationally motivated cosmos. The only thing was to ignore it, which I managed more or less successfully to do.

That was the year I was told how mammals were born. This seemed natural enough, but there remained the question: if the baby came from the mother, how did it happen that people often said it looked like its father? I thought about it and decided to ask Mother, because there was nobody else to ask. Her answer left me in the dark. It was a great mystery that some people claimed to understand, she said, but really no one understood how it worked.

Another conversation with Mother that year has remained with me. She had a cousin Margery who at one time had gone off to Germany to study opera singing. There she enjoyed herself so much that she stayed on for eight years without returning to America. When she got back home to Providence, she went to her father, who was Grampa's brother, and said: "Why didn't you tell me we were from a Jewish family?" This started an immediate commotion, with all the members of the family joining in, including my great-grandmother, who was particularly incensed and who was crying in broken English: "Eight years over there and that's all she has to tell us!"

"Yes," Mother mused. "She said it was a Jewish name. Ven-nevitz or some such thing."

"But why would she say that?" I did not know Margery, but the fact that she had spent eight years in Berlin invested her with a certain importance in my eyes.

Mother shrugged. "Funny. Margery said: 'Yes, if you'd only told me, I wouldn't mind.' Oh, Grandmother Winnewisser was furious! 'The leedle opshtart! Chooish! Ha!' I can still hear her."

"But it wasn't true," I said, not adding: "Was it?"

She laughed. "If it was, *I* never heard anything about it. Your great-grandfather was a firebrand. He came over in 1848. He didn't think much of religion. All the men in the Winnewisser family are like that."

The time came for graduation exercises; I was leaving the Model School at the end of January (1924). Because a new high school had recently been built in Flushing, it was decided that I should go there. This involved spending an hour and a half of each day on a swaying old trolley car. Daddy repeatedly warned me not to try to read or write while riding on the streetcar, but a good part of my homework was done each day en route to and from Flushing. High school demanded much more of my atten-tion than grammar school; painlessly I abandoned most of my early devices for persuading myself that the world was not really there and settled into learning Latin and algebra.

That winter Mother's health, never robust, was less good than usual. She had a maid, but Daddy thought she needed a house-keeper who could take charge of everything, so that she could be free of all responsibility. The housekeeper was Fanny Fuller, an old friend of Gramma's from Bellows Falls in the nineties. At that time Hetty Green, who was then the wealthiest woman in the United States, lived there too, on the next street, and, of course, knew Gramma and Grampa. I had been brought up on their an-ecdotes featuring Hetty Green's strange behavior. She was dead now, these many years, but she had a daughter who by then had become Sylvia Astor Wilkes and from whose home in Greenwich Fanny came to us. They arrived one Sunday afternoon in an enormous Rolls. In front were a chauffeur and a footman, and in the back were the two women carefully holding the sides of Fanny's large wardrobe trunk. When Mrs. Wilkes came in, she explained to Mother that since the trunk had to come, she thought it would be more economical to bring it by car than to send it by express. Then she decided that since the car was coming, she would take advantage of the opportunity and come along, too. At one point she asked Mother if she went regularly to the opera. "Heavens, no, Sylvia!" Mother laughed. "It would help you a great deal," Mrs. Wilkes told her severely, and so she began to take Mother to the Met on Thursday afternoons. Daddy was against it because he thought it too strenuous. (Months later when Fanny left, Mrs. Wilkes followed the same procedure with the trunk: between them the two men carried it out and got it into the back, and then she sat on one side of it, and Fanny sat on the other side, and they drove away.)

Uncle Paul and Uncle Fred had just bought a cabin boat and sailed the entire family to Florida. They had not been there very long before Gramma came down with pneumonia. We were playing mah-jongg one evening, Mother, Daddy, Fanny, and I, when the Western Union messenger brought the final telegram. Mother opened it and glanced at it, and then she tossed it into the middle of the game, into the space enclosed by the wall of tiles. "Is she dead?" said Fanny.

There was no reply. I began to turn all the tiles facedown, preparatory to packing them back into the drawers. "You'd better get up to your homework," Daddy told me. However, I finished putting away the mah-jongg set before I left the room.

In biology class I made the mistake of asking the teacher in all good faith if there were the same discrepancies between the male and the female reproductive systems in human beings as in mice. Miss Vickers thought I was having her on, as did the students, who laughed. "That's enough out of you," she snapped. I concluded that my suspicion had been correct and that I was on the way to discovering the great secret.

So there was a real difference between men and women, besides the obvious fact that women had fat chests.

When June was nearly finished, I took my examinations and the term ended. We were getting ready for the annual removal to

Massachusetts, and the weather was being hot and sultry. One evening just after sunset I decided to go down the hill to where the nearest shops were and have something cold at Roth's soda fountain. The shop was on a corner, with a swinging screen door giving on to each street. As I pushed open the screen door, something happened to me. The best way of describing it is to say that the connection between me and my body was instantaneously severed. The soda fountain was there in front of me, but I could not go to it. Instead, I turned right, walked to the other door, and went out into the street. But then I had to turn to the right again, go around the corner, and back to the first door. I repeated the operation and saw Mrs. Roth look up at me with surprise as I went out for the second time. I was caught in something that I could not break out of, and I tried desperately not to go into the shop a third time. However, I did go in and marched straight through and out the other door. And now the experience took on all the qualities of a dream. As I turned right to go back to the first door once more, out of the corner of my eye I saw a blue Buick coming down the hill and recognized it. I ran toward it and got in. Mother and Daddy had decided to call on some friends on Hilldale Avenue. They asked me if I felt all right, and I told them I was tired. "We shan't stay long," Mother said. "You've had a grueling week, with those exams in all that heat."

I could not talk about what had happened, because I was convinced that only the incredibly opportune arrival of the car had saved me. From what, I could not have said, but I was sure it would have included walking endlessly in a circle clockwise. The experience frightened me, and I suspected that if I were to put it into words, it would somehow become more threatening and true. Still, I could not get it out of my mind.

Aunt Emma had returned to visit us. On this occasion she was really sick, a veritable skeleton that lay in bed moaning most of the time; it went on day and night, week after week. Often the moans became screams, which rose and fell like sirens wailing. This gave me gooseflesh: my room was next to hers, so that I could hear all the details. Sometimes she cried: "When's he coming?" over and over again. Not that there was anyone in her room to answer her. I knew that Daddy and Mother were at sword's points about having her there at all. Daddy objected to the doctors who came so many times each day, and I finally gathered by eavesdropping that he was also against her being given so much morphine. I asked Mother about it, and she said yes, the doctors were obliged to give her shots regularly because when they wore off, the pain in her head became unbearable.

After the early doctor had come and gone each morning, I would look in the bathroom wastebasket to see if he had left there a little glass tube with a very official-looking paper seal featuring the word "Morphine." Thinking these tubes to be of interest, I began saving them from destruction.

During lunch at school I sat at table with a boy who was holding forth on "dope fiends." He claimed cocaine was a powder and morphine was a liquid. I, who had examined the little tubes, had seen that morphine came in pill form, too, and I told him so. His reply was that I was crazy, and where had I seen dope of any sort? "I'll prove it to you," I said. That night I filled one of the tubes with a mixture of baking soda and dusting powder for after the bath; then I put it with my schoolbooks in my briefcase.

The next day at lunch I brought it out and triumphantly handed it to the doubter. There were no pills, but there was powder, and the label with all its impressive fine print convinced him. His expression changed, and he began to tell me that I could be arrested for having such an object in my possession. An argument ensued in which students sitting at other tables became interested, with the result that a senior stepped in and confiscated the tube of powder, after which he strode purposefully out of the lunchroom. I was not too worried, since it was all only a hoax. Perhaps an hour later I was summoned to the principal; he took a very dim view of the escapade. "We know it's just talc in the bottle," he told me. "We've analyzed it. What we want to know is where you got the bottle."

"At home, out of the wastebasket," I said without hesitation. "The doctor throws them away all the time."

Then he asked for the telephone number of my father. I gave him the home number, hoping he would not call. He did, however, and got Mother on the line. She confirmed my story, but he wanted to speak to Daddy as well. She said it would be absurd to bother him at his office with such an insignificant thing. Actually she hoped Daddy would not hear of it at all, since it would give him more leverage in his argument against Aunt Emma's being at our house. The reason, which I did not learn until several years later, was that Aunt Emma was undergoing disintoxication; her symptoms were merely those of withdrawal. "The place for her is in a hospital," Daddy had reiterated many times, intimating that the whole thing was distasteful to him.

The school did eventually get Daddy on the telephone. That night he said to me: "Now, just what was all that about? You certainly can be counted on to do the wrong thing in a big way, can't you?"

"Yes, whatever *possessed* you?" Mother cried, much more annoyed with me, now that he knew about it. "The *last* thing you should have done!"

Daddy seemed almost grimly pleased, and I could not understand why. "The whole situation's impossible," he told Mother gruffly. "You can see that." But she could not see it; it was the least she could do for her own sister, and besides she was already much better. Aunt Emma stayed on all winter, until ultimately she put on a little weight and could move around without help. Even then she smoked three flat fifty tins of Luckies every day. If instead of lying, they had only told me the truth about her, that the morphine itself was the disease, I should not have done what I did. Imagining that I were given the power to relive my childhood, but under any conditions I chose, I should be content with the same sequence of events all over again, provided my parents made it clear to me that they trusted me.

IV

Until now Aunt Mary had remained in the background, a serious, sweet woman who lived in a big house and called Daddy, Mother, and me "my lambs." It is hard to think of her without thinking of Holden Hall, the old house where she lived. The house, high on a hill, had been built by Fox Holden, her grandfather. From my earliest childhood I had loved to wander through the high-ceilinged rooms from floor to floor, until I came to the mysterious tower room that smelled of sun and dust. This had couches along the walls and two sets of heavy curtains and was called the Meditation Room. It was here that Aunt Mary, along with a few friends, came each morning for an hour of silent communion. The friends would be staying with her; there was always someone, and often there were several. These women were in a sense addicted to Aunt Mary's presence; occasionally they "went to pieces" when they were separated from her.

Aunt Mary's particular system would seem to have been a combination of Hindu mysticism, suggestion, and pragmatism. During the meditation period she sometimes burned HPB cubes. The incense bore the initials of Madame Helena Petrovna Blavatsky, the founder of modern Theosophy, whom Aunt Mary had known and whose photograph she kept in a massive silver frame on her library desk. The smoke, she claimed, could induce a trancelike state if all those breathing it were not only concentrating their attention upon the same idea, but also touching one another. She also practiced a form of tantrism, insisting that the repetition of certain words was spiritually beneficial in itself.

Dr. Holden originally had conceived the house as a Spiritualist center for western New York State. No sooner was it finished than they began to hold nightly séances in it. The walls resounded with tappings and creakings. I once found a pile of notebooks in one of the storerooms on the third floor; these contained verbatim records of the séances. Apparently one of the most available spirit voices was that of Governor De Witt Clinton, who dropped in regularly at the evening meetings and was questioned at length on the digging and administration of the Erie Canal. There was another frequent visitor, referred to merely as Old Mrs. Guernsey. She had many opinions on everything, however, and her replies seemed to satisfy the questioners.

After the death of Dr. Holden, Spiritualism was replaced in the house by Transcendentalism. Christina Holden, Aunt Mary's mother, made a brave but vain effort to interest various religious thinkers in her Transcendentalist Center. (I have a letter from William James, Sr., regretfully declining to take part in it—not, as he said, on philosophical grounds, but because in his experience such places gave rise to much vague speculation and served little practical purpose.)

Aunt Mary had married; but both her husband and her daughter had long since died, and she had stayed on alone in the big house, sometimes without even a servant who slept in. Winters she lived in Florida, preparing the subjects for meditation to be used in the summers. When I was fourteen, she invited me, along with my cousin Elizabeth, who was seventeen, to spend several weeks at Holden Hall. I was delighted because I loved the house and the pleasant life that went on in it and also because I was very fond of Elizabeth. She was an adult who took me seriously.

I had not been there many days before I became aware that Aunt Mary was staring at me very often and with a curious and rather frightening expression. At first it occurred to me that in some mysterious fashion the morphine escapade might have reached her ears, but I decided that was too unlikely, and from there went to attributing her behavior to the little eccentricities that come with age. Thus I was not surprised when one evening after dinner she said to me: "You're tired. You ought to go up to bed now. Elizabeth and I are going to talk a while in the library."

I went to bed, but under some pretext to give as alibi if I were discovered, I got up a half hour or so later and opened the door into the hall in the hope of getting a scrap of the secret conversation from which I had been excluded. The house was completely silent, save for the faint and muffled voices down in the library. Suddenly Aunt Mary opened a door, and I heard her say clearly, with the inflections of a recapitulation: "Well, I can only say that to me Paul has all the earmarks of a boy who has started on the downward path."

Quickly I shut the door and got into bed, puzzled that they should have been discussing me and indignant that Aunt Mary should have spoken in that way about me without provocation. I went over the past few days in detail, trying to find a reason for it, something I might have said that was capable of a drastic misinterpretation. I went to sleep still wondering what had so inexplicably turned Aunt Mary against me. The next day at the first opportunity I got Elizabeth alone and questioned her. "What does she mean, downward path? Path to where? What does she think I'm doing, robbing banks?"

"Oh, she thinks you have the wrong friends," Elizabeth began cautiously. "You know, the sort that hang out on street corners and whistle at women going by."

I could hardly believe what she was saying. "But what's the matter with her?" I cried. "I *haven't* any friends!"

She smiled sagaciously. "You know the family. You know how they talk. If anybody is the least bit different from the way they think he should be, they get all excited about it. To them everything's the same as it was thirty or forty years ago. Aunt Mary's fine. She understands more than anybody else in this family. But she's worried about you."

That was precisely what disturbed me. She had no cause, nor even any right, to worry about me. This meant that her negative feelings about me had to do with something intangible, with who

I was, rather than with anything I had done. To me this smacked of persecution and was intolerable. At the same time it meant that her misgivings were at a deep enough level to make it unlikely that she would mention them to my parents. Daddy had little patience with her mystical side, and Mother, although she would have been receptive enough to it, was never encouraged to deal with it. Aunt Mary did not wholly approve of Mother because she used cosmetics, drank cocktails, and smoked cigarettes. All three of these she branded as unnecessary, vicious habits, each a separate insult to the body and thus to the entire being.

On the next property but one from Horseshoe Cabin in Glenora there was a house called Lasata, which belonged to the three Hoagland sisters. Miss Anna was delicate, Miss Jane made pottery, and Miss Sue was dour and read Spengler. Wintertimes they lived together in a big old house in Brooklyn, a place which in those days was quiet and had many gardens. From perhaps the age of ten I had been allowed to spend weekends with them; I enjoyed seeing the Brooklyn Museum or going to a symphony concert at the Academy of Music. We usually also managed to go to a film or two, which was important to me, since ordinarily I was forbidden this pleasure, save to see carefully selected films like *Nanook of the North* or Harold Lloyd's latest.

One summer when I went to visit the Hoaglands at Lasata I found a fourth woman there. Everything about her was completely different from them: appearance, speech, behavior, and ideas. Her hair was very black, and her eyes seemed to crackle with darkness. She had a hoarse voice which varied enormously in pitch as she spoke, and she lay on a chaise longue like a princess and pounded the floor with a cane when she wanted the maid. I soon learned that she was half Cree Indian and had just arrived from Cape Town. Such credentials seemed to me impeccable: she must be a most interesting woman. However, when I mentioned her later at Horseshoe Cabin, I realized that I had stirred up a nest of hornets. "An immoral woman," said Daddypapa. From what Daddymama had heard, Mrs. Crouch was "an unscrupulous adventuress" and had a "stranglehold on poor Sue." I determined to become friendly with her, this despite the fact that I knew she had a son and a daughter of her own, both only three or four years older than I. These two arrived; they were allowed to smoke and drink and to stay out as late as they felt like it at night, which glamorized them for me to such an extent that they seemed scarcely real. The unusual degree of freedom they were accorded probably made them more tolerant of me than they would have been otherwise.

I was busy writing a collection of crime stories called "The Snake Woman Series." In each tale there was a death which, although unexpected, could be reasonably laid to natural causes. However, in each case the reader had to explain away the brief but inexplicable appearance on the scene of a woman named Volga Merna. Since the other characters were not able to remember what she looked like or what she was doing, she was never suspected. Nor was it explicitly stated that she had any part in the crimes; the reader could decide. Once again I had found an audience. I read all of "The Snake Woman Series" to the Hoagland sisters and their guests that summer.

The hostility between Horseshoe Cabin and Lasata flared openly only once. Daddypapa was in the habit of raising the flag at sunrise and lowering it at sunset; this was, as Mother described it, a hangover from his Civil War days. He would stand at attention a moment, salute sharply, and then bring the flag down from the top of the pole. One evening Mrs. Crouch passed by just as he was going through his routine. She greeted him, but he was too deeply preoccupied to answer, or perhaps he did not hear her. She stood still, watching him, until he had the folded flag under his arm. Then with great scorn she spat out the word "Imperialist!" and went on her way. Daddypapa told about it with more amusement than anger, but Mrs. Crouch said indignantly: "It's men like your grandfather who've made the world the horrible place it is today." I had no idea of what she was talking about and assumed she meant simply that he was old-fashioned; thus her vehemence delighted me.

That autumn I decided to change to Jamaica High School, despite the suffocating classrooms without enough seats and the staggered schedule that started the first class at eight in the morning. I was tired of the trolley ride. When I announced my intention, Daddy said: "I know why he wants to switch schools. Because here they don't know yet what a damn fool he is."

Perhaps it was the chaos in the ancient school building, or perhaps it was merely that I was getting older, but I discovered that I was enjoying going to school, and for the first time. As a concomitant of that new experience, I also found that it was possible for me to fail in a subject. This was an eventuality that had never even occurred to me; nevertheless here I was, unable to get a passing mark in geometry. Geometry was a particularly bad class; we sat on the windowsills and on the floor, crowding against one another. Once I brought out a copy of *New Masses* and passed it around while the teacher was explaining a theorem. After class a boy named Goldberg came over to me and said, glowering at me: "What are *you* doing with *New Masses*?" I countered by saying: "Why, what's the matter with it?" "It's not for you," he told me, and walked away. This left me speechless; for months my mind replayed the scene. Why did Goldberg think I was unfit to be reading *New Masses*?

I was appointed humor editor of the school magazine, a humble post from which I hoped to move to that of poetry editor; my ambition did not reach higher. I spent most of my leisure time that year in bookshops looking for bargains in used lending-library copies. I bought all of Arthur Machen, whom I particularly liked. And one spring evening I bought my first Gide: Knopf's edition of *The Vatican Swindle*. (A later edition was called *Lafcadio's Adventures*; God knows why.) Like my fifteen-year-old counterparts all over the world, I was seduced by Lafcadio's *acte gratuit*. I still prefer *Les Caves du Vatican* to Gide's other novels.

Miss Jane Hoagland talked a good deal about what she called "the bohemian life"; it existed only in Greenwich Village, she said. She knew painters and poets who lived there, and sometimes she would take me along with her to a "studio." It struck me as repellent that people in the arts and in letters should make themselves look different from ordinary citizens. My own conviction was that the artist, being the enemy of society, for his own good must remain as invisible as possible and certainly should be indistinguishable from the rest of the crowd. Somewhere in the back of my mind there was the assumption that art and crime were indissolubly linked; the greater the art, the more drastic the punishment for it. Of the Village visits with Miss Jane, the only one I recall is the one we made to Buckminster Fuller's, to see his Dymaxion house. He had an enormous model of it which delighted me. It was a polyhedron with surfaces of what he described as a casein product. Of course, it did not touch the earth at any point, and as I remember, it could be rotated on its axis to face in whatever direction one desired. I arrived back home full of enthusiasm for Fuller and his fantastic house. (It *was* a daring project in 1926.)

"Trust you to dig up something that impractical," said Daddy.

"Well, no, not the way he described it," I began.

"Oh, I wouldn't live in it!" Mother exclaimed. "A glass house stuck up on a pole, where everyone can see me? I like my privacy. I think I'd honestly rather live in a cave."

"But he explained how the walls could be regulated. You could have them at any point between opaque and transparent."

"I don't *want* my walls to be transparent, ever, thank you."

"What'd you·say was this genius's name?" Daddy asked in his most snide manner. He was so sure it was going to be a non Anglo-Saxon name.

I told him.

"Fuller," said Mother reflectively. "Did you ask him where he was from?"

"What's in a name?" said Daddy scornfully.

At that time I became increasingly conscious of being in a state of nervous excitement. Often my heart pounded, and there was a hissing in my ears. Sleep became a problem. I would lie awake most of the night, listening to the clocks strike the hour and the half hour. I could not be interested in something without getting excited, and when I was excited, a motor began to buzz in the back of my neck. It made me feel that I was trembling, but this must have been my imagination, for no one ever mentioned it. Daddy, however, often said to me: "Calm down, young man, calm down."

Part of the musical education I was receiving consisted in being present at the Saturday Philharmonic concerts at Carnegie

Hall. These were complete with commentator and lantern slides, but for me any orchestral sound was a delight. The drabness of the auditorium contrasted strangely, I thought, with the glamorous sounds that filled it. Nineteenth-century works made up the programs, until one day they played *The Fire Bird*. I would not have expected an orchestra to be able to make such sounds. I was electrified and on my way home stopped at a phonograph shop to see if it was available on records. Fortunately Victor had just issued two 12-inch discs. I bought them and played them, constantly but very softly, on the portable phonograph I had in my room.

The new high school building was ready for use in September, 1926. After the "firetrap," the imposing new edifice was a delight. I went into the sixth term—that is, the second semester of the third year. As my life tended to become more social, experience began to cut less deeply into my subconscious, since it is precisely at this point where memory becomes less distinct. The recall is not blocked; it is simply that I was very busy living. Relationships with other people are at best nebulous; their presence keeps us from being aware of the problem of giving form to our life.

The *New Yorker* had begun to appear; I bought it each week on my way to the appointment at the orthodontist's. In the beginning it used center color spreads of cartoons by Gluyas Williams, Ralph Barton, Rea Irvin, and Peter Arno, but almost immediately this feature was discontinued, and the magazine assumed its present format, albeit somewhat more svelte. In the spring of 1927 a "Letter from Paris" in its pages reported on the founding there of a new international magazine called *transition*. I hunted it out in small bookshops on Sixth Avenue, and found it. No publication had ever made such a profound impression on me. Quite apart from the frontal assault of Surrealism, the existence of which I had not even suspected, I loved its concise format, the strange muted colors of the soft paper they used as covers, and the fact that each page had to be cut with a paper knife. Above all, each month when I bought the new issue, I had the illusion of being in Paris, for the feeling of the city I got from reading its pages coincided with my own idea of what Paris must be like, where the people were desperate but sophisticated, cynical but fanatically loyal to ideas. Paris was the center of all existence; I could feel its glow when I faced eastward as a Moslem feels the light from Mecca, and I knew that some day, with luck, I should go there and stand on the sacred spots.

I was elected president of the school literary society which met each Friday evening. Having at last attained the post of poetry editor of the school magazine, I was able to use its small office during certain hours. There I sat at the typewriter practicing the invention of poetry "without conscious intervention." At length I could type an entire page literally without any knowledge of what I had put there. These "poems" I sent out to transition, 40, rue Fabert, Paris, certain that nothing in the presentation of my manuscripts betrayed the shameful fact that I was a high school student. The material itself, being beyond my control, also escaped my judgment, but this did not matter; the important thing as far as I was concerned was that no one seeing it should guess that I was only sixteen.

I still had lunch occasionally with Annie Carroll Moore (except that she had changed her first name to Anne). When I stopped by at her office in the library to call for her, she still invariably gave me a book. It was she who first told me about the University of Virginia. In some way she managed to infect me with her enthusiasm, and soon I was sending off to Charlottesville for information. It became an accepted fact around the house that I was going to Virginia. But since I was being graduated from high school in January and could not enter college until September, there remained the question of what I was going to be doing with myself during all that time. It was unthinkable, of course, that I should do nothing at all.

Having painted some pictures, I took them to the Hoagland sisters' house in Brooklyn. There, as a measure of encouragement, two or three people asked to buy paintings. Not only was I pleased with the money, but I found it a good arguing point to use in my campaign to be enrolled at an art school after graduation. "You want to be a well-rounded dilettante?" Daddy asked, disgusted. "It's only for four months," I told him.

I suspect now that he thought I might become so engrossed in working at painting that I would abandon my intention of going to college, in which case he would have been delighted. He was not eager to see me go off to Virginia or anywhere else. I had no objective which required a degree, and he felt that whatever money was spent on my education counted as a total loss. Art school could be considered as possible training for a profession of sorts.

Several months before graduation I was already examining the art schools of Manhattan. Most of them were drab and depressing. The Art Students League frightened me off with its official-looking entrance. I settled on a tiny school which was entirely contained in the top floor of an ancient and long since demolished brick dwelling at 212 Central Park South. There could not have been more than a dozen students altogether. Let us say that seven worked in the front studio and five in the back one. The windows of the large room looked out over the trees of the park, and I decided that in spite of the three long creaking staircases I liked the place.

My announcement of this at home was greeted with derision. "School of *what?*" Daddy demanded, cocking his ear dramatically and screwing up his face.

"Design and Liberal Arts."

"They come up with the *damnedest* expressions."

"Of course they don't bother to teach fundamentals any more," Mother declared. "It's all Expressionism."

"Will you tell me what liberal art is?" said Daddy evenly.

Since I did not answer, he smiled triumphantly. Nevertheless I enrolled and paid the tuition in advance, so there would be no complications when the time came.

The graduation exercises took place; apparently they made no impression whatever on me, since I recall nothing about them. Then each morning I was reporting to the School of Design and Liberal Arts, where I took my place with the others and learned to draw absurd objects like pitchers, cylindrical containers of paper, and earthenware jugs. Soon, however, we started on plaster casts, in order to become acquainted with anatomy, and then the models arrived. I had never seen an unclothed human body before, either male or female, and after the first few weeks of observing the phenomenon I had no desire ever to see another. It had not occurred to me that human beings could look so repulsive. The women had three times too much flesh, and the men were covered with body hair. I asked Miss Weir, the directress, why we spent so much time drawing naked people; her astonishment was tinged with indignation at my insensitivity. "The human figure is the ultimate esthetic phenomenon," she declared. This struck me as pure convention, wholly arbitrary; it seemed to me that one could just as easily make the statement about spheres or trees. I suggested that a healthy cat or horse was a far more beautiful creature than any human being, but she would have none of it. When later in the season we came to painting the figures in oil, I used only blues for the flesh. This did not please anyone, including the models themselves, who during rest periods wandered around the studio, still naked and smelling of sweat, to see what we had done. One woman in particular was outraged when she saw herself all in brilliant blue, bloated like a corpse; she conceived a violent dislike for me then and there. Fortunately we changed models every week.

I arrived home one afternoon to find that a small packet had arrived for me from Paris. I tore it open. It was a copy of *transition 12*, with my name among those on the cover. I had imagined the moment so many times that the reality was almost like a *déjà vu*. I jumped into the air and let out a shout of triumph. There was no one in the house to notice such unusual behavior, but very likely I should have done it anyway. Then I took a paper knife from the desk beside me, sat down quietly, and slit the pages until I found my contribution, somewhere in the middle; a long surrealist effort called "Spire Song." There was a note inside from Eugene Jolas, saying they would be using a prose piece called "Entity" in number 13. My joy and excitement were such that I remember little else about the spring of 1928.

For months afterward I had only to remind myself of this great stroke of luck, and I would feel a momentary surge of euphoria. Now when I sent poems out, I could add a note about myself, with my *transition* pedigree. At no point did I ask myself whether or not I had anything to say which could be of interest to someone else. My desire was to impose my personality by any means available; I did not conceive of anything beyond that.

In the back studio, where fashion design and layout were taught, there was an English girl I thought particularly beautiful. From the time when I first went to school I had always chosen one girl whom I could admire at a distance, the distance being purely subjective, since often she sat at the desk directly in front of me or across the aisle. Margaret Gill, Evelyn Lane, Edna Krebs, Virginia Andrews, and the rest of the list—all were superlatively beautiful and equally unapproachable. I was seventeen now and still had never had a date with a girl. The few I should have liked to go out with when I was in high school were not allowed out; the others did not obsess me and were of no interest. Now, however, I had for the first time a girl whom I could take out to dinner and who, furthermore, lived in her own room in the Village. We could go back there for a while in the evening, but her father had a room on the floor above and often stopped by to see her on his way to bed. Nor could I remain late. No matter how carefully I let myself in, my parents invariably heard me, checked the hour, and upbraided me in the morning. In general, coming home after one o'clock guaranteed an unpleasant breakfast the following day.

At the end of the term I was given a prize for what was called "greatest output and originality." I took this to mean that I worked fast and learned slowly. I conceived of originality as a quality which a happy few succeeded in retaining, in spite of having been forced through the process of education. Suspecting that the prize had been invented with me in mind as recipient, I asked, and found that I was right. "I had to make it up," the directress explained. "You had to have a prize, but I couldn't give it for quality."

Nearly four months remained before I was due to report to the bursar's office at the university. Daddy saw this as the ideal moment for me to get some practical knowledge. He spoke to one of his patients, the manager of the local Bank of the Manhattan Company, who agreed to hire me to work in the Transit Department. It seemed incredible that the bank should be willing to pay indefinitely for work which involved no effort—namely, the pushing down of the keys of an adding machine. My only other duties consisted of carrying a briefcase full of checks around to the main bank at 40 Wall Street. This variation in my routine came irregularly and was always welcome. I made the trips last a long time by using local, rather than express, trains on the subway and elevated lines and by planning the most circuitous routes. In those days the trains were relatively empty between rush hours. After the glare of the summer sun in the streets the cars seemed pleasantly cool. And the best way yet devised for seeing New York was to take the elevated, particularly the Second and Third Avenue lines, both of which provided dramatic views of lower Manhattan.

Even the days when I did not go out of the bank at all and merely sat under a fan adding long lists of digits, even these days were enjoyable, because I was completely relaxed; no mental effort whatever was being required of me. And it was fun to be saving up money to spend later once I was alone in Virginia. For it seemed already settled that Mother was going down to Charlottesville with me. I protested that there was no point in her tiring herself by making so long a trip when it was unnecessary.

"By rights your father should be going with you," she said. "But he's not, and you certainly aren't going galumphing down there by yourself. Besides, I've never seen the place." This prospect somewhat depressed me; it was not my idea of how a young man traditionally arrived at college, and it seemed an inauspicious beginning. When we got there, however, it was immediately clear that most of the freshmen were undergoing the identical experience: the hotels teemed with mothers and sons.

On the first day, Mother and a Southern lady with magnolias in her voice approached each other in the lobby and began to talk. At one point names were exchanged. "Is that the V'ginia Bowles?" asked the lady. "No, the Massachusetts Bowles," Mother said. The lady waited for just the amount of time it took to get the magnolias out of her voice before she said: "I see."

"All these years," Mother mused later. "You'd think by this time they'd have found something else to occupy their minds. But that's the sort of thing you're going to run up against here."

The prophecy proved to be quite wrong: no one cared whether you came from North or South. You learned to greet other students by saying: "Mawnin', gemmun" (or "Evenin', gemmun," if it happened to be after midday), and if you were a freshman, you had to wear a hat. That was the extent of your social obligations.

Most of the students roomed and ate in private houses. Soon after my arrival I noticed that my appetite had begun to increase considerably, and I found myself enjoying the act of eating. It was a novelty to look forward with such eagerness to the next meal. Mrs. Saunders on Chancellor Street, at whose house I ate, was reputed to serve the best food; very likely this had something to do with my introduction to the pleasures of hunger and its satisfaction. The principal factor, however, was merely the absence of parental criticism at mealtime.

I lived at the McMurdos', where there were five other students: Jenkins, Chapman, Grey, Shower, and Andrews. I got on with them all except Andrews, whose room was opposite mine. He resented the fact that I locked my door when I studied and refused to answer when he pounded on it, and so he made a great show of pretending to think I spent my time masturbating in there behind the locked door.

When I was not studying, I was out walking. In those days the countryside around Charlottesville was beautiful. There were very few cars on the roads, and the general decay into which most of the American landscape has now fallen had not yet become noticeable. I walked along paved roads and country lanes, as well as on the railroad tracks. I tried every direction, soon discovering that the west was the most satisfying, for it was out that way that the road crossed the Blue Ridge. The forest up there fascinated me; I kept returning when I should have stayed in Charlottesville studying. A certain familiarity with the back roads of the region was considered necessary in any case, since one had to use them in order to reach the dark and hidden farmhouses that sold liquor. You took along your empty gallon jugs, and they gave you new ones filled with colorless whiskey. When you got home, you drained off the fusel oil and added dried peaches and a bag of charcoal; the next night your whiskey was aged. It didn't taste very good in a julep, and it was considerably worse with Coke or ginger ale. The best way to drink it was neat, fast, and in great quantity. That way the taste buds were quickly put out of commission. I had done very little drinking in my life; now I felt called upon to do as much as I could.

There was a variant, introduced by students of the Medical School: you bought a pound tin of Squibb's ether and sniffed it from a small glass between drinks. It was only a step from this to buying several cans and soaking a sheet in their contents. I hung such a sheet in my room one night and met with great opposition from all sides. The stench of ether filled the house and distracted the guests at the party the McMurdos were giving downstairs.

In my French class one student wearing jodhpurs and boots regularly came in with his dog and gun. He stood the rifle by the door, and the setter went to lie quietly under Professor Abbott's desk. I made field trips with my geology class in search of hematite, schist, and crinoids. While some of the students straggled in order to stay far enough behind to be able to take quiet nips from their hip flasks, Professor Roberts explained ontogeny in phylogeny to those who had not fully understood it in class. Professor Pratt's "History of Music" was the only course whose factual material I have retained more or less intact.

I came into contact with my first group of intellectual snobs and understood that their principal interest was not in literature and art, but in talking about those things. However, I learned from them. That autumn I first read *The Waste Land,* first heard Gregorian chant and Prokofieff, first listened with pleasure to Duke Ellington and his band from the Cotton Club. And I bought my first blues records at secondhand furniture stores in the black quarter of Charlottesville.

I went home for Christmas. It was the winter when people discussed the words to Cole Porter's "Let's Do It." On New Year's Eve I was violently sick from drinking too much speakeasy beer that had been needled with ether. I returned to Virginia the next day in a morning-after mood which did not disappear when its physiological causes no longer existed. Having seen Virginia from the vantage point of New York in some way changed my feeling about it. I was inclined to agree secretly with Daddy, who declared that in his opinion the university was not a college, but a country club. The persistent malaise was heightened by a bout of conjunctivitis which landed me in the hospital, where I spent a drugged week with my hands strapped to the bed.

Having so many outside interests, I spent less time studying. It was therefore a surprise to find at the end of the first term that I had managed to get onto the dean's list, after all. This was a roster of students who had received consistently high grades; having your name on the list meant that you no longer were required to attend classes. You had only to pass your final examinations. This left me free to spend an occasional weekend in Richmond or to go on such long hikes that I had to pass the night at a hotel in Staunton or Waynesboro. One evening when I was far from any settlement, on top of the Blue Ridge, I asked for shelter at a lone farmhouse. No one in the family had ever been to Charlottesville. They fed me and let me sleep on a mattress. In the morning they served me the biggest breakfast I had ever seen.

Except among the snobs, James Branch Cabell was spoken of with reverent loyalty by literary-minded students and professors. *Jurgen* had been published just then; it was thought to be significant. I looked at it briefly in the university bookshop and decided it was not for me. Instead, I bought Djuna Barnes' new novel *Ryder,* because she had been among the contributors to *transition.*

Victor had just launched its first long-playing phonograph. I bought a big console model, which threw the records from one part of the machine to another and all too often either cracked them or took a large bite-shaped piece out of them. This feature was not called to my attention by the salesman, although I called it to his after the purchase. "They haven't perfected it yet," he said when I showed him my collection of damaged records.

Then I had what I thought was my first compulsive experience. (It was not until a good many years later that I connected it with going in and out of Roth's candy store.) I got back to my room one afternoon at dusk and, upon opening the door, knew at once, although I had no idea of what it was going to be, that I was about to do something explosive and irrevocable. It occurred to me that this meant that I was not the I I thought I was or, rather, that there was a second I in me who had suddenly assumed command. I shut the door and gave a running leap up onto the bed, where I stood, my heart pounding. I took out a quarter and tossed it spinning into the air, so that it landed on my palm. Heads. I cried out with relief and jumped up and down on the mattress several times before landing on the floor. Tails would have meant that I would have had to take a bottle of Allonal that night and leave no note. But heads meant that I would leave for Europe as soon as possible. I went back outdoors and walked some more, not returning to my room until I had sent a telegram to Mrs. Crouch in New York, announcing my decision and, at the same time, soliciting a favor. I wanted her to help me get a passport. It was with a conspirator's finesse that I chose her as confidante, aware that she could hardly be expected to resist such a splendid opportunity to shock all the members of my family at one fell swoop. And she would be certain to see the blow she was going to deal them in a symbolic light, particularly if I was there to induce her to start the legend off in the proper direction.

When I had a go-ahead wire from Mrs. Crouch, I began to move. Since the McMurdo furniture had not satisfied me I had bought my own, including a Persian rug. Now I sold everything except the phonograph, leaving the bed until the last afternoon. I had determined to keep completely silent about my departure. The night I left, however, because I needed someone to help me carry my suitcases, I confided in a student named Cesare Lloyd, and it was he who helped me lug all my belongings to the station at three in the morning. As we walked along the railroad track on our way down from University Heights to the main station, there were flashes of lightning and rolls of thunder, which I was pleased to take as an auspicious omen once Cesare had suggested it. Since there was no limit to where I might go if opportunity presented itself, the escapade presented itself to me in the guise of an expedition, and thus I wore hunting trousers and boots.

I spent my initial night in New York at a tiny, ancient hotel on Ninth Avenue. There were bedbugs, the first ones I had ever seen. I told the manager. He shrugged. "You don't like the room it's a free country." Mrs. Crouch and Miss Sue were delighted with my plan of escape; they thought it wonderful that I was showing originality and determination. "You've made the right decision," they assured me. "You'll fit into the life over there."

"What a blow this will be for the Bowleses," added Mrs. Crouch, shaking her head.

I only hoped to be gone by the time the family found out what I had done. First I had to make a trip out to Jamaica and get a photostat copy of my birth certificate. Mrs. Crouch took it with her when she went to get me my passport. This stage in the proceedings seemed to me crucial; doubtless because it involved deception, I felt that it was particularly likely to misfire.

Inexplicably, I was lucky. Either one of them by herself would have been convincing, and they had both gone. That night I was invited to their apartment for dinner. When I arrived, Mrs. Crouch announced that I was a free man. She began to search in her handbag and pulled out an envelope. "We perjured ourselves," said Miss Sue.

Mrs. Crouch had told them she had come to get a passport for her nephew, whose parents wanted to send him to Europe to school and were both indisposed and unable to appear in person at the office. There was no difficulty at all.

The next day I went to the Holland-America Line and got passage on the *Rijndam,* a very old ship making its last transatlantic voyage. My ticket to Boulogne-sur-Mer cost $125; this left me with less than $50 in my wallet, and the ship was not sailing until the following week. Mrs. Crouch came up with another suggestion. There was an empty furnished apartment on Washington Square that had been left behind by her daughter Mary, who had just got married and gone to Cannes. She gave me the key, and I moved in immediately. The place belonged to someone who worked for Condé Nast and was one of those establishments where everything was upholstered in satin.

It was comfortable, smelled wonderful, and felt good everywhere to the touch. After I had lived there a few days, the owner and his wife came by. They tried to let themselves in, but I had the chain across. This put them into a state of excitement. "Who's in there?" they cried. When I let them in and explained the situation, they insisted that Mrs. Crouch had no right to have put anyone into the apartment since it was not rented in her name. They found pretexts for going into all the rooms to examine them, and I followed, saying that my ship was sailing in a day or two. Finally they agreed to let me stay on. This was fortunate for me, or I should have had to move into a hotel. And my money was diminishing slowly each day, even without having to pay for a room.

I had rather hoped a little cash might be forthcoming from my two protectors at the moment of embarkation. Instead, they loaded me down with books to read on the sea voyage and gave me three letters of introduction to friends in Paris. They did not come along to see me off. The *Rijndam* left from Hoboken. It was a blustery March morning, and as the ferry cut through the choppy waters of the Hudson, I kept a paranoid lookout for my parents, arguing that it was still just possible for them to have found out and to stop me from sailing.

Who did come along to see me off was Lucy Rogers, two or three years younger than I. I had seen a good deal of her during several summers at Glenora. Mrs. Crouch and Miss Sue had unofficially adopted her and had sent her to school in France for a time, so that she knew the three women to whom the introductory letters were addressed. Until the guests had to go ashore, we sat in the incredibly old-fashioned salon discussing the best way to approach Miss Lynch, Madame Daniloff, and Madame Caskie. There were only eight other passengers on the ship; an elderly Dutchman bought drinks for everyone and continued buying them until we sailed.

V

Among the books I had with me in my cabin I can recall only two. Having read Gide's *Counterfeiters* two years before, I had gone to Brentano's and bought his working notes for the novel, *Journal des Faux-Monnayeurs.* The other was one of the books Mrs. Crouch had handed me: *The Hammer and the Scythe,* an early apologia for the USSR. I found it very dull.

The passengers all ate at one long table, presided over by the captain. I sat opposite a medium-pretty French girl, who was on her way to have her first baby at her mother's house in Paris. She was the most pleasant and amusing of those aboard, and so I talked with her. I had seen her out on deck while the ship was still in port, bathed in tears as she kissed her husband, over and over again. He was the Comte de Guendulaine, and he had brought her from his property in southern Mexico to New York, to put her on the *Rijndam.* I learned a good bit of colloquial French from Christine during the ten-day voyage. She did not speak much English, but she had to use it with the Dutch on board. When we got to Boulogne, it was after midnight, and the sea was very rough. To disembark we climbed down a ladder they slung over the side of the ship and dropped into an open dinghy below. When all four of us were in the bobbing rowboat, Christine called up to a Dutchwoman who was waving her handkerchief: "Don't make big ties!" Since she said it several times, I asked her what she meant. *"Ne faites pas des grosses larmes,"* she explained. *"Comment je le dis?"*

I began: "Well, *larmes* is *tears*. But you can't say it that way, in any case . . ."

She was impatient. "Tears, ties, ears, eyes! *C'est impossible. Tous les mots se ressemblent.*"

In the hotel room I sat for a long time looking out at the empty port, trying to persuade myself of the reality of the situation. I touched the curtains and said to myself: "They are France. This is France. I am in France."

The next day Christine and I boarded the train for Paris. At the Gare St.-Lazare we were met by her mother, the Comtesse de Lavillatte, and her brother, whom she presented as the Duc de St.-Simon. Like Christine, they had excessively long French noses. The taxi ride to the Rue St.-Dominique seemed endless, with all three of them talking at once, and the car horns in the street sounding like Gershwin's trumpets at the beginning of *An American in Paris*. I was listening for them and decided he had done a good imitation.

There were more brothers, sisters, and cousins at the house to meet Christine, including an eight-year-old boy who, when asked during lunch if he too wouldn't like to go to Mexico, looked across at his sister and shook his head saying: "You get too fat there." Then they all began repeating the phrase to one another. *"On y grossit trop!"* The tremendous merriment called forth by this phrase was predicated on the assumption that it had been pronounced in innocence. But while they were still laughing, I watched the boy and knew from his expression that he was quite aware of the cause of his sister's present stoutness. I felt a twinge of envy, thinking what a fortunate child he was to live with such a gullible family. After lunch we all sat on tiny gilt chairs drinking coffee and liqueurs, and the Duc de St.-Simon gave me a cigar. I hoped no one would guess that I had never smoked one before.

I now had exactly $24. That evening a brother of Christine's walked with me to see Madame Gaubert, who accepted *pensionnaires*. There in my room after dinner I took out the letters of introduction and studied them once again. Lucy had told me that Madame Daniloff was a charming and generous woman, who could surely be counted on to give me a dinner now and then.

Miss Lynch was an osteopath who practiced in a big office on the Rue de la Paix. Madame Caskie was an Irish actress who lived on the Left Bank. I decided that the osteopath's office was the place for me to go the next day in order to find work. There was, of course, the question of a work permit, which although necessary was impossible in my case, since the document, if granted at all, took three months to issue. I had to work immediately.

At Miss Lynch's I was turned over to a Monsieur de la Batut, a receptionist in her office. He took me to lunch and then to the *Herald Tribune* office on the Rue du Louvre, where he knew someone. In 1929 the paper had two Paris offices; the main one was on the Avenue de l'Opéra. I was briefly interviewed and told I could have a job as telephone switchboard operator. "But the work permit?" I murmured. "As an American firm we have a way around that," my interviewer said.

The following morning I started work. It consisted of standing beside an Armenian girl whom I was to replace at the end of the week and watching the board for a *papillon* to show somewhere on it. When a *papillon* showed white, you had to plug in a line opposite it. The pay for doing this was to be 200 francs a week, or $8. The Armenian girl showed me some cheap restaurants; we ate together at noon each day and once or twice at night. But she was leaving Paris immediately. When she had gone, I was left to manage the switchboard by myself. The work made me nervous, principally because it involved listening to numerals that reached my ears via a distorting acoustical apparatus, and then repeating them to the central operator. I had to remain always on the alert, in order not to make a mistake. Since I was under the impression that I was proficient in French, it became a matter of personal pride never to give anyone a wrong number. What would Elliot Paul think, for instance, in case it should be he on the wire? For he worked upstairs somewhere in the editorial department, reading proof, they told me, and he was a co-editor of *transition*. I would see him, complete with beard and cane, going in and out, since everyone had to pass by the telephonist's cage in the entrance hall. I used to imagine ways in which I might get to speak to him, merely to let him know I was there. They were all impracticable. One day after lunch he appeared from the street and walked straight to the cage. "Come outside," he told me. There was a taxi at the curb, in front of the entrance, and its door was open. "Look inside," he said. I did. The interior of the cab was entirely upholstered in false boa-constrictor skin. "Do you see what I see?" he demanded. "Just tell me that."

"You mean the snakeskin?"

"Ah!" He was satisfied; slamming the door and with a wave to the driver, he went inside and climbed the stairs, staggering a bit. It seemed like a poor occasion for trying to talk with him.

Another day I went all the way to the Rue Fabert, where *transition* had its offices, climbed upstairs, and stood outside the door for a while. Then, I decided that it would be absurd for me to go in and announce myself. No one could be in the least interested. I made no further effort to meet the editors of *transition*.

Madame Daniloff lived in what was then the suburb of Boulogne-sur-Seine. I presented myself there one evening soon after taking the job at the *Herald Tribune* and was warmly embraced by the matronly Russian lady with her hair piled high on her head. She had received a letter from Mrs. Crouch. The apartment was bare, very simply furnished. In one room with books piled everywhere sat General Daniloff, her husband, who had recently published a two-volume life of Marshal Foch. The general had little to say; he agreed with Madame that I must have something to eat. They lived alone and had already had their dinner, but she prepared me a Gruyère omelet and a salad, both of which tasted better than anything I had been able to afford in the *prix-fixe* restaurants I regularly patronized.

A stray cat returns to the place where it is fed. I began to make regular evening visits to the Daniloff apartment. Since then I have known other Russians of the *ancien régime* and listened to the excessive modulation of their spoken language; Madame Daniloff, being a demonstrative woman in any case, outdid them all. When she spoke Russian, her contralto voice rose abruptly to shrieking heights on certain accented syllables in nearly every sentence. The effect was baroque and dramatic, but the general, who was her only interlocutor in these instances, was in no way affected by the display and scarcely noticed her.

One night I took three of Mrs. Crouch's farewell gift books

along with me to Boulogne. She had suggested that when I was finished with them, the Daniloffs might like to have them. When Madame saw *The Hammer and the Scythe,* she screamed, touched her throat, and turned her face away for a moment. *"Mais qu'est-ce que vous faites avec ce livre?"* she demanded. *"Ne lisez pas cette saleté!"* She delivered an impassioned attack on the Soviet Union, finishing by calling it a government of dogs. She then picked up the book with a great show of distaste and carried it out of the room. It was with my topcoat by the door when I left. I had the impression that Mrs. Crouch had foreseen the episode more or less as it had happened, and I was amused by her deviousness.

Paris was a continual joy—even walking to work in the morning. The era had not yet arrived when the traffic was thick enough to cancel the smells of spring in the air. Some nights the mere fact of being there excited me so much that there was no question of going to bed until I had walked all the way across the city, say from the Place Denfert-Rochereau to the Place Clichy. Then I would have to get back to whatever hotel I was living in. The next day I would feel voluptuously weary, in a vaguely floating condition. The day in the cage would pass more swiftly as a result. And before me I had the prospect of a night of sound sleep. For sleep was still a problem. I kept changing hotels each two or three days, because the kind of hotel room I could afford always had bedbugs. In the case of one room which had seduced me with its picturesqueness, I made the error of paying a month in advance. The first night an army climbed up the legs of the bed and attacked. I complained bitterly to the proprietress, who then stood the legs of the bed inside small tins of kerosene. That night they swarmed up the wall, across the ceiling until they were directly over the bed, and then went into free fall.

When I told Madame Daniloff of my difficulties, she overreacted once again. *"Des punaises!"* she cried. *"Quelle horreur!"* Immediately she embarked on a campaign to induce my parents to send me a regular sum of money on which I could live. I objected that they would never agree, and I had to admit that they still had no idea where I was, inasmuch as I had not written home since I had been in Charlottesville. This news spurred her on; she could not fathom my secretive attitude and put it down to pride.

For my part, at that point I fully expected never to see my family again. I had taken matters into my own hands, and that they would not forgive. When I told her that, she merely laughed. "You are too thin and nervous," she told me, and she took me to an old Russian doctor, who she said had been the great physician of Petrograd. The doctor talked and made tests and went on talking. "Do you practice self-abuse?" he wanted to know. I was annoyed at being asked such a question, but I answered him, saying: "Once in a while."

"Ah!" He was triumphant. "And wouldn't it be better to go each morning and run in the Bois de Boulogne?"

I decided he was senile and agreed. When we rejoined Madame Daniloff in the reception room, they spoke lengthily in Russian, and she showed signs of great relief. Then I paid the doctor a quarter of my week's salary, and we left. After that, she regularly admonished me: *"Et maintenant ne faites plus de bêtises."* Her apparent relief did not keep her from insisting upon writing Mother a letter in English. Subsequently I saw it. I needed to go away for a cure, she had written. And farther down on the page: "A few weeks of cure will make Paul well."

Mother must have been glad to hear I was alive and to know where to reach me, but not understanding the French usage of the word *cure*, she assumed that somehow I had begun to take drugs. Her return letter to me spoke of using willpower and of knowing that one really wanted to break the habit. Not a penny was forthcoming, naturally enough; I had prophesied that beforehand. Poor Madame Daniloff found it difficult to believe that any parents could remain impervious to the plight of their only child. She did not know the New England mentality, according to which reparations must accompany transgression. Mother's rigid answer to her, which came the same day as her letter to me, left her wide-eyed with shock. However, she persevered and wrote to Mrs. Crouch's daughter Mary, who was in London. This brought results: money arrived immediately, enough so that I could quit the *Herald Tribune* job and have time to look for less exacting work. I wrote to Mary thanking her. Almost simultaneously I realized with a shock that now I was not chained by the necessity of earning the money for my food and lodging; I understood that for the first time I was free. It was a heady sensation, but I did not savor it all at once. Every two days I made a trip out of Paris and each time covered territory that lay a little farther from the city. Finally one day I took a ticket for Chamonix and set off on the train in my boots and breeches, carrying nothing with me. The next ten days I spent climbing up and down the mountains and going around Lake Geneva.

The Alpine landscape looked like a vast florist's display window, with purple hyacinths blooming at the foot of snowbanks and streams of clear water rushing through the meadows. The only sounds to come up from the valleys were cow bells, goat bells, and church bells. I followed the main thoroughfare from Chamonix, yet during the first day on the road I saw only one automobile. At Orsières I spent Ascension Day sitting at the piano in the little salon of the inn, writing a piano prelude. Lausanne was a pleasant town, but not Geneva, which seemed too much like an American city. I crossed back over into France at Annemasse, where an argument with a customs inspector over a box of Swiss cigarettes caused me to miss my train connection. Once again I set out on foot. Two or three days later, with the aid of a local train here and another there, I found myself down in the *département* of Basses-Alpes. The weather was perfect, and I walked from one village to another in a state of semi-euphoria induced by the unfamiliar countryside. My experiences with nature and the open road had been limited to the relatively comfortless landscapes of the eastern United States; it was not surprising that I should have been impressed by what I found in France and Switzerland.

Renting a room at a country hotel meant being at the mercy of the weather, since I would take advantage of my stay by washing my shirt and tacking it up to dry. First I had to pry out the thumbtacks that held the regulation room price card to the back of the door. If it rained, the shirt was still wet in the morning. I had a raincoat, but I never started out when I thought there was going to be rain.

I came down into Nice on the train at night. Even though I could not see the difference in the light, the smell and texture of the air told me that I was in a new climate. I had never before seen subtropical vegetation, thus the presence of palms and mimosas in the streets inevitably gave the city an air of voluptuousness.

I stayed on for a week, rising each morning at daybreak to have a sunrise walk along the sea to Mont Boron, where there was a small *bistrot* right on the waterfront. There I would have my coffee and croissants, and sit a long time reading and writing and simply looking at the water. A few horse-drawn vehicles and an occasional trolley car went past. I read and wrote most of my mail here. One day I had a long letter from Mary, who said she'd see me shortly in Paris and to make whatever money I had last until then. I took this as my cue to go back to Paris fast and see about the work I was supposed to be trying to get.

Mary, beautiful and incredibly elegant, sat facing me in the room at the Hôtel de la Trémoaille and quickly dumped all the money out of her handbag onto the table. "Put it away fast. Jock'll be here any minute." Jock did come: he was thin and much more agreeable than I had expected. We had several meals together before he and Mary left Paris. One day we went to see Madame Daniloff, who squealed with delight. That day it was arranged that she would speak to her friend Sergei Prokofieff and ask him if he would take me on as a pupil. It must have been assumed that he was to be paid for the lessons, but I heard no mention of it. In any case, the idea rather unnerved me: I could not imagine the kind of life such study might entail. When a favorable answer came from the master, I was more worried than flattered. By then Mary had gone on to Vienna, and I could no longer confer with her.

Madame Daniloff and I went to see several of the Russian operas being given at the Théâtre des Champs-Elysees. So far I had gone to the opera only three or four times and considered it either a distracting manner of presenting music or a dull form of theater, depending upon how one looked at it. *Tsar Soltan* and the others somewhat altered my opinion. When the Diaghilev Ballet came to Paris, I went and sat in the cheapest seat. Visibility and sound were both excellent. I had chosen the program carefully (Rieti's *Bal*, Sauguet's *Chatte*, Prokofieff's *Pas d'Acier*) and came away from the Théâtre du Chatelet in a state of exaltation. The net result, nonetheless, was that I felt still more unworthy of meeting Prokofieff than I had before. Because I was so affected by his ballet score, I decided that he could not possibly find anything worthwhile in what I had written. I was correct in that; my error consisted in imagining that this had anything to do with whether or not I ought to study with him.

I had made an appointment with Prokofieff, who lived in Passy, on a Sunday afternoon at three o'clock. At two I packed up my belongings, and leaving them in the care of the concierge at the hotel, took a taxi to the Gare de l'Est, where I bought a ticket on a train that left at three. The train happened to be going to Saverne, a place-name which meant nothing to me. This was an act without conscious motivation; I was not able either at the moment or in retrospect to discover what determined my decision. Again and again I relived the afternoon in memory, hoping to catch the precise instant when I became aware that I was going to the Gare de l'Est, but I was never able to find it. Clearly I felt that the action precluded the necessity of making a choice, that once I was on the train there would be no question of my having to decide anything one way or the other.

When I got to Saverne I began to walk—straight out of the town into the country, and on. Eventually I got to Strasbourg, crossed the Rhine to Kehl, and walked on into the Schwarzwald. The Germans were friendly but wholly uninteresting. I understood why they stressed the word *Kultur:* they had none and hoped to make one by dint of talking about it. However, the beer and the strawberries were very good. I wandered for a week in the Black Forest and crossed the river back into France one midnight at Altbreisach.

I felt that Madame Daniloff would now ask too many questions which I should be unable to answer to her satisfaction, and so I did not go to see her once I got back to Paris. Instead, I concentrated on finding work once again with an American firm. In the meantime the Duc de Saint-Simon had written to a friend of his in New York, suggesting that he see Daddy and try to get him to agree to send me a regular allowance. The friend was a public figure, Judge Victor Dowling, whose connections with Tammany Hall were widely known. (Also, as Daddypapa subsequently remarked of him: "He's a notorious Catholic.") The dialogue was clearly destined to come to nothing. But I unearthed a job in the foreign department of the Bankers' Trust, Place Vendôme, where all I had to do was use a comptometer and give people marks in exchange for lire, or francs for pounds. And the wages were $10 a week rather than $8. This work might have gone on longer had I not made a serious error during the second week: I gave an American woman $1,000 worth of francs rather than $100, and it was not discovered until several hours later. They told me that it was my responsibility to go out and get the $900 back from the client. As I started out from the Place Vendôme, I imagined myself being interrogated by the police. In reality it proved very simple. The woman lived at the Plaza-Athénée and received me pleasantly, claiming that she had not yet examined the bundle of francs I had handed her. I returned to the bank with the money and was congratulated on my good luck. However, any work which included such narrow escapes seemed too dangerous, and I determined not to return to the bank the next day.

That night I went to the Dôme and sat on the *terrasse,* around on the rue Delambre side. Two couples, one in their twenties and the other in their thirties, were sitting at a nearby table; presently the girl asked me to join them. Her name was Hermina, and she was Hungarian. In the course of the conversation she invited me to spend the weekend with them camping beside the Seine. The next morning early I met them at the Dôme, and off we went in their car, the five of us, to a place about an hour and a half east of Paris. They had a campsite right on the river outside a small village. We slept in a tent, which we had to go and fetch from the farmhouse where they stored their equipment. The following morning as we bathed in the river, a fat man rowed his boat to within 200 feet of us and began a heated harangue, shouting that he intended to go to Creil and denounce us to the police. "*Ça a un nom, ça!*" he yelled. "*Ça s'appelle détournement de mineurs!* Each week a different one!"

Hermina called back: "*Assez! Allez vous branler ailleurs*" and the Frenchwoman let down her *cache-sexe* and rotated her buttocks at him, screaming: "*Ça y est? Ça y est?*" He rowed off, shaking his fist at us. After lunch Hermina and I took a walk, still in our bathing suits, which made it bad for me when I ran innocently into a patch of high nettles. Never having seen or heard of the plant before, I first thought I had brushed against a wasps' nest. We climbed through the woods and came out on top of a hill in a cherry orchard. The nettle stings were not the only initiatory experience for me that Sunday afternoon. There among hundreds of excited ants that rushed over us, while Hermina declaimed such sentiments as: "I'm the flower, you're the stem," I had my first sex. When I put my bathing suit back on, I realized that in addition to the nettles and ant bites I was painfully sunburned.

We drove back to Paris. "You'll come next week?" they said, and I agreed. But a few days later I had a note from Miss Sue and Mrs. Crouch, who had arrived in Paris en route to their house near Arles. I went to the station to meet their boat train. My appearance disappointed Mrs. Crouch; she remarked in accusing tones that I looked the same as I had in New York. I said I was wearing the same clothes. "I'd hoped you'd be wearing a beret and maybe a cape like the students wear." Miss Sue remarked that all those things were only outward manifestations, and as such of little importance.

"Or you might have grown a little pointed beard like a Frenchman," Mrs. Crouch went on, still speculating. "Something to show that you've broken away once and for all."

"But how do you know he *has*?" objected Miss Sue.

"Well," declared Mrs. Crouch, as though I had not been sitting there, "if he goes back I shall be very much disappointed in him. After all, it would be an admission of failure. No young man can accept that. But neither can he go on taking money from Mary, of course."

They invited Madame Daniloff and me to lunch at the American University Women's Club where they were staying, and Mrs. Crouch began an argument with the poor lady about the achievements of the Soviet Union. Madame Daniloff grew highly emotional and trembled as she talked; she wanted to hear no good spoken of the Bolsheviki, and she felt herself obliged to refute each statistic. Present at the lunch was an American girl named Kay Cowen, whom I liked immediately. She had just returned to Paris from a sojourn in a place which, to judge from her description and the few photographs she showed me, was one of the world's really extraordinary cities. It was called Marrakech. Unfortunately she stayed only a few days in Paris, but even so I saw her several times. Before she left she took me to see Tristan Tzara and his wife. Except for his monocle he looked more like a doctor than a Surrealist poet. He had a great collection of African masks and artifacts, the like of which I had never seen even in a museum. "You must go back and see them after I've gone," said Kay. I did, but not that year. Later I heard that upon arriving in New York, Kay had gone to visit my mother to assure her that she need not worry about me.

In the late 1880's Daddymama and Daddypapa made a tour of the Deep South. They considered it a picturesque region full of touristic interest. Somewhere in Alabama they heard of a "good" family which had undergone a tragedy. There were several children of varying ages; both parents had just died and almost simultaneously. Daddymama felt impelled to help; her heart went out to the oldest boy, Hubert, who was the age of her own elder son. When they returned to Elmira, they had Hubert with them. He was never formally adopted, but he lived as one of the family for several years, until he had set himself up in business and become successful. "The responsibility for his entire family had fallen on his shoulders," Daddymama told me, "and his shoulders were too frail. We wanted to help make them strong. And that boy worked hard, let me tell you." Hubert's business was eventually so remunerative that he was able to support his sisters and their families all during his lifetime. He was one of the first American couturiers; he established his salon (and sweatshop) on Fifty-seventh Street just around the corner from Fifth Avenue. I remember his occasional visits for dinner during my childhood. He wore silk shirts with sapphire, ruby, emerald, or amethyst cuff links depending on the color of the silk. And he always had on spats. His conversation consisted of gossip about Café Society. (The term had not yet been invented, but the phenomenon was there.) This gossip was judiciously larded with off-color jokes and anecdotes—rather more sophisticated than my parents would have heard from their suburban friends, because Hubert made six European tours each year and collected his conversation in

Paris, Karlovy Vary, Cannes, St. Moritz, and Biarritz. It was inevitable that he should arrive in Paris and equally inevitable that he should get in touch with me. I had not seen him in ten years, but I remembered him as soon as I saw him at the Hôtel Daunou; he had not changed, except that he was not wearing spats, perhaps because it was summer.

He greeted me by saying: "My, my! How much like your father you look when he was your age. What a handsome boy he was, too. Better-looking than you." Since I was not handsome, I found his praise of Daddy unconvincing. "Where are you staying?" he wanted to know. I told him. "It's so far away," he said. "Why don't you move in here with me?" And so I moved into the Hôtel Daunou (Over Harry's Bar; say "Sank Roo Dough Noo") and received a further sexual initiation, equally cold-blooded and ridiculous. "Your father gave me a check for two hundred dollars to buy you some clothes with," Hubert told me, "but I'm going to destroy it." "And the clothes?" I said. "Oh, we'll get them. Don't you worry."

We bought very little, but Hubert took me around to his tailor Dusautoy and had him alter a new suit he had ordered, so that after two fittings I was able to wear it. Certainly it was unlike any suit I had ever worn before: it was double-breasted, and the material was a chocolate brown cheviot with a white pin stripe. "There's only one place for shoes: Hellstern's." We went there. "You must carry a cane," Hubert decided. "And we'll go somewhere next week. Where would you like to go?"

"Venice," I said.

"All right. I'll go to Cook's tomorrow."

The pleasant and entirely unfamiliar experience of being made to feel important was somewhat counterbalanced by the long hours of boring conversation I had to make. At Cook's Hubert met a woman who had just returned from Venice where she said the heat was unbearable. We ended up at St. Moritz with an open car and chauffeur. Thus instead of St. Mark's I saw the Villa d'Este in Como, and instead of riding down the Grand Canal I rode over the Stelvio Pass into the Austrian Tyrol. I suffered from nosebleeds and put on weight.

Back in Paris I visited the Comtesse de Lavillatte who invited

me to Guéret, in the Creuse. Most of the members of the family
whom I had met in Paris were there, but not Christine, who was
in a nursing home awaiting the birth of her baby. The Château
de Lavillatte had a round tower at each of its four corners, and
my room was in one of them; it was circular, and its walls were
covered with *toile de Jouy*. A very old servant named Petitjean took
care of me. Whenever he brought me water, he would set down
the ewer and say: *"Débarbouillez-vous."* When I asked at table
what the expression meant, there was both laughter and conster-
nation. "You must forgive Petitjean," they said. "He's only a
peasant."

The countryside was tender and lush, and there were showers
every day. The countess spent most of her time sitting placidly in
the salon doing petit point. The house was drafty; breezes moved
the tapestries hanging on the walls. In the dark halls the suits of
armor were scarcely visible. The quiet was so complete that if I
listened, I could hear the bees humming outside the windows.

I had agreed to meet Hubert in St.-Malo, and to go from there
with him to Deauville, which in that era was Café Society's summer headquarters. "I never miss it," he said. Also, he was a devout gambler and believed that his luck was better at the Deauville Casino than at any other. I arrived in St.- Malo several days
ahead of him and went to see Mont-St.-Michel, staying in one of
the little rooms that La Mère Poularde put at the disposal of her
dinner guests. Since her kitchen was on one side of the main
street and her restaurant on the other, the waitresses were constantly rushing back and forth with trays and dishes; in spite of
that, the food was excellent. I mentioned this to Hubert when he
got to St.-Malo. "I'm going to take you to a really fine restaurant," he told me. We drove to Dîves-sur-Mer, to the Auberge de
Guillaume le Conquérant. The proprietor, an extremely old man
who wandered about the premises with a parrot on his shoulder,
ate with us in the garden and talked about Proust, who had been
one of his clients. He was particularly proud of the fact that the
auberge figured in *A La Recherche du Temps Perdu*. Since I had not
read the book, his reminiscences meant nothing to me; I was
more interested in the parrot.

It was at this point that Hubert began to work on me, hoping to persuade me to go back to the United States. "The *Paris* is leaving Havre on Monday. Why don't you take it?" I objected that having treated my parents as I had, I could not expect them to welcome me with open arms. But he ridiculed this. "Nothing could make them happier than to have you back with them." (*They* might be happy, I thought, but I?) "It's out of the question," I said.

We went to the Casino; there was some difficulty about getting me in the first time because I was under age; but he bribed someone, and they waived the rules. At *petite boule* I won about $250 one evening and then wanted to stop. Hubert tried to take me into the baccarat room with him, saying I was his mascot, but here they flatly refused to allow me in. I waited for an hour in the bar, drinking porto flips. Eventually he came out, having lost the entire $4,000 he had allowed himself for that night. He did not seem depressed, but I was scandalized; it gave me a sick feeling to see money treated so lightly. I got very drunk after we left the Casino—so drunk that the next morning I could recall nothing. All I knew was that I had an abysmal hangover and a great desire to escape from what seemed an intolerable situation. At lunch I asked Hubert if he had destroyed the check Daddy had given him. He had it with his luggage in the hotel room. "I'll take the *Paris* on Monday," I heard myself saying. Hubert was delighted. "My, my! How glad your people are going to be to see their boy. And to think that Uncle Hubert is responsible for it!" From then on I behaved in a sullen fashion with him: I was annoyed that he should take the credit for my decision.

We drove to Le Havre; Hubert bought the passage in the morning and I embarked in the afternoon. The voyage took a week, and I recall nothing about it except that I spent most of my time with a family named Schuster, who along with another family named Simon had published the crossword puzzle books I had been buying for several years. I went to see them in New York later.

VI

My parents seemed genuinely glad to see me; before I arrived, they must have agreed between them not to question or criticize. I thought I detected perhaps even a shred of respect in their attitude. Only once, when I was alone with him in the car, did Daddy refer to my flight. "That was a terrible thing you did to your mother," he told me. "You've noticed her hair has gone gray as a result." I said I had not. "Well, notice!" he said angrily. "That's the main trouble with you. You're so busy thinking about yourself and what *you* want. You never see anything around you. There are others in the world, too, you know." This struck me as relatively mild reproof; I felt that I had gained several points.

We went to Glenora, where the people seemed more interested in me than they had before. I could not detect a note of disapproval even in the attitude of the family. "An extremely educational experience for him," Aunt Mary said. "First-rate, first-rate," murmured Daddypapa when I showed him the photographs I had taken on my wanderings afoot.

Among the people visiting Glenora were two brothers, Charles and Frederic Jackson. Charles wrote short stories which he read aloud to me. Later he wrote a novel called *The Lost Weekend.* I did not understand the stories, but they struck me as sufficiently sinister to be interesting. He also presented me with his copy of *Swann's Way,* scribbling a quote from Whitman on the flyleaf. Since I despised the Good Gray Poet, having been taken to see his house as a child, the inscription somewhat dampened my desire to read the book. I read perhaps twenty pages and quickly put it aside.

Back in New York, Daddy said to me: "If you think you're going to spend the rest of your life lolling around this house, you've got another think coming." I looked for work, remembering my pleasant stint in the bank the year before. All I could find was a job at Dutton's Bookshop on Fifth Avenue. I was stationed on the balcony, selling Everyman's Library volumes and travel books. This was enjoyable, too, in itself. But I had to take the Long Island Railroad each morning and afternoon in order to get to and from the city. After a few weeks, having had my fill of commuting, I rented a room on Bank Street in the Village, a block farther west from where Peggy still lived with her father. It was the big first-floor front room of an old house, and thus it was equipped with a fireplace. I had an extra key made for Peggy. Sometimes on returning from work in the afternoon, I would find her there and a roaring fire in the grate. I discovered that she gathered the wood herself on the docks along the Hudson, which was only two blocks farther west. She would bundle it up in her coat and carry it over her shoulder back to the room. Since it was a camel's-hair coat which her father had just bought for her from Abercrombie and Fitch, I put a stop to the wood gathering.

Having merely disappeared one morning from my parents' house and not gone back again, once more I precipitated a crisis there. They came to Dutton's to talk with me. "But are you *married* to Peggy?" Mother wanted to know.

Each day as I sat at my desk on the balcony I wrote several pages in longhand of a work which I had titled "Without Stopping." The important thing was the constant adding of pages to the pile. I decided to write it as it came to me and prune it later; I was afraid that if I stopped to exercise choice, I would also begin to consider the piece critically, which I knew would stop the flow. And it was the flow above all which preoccupied me, because the writing of "Without Stopping" was therapeutic. Seeing the number of pages grow gave me the illusion of being on my way somewhere. I was all too aware that the bookselling job imposed a condition of stasis.

I presented the material as fiction, and it read like fiction be-

cause I included long "stream-of-consciousness" sections. However, it was also an accurate day-to-day account of certain walking trips I had made in regions that lay within an hour's train
ride from Paris and contained directions, signposts, and adver-
tisements found along the way, as well as reports of arguments
with peasants and shopkeepers.

Living in Manhattan, I had time to look up various people I
wanted to see. One of these was Dorothy Baldwin, who had led
me through the wasteland into the wasps' nest as a child. She
and her husband, a painter named Maurice Becker, lived in a
studio in the Village. There were always other painters there. I
remember Stuart Davis, whom I liked, and John Marin, a
strange-looking little man to whom everyone listened intently. At
some point it was decided among them that I should go and see
Henry Cowell, in order to show him my music. I longed to be assigned a civil status. If a composer said to me: "You are a composer," that would be all right. Or if a poet said: "You are a
poet," that would be acceptable, too. But somebody had to say
something. I looked forward to my meeting with Cowell as if he
might provide the necessary magical act that would transform
my life. Perhaps I was correct; in any case he examined the
music I took him and made me play it for him. Then he consented to play me several of his own piano pieces involving the
use of "tone clusters" and occasionally of glissandi made directly
on the strings. I was highly intrigued by this demonstration of the
piano's unsuspected sonorous possibilities, and thus even more
dissatisfied with my own very unsensational little numbers. Before I left, he scribbled a note to Aaron Copland which he suggested I take to him. When I got down into the street, I read it.
Paraphrased, it said: "Dear Aaron: This will introduce Paul
Bowles. His music is very French, but it might interest you. See
you soon, Henry."

During my Christmas vacation the year before, I had attended
one of the Copland-Sessions concerts at Town Hall; because the
critics the next day were less than laudatory in their remarks—
even rather snide, I thought—and because I had heard Copland's music ridiculed by several older people whose taste seemed
antiquated, I assumed automatically that he was the most impor-

tant composer in the United States. Thus I determined to deliver the note in spite of what I considered its derogatory tone. A few days later I telephoned Copland and made an appointment. At that time he lived on the second floor of the Hotel Montclair at Lexington Avenue and Forty-ninth Street. I arrived right on time and stood outside the door a while before knocking. From time to time I heard a note being struck on a piano. When I knocked, someone called: "Come in," and I opened the door. There was a thin man sitting at the piano; he looked up, said: "Aaron will be back in a minute," and went on working. Copland came in; he seemed flustered. "This is Roy Harris. And what's your name? You told me on the phone, but I've forgotten." I handed him Cowell's note. He read it and burst out laughing before stuffing it into his pocket. I thought him unusually likable. During the following weeks I returned several times to see him, and finally he agreed to give me a daily lesson in composition. This went beyond my most sanguine expectations. I ceased working at Dutton's and even moved back home in order to have a piano at which I could work. We began by studying the Mozart piano sonatas, which I had to learn to play and at the same time to analyze formally.

In spite of my delight at having found a mentor who was willing to take me in hand, my parents decided that I should return to the University of Virginia immediately for the second semester of my freshman year. There I took an apartment in a building called Preston Court, and because it was on the expensive side, I shared it with a student named Rosser Reeves, whom I had known the preceding year. He was one of the extrovert intellectuals, an admirer of Cabell and Joyce, but we got on perfectly and never had a disagreement. Since I was still favored by being on the dean's list, I spent much of my time wandering in the Ragged Mountains nearby and down in Richmond, where I had a good friend in Bruce Morrissette, a student with an exceptionally fine intelligence. During the spring Aaron Copland came down to Charlottesville. This I considered a great feather in my cap, and so I saw to it that he was entertained constantly. At one musical evening Aaron was prevailed upon to play a movement of his Jazz Concerto; it was then that I understood the extent of the provincialism at the university. Instead of finding it enormously exciting as I did, the guests seemed to think it some sort of hoax; it was not possible that he expected them to take such noises seriously. Aaron was not in the least fazed by the adverse reactions: of course, this raised him in my estimation. Later Miss Moore came for a weekend, and I took her up to the top of the Blue Ridge to the same isolated family I had found a year and a half before. The untimely death of a cow kept them from exercising the rare hospitality which had so impressed me on my earlier visit. We came upon the animal as we walked through a pasture on the way up to the cabin; one small boy stood nearby staring at it in silence. Soon members of the family came hurrying down the hillside. They were untalkative about it, but their expressions and behavior could scarcely have shown greater grief if the creature lying there surrounded by spring flowers had been human. The following Sunday Miss Moore devoted an entire page in the *Herald Tribune Books* section to the excursion and the incident of the cow.

In Paris I had been lent *Lady Chatterley's Lover* and had been struck by what seemed to me Lawrence's perverse insistence upon presenting copulation as a sacred activity. I had read Cleland's *Fanny Hill* and his *Amatory Experiences of a Surgeon*; those I could understand because the author had presented them honestly as examples of pornography, but the hieratic overtones of *Lady Chatterley* enraged me, and I would not hear of D. H. Lawrence. John Widdicombe, still at the university, tried to interest me in *Sons and Lovers*. I made a not very serious attempt and was unsuccessful. Although I knew enough Freud to believe that the sex urge was an important mainspring of life, it still seemed to me that any conscious manifestation of sex was necessarily ludicrous. Defecation and copulation were two activities which made a human being totally ridiculous. At least the former could be conducted in private, but the latter by definition demanded a partner. I discovered, though, that whenever I ventured this opinion, people took it as a joke.

When I learned that Martha Graham would appear in the *Sacre du Printemps* with the Philadelphia Orchestra, I bewailed being so far from the scene of action. "Why don't we hitchhike?"

suggested John Widdicombe. We did that, spending one night in Baltimore. He had wired friends in Bryn Mawr and Princeton, so that by the time we all got to our seats we were a large group. Since this was the first time I had heard a performance of the *Sacre,* it was understandable that I should have listened more than I watched.

We spent that night and the following day in Princeton. Harry Dunham, who had gone along the evening before, asked us to lunch at his club, and there I met a student who was about to start a magazine and wanted material, preferably fiction. Thinking of what I had written while I sat on the balcony at Dutton's, I said I would contribute a short story. The magazine, *Argo,* appeared later that year, carrying an excerpt from "Without Stopping," called *A White Goat's Shadow,* my first published piece of fiction.

When summer came, Aunt Mary asked me to stay with her at Holden Hall. A distant cousin of hers was spending the season there and had two of her young sons with her. Oliver Smith, who was twelve, spent literally all his time designing houses, which he did with astonishing skill, both the floor plans and the elevations. There was a piano in Aunt Mary's music room, but the house had to be kept free of unharmonious vibrations in order to facilitate meditation, so I put in my two-hour practice period at the home of a woman who lived nearby. I was learning two works that summer: Hindemith's *Übung in Drei Stücke* and the piano reduction of Stravinsky's *Histoire du Soldat.* After hearing me work each day for a month or so, by which time I had memorized several sections of the Stravinsky piece, the woman said to me: "Keep it up. You'll get there. You don't pound like the rest of 'em when they begin. If you could just hit the right notes, now, it would be fine."

I had written to Yaddo, the artist colony outside Saratoga, asking that they invite me in September, since Copland was to be there, and I wanted to go on working with him. Nina Smith offered to drive me to Saratoga, and the two boys came along. When Oliver saw the impressive house and my room in it, he made a remark which enraged Nina: "Oh, Mother! I wish I were Paul." The day ended with scolding and recrimination.

"You don't wish anything of the sort. I don't want to hear you make such a statement again. I'm ashamed of you! The idea!"

Yaddo was quiet and comfortable, an ideal place to work. Aaron was the only guest who did not live in the main house. He had a studio in some woods by a pond, where he sat composing the *Piano Variations.* Sometimes, when I took walks around the estate, I would come within hearing range and would sit down on a log or a rock to listen and discover what phrases had emerged and taken on definitive form since the last time I had eavesdropped.

Everyone talked at mealtimes, and much of the talk was about politics. Expectedly, more than half the guests were Marxists. They had a humorless understanding among themselves, rather like schoolteachers, I thought, and they indulged in the compulsive identification and unmasking of others as enemies of the cause. Thus conversation was likely to take the form of prolonged and sometimes bitter argument. "*Why* am I against you if I'm not with you?" What interested me more was the fact that I was anagrams champion at Yaddo. I was convinced that my self-imposed Surrealist practices were responsible for this ability. When I realized that I could imagine all the letters of a word, seeing them in suspension, as it were, merely as disparate elements, and yet could form other words from them only if I delegated all the work to my subconscious, I attributed the phenomenon to my habit of never starting to write until I had entirely emptied my mind.

Aaron had an old car which he called Nicodemus; I thought his driving reckless and constantly told him so, but he merely laughed. When the frost had begun to turn the hillsides orange and red, he suggested we drive to Vermont to visit Carl Ruggles. It fascinated Aaron that here was a real old-time New Englander not afraid to be himself right in his own environment. We found him in a farmhouse, a tiny old man sitting at the piano playing Mendelssohn, surrounded by musical friends, all of them singing from the score. He did not play any of his own music. Instead, he went on vigorously extolling the oratorio in front of him. One would have said that in his opinion there was no greater composer than Mendelssohn. When we left, Aaron said, laughing delightedly: "You see what a real old eccentric he is? Mendelssohn, of all men!" We went on down to Massachusetts and spent an afternoon with Roger Sessions, whom I found formidable, perhaps because Aaron showed him two movements of a little piece I was writing. After playing them over for a time, Sessions confessed that he did not find they had any particular merit. "Not even freshness?" asked Aaron. Sessions shrugged.

Back in New York, I brought Aaron and Harry Dunham together. My Aunt Adelaide had left me a tiny amount of money, but I could not have access to it for another year. Harry was going to get a little on his twenty-first birthday if he kept his promise not to smoke before that. Aaron thought I should go to Paris and study with Nadia Boulanger. Harry, suggestible and generous, offered to give me half of what he would get in November, 1931, if I thought that would help. It would, except that Aaron was going to Berlin soon, and I dreaded the hiatus in my study which that would cause. My consuming desire was to accompany him to Berlin and work there with him until autumn, when I could start with Boulanger. The problem thus was to get hold of money quickly. This was solved during a visit of Harry's parents to New York, when I had to meet them and explain the situation to them. They did not react at all well to me; I could see that they considered me an objectionable character and one likely to wield a destructive influence over their son. Mrs. Dunham felt that she knew about music: her sister Lucy Hickenlooper had changed her name to Madame Olga Samaroff and become a concert pianist, finally marrying Leopold Stokowski. As far as she was concerned, Aaron Copland had nothing to do with music, nor did she know or care about Nadia Boulanger. I think Harry had some trouble getting the money from his mother and father, but he succeeded eventually. I saw Mrs. Dunham again that winter with Harry's sister Amelia in Princeton, and I shall never forget the honeyed hatred of her voice as she said to me: "When are you going?" I replied: "As soon as possible," to which she said: "Good."

I had been writing poetry regularly and sending it to magazines. I even went so far as to write several in French, which were published at various times in a Belgian review called *Anthologie*.

Since *transition* had carried notices to the effect that it paid 30 francs a page, I wrote them telling them they owed me 150 francs for the two pieces they had used in numbers 12 and 13. I also enclosed more material. A check arrived not long afterward, but there was no mention of any further publication. However, I had the pleasure of seeing four of my poems appear in *This Quarter,* which I considered a very important review.

Bruce Morrissette, still at the University of Richmond, wrote asking me if I would like to edit an issue of *The Messenger,* which was the college's literary magazine. I jumped at the opportunity and immediately sent off a dozen or so letters to writers, none of whom I had ever met or corresponded with, but who I thought might be willing to contribute. Surprisingly, most of them answered, and I got back material from William Carlos Williams, Gertrude Stein, and Nancy Cunard, among others. I continued to write to Gertrude Stein and sent her a copy of the magazine when it was printed.

I began to study German, buying grammar, verb book, and dictionary, as I had done the preceding year to study Italian. "You'll like German. You'll find it easy," said Mother, who had studied it in school. I liked it, but I did not find it easy, nor did I ever manage to learn to speak it properly.

During my early childhood I had been good-natured and unusually tractable, but subject to occasional outbursts of temper. As I grew more devious and circumspect, the rages ceased to occur. It was natural for me to assume that I would cease to be visited by them. Thus at the age of nineteen I was astonished one night to discover that I had just thrown a meat knife at my father. I rushed out of the house, shattering the panes of glass in the front door, and began to run down the hill in the rain. Before I had gone three blocks Daddy caught up with me in the car, then parked and came along behind me on foot. I stopped and turned around to face him.

"I want to talk to you," he said. "You can't do this again to your mother. It wasn't my idea to come after you."

It was true that I had not thought of her at any point. I let him persuade me to go back to the house. We were both very wet. Mother was in tears when we arrived. I walked past her without

looking at her. "You have no heart at all, have you?" cried
Daddy.

I had started upstairs, but on hearing that I stopped.

"You can't stand me because every time you look at me you
realize what a mess you've made of me!" I shouted. "But it's not
my fault I'm alive. I didn't ask to be born."

"What . . . kind . . . of nonsense . . . is that?" he said, as if
with difficulty, raising his face and hands toward the ceiling.

I went to my room and shut the door, feeling like a person who
has been goaded by a provocateur into revealing what he should
have kept to himself—totally dissatisfied with my own behavior
because it had been a result of weakness. And the throwing of the
knife, which was now a fact rather than a fantasy, worried me
with its implications of future danger. If it were so easy to lose
control in this situation, it would be just as possible to lose it in
one where the results might be tragic. As usual I reminded myself
that since nothing was real, it did not matter too much.

I took passage on an old American freighter called the *McKees-
port*. There was only one other passenger aboard, a French count
just divorced by his American wife in California, with a big
album of photographs of her which he brought each time he
came to the dining room. Most of the time he stayed in his cabin.
This was understandable, since we ran into a violent storm the
second day out of New York, and for days the ship heaved like a
water buffalo in a mudhole. Both the dining room and my cabin,
adjacent to it, remained awash, with the water sloshing from one
side to the other and splashing against the walls. I piled my valises on the empty bunk and had the steward put my steamer
trunk on blocks and wedge it between the wall and the chest of
drawers. I might better have let myself be seasick, but I made it a
point of honor not to, and walked the deck for hours in the wind
and rain, breathing deeply. The ploy worked; I did not throw up
at any point. After a week of storm and motion, I spied a gull one
morning behind the ship and hopefully asked the captain if we
were approaching the Scilly Islands. "Naw, we're off the Grand
Banks," he said. It took us another eight days to get to Le Havre.

And there was Paris, with the trees in the Tuileries beginning
to bud and the sweet smell of the Métro disinfectant wafting up

from under the ground just as I had remembered it a thousand times during the past twenty months. I had only three weeks to spend there before Aaron would come from New York to pick me up and take me on to Berlin. One of the first things I did was to go around to 27 rue de Fleurus and find Gertrude Stein's door. When I rang the bell, a maid answered and said Mademoiselle was busy. I could hear the sound of women's voices coming down from the stairwell, and I said I had just arrived from America and must see her, if only for a moment. The girl made me wait outside. Soon Gertrude Stein appeared, looking just as she did in her photographs, except that the expression of her face was rather more pleasant. "What is it? Who are you?" she said. I told her and heard for the first time her wonderfully hearty laugh. She opened the door so that I could go in. Then Alice Toklas came downstairs, and we sat in the big studio hung with Picassos. "I was sure from your letters that you were an elderly gentleman, at least seventy-five," Gertrude Stein told me. "A highly eccentric elderly gentleman," added Alice Toklas. "We were certain of it." They asked me to dinner for the following night to meet Bernard Faÿ.

At the dinner there were only four. I was plied with questions; my answers seemed to please and amuse them. I liked Bernard Faÿ. He had the patience and charm that sometimes come as a result of prolonged physical suffering. Earlier in his life he had contracted polio and now had great difficulty in moving. Gertrude Stein insisted that I was really a Freddy and not a Paul. Accordingly, all three of them from that moment on refrained from using my name and addressed me only as Freddy. (Eventually Alice Toklas shortened it to Fred for her own use.)

"This is the season for *lancer*-ing Freddy," announced Gertrude Stein, who was in a jovial mood after dinner when we sat around the studio. "We're going to *lancer* Freddy." They discussed various people to whom I should be presented, laughed a good deal, and that was the end of it. The subject never came up again. A few nights later we all ate at the house of Bernard Faÿ's brother. A magazine called *The New Review* had recently been launched in Paris; its editors were Samuel Putnam, Ezra Pound, and Richard Thoma. At Thoma's that morning I had met Pound, a tall man with a reddish beard, and later had lunch with him, after which we had gone out to Fontenay-aux-Roses together to see Putnam. I had liked Pound and brought his name up during dinner. "Oh, I won't see Ez anymore," said Gertrude Stein. "All he has to do is to come in and sit down for a half hour. When he leaves, the chair's broken, the lamp's broken." "And the teapot," Alice Toklas added. "Ez is fine," Gertrude Stein went on, "but I can't afford to have him in the house, that's all." This struck me as very strange until one afternoon during tea at Bernard Faÿ's I learned that Gertrude Stein had recently sent many of her acquaintances a standard note stating that henceforth Miss Stein would do without his friendship. The arbitrariness of such behavior defied belief, but two who had received such notices, Virgil Thomson and Pavel Tchelitchew, were present to attest to it. This was the first time I had met Thomson; I was rather put off by the casualness with which he pronounced his judgments. Being naïf, I imagined that the willingness to be amusing reflected inevitably a lack of serious purpose.

One day when I was at Gertrude Stein's, Maria Jolas came by. "I believe you've published some of Freddy's things in *transition*," Gertrude Stein said to her when she introduced me. Mrs. Jolas looked very vague. After she had left, we discussed her strange lapse of memory, which my hostesses insisted was feigned. Alice Toklas suddenly said: "You didn't by any chance ever write and ask to be paid, did you?" They joined in a great burst of laughter when I answered defensively: "They'd been owing me for a year." "That's the end of *transition* for Freddy!" Gertrude Stein announced with satisfaction. I realized then that she did not like the magazine or the people who ran it.

Another day Thoma took me around to the rue Vignon to visit Jean Cocteau. A maid let us into an antechamber one of whose walls was a huge blackboard with scrawls and doodles on it. This was where friends left messages when Cocteau was not in. On another wall was a very large sheet of brown wrapping paper where Picasso had inked some hieroglyphs and figures. We waited a moment, and then Cocteau appeared and led us into a much bigger room. He was extremely thin and intensely nervous, and the constant, expressive agitation of his hands was like a choreography perfectly devised to fit the course of his speech. For two hours he carried on a conversation without remaining seated for more than a minute at a stretch. The rest of the time he was a man playing charades, illustrating his remarks by the use of mime and caricature and changing his position and voice to give verisimilitude to his accounts. Once he crawled across the floor in imitation of a bear, and for a while he was a succession of disdainful ushers at the new Paris Paramount Theatre, which he loathed. Naturally I was fascinated by this performance; on another occasion I went back to see him, but was met at the door by Jean Desbordes, who before shutting it said firmly: *"Monsieur Cocteau est au fond de son lit."* When I told Thoma, he said: "Oh, he was smoking opium." I had just finished reading *Opium, Journal d'une Désintoxication*; ingenuously, I imagined that once disintoxicated, a smoker smoked no more.

Aaron Copland was about to arrive in Paris. I knew he would be much impressed when I told him that since seeing him I had met Pound, Stein, and Cocteau; accordingly when an American painter asked me to his *vernissage,* saying that André Gide would be there, I made a point of being present. I did meet Gide; we stood in a corner talking for perhaps two minutes, and I was so elated by the idea of being face to face with the master that I had no precise idea of what we were talking about. That was that, but at least I would have one more name to add when I came to give Aaron the list. One might expect a young man of twenty to have progressed beyond this sort of thinking and behavior or at least to be aware of its absurdity, but not at all. I went to the Gare St.-Lazare to meet Aaron, and we had scarcely settled ourselves in the taxi before I began. I had a plum for him, too: Gertrude Stein wanted me to bring him to dinner the following evening. The dinner went off very well. When we had left and were walking in the street, Aaron said: "When I opened the door and saw her sitting there, the only thing that went through my mind was: 'My God, the woman's Jewish!'"

So we went on to Berlin. Aaron had arranged his living quarters in an apartment on the Steinplatz, in the northern part of the city. I had to look for mine, but I found them the first day through an agency. My room was in the house of a Baronin von

Massenbach, who turned out to be English by birth and more violently pro-German than the Germans themselves. I had a big balcony overlooking the Güntzelstrasse, near the Kaiserallee, and I could walk to the Kurfürstendamm in fifteen minutes. Architecturally Berlin was hideous, but as a compensation its streets were spotless and bordered by miles of carefully tended geranium beds. Each morning I had my breakfast on the balcony; it included an enormous bowl of *Schlagsahne* to put in my chocolate or over the strawberries. Very likely I was laying the foundations then for the liver complaints which plagued me many years later, but the breakfasts of the *Baronin* in the spring sunlight were one of the high points of the Berlin sojourn.

Berlin teemed with trolley cars in 1931, and there was little motor traffic. The sunlight was not the tentative, diffuse glow that hangs in the sky above today's cities; its unfiltered rays reached the ground. You could sit in a sidewalk café on the Kurfürstendamm and get a real sunburn. It was a new experience to be in a metropolis where one felt in constant touch with nature. The German obsession with nature had its comic side, of course, exemplified by such places as the Wellenbad at Halensee, where a monstrous contraption had been installed at one end of the pool; its mechanical heavings created huge waves which broke in surf at the opposite end. The important thing was to have a tan and to show as much area of bronzed skin as decency allowed. Pallor meant poverty, the East End, that vast slum beyond the Alexanderplatz, and no one wanted even to be reminded of the existence of such a region. The frantic insistence on enjoyment was in part a result of the suppressed knowledge that a few miles away great numbers of people were hungry.

Edouard Roditi was one of the poets to whom I had written the year before in order to get material for *The Messenger*; he had not only sent poems, but had also written several letters subsequently, in which he had given me a list of people to see in Berlin. Among them were Renée Sintenis, the sculptress; Wilfred Israel, who owned Wertheim's, Germany's largest department store; and two English writers, Christopher Isherwood and Stephen Spender. I presented the letters written to Germans first. When I came to Isherwood, he said he would take me himself to meet Spender. We walked one afternoon from the Nollendorf-platz to the Motzstrasse, where Spender had a room at the top of a house. Its windows faced west, and the sun was about to set as we walked into the room. Spender, who had reddish hair and was very sunburned, stood in the red light, looking as if he were on fire. I noted with disapproval the Byronesque manner in which he wore his shirt, open down to his chest. It struck me as unheard of that he should want to announce his status as a poet rather than dissimulate it; to my way of thinking he thus sacrificed his anonymity. To me name was all-important, the actuality represented by it less so. In a grammar-school reader I had once found a sentence: "Reputation is what people think about you; character is what God knows about you." References to God confused me. How was one to interpret them, since it was agreed that God was a figment of man's imagination? I ventured the opinion to Mother that this particular statement meant nothing at all. "Oh, yes, it does," she said. "It really means that character is what you know about yourself." In my fantasy the part of me about which there was anything to know did not exist; thus the knowing or recording part of me could scarcely learn anything about it. My deduction was that reputation was conclusive. Whether Spender wrote poetry or not seemed relatively unimportant; that at all costs the fact should not be evident was what should have mattered to him.

I soon found that Isherwood with Spender was a very different person from Isherwood by himself. Together they were overwhelmingly British, two members of a secret society constantly making references to esoteric data not available to outsiders. I reported all this to Aaron, who was amused, and who suggested that we all eat lunch one day. In this way we began meeting at half past one each afternoon on the terrace of the Café des Westens. Christopher often brought along Jean Ross, a pretty, dark-eyed girl who lived in the same rooming house on the Nollendorf-platz. She too was British, but from Cairo. (When Christopher wrote about her later, he called her Sally Bowles.) At all our meetings I felt that I was being treated with good-humored condescension. They accepted Aaron, but they did not accept me because they considered me too young and inexperienced or perhaps merely uninteresting; I never learned the reason, if there was one, for this exclusion by common consent.

I found German hard to acquire without regular lessons. After a month of riding on the tops of Berlin buses, I remarked to Aaron that usually I rode free of charge, since the man who came around to sell tickets seldom asked me to buy one. "But he always says: *'Noch jemand ohne Fahrschein,'* doesn't he?" asked Aaron. I had no idea of what the man had been saying, and I thought of the many times when I had looked straight at the ticket seller and not reacted to his words. It seemed a haphazard system they used, but now, knowing about it, I could no longer ride without paying. I ceased making an effort to learn the language. At least I knew the meaning of *"Fenster zu!"* the unceremonious phrase which my neighbors across the Güntzelstrasse shouted each time I began to work on the Baronin's big Bechstein. (Inspired by Aaron, I was writing a loud, dissonant piece for piano.) And I knew the word *Ausländer,* which the intolerant Berliners regularly applied to me; I had never been in a place where I felt so decidedly unwanted. In my fantasy I augmented this disagreement between us into a continuous feud and sought out details of behavior which I had learned would goad them into angry expostulation. I could get a reaction by tapping a fast rhythm with a coin on a café table, or by resting one foot on a chair opposite me, or even by ordering two *Schwedenfrüchte* in succession. Anything they were not used to seeing infuriated them because it was not in their manual; naturally this was too inviting a game for me not to be drawn into it.

Stravinsky's *Oedipus Rex* was about to be given in Munich. Since I had never heard it, I set out for Bavaria a week beforehand in order to be certain of not missing it. The city was bursting with vegetation, and the Isar churned through it, full of mountain water white as milk. I went on to Salzburg and the Salzkammergut for three days; in a village called Würgl I climbed through a glen and slipped into ice water up to my waist.

While I was in Munich, I received three letters of invitation: one from Gertrude Stein asking me to visit her in the country, another from the Comtesse de Lavillatte suggesting a stay at the château, and one which I had to decide and act on immediately. This letter was from another friend of Edouard Roditi's, an Egyptian named Carlo Suarès, who wanted me to go the following week to Holland and meet Krishnamurti. I wired Aaron that I should not be getting back to Berlin when I had planned to, and as soon as *Oedipus Rex* was presented, I left for Heidelberg. I wanted to explore the *Schloss,* but by myself. The only way of doing this was to get in at night. I had a small flashlight; with the aid of that and the moon, which was much brighter, I went over the building at my leisure. It was in an advanced state of disrepair then, with holes in the floors and bats overhead. I tried to feel that I was living in a poem by Novalis. The next day I continued to Deventer in Holland. Suarès met me at the station and we drove to Kastel Eerde, outside Ommen. The property had been given to Krishnamurti by a Dutchman, who a few years later changed his mind and asked that it be returned to him. Suarès was an Alexandrian banker who lived in Paris, where he edited *Carnets,* a monthly magazine devoted largely to studies of Krishnamurti's writings. Most of the texts he published in the review were his own, but now and then he printed a piece by Joe Bousquet or René Daumal on the same subject or a ramification of it. From time to time he spent a fortnight at Kastel Eerde with Krishnamurti. Madame Suarès was also a Krishnamurti follower; she sometimes accompanied him to Ojai in California and spent the winter there. I knew Krishnamurti's face very well, having seen it over a period of many years in the photograph of him which Aunt Mary had on her desk at Holden Hall, and when I met him, I was astonished to see that he still looked like a youth, although he must have been nearly forty by then. The first morning of my visit he came out of the castle and stood on the bridge that spanned the moat, tossing bread to the one swan that lived there. His shirt was open at the neck, at least as low as Stephen Spender wore his, and he had on white flannels and a scarlet blazer. Every morning after breakfast he appeared in the same costume and scattered the pieces of bread over the dark surface of the moat. The swan came sailing around the corner, white and fierce. It was an unfailing ritual.

In actuality I did not stay in the castle. I only ate there. The non-Indians lived in a dozen or so comfortable apartments that had been built on one side of the entrance driveway. In the castle itself was a man named Rajagopal who was constantly with Krishnamurti; they were often in the company of two or three other very serious-looking Indians, possibly secretaries or simple followers. In the apartments there were several Americans, a Frenchwoman with a small girl named Rolande, and Madame Pushkin, a very old Russian lady who had direct family ties of some sort with the poet. I went on walks in the lush Dutch countryside with Krishnamurti and Suarès. And I took an unforgettable stroll one sultry afternoon under the dramatic Dutch sky with Madame Pushkin and Rolande. A thunderstorm was rapidly approaching. The flat terrain made it clear that the rain would soon reach us. Rolande was all for running in order to get back to the castle before we were struck by lightning. There was something to be said for her suggestion, but Madame Pushkin went on ambling unconcernedly, assuring Rolande that if one were not afraid of lightning it would not hit one. Even eight-year-old Rolande was not going to swallow that. *"Ce n'est pas vrai!"* she cried. *"C'est une décharge électrique. Papa m'a expliqué."* But Madame Pushkin actually believed what she had said; she went on to tell Rolande that the power of the mind enabled one to go along with natural forces rather than combatting them. Rolande, skipping nervously, kept interrupting her, saying that it was impossible, and how could the lightning know whether somebody was afraid of it or not? As if in answer, a bolt struck a huge oak tree that stood alone a quarter of a mile out in the meadow. After the crash, Madame Pushkin sighed, turned to the child, and said: *"Ah, ma pauvre fille, comme tu es déplaisante!"* We continued in silence, albeit somewhat faster, until we got to Kastel Eerde.

I made plans to see Suarès the coming winter in Paris and returned to Berlin to work. Aaron was critical of my lack of seriousness in having spent so much time on holiday but I could not make myself feel guilty.

One weekend we went to Rheinsberg, where the hotel proprietor behaved in a typically German fashion. He allowed Aaron to sign the register as *Komponist,* but when he saw that I too claimed to be a composer, he objected, saying that I might sign myself in as a student if I wished, but certainly not as a composer. Aaron tried to argue with him, but to no avail. He crossed out what I had written and finally, as a special favor, he was careful to tell us, he rewrote my civil status as *Jazz-Komponist*. That was the best he could do for me. Back in Berlin Aaron told this as a joke; by that time I too could think it amusing.

Sometimes when I went around to see Christopher Isherwood, he would not be in, and I would ask for Fräulein Ross. Invariably I would find her stretched out in bed, smoking Murattis and eating chocolates; almost as invariably a German friend or two would appear, and she would involve herself in long conversations with them, only a small part of which I understood, punctuating her remarks here and there with her inevitable *"Du Schwein!"* Aaron told me I was not working hard enough. This was not surprising, since I wasted so much time moving around Berlin trying to see people. I decided, for instance, that I had to know Naum Gabo, the constructivist sculptor, and spent a whole day in his studio out at Potsdam, when I should have stayed at home doing figured basses. Another day I followed up a series of introductions which finally led me to the office of Walter Gropius, the architect, who looked like any businessman sitting at his desk, and who must have been mystified by my desire to talk with him, particularly since I had nothing at all to say. When Aaron announced that there was to be a Musikfest at Bad Pyrmont and that he thought we should go, I leaped at the opportunity because Bad Pyrmont was not far from Hannover, and in Hannover lived Kurt Schwitters, whom among all Germans I wanted most to meet. However, I said nothing about that until we were in Bad Pyrmont. The only concert of the festival I remember was the one at which Bela Bartok and his wife, both with cameo profiles, played at two huge black pianos facing each other across the stage. I have no idea of how I worded the wire I sent to Schwitters, but I recall my feeling of triumph when I went to the post office and read his answering telegram inviting me to Hannover. I set out the next morning, Aaron having gone back to Berlin.

Schwitters lived in a stolid bourgeois apartment house. The flat was relatively small and somberly furnished. I slept on a small glassed-in porch off the dining room. There was a huge chest near my couch; the first night I was astonished to hear distinct stirrings inside it. At breakfast I felt impelled to mention the phenomenon. The twelve-year-old Schwitters boy had filled it with guinea pigs. We went that day to the city dump and walked for two hours among the garbage, ashes and pieces of junk, collecting material for the Merz-Bau in the apartment below. On the trolley car returning from our outing people eyed us with curiosity. Schwitters, his son, and I each carried a basketful of refuse: we had bits of paper and rags, broken metal objects, even an ancient, stiff hospital bandage. It was all to be transformed into parts of the Merz-Bau. The Merz-Bau was a house within an apartment, a personal museum in which both the objects displayed and the exhibit rooms were inseparable parts of the same patiently constructed work of art.

Merz-Kunst was Schwitters' own brand of Dada, its lineage most evident in his poems and stories. That evening Frau Schwitters placed a big pan of strawberries on the dining-room table. Somehow we got the idea of making *Maibowle*. I went out to a nearby shop and bought a bottle of gin, which the Schwitterses claimed never to have tasted. Frau Schwitters made the *Maibowle*, and we all drank it, including the boy. It had a foul flavor, but the strawberries improved after they had soaked up the gin. When Schwitters was feeling happy, I begged him to recite some of his syllable poetry, which he did with great gusto. One which I liked particularly began:

> Lanke trr gll.
> Pe pe pe pe pe
> Ooka. Ooka. Ooka. Ooka.
> Lanke trr gll.
> Pi pi pi pi pi
> Tzuuka. Tzuuka. Tzuuka. Tzuuka.

I notated the words, the rhythm, and the vocal inflections and later used it without changes as the frame for the theme of the rondo movement of a sonata for oboe and clarinet. At my host's insistence I played two or three of my own pieces to them. Schwitters asked his son: "How do you like that?" and he replied: "*Schrecklich!*" without bothering to explain his reaction.

I went back to Berlin. The nights got shorter and shorter, until there were only two hours when the sky was uniformly dark. The sparrows began to chirp soon after two o'clock in the morning. The feeling came to me that I had had enough of this strange, ugly, vaguely sinister city, and I began to look forward to returning to France. The uneasiness Berlin induced had nothing to do with the little swastikas that were constantly being glued up everywhere by unseen hands. Hitler was unimportant, a feeble-minded Austrian fanatic with a gang of young hoodlums. Everyone said that. Everyone, that is, except a few people I met one day in the Baronin von Massenbach's salon, who believed he was going to save Germany, and an extraordinary young aristocrat named Von Braun, who invited me to his house for lunch with several of his friends, only to pause before sitting down to eat and point dramatically to his family tree on the wall, saying: "This is what Americans can never have. An American is worth only the number of dollars he has in his pocket." Then he sat down, and we ate, while he explained that Hitler was the only hope for cleaning out the rot that had attacked the German people's spirit. Had I met these people only a year later I should have recognized them as Nazis, but in 1931 they were only crazy Germans. It was not they, but a ride I took one day on the Ringbahn, that made Berlin seem sinister. With the exception of the quarters I already knew, the city was a gigantic slum, a monstrous agglomeration of uninhabitable buildings. Merely to see its geographic extent and the degree of unrelieved poverty it represented made me uneasy. The aura of desperation that I had found stimulating suddenly seemed ominous.

Just before I left for Paris, I met Julien Levy. At that time he was about to open a gallery in New York where he would show nothing but photographs. A week later in Paris it was Bastille Day, Aaron had gone to London, and I sat on the *terrasse* of the Dôme. Some friends walked up, bringing with them a fantastic girl in a very small bathing suit. Apart from being beautiful, she looked as though she had just come off the beach at Juan-les-Pins. Which, she explained charmingly, was exactly what she had done. In a fit of pique she had got onto the *Train Bleu* just like that, with no clothes and no luggage. And there was no way of buying anything for another three days because it was the *Quatorze Juillet*. What was she going to do? She shrugged, and we laughed. It soon became necessary to do something, however, inasmuch as the waiter arrived before long to say that the *patron* could not permit nudity on the *terrasse* of the Dôme. We were ordering plenty of drinks, the *soucoupes* were piling up, and we felt moved to protest. The *patron* sensibly suggested that we sit downstairs in the *sous-sol*. Jacqueline thought it a perfect solution; she had had enough of being stared at. We continued to drink in a corner of the basement near the *W.C. pour Dames*.

At some point Julien Levy came by and sat down to join us in our drinking, his beady eyes already on Jacqueline. When he heard of her plight, he grew very serious and began to rack his brain to think of some woman Jacqueline's size who might be in Paris during the holidays. "Don't you know anyone?" he said suddenly to me. I said no, I didn't, and then I took out my wallet and went through the cards and slips of paper until I came across one that read "Eva Goldbeck," with an address on the Boulevard Raspail. She was Marc Blitzstein's wife, whom he had suggested I go to see. "I've got someone here who might have something. I don't know her, though."

Julien thought I should call her immediately. I did. She was in, and I asked her if I might come over right away. She finally agreed, and I went back to the table triumphantly. One drink later I got up and set off for Eva Goldbeck's. She let me in, but she seemed disconcerted by the fact that I had been drinking and mystified by the course our conversation took. "Marc said you might look me up," she told me.

"You haven't got a dress you could lend me, have you?" I tried to paint her a picture of the serious emergency that existed back at the Dôme, but she looked confused and disapproving. "Came to Paris in a bathing suit?" she repeated.

"She's afraid she's going to be arrested," I went on. "That's why if you had any old thing, anything, it would save the day."

Eva Goldbeck looked doubtful, but she said: "Wait." She came out of her bedroom a moment later with three dresses on her arm. I took them, thanked her, and ran off, promising to bring them back as soon as Jacqueline could get to a shop.

Jacqueline was a tall girl, and Eva Goldbeck was short. Still, the discrepancy was not enough to explain what happened to the dresses when I carried them back to the Dôme. Jacqueline bore them off to the *W.C. pour Dames.* Fifteen minutes later she came back to the table looking glamorous in all three of the dresses. They had been partially ripped open and recombined with great skill. *"Dis donc,"* she said to me. "Your *petite amie* is not going to like it much when you take her clothes back to her." I assured her it would be all right, but of course I never took them back. (Two or three years later I learned from Marc Blitzstein that it had not been all right, at all.) The rest of the day has been lost in the mists of alcohol; I hope Julien remembers it, since it was he who finally carried Jacqueline off to his hotel, where she spent the remainder of the holidays.

A few days later I left for the Château de Lavillatte. This time there were several small children in residence. They had a toy phonograph which they played all day, and their favorite record was a popular song called "Constantinople." I was busy sending messages to Gertrude Stein, trying to arrange things so that I could go directly from the château to her. The Comtesse de Lavillatte, who was still occupied with her petit point, became curious. "Who is this woman?" she demanded. When I said she was a famous poet whose works few people understood, she asked me to quote a line. I translated one I remembered from "Tender Buttons": "A little lace makes boils." She nodded her head in agreement and said without looking up: *"Ah oui, et la broderie anglaise fait des pustules."*

Gertrude Stein met me at the station in Culoz, along with Alice Toklas and Basket, the white poodle, and on the way to Bilignin I repeated Madame de Lavillatte's remark. She was overjoyed. "You see? You see how wonderful the French are?" she cried. Then Alice Toklas asked me what I thought of Germans. When I started to tell her, Gertrude Stein interrupted, saying: "We think they're *awful.*" There was no need to say any more on the subject.

The house looked very old; it was like a miniature château, with floors that slanted in various directions. It stood directly on the only street in the hamlet of Bilignin; there were often cows in front of the door. The walls were very thick, and inside the house it was beautifully quiet, a bit like the Happy Hollow Farm, I thought, with distant sounds of lowing cattle and crowing cocks. If you went straight through the house, you came out into a garden whose farther edge was a parapet. A valley lay below, its green lushness made sedate by rows of tall poplars that rose above the surrounding vegetation. (From the opposite side of the valley on a clear day, they said, you could see Mont Blanc.)

It did not take me long to understand that while I undoubtedly had her personal sympathy, I existed primarily for Gertrude Stein as a sociological exhibit; for her I was the first example of my kind. I provided her initial encounter with a species then rare, now the commonest of contemporary phenomena, the American suburban child with its unrelenting spleen. She wanted to hear every detail of life at home. Mother's activities particularly fascinated her, so much so that she wrote to her after I left. (Later, when I discussed it with Mother, she said: "Oh, yes, I answered old Sophie and poor Alice B. Luckless. I sent them some recipes of Grandmother Barkers'.") After a week or so, Gertrude Stein pronounced her verdict: I was the most spoiled, insensitive, and self-indulgent young man she had ever seen, and my colossal complacency in rejecting all values appalled her. But she said it beaming with pleasure, so that I did not take it as adverse criticism. "If you were typical, it would be the end of our civilization," she told me. "You're a manufactured savage."

Each morning Thérèse brought my breakfast tray to my room. After that she lugged up a two-foot-high pitcher of cold water so that I could wash. I was supposed to stand in the middle of a small circular metal tub and pour the water over myself. A little later she would bring a canister of hot water for shaving. Not of the opinion that cold water is useful for bathing, I would wash as well as I could with a washcloth, using the small amount of hot water and leaving the cold untouched. After a few days had gone by, Gertrude Stein began to question me. "Thérèse says you don't bathe in the morning." When I protested, she closed in on me, saying that I must use cold water. I had been through the cold water bit as a boy, when Daddy had obliged me to take a cold shower every morning, and I had made up my mind I was not going to use the cold water.

I told Gertrude Stein this; she shook her head impatiently. "It's of no interest whether you like it or not. We're not talking about that. All I'm saying is, you've got to use the water Thérèse brings you. It's simple." Then she delivered a short lecture on Americans. They were the dirtiest people on earth, really, she said, because unless they had access to a bathroom, they refrained from bathing. From then on she took to standing outside my bedroom door in the morning, calling out in a low melodious voice: "Freddy. Are you taking your bath?" I would make the appropriate noises and say that I was, indeed. "I don't hear anything," she would pursue, after a short silence. "Well, I am."

She would wait again, perhaps thirty seconds, before saying: "All right. Basket's waiting for you."

The huge poodle, Basket, being all white, also had to have a thorough bath in a tubful of sulfur water every morning. This was performed faithfully by Alice Toklas, who spent an hour at the task. The dog was bathed quite as if it had been a baby, and it squealed and whimpered during the entire hour. When for some reason the bathtime was postponed until later, it began to cry at the usual time and continued until the bath had been given. When the washing was finished, and the tub, brushes, and swabs had been put away, it was my job to give Basket his drying-off exercise. This consisted in running back and forth through the garden with the dog after me. For this work I had to wear a pair of lederhosen which reached just above my knees. These were what Gertrude Stein called my "Faunties." (She referred, of course, to the trousers little Lord Fauntleroy wore.)

"Ah, you've got your Faunties. That's right. Get out there and run Basket." If he could manage it, Basket liked to reach up as he ran and scratch the backs of my legs with his toenails. Gertrude Stein would lean out a second-story window watching us, occasionally crying: "Faster, Freddy, faster!" This advice was scarcely necessary, considering the sharpness of his nails. There would come a moment when I would call out: "Isn't that enough?" Invariably she answered: "No! Keep going!" There was no way of doubting that she enjoyed my discomfort. But since such behavior seemed to me a sign of the most personal kind of relationship, I was flattered by the degree of her interest.

A telegram arrived one day, asking if the sender might come to Bilignin the following Sunday. It added: AM IN EUROPE SPECIFI-CALLY INTERVIEWS YOU AND GB SHAW, and it was signed FATTY BUTCHER. Gertrude Stein was delighted with the name; neverthe-less, she murmured: "What does he want with Shaw?" Instead of the heavy man we were all expecting, Sunday brought two ex-pensively dressed American ladies, one of whom introduced her-self as Fanny Butcher of the Chicago *Tribune*. A maid took their wraps upstairs, where Basket promptly went and shit on them. The fact was not discovered until much later, as they were leav-ing. Gertrude Stein apologized, shrugged, and said: "He doesn't like to have people come." A maid did some rapid cleaning, and Miss Butcher went away happy with her interview.

Mealtimes were fun, because then each of my hostesses ex-pressed herself. This gave rise to a certain amount of contradic-tion; indeed, the words sometimes went across in front of me from one end of the table to the other like a ping-pong ball. "But, Lovit, I didn't say that." "Ohh, yes, you did, Pussy." Neither ever lost a shred of her equanimity, although it was always quite clear when Gertrude Stein was annoyed, because her face col-ored perceptibly. When there was an argument over a detail, Alice Toklas usually proved herself right, but then, having lost her point, Gertrude Stein would smile crookedly and with a cer-tain mock commiseration, as if to imply the absurdity of caring whether one had been right or wrong in such a trivial matter. They were both fervent gourmets, but Alice Toklas liked her food hot, whereas for Gertrude Stein its temperature had no impor-tance. She enjoyed dallying in the garden after lunch had been put on the table, in order to watch what she considered Alice Toklas' obsessive anxiety about getting inside and sitting down before the meal cooled off.

Gertrude Stein asked me one afternoon to get some of my poems and let her see them. After she had looked carefully at them for a while, she sat back and thought a moment. Then she said: "Well, the only trouble with all this is that it isn't poetry."

"What is it?" I demanded.

"How should I know what it is? You wrote it. You tell *me* what it is. It's not poetry. Look at this." She pointed to a line on the top page. "What do you mean, *the heated beetle pants?* Beetles don't pant. Basket pants, don't you, Basket? But beetles don't. And here you've got purple clouds. It's all false."

"It was written without conscious intervention," I told her sententiously. "It's not my fault. I didn't know what I was writing."

"Yes, yes, but you knew *afterwards* what you'd written, and you should have known it was false. It was false, and you sent it off to *transition*. Yes, I know; they published it. Unfortunately. Because it's not poetry."

Gertrude Stein had just inaugurated what she called the Plain Edition; this was to comprise a series of volumes published at her own expense. The first title was *Lucy Church Amiably*. It was a descriptive novel whose principal character was a small church in the nearby village of Lucey. We drove twice to look at it; she was fascinated by the juxtaposition of the building's somewhat Slavic-looking steeple and the very French landscape in which it stood.

There was an afternoon when I read to her for a long time from her own *Operas and Plays,* the Plain Edition proofs of which she was then correcting. Occasionally she would laugh appreciatively, and once she stopped me, saying: "That's wonderful! Read that paragraph again, will you, Freddy?"

One day she announced that we were all going to Aix-les-Bains to market. Alice Toklas shuddered and murmured: "Oh, Lovit, not by the tunnel!"

"Of course we'll take the tunnel. We're not going all the way around the Dent du Chat."

"It drips," Alice Toklas explained to me. "I don't like tunnels. Of course Gertrude loves them. She'll always take a tunnel if she can."

We took the tunnel; Alice Toklas showed her misery, and even Basket seemed disturbed by it. At Aix-les-Bains I sent a wire to Aaron in Oxford, where he was attending a music festival of the ISCM, telling him that he was invited to Bilignin and to let us know when he would arrive. In the market Gertrude Stein's eye lit on an enormous gray eel, which, in spite of Alice Toklas' protestations, she insisted upon buying. Along with the other provisions she bore it off to the car, and we went back through the tunnel to Belley and thence to Bilignin.

While it was being cooked, the eel gave off a revolting stench, and when the lid was lifted from its terrine in front of Gertrude Stein's radiant face, its appearance was totally unappetizing. I decided to subsist on a vegetarian meal that day, but it seemed there was to be no question of that. "You eat what you're served," she told me sternly. "It's all good food." She gave me a large helping, and I managed to get it down.

When Aaron came, they had talks about me, both privately and in front of me. "Why does he have so many clothes?" Gertrude Stein wanted to know. "He's got enough for six young men." Then she would ask Aaron if I really had talent as a composer and if I really worked at my music. Aaron said he could imagine someone who spent more time at it than I. "That's what I thought," she said. "He's started his life of crime too young." Aaron snickered and told her never to pay any attention to what I said—only to what I did.

"I know," she agreed, looking narrowly at me. "He *says* he bathes every morning."

At lunch one day we discussed where Aaron and I ought to go for the summer. I was holding out for Villefranche, and Aaron kept mentioning St.-Jean-de-Luz over on the Atlantic. Gertrude Stein thought both very bad ideas. "You don't want to go to Villefranche," she said. "Everybody's there. And St.-Jean-de-Luz is empty, and with an awful climate. The place you should go is Tangier. Alice and I've spent three summers there, and it's fine. Freddy'd like it because the sun shines every day. At least, in the summer."

At each succeeding meal we got more information about Tangier. Finally we came to a decision: Aaron and I were leaving for Tangier. The last afternoon as we sat in the garden, Gertrude Stein suddenly said to me: "What about those poems you showed me last week? Have you done any work on them?" I said no, because once a poem had been published there seemed to be no reason to rewrite it. She was triumphant. "You see?" she cried. "I told you you were no poet. A real poet, after one conversation, would have gone upstairs and at least tried to recast them, but you haven't even looked at them."

I agreed, chastened. The next morning we hugged, kissed on both cheeks, and that was the end of the visit. "Quite a woman, quite a woman," Aaron murmured as we drove off in the taxi. Thinking how mysterious it was that she should be lovable, I said she reminded me of my grandmother.

The trip to Morocco would be a rest, a lark, a one-summer stand. The idea suited my overall desire, that of getting as far away as possible from New York. Being wholly ignorant of what I should find there, I did not care. I had been told there would be a house somewhere, a piano somehow, and sun every day. That seemed to me enough.

VII

As we went aboard the *Imeréthie II*, they told us of a change in itinerary. The ship was not going to touch at Tangier, after all, but at Ceuta, in Spanish Morocco. On the second day at dawn I went on deck and saw the rugged line of the mountains of Algeria ahead. Straightway I felt a great excitement; much excited; it was as if some interior mechanism had been set in motion by the sight of the approaching land. Always without formulating the concept, I had based my sense of being in the world partly on an unreasoned conviction that certain areas of the earth's surface contained more magic than others. Had anyone asked me what I meant by magic, I should probably have defined the word by calling it a secret connection between the world of nature and the consciousness of man, a hidden but direct passage which bypassed the mind. (The operative word here is "direct," because in this case it was equivalent to "visceral.") Like any Romantic, I had always been vaguely certain that sometime during my life I should come into a magic place which in disclosing its secrets would give me wisdom and ecstasy—perhaps even death. And now, as I stood in the wind looking at the mountains ahead, I felt the stirring of the engine within, and it was as if I were drawing close to the solution of an as-yet-unposed problem. I was incredibly happy as I watched the wall of mountains slowly take on substance, but I let the happiness wash over me and asked no questions.

We landed at Oran that afternoon. It was hot and dusty, and to me, beautiful and terrible. Because I remembered the absurd name of a suburb from having studied a Baedecker obsessively when I was working at Dutton's, I wanted to climb aboard a tramcar and ride out to a place called Eckmühl-Noiseux.

We swayed through the city that reeked of light on an open trolley car to the outskirts. Cicadas screamed in the trees overhead and in the canebrakes that covered the slopes of the ravines. At Eckmühl-Noiseux we got down, but only because it was the end of the line. The sun was incandescent; people must have been asleep, for there was no one around. Returning on the same car to the center of town, we changed to another one that was going to Mers-el-Kebir. The cicadas screamed here too, the savage cliffs increased the sun's searing heat, and when the wind hit, it was like having a hot scarf thrown over one's face. At the fortress we were suddenly challenged by an Algerian soldier, who pointed his gun at us and bellowed: *"Halte!"* Then he told us to turn around and start walking, and he kept us covered until we were back on the road. "Well, I'm glad we're not going to live in *this* country!" Aaron said. "Morocco's much wilder," I told him; I had been listening to conversations among the French aboard the *Imeréthie II.*

The next afternoon we put in at Ceuta. We disembarked with so much luggage that we needed a small detachment of porters to carry it. As we sat in a sidewalk café in the central plaza, we looked around at the extraordinary animation of the people in the street. I had the impression of something great and exciting happening somewhere offstage. Neither of us had ever before seen the Spanish. Soon Aaron shook his head and said: "They're like a lot of Italians who've gone raving mad." Alfonso XIII had abdicated only four months earlier; their agitation may have been part of the general euphoria that was so apparent all over Spain during the years of the republic.

We got aboard a narrow-gauge train which yanked us along the coast southward. In Tetuán the impression of confusion and insanity was redoubled. The Moroccans were even more excited and noisy; furthermore, they engaged in passionate arguments which continually seemed about to degenerate into physical violence. We sat and watched while buses came and went, unloading chickens and sheep along with the sacks and chests they brought down from the roofs of the absurd old vehicles. Each Moroccan gave the impression of playing a part in a huge drama; he was involved not only with the others in the dispute, but also with the audience out front (a nonexistent audience, since no one was paying any attention but Aaron and me). He would face his invisible public and subject it to formalized grimaces denoting exasperation, incredulity, indignation, and a whole gamut of subtler states of mind. "It's a madhouse, a madhouse!" declared Aaron. "It's a continuous performance, anyway," I said with satisfaction. Even before getting to Tangier, I knew I should never tire of watching Moroccans play their parts.

Gertrude Stein's habitual hotel, the Villa de France, was filled with vacationists; our cabdriver took us to the Minzah, a new hotel built at the end of the twenties and which now, in 1971, is still Tangier's best. We spent ten days or so looking for a house in town big enough so that we would not be in each other's way. One afternoon I took a tiny bus in the Grand Socco and stayed on it to the end of its run at the foot of a forested mountain, then began to climb the dirt road that led upward, until suddenly I came upon the house. When I got back to the hotel, I was able to talk of little else. The next day we hired a carriage in the Grand Socco and explored the property. Aaron hesitated because the house was big, run-down, unfurnished, and isolated. However, we decided to take it and immediately began buying the necessary beds, tables, chairs, and cooking equipment.

This was easy, if not economical. The complicated part was getting the piano. In the Calle de Italia we found an old black upright marked "Bembaron et Hazan," hopelessly out of tune, but which we were obliged to take if we expected to work at all. The salesman who rented it to us assured us that he could get a tuner to set it straight, so we arranged for the men and the donkey to deliver it. When they arrived and the donkey saw the gate, it decided not to go through it. In the struggle the piano crashed to the ground with an attractive but unreproducible sound, and Aaron and I saw our working possibilities growing dimmer as the two Moroccans pushed, heaved, and banged the instrument about some more. When it was finally left in a corner of the empty salon, however, it seemed to be no more out of tune than it had been in the shop.

Each day we went back to the piano store to find out when the tuner was going to appear. One morning they said to us: "You're in luck. The tuner came by a while ago, and we're sending him to you this afternoon." The man arrived at the house wheezing from the climb and got to work. Aaron and I sat in the garden listening; it soon became apparent that the man had no idea of how to tune a piano and no sense of pitch. However, we did not bother him. Presently there was silence in the salon, and the silence continued. I went inside. He was sitting with his head resting on his arms, and his arms folded on the keyboard. I coughed, but he did not react. Then I saw a pint bottle of cognac on top of the piano and realized that he had drunk himself to sleep. We awoke him; he seemed embarrassed, but jauntily ripped off some ragged arpeggios and barged into the "Pilgrims' Chorus" from *Tannhaüser*. The piano sounded, if possible, even more sour than before. Drastic action was essential. "The piano is tuned," said the man. "No," said Aaron. "You sit there, and we're going to tune it." And so for another two hours he loosened and tightened the strings while we cried *"Más alto!"* or *"Más bajo!"* until eventually the instrument sounded like any other piano in need of tuning—that is to say, one at least could tell what each note was supposed to be. By that time the tuner had finished his bottle and was in a mood not to mind the long walk back into town. The next morning Aaron got to work on his Short Symphony, and I on my little Sonata for Oboe and Clarinet.

If I said that Tangier struck me as a dream city, I should mean it in the strict sense. Its topography was rich in prototypal dream scenes: covered streets like corridors with doors opening into rooms on each side, hidden terraces high above the sea, streets consisting only of steps, dark impasses, small squares built on sloping terrain so that they looked like ballet sets designed in false perspective, with alleys leading off in several directions; as well as the classical dream equipment of tunnels, ramparts, ruins, dungeons, and cliffs. The climate was both violent and languorous. The August wind hissed in the palms and rocked the euca-

My mother, Rena Winnewisser, about 1892, Bellows Falls, Vermont.

My grandparents at Happy Hollow Farm, 1916.

Photo by Harry Dunham.

My mother in 1937.

In a burlesque theater on the Bowery, 1938.

Photo by Victor Kraft.

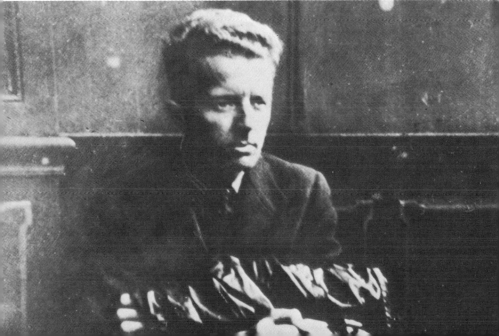

Photo by Paul Bowles.

Jane in Costa Rica, 1938.

At home in the little penthouse, New York, 1944.

Photo by Karl Bissinger.

Jane at Tenth Street while she was writing *In the Summer House,* 1946.

At Merkala Beach, 1949. Taken the month *The Sheltering Sky* was published.

Photo by Cecil Beaton.

Portrait of Jane by Maurice Grosser.

On the roof of the house in Amrah, Tangier, 1952.

lyptus trees and rattled the canebrakes that bordered the streets. Tangier had not yet entered the dirty era of automotive traffic. There were, however, several taxis stationed along with the carriages in the Grand Socco, one of which Aaron and I took each evening to get home after dinner. Just as the absence of traffic made it possible to sit in a café on the Place de France and hear only the cicadas in the trees, so the fact that the radio had not yet arrived in Morocco meant that one could also sit in a café in the center of the Medina and hear only the sound of many hundreds of human voices. The city was self-sufficient and clean, a doll's metropolis whose social and economic life long ago had been frozen in an enforced perpetual status quo by the international administration and its efficient police. There was no crime; no one yet thought of not respecting the European, whose presence was considered an asset to the community. (This was not entirely true with regard to the Spaniards, of whom there were so many thousands that they scarcely counted as Europeans.)

Immediately after breakfast each morning Aaron gave me my harmony lesson; it included correcting the figured basses I had prepared the day before. I was still in the process of analyzing the Mozart piano sonatas. I worked lying in a deck chair in the lower garden, where I would not hear Aaron's chordal laboratory. Afternoons Aaron, who drank wine at lunch, took a nap upstairs, while I worked at the piano. We had a cross-eyed servant named Mohammed, who prepared breakfast and lunch and took care of the garden. In the late afternoon we walked down into town and had dinner on the beach.

Gertrude Stein had told us that a Dutch Surrealist painter named Kristians Tonny was in Tangier. He was living, she added, laughing sourly, with a girl named Anita, who it was clear did not have her approval. Since it was a foregone conclusion that we were going to see these two at some point, there seemed no reason to hasten the meeting. I foresaw a static evening with a square-headed Dutchman who would show us his canvases one by one, and I did not think it would be fun. Aaron, more interested in people than I, wanted someone to talk to, so we soon made arrangements to call on Tonny and Anita. I remember being pleasantly surprised by them: Tonny seemed more French than Dutch; he had been educated in France. His drawings were quite wonderful: Moroccan landscapes out of Bosch, alive with hundreds of tiny figures wearing djellabas and haiks. The second time we met, Tonny remarked to Aaron: "The young man with you is slightly off his head, isn't he? I noticed it the other night right away. I heard shutters banging in the wind in there somewhere." I found this a sympathetic observation and liked him better for having made it. They had a friend who was a soccer star on the Moghreb team. We went to a game and on the way back to town afterward saw members of the Hillal team ambush their rivals. Fists, rocks, and knives were used, and it was all because the Moghreb had won the game. Tonny and Anita smiled at our astonishment and said this always happened.

When I wrote Gertrude Stein, describing our difficulties with the piano, she replied that Chopin had had even worse ones when he went to Mallorca with George Sand. "So cheer up. It's the common lot," she told me. And she added: "This time you seem to have left nothing behind but an aluminum penny German piece and a very pleasant memory."

Aaron and I gave up the Tangier house in the autumn after selling all the furnishings we had so recently bought, and set out for Fez. Tonny had visited the city, staying at the house of a Swiss named Brown, to whom he gave me a note. Although Aaron was not delighted with Morocco (claiming that all the things that struck me as so exotic were nothing new to him because he had seen and heard their counterparts as a child on President Street in Brooklyn), he agreed to spend a few days in Fez before returning to Germany.

We arrived in Fez at sunset and took a carriage through the Mellah to Fez-Djedid. Tangier had by no means prepared me for the experience of Fez, where everything was ten times stranger and bigger and brighter. I felt that at last I had left the world behind, and the resulting excitement was well-nigh unbearable. Still, I was not too agitated to be able to notice a hotel sign some distance down a side alley as we drove along. I stopped the carriage and ran to examine the place. It was called the Hotel Ariana. As soon as I saw the three outside rooms upstairs, I knew it was the right place, because they gave directly onto the ramparts of Fez-Djedid. You could step out the windows onto the top of the rampart wall. Below was the garden of Djenane es Sebir with its willows overhanging the Oued Fez, and to the right an ancient waterwheel turned slowly, dripping and creaking. The hotel was a primitive little establishment, but Madame did serve breakfast. In the morning Aaron and I would step out the windows of our respective rooms and have our coffee and croissants on the ramparts. We ate other meals at a Jewish restaurant in the Mellah.

A wire came from Harry Dunham saying that he was en route from Dresden to Fez and would arrive within a week. I suspected that Aaron was finding Fez even less agreeable than Tangier. In any case, he had to return to Berlin. I was very sorry to see him go, and probably if Harry had not already been on his way, I should have gone back to Paris. But Harry did come. He had decided to take a year off from Princeton in order to study the dance in Germany; in the meantime, however, he had discovered the delights of photography. As a result, he arrived in Fez in a febrile state and spent most of his time climbing into all kinds of places where he was not supposed to be, being screamed at by Moroccans and French alike, but snapping his pictures, several hundred of them each day.

Harry was from Cincinnati and often mentioned the old slave quarters behind his parents' house there. If we took a municipal bus to get back to the Hotel Ariana from the Ville Nouvelle, he would refuse to sit next to a Moroccan, for fear of catching vermin. Yet he thought nothing of being crowded in among French workmen who were infinitely less clean than the Moroccans. He did not like it when I pointed this out to him; his face would darken and he would say: "You don't understand. I was brought up differently."

Even with my past practice of pretending not to exist, I could not do it in Morocco. A stranger as blond as I was all too evident. I wanted to see whatever was happening continue exactly as if I were not there. Harry could not grasp this; he expected his presence to change everything and in the direction which interested him. I told him that was not an intelligent way to travel. Obviously he could not change; he continued to make his presence felt in situations where I believed we should both strive for invisibility. Harry thought in terms of confrontation rather than conspiracy. I, however, was so used to hiding my intentions from everyone that I sometimes hid them from myself as well.

We made a trip to Sefrou and walked for some distance out of the town, following a river which little by little became recessed in a gorge. A peasant passing by told me in bad French that farther up there was a cave behind a waterfall. He then added that people went there to sacrifice chickens and occasionally goats. Immediately Harry wanted to find the place in order to photograph the cave. I refused to continue translating at that point and sent the man on his way. Harry was annoyed, but so was I. I asked him if it wasn't enough to know the cave was there, and that for centuries the stones at our feet had been washed by sacrificial blood. "Why do you have to have a picture?" Harry shrugged and went on taking photographs.

One morning, taking along my introduction from Tonny, I went with Harry to see Brown. He had an old Moroccan house in an orchard outside Bab Sidi bou Jida; it was one of the very few places in Fez with a swimming pool. Richard Halliburton, the Baron Munchausen of the twenties, had been staying there and had left that morning for West Africa. There were several guests for lunch, but Brown added us to their number, and we all sat at a long table on the terrace. Thus we met a young Fassi named Abdallah Drissi, who insisted that we visit him for tea later in the afternoon.

Abdallah's manner of living was extraordinary. He and his married older brother (who, as he immediately explained to us, were the only two remaining direct descendants of Moulay Idriss, the founder of Morocco) had inherited a vast palace in the Nejjarine quarter. Most of the aristocracy had been ruined financially by the French presence, but not this family. The brothers owed their continued prosperity to the fact that they regularly collected money and large quantities of salable goods from the zaouias roundabout. When Abdallah wanted something, he clapped his hands, and the slave on duty in his courtyard appeared. (He consistently used the word "slave" rather than "servant.") The order was relayed to responsible people in another part of the house, who saw that it was carried out to the letter. Thus a few days later when he wanted to take us on an evening excursion to Sidi Harazem, one brief command dispatched two slaves ahead of time to Bab Fteuh. When we got there, the carriage was waiting, packed with food, braziers, charcoal, lanterns, rugs, and cushions. The slaves came along to prepare the food and tea at the oasis. Wherever Abdallah went, men insisted on bowing low to kiss the sleeve of his djellaba. This annoyed Harry, although he did not explain why.

I learned that Harry's parents had no idea that he was not in Dresden studying. His twenty-first birthday would be in another three weeks; he had to go back there in time for that, in order to send them a cable on the day (it was that kind of family) and also to arrange for his sister Amelia to visit him. Before returning he wanted to see Marrakech. We spent a night in Casablanca, to which I vowed I would never return if I could help it, and we left the following day for *la ville rouge.*

In Marrakech we stayed at a tiny hotel near the *quartier réservé.* It was run by a typical colonial couple who thought it their duty to warn us continually of the dishonesty and savagery in Morocco. When we came in at night from the street, we stepped over (and sometimes on) a boy whose job it was to lie across the doorway until dawn. Harry was indignant to see this and asked the woman why she did not give him a mat to lie on. "Ha!" she cried. "That's all he needs. He's already so spoiled he's no good. I'd fire him except that he owes me two months' work for one of my husband's shirts he ruined trying to iron it. He's an animal, that one!"

This information scandalized Harry. The next day I found him sitting on the roof talking to the boy. "It's perfectly true," he told me. "Two months for scorching a shirt. And the man's wearing it, what's more."

"They'll have their revenge some day," I said. "Don't worry."

"But that's not the point," he objected.

A quarter of an hour later when I went back to the roof, I saw that something had happened. The boy was looking at Harry as

if he were the incarnation of God, and Harry was looking reso-
lute and pleased. "I asked Abdelkader if he'd like to go to Paris
and he said yes."

"But why?"

"I want a valet. I've never had one, and this is a good chance."

Harry went downstairs and calmly told Madame he was taking Abdelkader with him to Paris. I stood on the balcony above
the courtyard and listened to the Frenchwoman's shrieks. *"Il me
doit deux mois de travail!"* she kept crying. In spite of having no
French, Harry had got his idea across.

When I saw Madame that evening, she was still very much
excited. She rushed up to me, saying: "You know, if your friend
attacks him, he'll defend himself." It was clear that she believed
Harry's intentions regarding Abdelkader were sexual. "If he tries
to take him away, I shall call the police!" she shouted. At that
moment Harry came into the courtyard and, passing behind us
into the kitchen, suddenly stood in the doorway pointing a re-
volver at Madame. She swayed, nearly losing her balance, and
screamed: "Lucien!"

The husband appeared from a back room and, seeing Harry,
stood perfectly still. Harry swung around and aimed at him.
Then he laughed and laid the weapon down on the table. The
man immediately rushed over and seized it. By this time Abdelkader and a maid had come onto the scene and were watching
with round eyes. Monsieur, Madame, and Harry now began to
shout all at once. Harry's invective was in German, although I
doubt that any one of them was aware of that. They were all red
in the face, and they went on bellowing at one another for five
minutes. We changed hotels that night, but the next day we had
to confront Monsieur and Madame once again at the police station, for Harry had gone early in the morning to announce his
intention of removing Abdelkader to France and to fill out the
necessary papers. Since Abdelkader was working at the hotel, he
had to be cleared by his employers, who steadfastly refused to
give him up until they were paid a sum which suddenly included
dishes and windows the boy had broken, as well as the scorched
shirt.

The police warned Harry that the proceedings could take a

long time, because Abdelkader's entire family had to be legally in accord with the project. Harry would go back to Dresden and I would stay on in Marrakech until I had straightened out official matters with both the French government and the Moroccan *adoul*. Then I would go straight to Paris with Abdelkader, where Harry would join me before Christmas. (He had just decided he wanted to spend the winter in Paris, rather than in Germany, because Man Ray was there, and he hoped to work with him.)

The proprietor of our new hotel was also a truck driver who regularly, twice a month, carried wine and food across the High Atlas to the Foreign Legion post at Ouarzazate. I questioned him at length about the place: he said no one could visit it without a pass from the governor. We checked on that bit of information and found it correct. Later he casually remarked that he himself would take us if we made it worth his while. He had done it once before, he said, arranging the matter at each checkpoint along the way by making generous gifts of extra bottles of wine and liqueurs.

A few days later we started out with him at three in the morning, a second truck following behind, as was the custom in those unsafe days. The trail over the Atlas was so hair-raising that the most sensible place to sit seemed the top of the truck, where at least we could see down over each precipice as we swayed along its edge. The road was in the process of construction, not a mile of it yet paved. Above the cloud line it was a mud track. We bogged down several times and once skidded to within inches of the abyss, when we got out and collected shrubs and stones to push under the wheels. And at each *poste de controle* the wine went out to the soldiers. Ouarzazate came into view just before sunset; we saw the painted towers of the Casbah above the palms, and when the truck came to a stop, the silence was broken by the faint sound of a bugle. A Greek had put up a hotel with eight tiny rooms at the edge of the camp. Each room had two army cots enveloped in one mosquito net that hung from the ceiling. There were no toilet facilities—not even a shed or a hole in the ground—nothing but the open desert. That night a sandstorm began to blow, so that the next day we could not leave the hotel.

The following day was calmer, but unfortunately a French commandant burst in for drinks at the bar and, seeing Harry and me sitting there studying our maps, lost no time in demanding our papers. Harry jumped up, clicked his heels together, and saluted in best Junker fashion, saying *"Ja, ja! Natürlich, natürlich. . . ."* This so aroused the officer's suspicions that even though Harry quickly went into English, he questioned the validity of the American passport and placed us under house arrest, saying that we would be put on the first vehicle that went out of Ouarzazate. "And I know who brought you here," he went on. "And every guard along the trail is going to get fifteen days in prison." When he had gone, the Greek explained that often when legionnaires deserted, they acquired false or stolen American passports.

The next day the officer came back, accompanied by a civilian. "You had better have some money on you," he told us. "You paid to get here, and you're going to pay to get out. This man can take you to Marrakech tomorrow morning, and I hope he makes you pay through the nose." The man, however, wanted less than the other one had charged for bringing us, doubtless because there was no wine to be distributed, and so everyone was content.

Harry went back to Germany, leaving me with enough money to see that Abdelkader got to Paris. I waited in Marrakech, going each day with him to the notaries. His mother and grandmother had to go along as well; they rode always in a separate carriage and heavily veiled. It seems to me now that those days consisted largely of endless carriage rides along the dusty alleys, through flickering sunlight and shadow, the other carriage with the two covered figures in it, going on ahead.

Time passed, and nothing happened. The police themselves now were hindering progress by being slow to get certain documents stamped and signed. There was nothing I could do about that. I left my address with Abdelkader and went back to Tangier, where I stayed with Tonny and Anita. They had just moved to a small Moroccan house on the hill above Dradeb, reachable only by using a steep path bordered by cactus and boulders. The house always had Moroccans in it. During the day the maids, one of them noseless, worked in the courtyard, and at night friends came in to play cards and listen to the phonograph. The games were Moroccan, played with *naipe* cards, some of which looked as if they were part of the tarot pack.

Anita had come down to Tangier ostensibly to join an old friend, Dean, who was barman at the Minzah Hotel. But little by little I understood that it was Gertrude Stein who had engineered her departure from Paris, in order to make Tonny work more at his painting. With this in mind, she also had persuaded him to sign a long-term lease on a studio in Montparnasse, offering to pay the first two months herself. After he had lived there for a while, he began to hear rumors about the true reason for Anita's disappearance from the Paris scene. He promptly broke the lease and, leaving everything behind, came as fast as he could to Tangier to be with Anita.

At this point it was natural that my hosts had only the most disagreeable things to say about the Misses Stein and Toklas. Tonny was so totally infatuated with Anita that he seemed not to be aware of her continuous flirtation with the younger male population of Tangier. Or perhaps he blamed it toally on the Moroccan youths, who swarmed around her like bees over a honeysuckle vine.

Abdelkader arrived from Marrakech one morning by bus and straightaway began to find grievous fault with the way Anita managed the little house. *"C'est dégueulasse, mon zami!"* He would run his finger along the floor beside the wall and bring it up to hold it two inches from my eyes so that I could judge the truth of his statement. One evening Anita, having invited several Moroccans for dinner, prepared a couscous into whose sauce she decided to pour a quart of gin. Very likely it was a unique occurrence in Moroccan culinary history; with the exception of Abdelkader (who sensibly refused to taste the dish) everyone was violently sick afterward. From then on Abdelkader would not eat any food which Anita had, being persuaded that she had mixed poison with the couscous.

Since it was clear that Anita and Abdelkader were never going to get along together, I made a strenuous effort to leave quickly for Paris. The morning we set out, Tonny presented me with a fine drawing that I had admired, but he handed it to me as I was getting into the little motorboat that was to carry us out to the Algeciras ferry, so that it was damaged by salt water even before I left Tangier.

In Marrakech Abdelkader had gone several times to the cinema; that was the extent of his familiarity with the gadgets of the twentieth century. Of course, he had seen trains and automobiles, but as we boarded the ferry, a look of suspicion and terror came into his face, and he said: "Is this a bridge that moves?" I told him it was a boat, but the word meant nothing to him. "My grandmother told me that in Europe they have bridges that move, and she said never to go onto one of them, or I'd be very sick." We had scarcely got out into the strait before he was lying flat on the deck in an excess of nausea. Occasionally he moaned: "My grandmother told me," but that was all. In Algeciras he had to go immediately to the market to buy oranges, and he flew into a rage when he discovered that Spanish oranges were not identical to those in Marrakech. "This country is no good, *mon zami,* and the people are all crazy." This was still his opinion when we got to Seville. There in the dining room of the Hotel Madrid on Calle Sierpes he somehow met a middle-aged couple from Chicago who were traveling with their daughter and accepted an invitation for us both to accompany them on a carriage drive through the city. First the American went to Thomas Cook's and bought $5 worth of small coins, which he instructed them to put into several small cloth bags. Then he hired a carriage with two extra folding seats, on which Abdelkader and I sat facing the three members of the family, and we set out on the tour of Seville. The idea was for us all to stand up and scatter coins whenever we went through a densely populated quarter. Obviously it did not take long to collect a very noisy mob, which followed the carriage and was kept from trying to climb aboard by the driver's whip. All this delighted the American gentleman so much that when we got back to the hotel he sighed and remarked: "Well, I had fifty dollars' worth of fun for five. I call that pretty good!" That night we all went to a cabaret where the girls danced *sevillanas* up on a stage. At one point, however, they filed down into the other part of the room and danced among the tables. As one of them swirled by us, Abdelkader reached out and touched her. Then he pulled his hand back as if he had been burned and with consternation turned to me crying: "But it's not a cinema? They're real?" And a little later: *"Elles sont vraies, alors? Ah, mon zami, c'est bien, ça!"*

In Madrid too, at the Prado, he stood looking at the Goyas, waiting for them to move. When they failed to change, he was disappointed, and we continued to explore the museum. We came to the Bosches; he was immobilized. Finally he said: "Come on! They're beginning to move. Let's go outdoors." In the street, after he had examined the world and satisfied himself that everything was still the same, he sighed and said: "Do you know who made all the cinemas in that house? I can tell you. It was Satan."

Abdelkader's ingenuousness was often staggering. The first morning in Paris we had breakfast on the Coupole's terrace. There were brioches topped with currant jelly in the dish bearing breakfast breads. He erupted in a series of anti-French remarks because he took it for granted that the jelly was coagulated blood. *"Ah, non, mon zami! Je ne mange pas le sang. C'est honteux!"* (In spite of this, a few weeks later, when I was thinking of having my tonsils out, he implored me to tell the surgeon to save all the blood that would come out of me when he operated, so that he could drink it.) That afternoon he said he was going to take a walk. He was gone several hours and returned to the hotel after dark, full of a story of having met a very nice old gentleman, quite like his brother, he stressed, who had invited him to his house and given him tea, *"comme elle le fait ma mère, la pauvre, je te jure,"* by which I understood that he meant mint tea. It was not surprising, considering that he had gone wandering off fully dressed in Moroccan regalia. The old gentleman, who spoke Arabic, Abdelkader said, had pressed 50 francs into his hand when he left and insisted that he accept a djellaba which was hanging on a coatrack. He explained in an aside to me that he had not wanted to accept the garment because it would be shameful, but to be polite he took it and left it outside the door in the street. "It was very old," he added.

During the day I had telephoned Gertrude Stein. It was Sunday, her at-home evening. I told her about Abdelkader, and she said to bring him along. We were let in by a maid, who opened the salon door for us. The room was full of people; Gertrude Stein stood in the middle of it, talking. Suddenly she gave one of her hearty, infectious laughs and slapped her thigh, as she was wont to do in such moments. *"C'est elle?"* said Abdelkader in a stage whisper, wide-eyed. *"Mais c'est un homme, ça!"* I hushed him, and we went in. Soon I was in conversation with an engaging little Catalan whose paintings I knew and admired, but whom I had never met: Joan Miró. I told him about Abdelkader's behavior at the Prado two days earlier. He agreed with Abdelkader about the Bosches: they did indeed move. In case I ever passed through Barcelona he gave me his address there. But he also had a *mas* in Mallorca, which, like a true Spaniard, he said was my house whenever I wished. Then he asked me for a piece of paper and a pencil and drew me a map of Spain that looked just like one of his drawings. Now and then I glanced about to see what Abdelkader was doing. At one end of the room Alice Toklas presided over the tea and food, and here he had settled himself, beside her. They seemed to be deep in conversation. When the guests had thinned out a bit, she called Gertrude Stein and me over to the table. "Let him tell you about the Tonny ménage," she told Gertrude Stein, and to Abdelkader she said: "Tell Mademoiselle, was the house clean?" *"Oh, non, madame, pas beaucoup. Elle était dégueulasse."*

Gertrude Stein grinned. They continued to ply him with questions; his replies all delighted them. Gertrude Stein turned to me. "Did you leave two and six on the dirty toilet cover?" I did not understand. "That's what Mr. Salteena did in *The Young Visitors,* and that's what Tonny and Anita were expecting you to do." "But they invited me," I objected. The two ladies joined in derisive laughter.

Harry arrived from Dresden to say that he had got a girl pregnant and was trying to persuade her to go to London for an abortion. My reaction was one of indignation at his carelessness, but he seemed rather pleased with the situation. Wires kept arriving, first from Germany and finally from London, but there was still a question whether she would go through with the abortion. Harry took a furnished studio at the top of 17 Quai Voltaire, the same building in which Virgil Thomson lived. The first thing he did after signing the lease was to go down the street to the Galerie Pierre, where Miró was having an exhibit of his works in a new medium, three-dimensional assemblages, and buy three of them to liven up the walls of the twenty-foot-high salon.

I went to see Nadia Boulanger, who was very pleasant, but who seemed not to have been expecting me. Or perhaps she had expected me several months earlier and had ceased to do so. At all events, she was not willing to accept me immediately as a composition pupil; she advised me to enroll in her counterpoint class at the École Normale, which I did with the intention of starting classes at the beginning of the year.

Aaron had arranged a London concert of new American music to be given at Aeolian Hall in Wigmore Street. He was to play his Piano Variations, and Virgil Thomson was to accompany the singers in his *Capital Capitals,* a cantata on a Stein text. Since my Sonata for Oboe and Clarinet was on the program, I had to be there beforehand in order to rehearse the players. Harry and I left Paris a week before the concert. At that time Mary Oliver and Jock were living at Pembroke Lodge in Richmond Park, and she very generously offered to let me stay there. It was the sort of house that had Titians in the dining room and Gauguins and Picassos in the bathrooms. Its only disadvantage for me was its distance from central London, where I had my rehearsals each day. But Mary had just designed two extraordinarily smart-looking cars for herself, and she put one of them at my disposal, complete with chauffeur and footman. Harry made the mistake of mentioning the abortion to Mary, and she immediately began trying to persuade him to visit a witch she knew in Hampstead. The mere sound of the word infuriated Harry; his father was a doctor, he said, and he was having no truck with witches. The abortion took place a few days later, and there was no more mention of it.

In London I finally met Edouard Roditi, who had sent me so many letters of introduction to his friends. He was tall, suave, and polyglot. We went to his father's large export-import office in Golden Square. It was an international firm; Edouard had spent a time working for his father in the Hamburg branch.

Harry's older sister Amelia appeared at Aeolian Hall the night of the concert. She disliked the program intensely; for some reason my piece, even more than the others, incurred her wrath, perhaps because it had been described in the morning newspaper as "pagan." We went back to Paris together. On the ferry she told me: "If I had a little boy and he wrote a piece like that, I'd know what to do with him."

I was vaguely curious. "What would you do?"

"I'd see that he got hospital treatment," she said fiercely.

Amelia moved into the studio with Harry. From the moment she saw Abdelkader she loathed him, and it became her favorite occupation to persecute him by following him around, issuing impossible orders in a language no one could understand. *"Faites ceça or no spazieren, you hear?"* Abdelkader would stare at her uncomprehending; sometimes he would cry: *"Ah, je t'en prie, madame, laisse-moi tranquille!"* I could see that the pattern of life at the studio would be ephemeral.

VIII

Instead of moving into the studio on the Quai Voltaire to sleep on the balcony and attending the counterpoint class at the École Normale, I met Anne. She was very beautiful and did tiny Klee-like engravings. Also she was a great ski enthusiast. We sat in Montparnasse bars and talked so much about skiing that before we knew it we were in a third-class coach on the train to Torino, drinking large quantities of red wine. I had been spending many sleepless nights, and the one on the train was one too many. When we got to Torino, I went directly to the hospital. Anne wired Harry, and he came to visit me. When I was able, Anne and I went up to Clavières, a recently opened ski resort near the border, on the Italian side. Anne did some skiing; I recuperated. But the last day we went on a picnic in the snow high above the valley. Unwisely for me we decided to wear bathing suits. Even before we got back to Paris, I had come down with a violent grippe and acute tonsillitis. I settled into Anne's flat with her, and she cooked for me and got me back on my feet. Then we heard that her husband might return from Germany any day. He did not live with her when he was in Paris, but he always came to see her. It was no pleasure, living in expectation of his imminent arrival.

I moved a Pleyel concert grand into the studio and began to live there. Harry was not in Paris at that moment, and Amelia had been disciplining Abdelkader by keeping him locked in the kitchen quarters. This was not as brutal as it sounds, inasmuch as his bedroom and bath were part of the kitchen unit where he was imprisoned. But as Amelia's fancy became more refined, she also began to starve him systematically. The day I finally freed him, he had had nothing to eat but *crème fraîche,* of which she had bought him a large supply the day before. By that time he hated Amelia much more than she did him.

A few days later I went to the *vernissage* of a photographic exhibit at La Portique on the Boulevard Raspail, taking Abdelkader with me. All Paris was there; the walls were hung with the work of Atget, Moholy-Nagy, Man Ray, and the rest of them. I met several people I knew and got separated from Abdelkader. Suddenly I heard his excited voice shouting above the several hundred other voices, saying: *"Monsieur Paul! Monsieur Paul! Viens vite!"* I hurried toward the sound and met him rushing toward me, still crying: *"Viens! Regarde!* There's the nice old man who gave me the fifty francs! Look!" Occupying a place of honor at the end of the hall was a huge photograph of André Gide, wearing a beret. It became the joke of the month around Paris.

Amelia's mind had an obsessive quality; she campaigned ruthlessly to implement her convictions. She was determined to get rid of Abdelkader, but at the same time, mindful of the fact that he was Harry's servant, she realized that whatever initiative was to be taken could not appear to come from her. I tried to comfort Abdelkader by assuring him that she would soon leave for America, but not with noticeable success. As for her intentions with regard to me, she announced them openly. "I'm going to get you into a hospital yet," she would say, squinting fiercely. I told Carlo Suarès about it as a funny story; he thought it ominous. "Be careful," he advised. "The woman's mad." Sometimes I took Anne to the studio; although Amelia emanated waves of hostility, she was too well brought up to show it in her speech or behavior.

When Amelia reduced her ambition regarding me to the point of demanding only that I undergo a spinal tap (since she now claimed to believe I was syphilitic), I moved to Carlo's flat. Mornings when I returned to work at the piano, she was seldom there. I was trying to finish a suite of six songs to texts of my own; I wanted to get them to the copyist quickly in order to send them to Aaron for performance at Yaddo in the spring. One day when

I went into the studio, I saw that the three Mirós were no longer gracing the walls. In addition, the place seemed strangely empty. I glanced into all the rooms: no sign of Abdelkader. Then I climbed to the balcony and found chaos. Most of Harry's and my clothes were gone, although there were a few spare shirts and pairs of socks lying about. While I was sorting the remains, I heard Amelia come into the apartment and ran downstairs to announce the bad news. When I saw her face, I realized that she already knew all about it.

"He wanted to go to Africa, so he went," she said. "I took him to Louis Vuitton and bought him some luggage, and he went."

The absurdity of buying Abdelkader Vuitton luggage did not strike me until later, when I was less emotionally affected by the sudden depredation. "And my clothes?" I shouted. "And all of Harry's?" She shrugged and said coolly: "If you have street Arabs in the house, you expect to lose things, don't you?"

"Abdelkader never stole. You *gave* him my clothes, didn't you?" She giggled in her most infuriating manner and said: "Certainly not. I told him to fill his valises, and then I took him to the Gare d'Orsay. That's all."

"And the Mirós? I suppose he took them, too?" I said witheringly.

She did not show any interest. "Oh, are they gone? I'm afraid I don't know anything about that."

I stopped by the concierge's flat on the way out and reported the disappearance of the Miró constructions. She seemed mystified; what pictures was I talking about? I described them. *"Ahh! Monsieur veut dire ces vieux morceaux de bois?* Those old pieces of wood? I thought you'd be glad to get rid of them. I threw them out."

Fortunately she had put them in the cellar, so that they were recuperable, if rather badly damaged. When Harry returned to Paris, he took them back to the Galerie Pierre for repairs. Miró himself did the work, and once again they adorned the walls of the studio.

Carlo's wife had just gone to California to be with Krishnamurti. I did not see much of Carlo, since he was generally out, but his two small children, aged five and seven, were there with a houseful of Italian servants. We all used to eat lunch together in the kitchen. The flat was a penthouse at the top of a high building on the Avenue de la Bourdonnais, and because the Eiffel Tower was directly in front of it, Carlo had installed glass walls in the three rooms facing the tower, so that the entire structure would be visible from there. Carlo was an intellectual Communist who had not joined the party; he talked a good deal about revolution. One afternoon I took Bernard, the seven-year-old, to hear Prokofieff play his three piano concerti with the Philharmonique. On the way home in the taxi Bernard turned to me and said: "Why are they all mad?" "Who?" I asked him. "All the people in the streets. My father says they're all mad. He says they're capitalists, and they're all going to be killed soon. But *why* are they capitalists?" I had no ready answer to that.

Winter in Paris was even worse than I had expected. The unvarying succession of short, cold, gray days, with never so much as a glimpse of the sun, necessarily ended by being depressing. I went twice to the École Normale and worked on the counterpoint exercises given in the textbook, but my enthusiasm for the course burned low. One evening I had dinner at a Left Bank restaurant with Virgil Thomson and several other people. Among these was John Trounstine, an American literary agent from Cincinnati who recently had sold a book called *Little Caesar* (subsequently made into the film *Scarface*). He mentioned wanting to see Spain. I began to speak so glowingly of it that he asked me if I would like to accompany him there. The prospect of escaping from Paris seemed too enticing to be disregarded.

In Barcelona I went to the Pasaje Crédito to look for Miró, but he was in Mallorca. We went south along the Mediterranean coast, via Valencia and Alicante to Elche, whose oasis of date palms started me on a lengthy panegyric of North Africa. It was not long before we had decided to go to Morocco.

In Granada I discovered that Manuel de Falla lived just down the hill from the hotel. One afternoon I went and knocked on his door. He and his sister, both well along into middle age, lived very simply in the most Andalusian of houses, surrounded by potted flowering plants. We spent half the afternoon sitting in the patio, eating from a huge bowl of fruit. French was our lingua franca. I told him of my admiration for *El Retablo de Maese Pedro;* he was more interested in his Harpsichord Concerto, which I had not heard. Another day I saw him in a long black cape, hurrying along one of the dusty back alleys on the hill of the Alhambra, en route to midday mass.

That early spring of 1932 in Spain was a time of collective happiness on a vast scale. In every town there was rejoicing; people were singing and dancing in each *plazuela.* The air crackled with *alegría,* and there were palms and flowers in the festive decorations that lined the streets. On the tables of the cafés they had put small signs advising that it was forbidden to give or receive gratuities. This prohibition was directly related to the general euphoria. It appealed to the common man's inflexible sense of *honor,* which we define as "Spanish pride." Spain was alive then; it has never lived since.

We crossed over to Tangier; the first day I went in search of Tonny and Anita, to discover that they had moved and were living on the Marshan behind the Moslem cemetery. In the middle of the graveyard itself I met Anita. Hesitantly she turned around and went back with me to the house, explaining that Tonny had just locked her out. When she knocked, I heard Tonny's voice on the other side of the door, roaring: *"Qui est là?"* She told him I was with her. "I don't want either you or Paul in my house!" he shouted. Anita shrugged, and we walked together into Tangier. Things were not going very well between them, she said, principally because of Tonny's boundless jealousy. For one thing, she had opened a small shop where she sold Moroccan objects to tourists. We went there; it was in an alley of the Medina near the Hôtel Continental. There was a reed mat on the floor and a decorated shelf where several wallets were on display—nothing more. Naturally, when Anita shut herself into the shop with her Moroccan friends, the gossips ran about saying that the place was really not a gift shop at all, but a brothel. There was another reason for Tonny's jealous rages, and that was the presence in Tangier of a man whom Anita had known previously in America. The West Indian poet Claude McKay (*Home to Harlem*) had taken a house in the country at the mouth of the Suani River. On the occasions when her life with Tonny became unbearable, she said, she would go and spend a week or so there with McKay. Then Tonny, after living alone for as long as he could bear it, would swallow his pride and walk out to the house by the river to fetch her and take her back to the Marshan. We all went out to see McKay; he was plump and jolly, with a red fez on his head, and he was living exactly like a Moroccan. At one point with a clap of his hands he summoned his Moroccan dancing girl, not yet twelve, and bade her perform for us. Trounstine was displeased by the entire scene. He was not liking Morocco very much, in any case.

In Fez he and I finally fell out. We were walking through the Andaluz quarter of the Medina, Abdallah Drissi and I in front, he and two other Moroccans behind. Suddenly he called ahead to me, accusing me of being in the act of telling Abdallah that he was Jewish. "I know what you're saying," he kept insisting. Without hesitation I hit him in the mouth. He left Fez that day, and I never saw him again.

Back in Tangier I met a man named Abdeslam ben Hadj Larbi, who liked to eat opium. I tried it; it only gave me a headache. He also had a very particular interest in Claude McKay, a phenomenon I was never able to analyze satisfactorily inasmuch as Abdeslam died shortly afterward. I can only assume that he had been paid by someone (which in those days invariably meant some government) to put McKay in an untenable position. At all events, Abdeslam and a friend broke into the house by the Suani River and stole McKay's passport, then went to the authorities and denounced him as a Communist. At that time a Trotskyist was considered a Communist, so that the accusation was not beside the point. McKay had shown me a letter from Max Eastman announcing his intention of visiting Tangier to stay in the house with him later in the year. For some unexplained but doubtless valid-seeming reason which I have forgotten, McKay decided that I was at the bottom of the conspiracy that had placed his pleasant Moroccan sojourn in jeopardy. One evening he came around to the bedbug-infested Hôtel Viena, where I lived, and demanded to see me. Because he was black and wore a fez on his head, and also because he was obviously in a state of great excitement, the Spanish proprietor refused to allow him past the desk in the courtyard. I came out onto the balcony and stood there while he shouted up imprecations and threats in his West Indian English, brandishing his cane at me, at the hotel employees, and at the *dueño,* who forced him out into the street.

I had very little money. Fortunately I had now passed my twenty-first birthday and would soon be able to have the small sum that had been bequeathed to me by Aunt Adelaide fourteen years earlier. Harry had left Paris and gone to Shanghai, where he said the action was. His address there struck me as poetic: Bubbling Well Road. Amelia's feeling about this latest escapade of her brother's was expressed in a letter to me from Paris: "If he wants to make a damn fool of himself, I suppose it's about time." The ellipsis here was typical of her manner of speaking. She also asked when I intended to return to Paris to be hospitalized.

I wired Abdallah Drissi, saying I was arriving in Fez. He met me at the station, and we drove in a carriage with all my bags as far as Bab Bou Jeloud. Then we plunged into the Medina on foot, a train of porters following behind, each with a valise on his head. I must stay in the Nejjarine house as long as I liked, said Abdallah.

As the door to the house swung open and I saw the expressionless face of the tall old Sudanese slave who stood behind it shouldering a key two feet long, I had a premonition of what life might be like if I stayed here. It is pleasant to be inside an ancient Fassi dwelling if there are other people around. But if one's host goes out and stays twelve or eighteen hours at a stretch, and if during that time no one is allowed to pass through the doorway, either coming in from or going out into the street, then one can begin to wish one were outside rather than in.

There was a beautifully tiled courtyard two stories high, with a colonnaded balcony. All I could see of the balcony from below in my quarters was the succession of huge cedar beams in its ceiling, meticulously carved and painted with geometric and, surprisingly, floral designs. Several times a day there would be a scurrying along the balcony as of several clumsy, perhaps blind, animals, often accompanied by squeals of laughter. These were groups of girl slaves who lived in another part of the house.

Abdallah told me there were twenty-two of them altogether. Sometimes I could see their fingers poking out through the carved wooden screen that protected them from view. It seemed hard to believe that they ever did anything besides frolic and giggle. Abdallah was noncommittal about them; after a blatantly noticeable outburst of screams and bumpings, I asked him: *"Mais qu'est-ce qu'elles font là-haut?"* He raised his eyebrows and said: *"Elles s'amusent."* But much of the time he was not there for me to question. I knew whether or not he was coming to a meal only when the servants brought the *taifor* to the entrance of the courtyard, and I saw for how many people it had been set.

A square of sky was visible at the top of the courtyard; it was surprising to see how it changed color during the course of the day. At afternoon's end the swallows began their chasing games; I would sit and watch them dart across the patch of empty blue. An ancient phonograph was there, with two records: Josephine Baker singing "La Petite Tonkinoise," and Mohammed Abd el Wahab doing a popular Egyptian ballad from the twenties. At my request these were supplemented by other scratchy discs, including some Andaluz *misanes*. After two weeks of this monastic life I moved to the Hôtel Ariana; as a reaction to having been so restricted in my movements, I now spent every day wandering and exploring the city.

It was then that I saw my first brotherhoods in action. At that time more than half the population of Morocco belonged to one or another of the religious confraternities which enable their adepts to achieve transcendance of normal consciousness (a psychic necessity all over the African continent) and to do so in Islamic terms. For most educated Moroccans the mere existence of the cults is an abomination; with the emergence of nationalism they were suppressed more or less successfully for two decades or more. When once again they were sanctioned, care was taken to see that the observances took place hidden from the sight of non-Moslems. Visitors might ridicule the participants, it was said, or consider Moroccans a backward people if they witnessed such spectacles. I had suspected that someday I would stumble onto a scene which would show me the pulse of the place, if not the exposed, beating heart of its magic, but it was a tremendous surprise to find it first in the open street. Yet there they were, several thousand people near Bab Mahrouk, stamping, heaving, shuddering, gyrating, and chanting, all of them aware only of the overpowering need to achieve ecstasy. They stayed there all day and night; I could hear the drums from my room, and during the night they grew louder. The next morning the mob was at Bab Dekaken, just outside the hotel. Then I realized that it was a procession, moving at the rate of approximately a hundred feet an hour, with such extreme slowness that as one watched no visible progress was made. Along the edges of the phalanx there were women in trance; pink and white froth bubbled from their mouths; small shrieks accompanied their spastic motions. When someone lost consciousness entirely and fell, he was dragged inside the wall of onlookers. It took the procession two days to get from Bab Mahrouk to Bab Chorfa, a distance of perhaps a mile. I should never have believed an account of the phenomenon had I not been watching it. But which one or more of the brotherhoods the participants represented, whether they were Aissaoua or Jilala or Hamatcha or something else, there was no way of knowing, nor did I ask. Here for the first time I was made aware that a human being is not an entity and that his interpretation of exterior phenomena is meaningless unless it is shared by the other members of his cultural group. A bromide, but one that had escaped me until then.

In those days most of my moving around Morocco was done in buses. Departure was more than likely to be at three in the morning. This seemed to me to shorten the trip. Somehow the dark hours that went by before daybreak did not count; my subconscious reckoned the time only from the first daylight on. On the way back to Tangier up in the hills of the Zerhoun, the bus rounded a curve and hit a cow. The vehicle raised itself in the air, came down, and continued. I glanced out of the rear window and had a fleeting but indelible vision of the cow, humped over, her tongue spilling onto the road, and the robed man beside her, frenziedly pulling at his hair as he jumped up and down.

I wanted to go to Agadir. People in Tangier said there was nothing there but a beach; that did not make it a less exciting project. It was in the Souss country, thus I knew I wanted to go.

Air-France ran a plane twice a week to Casablanca. It came down onto the pasture in Tangier four hours late. There were six other passengers; they all vomited en route. Since it was my first flight, I refused to allow myself that weakness, although at one point I felt tempted.

People had been quite right about Agadir: there was no such town. But there was the Casbah up at the top of the mountain, there was the white village of Founti below on the shore, where a chicken cost twenty cents, and there was a long wooden shack built on piles above the beach that served as hotel. The region, exploding with light and heat, had tremendous atmosphere, but as in all such places, its flavor was swiftly destroyed by commercial exploitation. Two years later a jerry-built pseudo-French town stood on the site. (Providentially this excrescence was pulverized by the earthquake.) Now that all trace of charm has vanished from the entire area, the Moroccans are making Agadir into a tourist center. Why not? Tourists will go anywhere.

At this remove in time, my motivation for returning to Paris is lost. However, before long, I was back there, complaining of the cold. I took a furnished room in the apartment of a widow up in Montmartre, put in a piano, and began work on a sonata for flute and piano. Each day I felt colder, although it was the end of May and spring was not unseasonably late in arriving. One day I had lunch with Carlo Suarès; he looked at me and said: "I think you have typhoid. I've seen it so often in Egypt." He made me take my temperature. I had a high fever.

At the American Hospital in Neuilly they put me to bed and made a long series of tests. The first diagnosis was Malta fever, since I admitted to having drunk goat's milk on many occasions. But Carlo's guess proved to have been correct. It was typhoid-A. There was, of course, no specific drug against the disease in 1932. Food was withheld, and the patient was given cold baths and packed in ice while the fever ran its course. The dangers were pneumonia and peritonitis.

The first two weeks I was too sick to know who came to call on me. After that I was allowed to sit up when visitors arrived. Amelia appeared, wreathed in smiles, and had the effrontery to say to me: "At last I've got you where I want you." I seized a glass of water that stood on the bed table and hurled it at her; she ducked and ran out, giggling. After that, the nurses did not allow her in to see me. They let Virgil Thomson in. By that time I had nearly a month's growth of beard, and it was a ghastly red. "You look just like Jesus," said Virgil. The next day I managed to get hold of a razor, and never since then have I gone even a day without shaving.

One afternoon I looked up and saw Abdelkader being shown in. I never had a satisfying explanation from him about how he had got from Marrakech back to Paris, but there he was, with one of my handkerchiefs showing from his breast pocket. He said he was working for someone called the Marquis de Villeneuve. I drew his attention to the handkerchief, and in his protestations of innocence he was able to make tears start from his eyes. Many Moroccans have this talent; I suspect it to be an adjunct of boundless self-pity. The fact that I accused him openly of stealing my clothes did not seem in the least to diminish his supply of goodwill toward me. He merely denied it. Amelia had given him everything, he claimed, only she had not bought enough valises to take it all in, and so he had had to leave many things behind. I was told subsequently by a Frenchman who had seen him in Marrakech that he spent entire days in the Djemâa el Fna selling his booty, piece by piece, to passing Moroccans.

A letter came from Aaron, saying that Ada MacLeish had sung my six songs at the Yaddo Festival and that the impression created had been excellent. "You're on the map now, and don't you forget it," he wrote. The letter was a great morale booster for me.

When Mother heard I had typhoid, she wired that she was coming to France to stay with me after I left the hospital. We spent a while outside Grenoble, in company with Bruce Morrissette and Daniel Burns, who had brought Mother down from Paris. Bruce had a motorcycle; he and I rode one Sunday on it to Belley for dinner with Gertrude Stein. That proved to be my last glimpse of her. I took Mother down to Monte Carlo, to relax for two or three weeks. Each day on the beach at the Sporting d'Eté we would see Gertrude Lawrence. "She looks like a beanpole," said Mother, "and she'd better be careful. Her back's as red as a lobster. You can't tell me that doesn't *hurt*." We went to Mallorca, where we met Bruce and Daniel and hired a car to take us around the island. After a week we returned to Barcelona. I wanted to visit the Gaudí landmarks: the Sagrada Familia, the apartments in the Paseo de la Gracia, and the Parque Güell, where I remember above all the statue of a girl carrying an open parasol over her head. The Gaudí touch was visible in the fact that the parasol had to be a real one. For some reason the authorities in charge of the park that year had chosen to supplant the parasol with a large black umbrella; perhaps they were aware of the Surrealist effect. Barcelona's Barrio Chino had the reputation, along with the Vieux Port of Marseilles, of being the most vicious quarter of any European city. (It is interesting that both should have been annihilated by Fascist warplanes.) Like good tourists, we visited the Barrio and were satisfied as to its depravity.

As a result of spending too long in the sun on the roof of the hotel, I managed to come down with a sunstroke. While I lay in bed with protracted fever and sloughing skin, Mother sat reading Richard Hughes' *A High Wind in Jamaica* to me. It was like being a child all over again. Another recuperation was in order. We went up into the Pyrenees to a Catalan shrine-resort, Nuestra Señora de Nuria.

Back in Paris Abdelkader met Mother and immediately sat down on her lap, playing absently with her pearls and saying: *"Je te jure, madame, je t'aime comme ma mère."* This unexpected behavior disgusted me and startled her. A few minutes later she drew me aside to ask me if I thought he was all right in the head.

I took Mother to see what people went to see when they visited Paris. She enjoyed the Bal Nègre in the rue Blomet and the Théâtre du Grand Guignol. In fact, she enjoyed everything; at the same time, there was no persuading her to defer her return trip, because as she said: "Your father will be getting most impatient." As soon as I had seen her onto the boat train, I hurried back to the Mediterranean to visit Virgil Thomson and Maurice Grosser on the Île de Porquerolles. I had with me on the train a copy of *Les Chants de Maldoror*, of which until then I had read only sections. I was far more enthusiastic about Lautréamont than about Rimbaud. His legend, at least the version of it presented by the Surrealists, was almost as compelling as Rimbaud's, and the work itself, constantly violent and totally devoid of subtlety, a good deal more easily approached.

Porquerolles was pleasant; I stayed about a week, two days of which I spent in bed with another sunstroke. Virgil paid me a visit the day I came down with it and went off to consult a local sorceress. It seems that she set an empty pot inside a caldron of boiling water and performed her divination according to its behavior. Her prediction was that I would be either dead or all right after sunset.

I went back to Monte Carlo and resumed work on my settings of passages of St.-John Perse's *Anabase*. Having heard that George Antheil was living at Cagnes-sur-Mer, I made a journey there and called on him. He and his Hungarian wife, Böske, lived in a little house right on the main square of the village. Once again I was gratified by a friendly reaction to my importunate behavior. It would have been so much simpler for them to put me off in one way or another; but they asked me to dinner, and George sat at the piano for hours reading and singing the scores of Kurt Weill's *Dreigroschenoper* and *Mahagonny*. I returned to Cagnes several times to see George and Böske; we went into Nice together to the movies. George was engaged in a propaganda campaign to interest composers in writing operas. He claimed it was the musical form of the future. He was writing one himself, on the life of Helen of Troy, using a libretto by the then-popular John Erskine, and he performed some arias from it. I had imagined something in the style of his widely publicized *Ballet Mécanique* and was a little disappointed to find that the music sounded more like Hindemith than like the extension of the Stravinskian esthetic I had expected to hear.

I stayed on in Monte Carlo until December, when the weather grew unpleasant and I began to dream once more of North Africa. Soon I went to Marseilles and got a ship across to Algiers. The first night in the bar I talked with a group of French army officers, one of whom told of a place in the desert called Ghardaïa, which he recommended highly for a winter sojourn. *"Il y a une palmeraie qui est une merveille!"* he said with enthusiasm. I determined to get there and see it.

On arriving in Algiers, I set out immediately by bus for Laghouat and arrived in time to go to bed the following evening. The next morning it was raining; the rain poured down all day while I waited in the execrable hotel, with the result that when the bus for Ghardaïa set out that night, it managed to go only about three miles before stalling in the midst of a vast and deepening lake. The passengers got out, pulled up their burnouses, and stalked about in the water, trying to find the road; but they were unsuccessful, so they got back into the bus to sleep until morning. The driver, a European, suggested that I return to Laghouat to spend the night. I was not eager to leave all my luggage on top of the bus, nor did I want to see the inside of that unappetizing hotel again; but he ordered a tall Algerian to put me on his back, he himself clambering onto the shoulders of another, and together we were carried to dry land. Then the Algerians returned to the bus, and we plodded through the mud, back to Laghouat, to the Grand Hôtel du Sud. The next morning we walked easily to the bus, the lake having nearly disappeared. I had been thinking about my valises and trunk, but that was only because I did not yet know the French Sahara, where, as the driver said, one could leave one's watch on a rock and find it a month later.

At Ghardaïa it had also rained, and for the first time, so they insisted, in seven years. A deep pond had formed at one side of the road leading into the town, and two or three small children, never before having seen water on the ground, tried to walk on it and were drowned. A great crowd of women surrounded the pond at all times of the day, scooping up the water to carry it home; this continued for the rest of the week until all sign of water had gone.

I was entirely delighted with the place, and set about trying to find a house. In this I was helped by a Lieutenant d'Armagnac, the regional commander, who found me a fine little dwelling with a garden outside it, the whole surrounded by a high wall edged at the top with sharp shards of bottles to keep out maraud-

ers. This property was not in the town or in any of the other villages of the so-called heptapolis of the M'Zab, but all by itself in
the wasteland, near the Route de Melika, and only a ten-minute
walk from the lieutenant's own house. He sent me one candidate
for the position of houseboy, a proud-faced young man apparently full of enthusiasm for the work, but who refused to look at
me while I interviewed him. This seemed to me to presage no
good; I asked the lieutenant if he thought him trustworthy. *"On
ne peut pas savoir,"* he replied. I decided to wait for another appli-
cant, and this time it was a man with only one eye, who had been
sent by the local Catholic mission. This man struck me as a good
bet, and I hired him. His cooking was rudimentary, but he was
intelligent and industrious; he also saved my life.

The M'Zab is in a particularly barren part of the northern Algerian Sahara, and December is a cold month there. That winter, because of my general depletion following typhoid, I was
more than normally sensitive to the cold. In any case, the little
house was like a freezing compartment. Outside the door the
palms baked under the powerful sun, but as soon as I stepped
within, I noticed the cold. The thick mud walls were all too effective in isolating the inside from the outside. I needed heat, and
the only equipment available was the classic *mijmah,* a terra-cotta
brazier for burning charcoal. As everyone who has ever handled
a *mijmah* knows, they must be lighted in the open air and kept
there until the coals are red. Asphyxiation from the *mijmah* is
common all over North Africa. The tiny rooms of the houses fill
quickly with carbon monoxide. However, I had never handled
braziers and knew nothing about them.

The morning of my misadventure I placed the *mijmah* on the
floor beside the mattress where I sat and went on reading. Nothing at all happened, except that suddenly I wanted very much to
slump over and lie with my head on the mattress. I did this,
feeling so very heavy that I could not even wonder at the suddenness of my great weight. There seemed to be no time left before
darkness would be upon me, but it was a comfortable darkness
into which I went willingly. Then the word *monsieur* was being
shouted at me, and I was yanked onto my feet and dragged out
into the kitchen. Later I remember being led stumbling across

the hot wasteland in the blinding sun, to Lieutenant d'Armagnac's house. For two days I lay there in bed with a cracking headache.

The lieutenant suggested that since there was no way of having heat in my house, I go up to Laghouat and stay at the Hôtel Transatlantique there until the weather got warmer, which he claimed it always did three or four weeks after the solstice. Leaving everything in the house save the clothes I should need, plus some music manuscript paper and the two volumes of *Le Temps Retrouvé*, I set out for Laghouat. The Hôtel Transatlantique gave me a very good monthly rate, all inclusive, so I settled in to a regime of comfort. Early each morning they came into my room carrying logs and built a roaring fire in the fireplace; when the room was warm, they brought my breakfast tray.

There was a church in town; I went to ask the curé for permission to use its harmonium. On receiving his sanction, I set to work writing a cantata on a text in French of my own devising. (Many years later this was given a performance at the Museum of Modern Art in New York, but since I was in India at the time, I missed it; it has never had a second hearing.)

A month later I went back to Ghardaïa. The lieutenant had been quite right: it was beautifully warm now. In spite of that, I did not move into my house again but stayed at the native hotel used by the bus and truck drivers. Having eaten good French food for a while, I could not face the prospect of the nearly inedible meals my one-eyed man would have prepared for me. Here at the hotel I met an American named George Turner, perhaps a year older than I, who had been wandering around the desert for several months. We began eating at the same table, and it was not long before we decided to try and make a trip by camel together.

I sold the few objects of furniture I had bought, packed my belongings, said good-bye to the lieutenant, and we started off by bus for Algiers, where George had to get mail and money from his family in Evanston. Every night we explored the Casbah. Considering the fact that the French police stayed out of the place altogether unless there was big trouble there, in which case they went en masse and made multiple arrests, we were foolish to expose ourselves to what I suppose was the very considerable danger involved. But if we were foolish, we were also fortunate: we never encountered any difficulties.

We went to Bou-Saâda for a few days, where we were followed wherever we went by an untiring guide insistent upon showing us something—it didn't matter what: the market, the sand dunes, the dry riverbed—anything at all. When he mentioned Ouled Nail girls who would dance naked for us, we relented and let him arrange it. We had spent one night in Djelfa sleeping in a room with three Ouled Nail women and had not got rid of the vermin until Algiers, where we scrubbed in a hammam; thus we were firm about not wanting to sleep at the bordel in Bou-Saâda. There was only one good-looking girl in the establishment; she was about sixteen, and she made a great show of being very shy. To have taken her to bed would have cost each of us fifteen francs; to see her dance naked, however, was going to cost seventy-five. Furthermore, said the woman with whom we were making the arrangement, it was not the custom for the girls to dance without clothing, and she was not at all sure that the one we had picked would consent to do it. George was for abandoning the project, but I insisted, saying I would supply the money if the girl could be persuaded. In the end she agreed, of course, but she was in an agony of embarrassment as she removed her garments. At one point she lost her nerve and scurried into the adjoining room where the woman was waiting. But the guide was sitting there too, and she came back in even faster than she had gone out. Her dancing was not very good, and it lasted only about five minutes. Nevertheless, her beauty was such that nothing mattered. Whatever she did with her body was esthetically satisfying. When she had finished, and we had paid the woman, the girl asked which one of us was going to stay with her. On hearing that neither of us wanted her, she seemed crestfallen and angry. We went back to the hotel. I had scarcely got into bed and turned out my light when I heard George's door open and his footsteps going along the corridor. The next morning he admitted that he had returned to spend a while with the girl, but being as secretive in his own way as I was in mine, he merely mentioned it in passing.

While we were in Bou Saâda, I decided to go horseback riding, an idea which I should have rejected as soon as it occurred to me. My mare bolted, the saddle slipped and hung upside down under her belly so that I was riding bareback as she galloped, and I landed facedown in a dry riverbed. By the time I had crawled up the bank the mare was already far away and tiny on the horizon, still galloping. My watch was broken, and I limped for the next few days.

We returned to Algiers, where I left my trunks and valises in a hotel, and then we set out once more for the south. In Touggourt there were difficulties with the police, the French being French, which is to say xenophobic and suspicious, but the difficulties did not extend beyond a session at the commissariat during which we were asked innumerable questions about the reasons for our presence in Algeria. Two days later I met the *bach'hamar* of the region and arranged with him for two camels and a driver to take us across the northern tip of the Great Eastern Erg to El-Oued. As provisions we bought a case of Vittel, a large tin of soda crackers, and five kilos of Deglat Nour dates. For sleeping we purchased camel blankets ten meters long, which when folded served as seats for riding. Neither beast was provided with a saddle.

East of Touggourt we passed through a long string of small oases where there were many locusts whirring through the air. Our driver was adept at catching them on the wing. He would rip off the head and legs and crunch the insects like celery, a satisfied expression on his face. Neither George nor I felt like sampling them with him, nor did we accept his offer of water from his *gourba,* which he filled with the very green liquid he found in the occasional water holes on the way. The driver's work was to walk along beside us and try at least to keep the two camels going in the same general direction, a by no means easy task, since they were only pack animals and not used to being ridden. If there were a bit of desiccated plant life anywhere, he let them wander to it and eat at their leisure and objected when we kicked their flanks to make them continue. Now and then, at the sight of some small white object in the distance, the camels would change direction and go to examine it. The object always proved to be a pile of bones or a single bone, and each camel always seized a bone and contentedly munched on it until the driver, who became quite frenzied at such moments, could wrest it away. He explained that if a camel had a bone in its mouth, it would not bother to stop and graze, and he wanted his animals to take in as much nourishment as possible en route.

There was no trail to follow, but when there was any uncertainty about the exact direction, one had only to climb to the top of the nearest high dune in order to see the next concrete marker erected by the French every few miles along the way. Nights we slept in the *bordjes,* also put there by the French for use by caravans. (A *bordj* is a compound surrounded by four high walls.) On one side it was arranged for camels and on the other for men. The "arrangement" was simply a row of cubicles with walls and ceiling, but no floor. You rolled yourself in your blanket and slept on the sand. At dawn you took hot tea and started out once more. By the third day I was so chafed from the outlandish motions of the camel as it walked that I decided to dispense with riding. George did the same. Throughout the trek the camel driver knitted as he walked; he was making a muffler, he said, the finished end of which he was already wearing around his neck, so that he went along looking down, plying the needles as he went.

After three days of travel we came into the region of the Souf, with its funnel-shaped oases sunk in the sand, and then into El-Oued, where we paid and dismissed the driver. At table in the dining room of the Hôtel Transatlantique they served local water, assuring us that it was not polluted.

They neglected to mention that it contained a high percentage of magnesium salts. At three in the morning I was visited by incredibly violent cramps and nausea; it was as if a bomb had exploded inside me. George had no such troubles, having drunk wine with his dinner. I was sick for a day, but it made no difference to our plans, as we had to wait another two days to catch the caterpillar truck for Nefta, in Tunisia—that is, if we wanted to go to Tunis, which we had finally decided would be our objective. The caterpillar was fun; it was rather like taking a prolonged ride in a roller coaster. We spent all morning going to the tops of dunes and down again. Two days later we were in Kairouan, where the vermin in the beds was indescribable. My cash had almost given out; George had just enough for himself. I tried in vain at the bank in Kairouan to persuade them to honor an American Express check. On leaving the bank we were apprehended by the police, who led us off to the commissariat. We were questioned at length. Then, for no reason I understood, they confiscated my passport and my folder of traveler's checks. The next day they returned everything, still with no explanation, and we proceeded by train to Tunis.

The first place I visited was the American Embassy, to get badly needed francs. The only trouble was that the dollar was no longer a valid currency. It seemed that a new President in the United States had closed the banks. I said what everyone to whom they had imparted the unwelcome news must have said: "What am I going to do?" They advised me to borrow francs from my friends, as they were doing. I did not bother to explain that I had just arrived in Tunis for the first time in my life and could not have found anyone who would have lent me the price of a box of matches. I went out and spent the francs I had been going to eat with, sending four cables to Europe, in which I begged to have whatever francs anyone could spare. Nearly a week went by. We took the electric railway out to Sidi-bou-Saïd. I wanted to meet the Baron d'Erlanger who had written a large volume on Arab music. He was not in residence, but his librarian was hospitable. All I saw of Carthage was a herd of cows eating flowers in a meadow. We ate at the cheapest places in the Medina; fortunately the hotel did not present its bill. The only wire to get a response was to be the one I had sent to Bruce Morrissette at Clermont-Ferrand. With the money he sent me I paid my hotel bill and bought a third-class ticket to Algiers. George had decided to continue north from Tunis and cross to Sicily, so we parted company.

I did not have enough cash to pay for meals on the way, but then I learned that there was no dining car on the train in any case. The first morning as I wandered up and down the corridors of the cars looking into the compartments, I came upon a scene which stopped me short. There were two Moslem youths in there, and one was giving the other an injection in the thigh with a hypodermic needle. Somewhat later I passed through the car, stared into the compartment again and saw the same scene being reenacted. The one who had given the injection then looked up and noticed me. Perhaps he had seen me staring in earlier. In any case, when he had put away the syringe, he opened the door and came out into the corridor. We talked. His brother had tuberculosis, he said, and he had taken him from Constantine to Tunis to see a doctor. They were now on their way to Souk-Ahras, a town near the Algero-Tunisian border, where he was going to enter him in a sanatorium. Meanwhile the doctor had told him to administer morphine regularly, at very short intervals. He confided sadly that he did not expect him to live. My own money difficulties seemed too petty to mention, but being full of them, I eventually did. He said there was no problem at all. I need only stay with his family in Constantine until the banks opened again. There was a hammam in the town, owned by a friend of his for whom he would give me a note. I would sleep there that night, and tomorrow evening at six he would meet me there, since he was getting down very soon at Souk-Ahras. He wrote me the little missive in French to give the hammam-keeper and signed it Hassan Ramani. Then he and his brother (who when he stood up did look very ill) got their things together and left the train.

I went on to Constantine, arriving there at dusk, and found the hammam. It was large and clean, and they even served me shish kebab and tea, so that I did not have to go out again into the deep snow that covered the streets. But once I was stretched out in a dark corner on a mat, with a blanket over me, I found it impossible to sleep for the noise. A customer arrived carrying a *guinbri*—one might describe it as a rustic lute—and began to play. And he played so well that several men got up and danced. There was loud hand clapping to accompany the music, and the ensemble was punctuated by hortatory cries and peals of laughter. From where I lay I could see the gyrating figures, towels around their heads and loins; at any other time I should have been delighted with the entertainment, for both the musician and the dancers performed with precision and style. About one o'clock I sought out the hammam-keeper and asked if it were

possible to be put in a quieter spot. Accommodating, he led me
up two flights of stairs, to the very top of the establishment. It was
completely empty, dark, and quiet. It was also much colder than
it had been down in the bath. He gave me an extra blanket, and
I spread my overcoat on top of that. In the morning I left my
luggage at the bath and went out to examine the town. The sun
had appeared, and the snow was melting, so that water dripped
and ran in all places. The city follows the contour of a vast natural bastion, along the edge of a very deep, narrow, winding gorge.
A swaying footbridge spanned the abyss. The invisible river that
roared far beneath was swollen with the melted snows of the
Hodna Mountains; a fine vapor rose constantly from below.
Storks stood quietly on the rooftops, and the sad smell of late
winter hung in the air.

Hassan Ramani met me at six that evening and took me to his
house on the outskirts of the city, and at the very edge of the
gorge. The family received me with enthusiasm; one would have
thought I was a returned prodigal son. Each meal was a banquet
with singing and dancing by the womenfolk. Daytimes we ate on
the long terrace overlooking the emptiness below, and the rising
mist nearly obscured the cliffs on the opposite side of the gorge. It
was all very fine, but I was eager to get to Algiers and see my
mail, so after three days I said good-bye and started out once
more.

In Algiers the banks had opened; the dollar was again negotia-
ble. I picked up my pile of letters, left instructions to forward further arrivals to Tangier, got together all my luggage, including
the seventeen jackal pelts and the python skin I had acquired in
Laghouat and had arranged to have shipped direct to Algiers,
and boarded the train for Morocco.

IX

Had I believed that my constantly changing life, which I considered the most pleasant of all possible lives (save perhaps the same one on a slightly more generous budget), would go on indefinitely, I should not have pursued it with such fanatical ardor. But I was aware that it could not be durable. Each day lived through on this side of the Atlantic was one more day spent outside prison. I was aware of the paranoia in my attitude and that with each succeeding month of absence from the United States I was augmenting it. Still, there is not much doubt that with sufficient funds I should have stayed indefinitely outside America. Gertrude Stein had said I was self-indulgent, but with all the displacements I had been able to finish writing the Flute Sonata, *Scènes d'Anabase*, the Piano Sonatina, and the cantata I had begun in Laghouat. This last was called *Par le Détroit*, a hermetic reference to my preoccupation in dreams with the Strait of Gibraltar. Perhaps the title *Dream Cantata* would have been more apposite, inasmuch as several sections of the work were composed in detail while I slept. On awakening I immediately wrote them out. Why this should have happened in the case of this one piece and at no other time, I have no idea. Since early childhood it had been a fantasy of mine to dream a thing in such detail that it would be possible to bring it across the frontier intact—the next best thing to being able to hang onto all those fistfuls of banknotes that must always remain behind when the eyes open. When the experience I had so often imagined actually came about, I was so gratified that I kept it all just as I had found it, exercising no critical judgment. In part I was impressed by the fact that I needed no keyboard instrument for writing it, since what I was bringing back from the dream was the printed music as I had memorized it.

As soon as I arrived in Tangier, I began a search for a house where I could put a piano. I had notes for a solo piano work, and I wanted to be able to play as long and as loud as I pleased; this meant that no one must be within hearing distance. I took a very simple Moroccan house up on the Marshan, across from the old palace of Caid Mac Lean. There was no running water on the property, but this made no difference since I slept down in the Medina at a hotel. I installed an old upright piano and got to work. In the morning I would buy food for lunch and carry it up to the house. Sometimes I ate on the cliffs opposite, lying among the rocks, looking out to sea. Sometimes I merely went outside the kitchen door and had my lunch under the fig tree there. I would work until the end of the afternoon, pack up my materials in an attaché case, and go back down into town. If my insistence upon prolonging the wanderings was compulsive, no less so was the fanatical manner in which I forced myself to work regularly each day. The truth was that Aaron's little warning of two years before, "If you don't work when you're twenty, nobody's going to love you when you're thirty," although scarcely meant seriously, had remained with me and taken root.

Back in 1930 I had published poems in a little magazine called *blues,* jointly edited by Charles-Henri Ford and Parker Tyler. Although originally issued from Columbus, Mississippi, it was soon being printed in New York, because Ford had moved there. He asked me, and I agreed, to appear at a poetry reading by *blues* contributors, held somewhere in the Village. I read only works which I had published in French; my impression was that no one in the audience understood them. After the reading a man came up to me and said: "You're way out over your head with these people, boy, you know that?"

Later I had run into Ford in Paris with Tchelitchew, the painter. Now suddenly he was in Tangier, awaiting the arrival of Djuna Barnes from Devonshire, where she had been visiting

Peggy Guggenheim. Until her arrival Ford had been staying with a young Spanish couple, Pito and Carmita. Djuna came and explained that she wanted to find a house. Someone suggested that since I used my house on the Marshan only to work in, it was logical that she should use it to sleep in. Charles-Henri Ford moved in with her, on the understanding that after one thirty in the afternoon I could always count on their being out of it. Before she would unpack, Djuna insisted on removing all seventeen jackal pelts from the walls where I had hung them; she also rolled up the python skin and put it away.

Soon Djuna and Charles-Henri found a more comfortable house in the middle of an orchard a few hundred feet up the lane. They lived Moroccan-style, on the floor. She was typing a manuscript called *Bow Down*; the title was later changed to *Nightwood*. We used to sit at the Café Central in the Zoco Chico, and because Djuna's makeup was blue, purple, and green in a day when no one used such colors, she was an object of interest to everyone. She did not at all mind being stared at; a brief imitation of Sir Francis Rose she did one day galvanized the spectators in the café, as well as the passersby.

I can only assume that I had come, more or less, to the end of my money; otherwise, I should not have gone across to Cádiz and bought a third-class passage on the *Juan Sebastian Elcano*, bound for San Juan de Puerto Rico. It was a very uncomfortable trip, made worse by the execrable food. Everything, including the drinking water, reeked of fish. We stopped at Tenerife and took on ninety-five workers on their way to Venezuela, and a great many roosters in cages, destined to perform at cockfights in Latin America. Several men kept busy with the fowl throughout the voyage, paring their spurs, rubbing them with unguents, and staging false confrontations between them, by merely holding them while they faced one another and grew excited.

After three weeks of sailing it was good to land at San Juan and have some fresh food. I wired my parents to let them know that at least I was back in the Western Hemisphere, stored my trunks and valises in a hotel, and took a rattletrap old bus up into the hills, to a village in the center of the island called Barranquitas. I stayed a week here in the country, eating fried bananas, *habichuelas,* eggs, and rice. Then reluctantly I boarded a ship of the Ward Line and sailed up to New York.

Almost as soon as I arrived, I went out to Greenwich to see John Kirkpatrick, to whom Aaron had introduced me, and gave him my Piano Sonatina, as well as some piano pieces I had written in Barranquitas. Later we went together to see Claire Reis, who ran the League of Composers' concerts, and he played the sonatina for her and a few invited composers, with an eye to including it on a program later that season. I remember Marc Blitzstein remarking to me afterward: "I didn't know you had it in you," which I was not able to identify either as praise or as general denigration. In any case, the reaction to the work was favorable, and it was scheduled for performance.

"Mercy! What are you going to do with those?" Mother cried when I unpacked the jackal hides. We stored them in the cellar, where they slowly rotted away. I spent that summer at Aunt Emma's in Westhampton, Massachusetts, trying to lose the incipient ulcer that threatened to take over my stomach. "You can't mistreat yourself the way you have without paying for it later," Daddy declared over and over.

Aunt Emma had divorced Uncle Guy and was living with a man named Orville Flint, of whom everyone in the family took a very dim view. His former wife had killed herself with a shotgun one evening at dusk as she sat in the parlor of the old house; Aunt Emma never went into the room where it had happened. "Sometimes I get to thinking about it," she told me, "and I wonder how she had the courage. *I* couldn't do it, I know that."

When I returned to New York in the autumn, Harry Dunham had taken the top floor of a large brownstone on East Fifty-eighth Street, and I moved into one of the empty rooms. I had been there hardly a fortnight before Harry's father, Dr. Dunham, was on the war path, threatening to cease sending him money unless I left. To his way of thinking I was a corrosive element in his son's life; I must be removed and kept at a distance.

For a long time now Aaron Copland had been thinking of forming a group of young composers, who would meet regularly and discuss one another's music. The autumn of 1933 was propitious to his project. I was rather more involved than anyone else in the business, since I had signed the lease on the furnished studio-apartment in West Fifty-eighth Street where the group met each Friday afternoon. Aaron and I each paid half the rent; occasionally he came and used the room with the piano, but most of the time I had the apartment completely to myself.

It was a heterogeneous assortment that came to the first gatherings. I remember Bernard Herrmann as the most aggressive member; he thought both my music and I were absurd and said so in no uncertain terms. The others were more tactful. They included Israel Citkowitz and the Wunderkind Henry Brant. Citkowitz was a prize pupil of Nadia Boulanger, and at that time I should guess the most musically educated of us all. In the midst of these and others, all of them not only articulate but vociferous —even combative on occasion—I would often ask myself what I was doing there, and I questioned the value of the venture. The fact that everyone enjoyed the occasions did not strike me as being of sufficient importance to counterbalance the feeling of futility that remained with me after each session. There were not many meetings after the New Year. Most of the group enrolled in Roger Sessions' harmony class at that point. I recall the odors that hung in the lecture room: the wet-putty smell of steam heat and the rubber reek of galoshes, damp raincoats, and umbrellas.

John Kirkpatrick performed my Piano Sonatina at the League of Composers' concert. (Marc Blitzstein, reviewing it, wrote: ". . . what is called damned clever. Whiter than even the White Russians. . . .") After the concert a strange little man came up to me and introduced himself. He was John Latouche of Richmond, he said, and a friend of Bruce Morrissette. I saw him several times at parties that winter and gradually came to think him brilliant and amusing.

Suddenly Aaron decided he had no further use for the studio in Fifty-eighth Street. Since I could not afford to pay the entire rent, it was only two or three months before I skipped the lease. (This proved later to have been a very poor idea: I was successfully sued by the corporation for the rest of the year's rent.)

Virgil Thomson came to New York and took me to the Stettheimers. Florine, the youngest of the three sisters, was designing

the sets and costumes for his Stein opera, *Four Saints in Three Acts.*
I went to vocal and instrumental rehearsals. The sound of his orchestra intrigued me: it had a slightly dry and wheezy quality,
which was because he had included two highly unorthodox instruments, the harmonium and the accordion. On opening night
in New York I sat with the Stettheimers in their box. After the
performance everyone went to a big party at Julien Levy's apartment, just redecorated for the occasion in what Virgil described
as "blood-red and pantie-white." To carry out the motif, there
was a small den whose walls were hung with a collection of
whips.

In the spring I lived in West Fifty-fifth Street, next door to a
factory where they pressed Decca records. The machines were attached to the wall next to the bedroom, and they functioned
twenty-four hours a day. My windows gave onto a courtyard
which was an epitome of New York: a scene of noise, grime, and
gloom. I tried to drown my melancholy in work, but I was ob-
sessed by memories of the air and light of North Africa. There
seemed no prospect of an imminent escape or indeed of a later
one. Nevertheless, in the face of logic I trusted in my luck, which
I considered had not yet failed me.

Three years earlier in Fez, Harry and I had lunched at the
house of Charles Brown, the Swiss gentleman who for many years
had been in charge of the American Fondouk there. The Fondouk had been established as a foundation in the twenties by an
American woman who could not bear the sight of the mistreat-
ment suffered by the pack animals in Morocco. (The custom was
—and still is—to keep an open sore on the haunch of the beast
and to prod the unprotected flesh with a steel-pointed stick carried for the purpose.) The aims of the organization were twofold:
to care for the maimed animals and to educate the men who
owned them. Brown had been happy and successful in his capacity of administrator, but now he had an enemy within the organization itself, in the person of Colonel Charles Williams, his immediate superior.

In a roundabout fashion I had heard that Colonel Williams, a
resident of Monaco, was on a brief visit to New York. I got his
address and went straight to see him. When I appeared in the

doorway of his hotel room, he greeted me with the words: "I knew your mother in Taormina. Delightful woman." Since I felt certain that he had merely invented the phrase for the occasion, it would have been a piece of rudeness to examine it too closely. "Did you, sir?" I said. I felt that he expected me to speak like that. Colonel Williams was seventy-five, with a bristling white mustache and a tendency to become very red in the face when things did not please him. He remembered Theodore Roosevelt with affection. When he began to discuss the American Fondouk, it soon became clear that the only aspect of the organization that interested him even a little was personnel; he intended to reorganize the administration in Fez, by which he meant that he was going to get rid of Brown. This involved going to Fez and seizing on a concrete pretext which he could use for the purpose. It meant going through inventories and records at the dispensary itself, a task for which he said he doubted he had the strength or the patience.

The situation was such that it seemed madness not to try and profit by it. I discovered that Colonel Williams had a voluminous correspondence, the steady flow of which he dreaded interrupting in order to do the necessary detective work. A few days later I got him to say that with a cook and a chauffeur he could not afford a secretary. But in Fez, I suggested, while he carried out his researches? He admitted that such assistance would be very useful. I typed some letters for him on the spot. I could see that he was very much pleased with them; he said he would telephone me soon.

When he called, he said I must go and be interviewed by the president of the American Society for the Prevention of Cruelty to Animals, whose name was Sidney Coleman and who was in charge of the foundation's disbursements. It was finally agreed, before Colonel Williams left for Europe, that I would meet him toward the end of August in Gibraltar, and we would go together from there to Fez. I told my parents that I had been offered a job, but they were unimpressed. "Oh, I wish you'd keep *away* from that old Africa!" Mother said with feeling, and Daddy grumbled: "He's just going for the trip."

During the spring, after getting permission from Cocteau, I

wrote a cycle of six songs to his texts, called *Memnon*. Then I set two songs to words of Gertrude Stein and immediately published them myself, using for the name of the press an absurd invention: *Éditions de la Vipère*. Over the following years I published other songs and piano music of my own, as well as music by David Diamond and Erik Satie, using artwork by Anne Miracle, Tonny, and Eugene Berman for the title pages. Since I printed only a hundred of each publication, all copies have long since disappeared; I did not even manage to keep one of each.

Harry had got involved in editing a film shot in Samoa; he asked me if I would enjoy furnishing a score for it. There was very little money involved, but I sprang at the opportunity of learning whatever I could about the medium. Shortly I was timing scene sequences and working at a Movieola counting frames. The film was atrocious, a leering commentary having been thought essential. I suppose it helped distribution; the movie was showing on and off for two decades in cheap houses on Forty-second Street and along Eighth Avenue. Its original title of *Siva* was altered after the initial showing to *Bride of Samoa*, which it remained thereafter.

In June I was once again eastward bound, this time first-class on the *Conte di Savoia*. On deck I met a girl named Gloria and then her father, Dr. Gilbert Grosvenor, who was the editor of the *National Geographic* magazine. I found him unfailingly interesting; he had been just about everywhere on the face of the globe. We discussed our separate experiences in Béni-Isguen, the "holy" city of the M'Zab, where as soon as a stranger arrives in the town, everyone who is in the streets rushes into the house, and all one hears as he walks along is the slamming and bolting of doors.

I traveled around Andalusia for three weeks or so and then went across to Tangier. One evening there was a knock on the door of my hotel room; it was John Widdicombe, who had come to Morocco for the summer. At one point he was to meet a friend named Fletcher, and together they planned to go into the Sahara. He wanted to feel the desert heat in August. We went to Casablanca, where I bought a phonograph and what the French called Chleuh records. (So-called Chleuh music is a popular genre evolved from the folk music of the Souss and sung in Tachelhait.) John made an excellent traveling companion: he was well educated, highly adaptable to unexpected situations, and blessed with a sharp sense of the ridiculous. Not so Fletcher, who was appalled by Morocco.

We continued to Marrakech. There in the Djemaa el Fna we saw a deformed man become a goat. He succeeded in bringing about a transformation within himself which made it possible for him to move like a goat, to sound like one, and, in an indescribable and faintly horrible fashion, even to have eyes and a mouth that looked like those of a goat. The actual possession was preceded by a long buildup with a nose flute and the classical caperings of the marketplace entertainer. When he began to roll in the dust, we walked on. (In Mohammed Mrabet's novel *The Lemon,* which I translated from the Moghrebi thirty-five years later, the boy Abdeslam tells of seeing a man become a camel and of the fear it arouses in him.) Having decided that we wanted to go to Taroudant via the Tizi n' Test, we asked at a garage where we saw some native buses if there was one that went there. The Moroccan in charge told us there was, and that it left at six thirty in the morning from that very garage. We were up at half past five and got to the garage with our luggage about quarter past six. There was a sleepy guard on duty who knew nothing about the bus. We waited. At quarter to eight the other man appeared.

"What happened to the bus?"

"What bus?"

"The bus to Taroudant."

"There's no bus to Taroudant."

"But you yourself told me yesterday it left at half past six."

He smiled. "Oh, I was just being nice. There's no bus."

Rather than return to the hotel we got a taxi to take us. It was a two-day ride on a dirt road through the High Atlas. We slept in a place about 6,000 feet up where the peacocks screamed most of the night in the trees outside the rooms. The next morning all the small boys of the village arrived bearing amethysts, which they put into our hands saying: *"Bour toi."* John thought he would amuse himself: he had them stand in a line, raise their fists and sing: *"C'est la lutte finale . . ."* which, being the "Internationale," he imagined would give the French military something to think about when next they passed through. For an hour he labored to teach them an approximation of the last part of the song; they got the melody better than the words.

After a few days in Taroudant we went on to Agadir. Since I was operating on a budget which I steadfastly refused to alter, I stayed again in the shack on the beach where I had been two years before, while John and Fletcher tried the new Hôtel Marhaba. There they met a nephew of Paul Valéry, who had a powerful racing car with him; he asked them to accompany him on a trip into the wilderness. They came back completely exhausted, but eager to see more. Because the week drew near when I was supposed to meet Colonel Williams, I said good-bye to them and returned to Tangier.

Right away I discovered that Colonel Williams was an inveterate complainer. He was convinced that there was a permanent and ubiquitous conspiracy in operation, whose purpose was to provide him with inferior accommodations, food, and service. All Spaniards were idiots, all Moroccans thieves, and all French intolerably rude. He carried a cane with him not because he needed it, but so that he could pound with it as he gave orders.

We spent some days in Tangier getting his correspondence cleared up and then we took berths on the night train to Fez. I learned the reason for his violent opposition to Charles Brown: it came solely from the fact that Brown met Moroccans socially and invited them to his house. It was fatal, said the colonel, to allow natives to suppose that you considered them your equal; they were not accustomed to it, and it could only make for misunderstanding and discord. It was a well-known fact that Brown had received Moslems at his house and even seated them at table with Europeans. Under no circumstances could he be allowed to continue working at the American Fondouk. "We'll get him out," he said in a satisfied tone, winking unpleasantly.

It was hot and sultry in Fez during September. My presence there was to make it possible for Colonel Williams to devote all his time to what he called "auditing"; it was this operation which was to dislodge Brown. He tried in various ways to get Brown out of town for a few days. After a time the man left of his own accord, to go to Rabat, and it was then that the colonel struck. Some small item in the preceding year's ledgers had not been properly accounted for; it was gross negligence. I had to write a letter of indictment to Mr. Coleman in New York. Eventually there was a terrible scene between Brown and the colonel which, mercifully, I did not witness. Brown was superseded by a retired captain of the British army who had been coached for the job by the colonel.

John and Fletcher arrived in Fez and moved into the Grand Hôtel, where we were staying. John must have got the idea for his practical joke soon after meeting the old man whose tirades amused him enormously. A few days earlier he had bought a djellaba and, wearing it, had arranged to pass me in the street, to see whether he was recognizable. I missed him completely. As a result, he decided to carry out his impersonation. Without confiding in either Fletcher or me, he got together an assortment of Moroccan and pseudo-Moroccan objects, including things he had bought for himself, as well as the hideous hotel bedspread and the rugs of his room. Then, wearing his djellaba and a pair of yellow goatskin slippers, carrying the smaller objects in an open basket, with the Manchester-made rugs and coverlet over his arm, he went and tapped at Colonel Williams' door. The colonel, roused from his afternoon siesta, opened it, saw a Moroccan salesman standing there, and tried to shut it again. John, having first put his foot inside, pushed all the way in, past the colonel's protesting presence, and, keeping up a barrage of street salesman's patter, began to spread out the things on top of the bed. *"Legarde comme c'est joli, mossieu!"* He thrust a hotel ashtray at the colonel, who by that time was cursing in English and attempting to get around John to the telephone. John, however, blocked him with a rug, repeating in a cajoling voice: *"Bour toi, mossieu. Cadeau!"* and stuffing the ashtray into the colonel's bathrobe pocket. The colonel's face had turned a very dark red, and John began to feel uneasy. He pushed him backward onto the bed, cooing: *"Oooh! C'est joli!"* swiftly gathered up his props and fled, coming directly to my room, doubled over with laughter.

At dinner the colonel spoke of nothing else. He had lodged a formal complaint with the manager of the hotel, and he was thinking of moving to the Hôtel de la Paix, where they were still faintly civilized. The three of us listened to his indignant account, occasionally murmuring: "Incredible!" or "My God!" We all had to look at him fixedly in order not to lose our composure and dissolve in hilarity. As a result of the prank, we did move to the Hôtel de la Paix, where we stayed for the remainder of our sojourn in Fez.

I was busy studying Spanish, which in essence meant writing out the conjugations of regular and irregular verbs. My choice of reading text was not ideal. I had decided on *Altazor* by Vicente Huidobro, much of whose vocabulary was invented by the poet himself and not to be found in any dictionary.

Fez in 1934 was still full of monsters. The cafés of Fez-Djedid swarmed with beggars deformed since birth by phocomelia, with unfortunate victims of Koranic law who had had both hands amputated, with faceless lepers and syphilitics, with men whose bodies had been twisted by disease or accident into fantastic shapes and who pushed themselves along using their spines as runners. There was also a large complement of simple madmen in circulation. John and I learned to avoid certain cafés around Bab Dekaken and the entrance to the Moulay Abdallah quarter, in order to escape being molested. Fletcher never frequented the native spots in any case. When John went to Meknès, he brought me back a gift: an illustrated book called *Variations sur le corps humain*. It might have been subtitled: *Guide Anthropomorphique des ruelles de Fès*.

John and Fletcher, apparently hoping to find greater discomfort than they had experienced on their short journey with Valéry's nephew, now planned to make another trip into the desert. Off they went. A fortnight later, emaciated and battle-scarred, they returned to Fez. The list of their troubles was impressive: first there was the unbearable heat, then they had been attacked by a pack of nomad dogs, had drunk copper-tainted water and been poisoned by it, had suffered food poisoning and had both been affected by sunstroke, although at different times. John had a nasty open wound in the flesh at the back of his leg just below the knee where one of the dogs had bitten him; it did not seem to have become infected, but he was justifiably anxious about the possibility of rabies. He left Morocco without bothering to see a doctor and wrote me later from Portugal to say the bite had healed at last.

Late in October when the air was clear between Fez and the freshly snowed flanks of Bou Iblane, I took a short holiday to visit the Tafilelt, in the southeast of the country. I wanted one whiff of the Sahara before leaving that part of the world. For it was certain that the end of this Moroccan interlude was near. Colonel Williams wanted to return to Monaco, and I, very poor as usual, would be left to my own devices. I went to Ksar-es-Souk and on to Erfoud, where there was a Foreign Legion post. Again a Greek camp follower had installed a "hotel"—perhaps the same one with whom Harry and I had stayed three years before in Ouarzazate. At sundown the gates of the town were shut; if you were unlucky enough to be caught outside after that, you stayed outside until the next morning. I was advised not to stray too far beyond the gates even in the daytime. The warnings did not keep me from examining the outlying oases, however. The palms of the region were scarce and squat. It all looked very poor; there was very little of the feeling of being overpowered by lushness, which makes a real oasis so satisfying.

There was fighting just behind Rissani, some thirty kilometers down the trail to the south. One moonlit morning about three o'clock I heard the galloping of horses and the muffled shouts of men outside my window. The Legion was mounting a punitive attack against "dissidents" for having ambushed and massacred a busload of travelers earlier that day. It was a startling sight, so many white-caped figures riding by, with not a light anywhere but the moon overhead. The last night of my stay at Erfoud a crowd of thirty or forty legionnaires came up on leave from Rissani. They all were Germans, and when they saw me, they insisted upon speaking their language with me. I replied haltingly, and they bought me beers *ad nauseam* and presented me with the snapshots which most of them seemed to carry with them. "You are lucky. You are going back to the world. We, who knows? We are forgotten men." I felt that they had been reading the wrong books about the Legion; only Germans can melt so swiftly into sentimentality. "These little pictures were taken in camp in Djebel Sarrho. Take them, show them to people so the world can see what a dog's life we lead down here in this hell." Tears for a moment. Then, arms around one another's shoulders, they would break into military songs, their faces all very purposeful and devoted. And always more beer. I returned to Fez with a good collection of photographs.

Having accomplished his purpose there, that of severing Brown from the American Fondouk, Colonel Williams was eager to get away from Fez. I had played with the idea of returning to Algeria to visit Hassan Ramani, but none of my letters had elicited a reply. Then I decided to write Gustave Bompain, the photographer in Constantine for whom Hassan had worked. That letter was returned to me stamped DÉCÉDÉ. RETOUR À L'EXPÉDITEUR. Reluctantly I went to Tangier and then on to Cádiz. Conditions in Spain were such that I was not allowed to leave the hotel save in the presence of both a *guardia civil* and a policeman. They accompanied me to the steamship office, to the bank, and eventually to the dock and onto the ship itself. It was the same dreadful ship I had taken the year before, the *Juan Sebastian Elcano,* but this time I had booked passage all the way to Puerto Colombia. And this time the food was even worse than it had been earlier. After two days I was put into the infirmary, where I spent the next three weeks eating rice, eggs, and apricot jam.

There was one advantage to being ill on the *Juan Sebastian Elcano*: I could not escape from the officers and crewmen who thought it their duty to come in at any hour of the day and chat with me. Thus I learned a good deal more Spanish during the trip than I should have done under normal circumstances, shut into my cabin by myself. Having brought along the phonograph and a lot of Spanish folk music, I also learned the difference between *cante jondo* and flamenco vocal style, which I had hitherto confused. By the time we reached the West Indies I felt well enough to go ashore at the ports of call. I bought as many kinds of fruit as I could find.

At San Juan a large woman and her teen-aged son boarded the ship, bound for Venezuela. After we had set sail for Santo Domingo, the son produced a cigarette-case full of *grifas.* I had never heard of marijuana until that moment; even after I had politely accepted one and smoked it, I could not imagine why the boy considered these homemade cigarettes more interesting than ordinary ones. The taste was unpleasant, and since I did not inhale, I got no effect. One night in Curaçao, however, we walked several miles out of Willemstad into the country, where we found a primitive cantina by an inlet. We drank some beers lying in hammocks while frogs croaked all around us. The Puerto Rican pulled out his *grifas* and we smoked. This time I did experience a strange sensation of being irretrievably *there* in that place, drowned in the noise of the ubiquitous frogs and insects. Because I also had the impression that my heart was beating in a manner both more violent and more rapid, I classified the experience as unpleasant and thenceforth refused the cigarettes when they were offered, on the grounds that he had only a certain number of them and had already expressed a doubt that he would be able to find more in Caracas. When we arrived at La Guayra, the teen-ager was suddenly beset by terrors; he said he could not risk taking his *grifas* into Venezuela. If they should be discovered by the authorities, his mother would punish him severely. He brought them all to my cabin and left them with me, advising me to hide them very carefully in my luggage. I hid them so well that I completely forgot about them for several weeks.

I went to Barranquilla and settled into a hotel. There was a magnificent violence to the weather; one lived in a world dominated by the sound of rain falling onto vegetation. As the thunder came nearer at the end of the afternoon, the air began to bear an odor of greenhouses and fresh fruit. This was the moment when the light in the sky turned amber and the streets emptied of people. With a sudden roar the rain arrived. There was no escaping its noise inside the hotel; all the rooms gave onto open patios full of plants with resonant leaves.

I inquired about passage to Bogotá and renounced the idea when they told me that even to get to the town from which one took a train for the capital would require nine days on a riverboat up the Magdalena. I had too little money to dare go so far from the coast. Then I met a man in the hotel who told me about Ríohacha in the Guajira Peninsula, where the Indians wore no clothes and walked about carrying bows and arrows. I boarded an old paddle-wheel boat one evening; the next morning we got to Ciénaga, where I took the train for Santa Marta.

In Santa Marta I went to the office of a local company that ran a coastwise ship eastward to Ríohacha. With a long face the owner told me that only a week earlier his boat had foundered and cracked up on its return voyage. There was thus no question of getting there.

At dinner the first night in Santa Marta the hotel waiter placed a carafe of darkish water in front of me. It looked so unpalatable that I asked him if they boiled their drinking water, and he said the proprietor himself did the boiling. The following day I felt like death. I had come down with something bad; I knew that much. The waiter brought boiled rice to me in bed. I decided to ask him again if he was certain that the water I had drunk had been boiled. This time he said: *"No, señor."* I could hardly believe my ears. "But you told me the proprietor always boiled it!" I cried. "Yes," he said, "but not for the guests. Only for himself and his family."

Four or five days later I was still in bed and feeling very low. When the proprietor told me about the *finca* of Señor Flye, I determined to visit it. Directly behind Santa Marta, its snows visible from the open Caribbean as one sails along the coast, is a configuration of mountains that reaches up 19,000 feet. Perhaps a third of the way up, the American gentleman had his coffee plantation, which the man said was just the place for me to recuperate. A week or two up there, and I would be feeling like myself. I must first get to a place called Jamonocal, as far as the road went, and from there it would be simple.

I found a truck going to Jamonocal. There at the edge of the forest I came upon a primitive general store run by two brothers. They looked sour and weather-beaten, very much gone native, and I was surprised when I overheard them speaking French between themselves. I used that language with them, and they decided to be helpful. Later in the day they brought me a horse that had been climbing up and down the trail all its life and put it at my disposal. I had only one small bag with me, which they strapped on behind the saddle. "All you have to do is sit there," they told me. "The horse will go straight to the *finca*. You should be there before dark."

The trail went up and up, through the rain forest. I never had seen trees even half as high as the giants around me, or such waterfalls, or such fantastic vegetation. Some four hours later, when it was already dark, the horse came up to a gate where a man stood holding a rifle. He was not inclined to let me pass: Señor Flye had to come make the decision, and he was not particularly pleased to see me, either. However, since I was ill, he said I might stay if I agreed to pay him $6 a day. I was scarcely in a position to bargain with him, there in the dark, perched on the horse. I rode up through the plantation to the house and was assigned a pleasant bedroom.

Mr. and Mrs. Flye had two couples from Bogotá staying with them—good bourgeois and high enough in the bourgeois hierarchy to be simple, straightforward people. I spent a pleasant week up there recuperating. Whichever direction I walked in, I came eventually to the edge of cleared terrain and thus to the primeval rain forest.

My malaise came and went, but it did not leave me. Mr. Flye prescribed Bayer's *Yatren,* a recently proven specific for amoebae. I got back down to Santa Marta the way I had gone up, took up my erstwhile quarters in the hotel, and went in search of *Yatren.* After a few days of taking the stuff, I felt a little better.

On the train going to Ciénaga there occurred a short, inexplicable drama. We were rattling along in a desolate region, through a mangrove swamp that stretched away indefinitely on both sides. Suddenly the train ground to a standstill. From the coach behind there came screams and shouts; then a man, stark naked, came bounding through the car's central aisle, followed closely by three soldiers brandishing swords. He ran to the front end and jumped off, the soldiers after him, and near enough to try to slash him with their swords. Everyone in the train was on the starboard side, leaning out. The four protagonists disappeared into the mangroves for a minute or two. Then the soldiers returned, sheathing their swords, jumped aboard, and gave a signal for the train to start again. The naked man was in the swamp. *Así es la vida.*

In Barranquilla I was able to secure passage from Puerto Colombia up to San Pedro, California. It was a Grace liner; I had
not bought steerage accommodations; nevertheless, as a result of
one of those very American office-work errors, that was where I
had to sleep the first night out, with the anchor clanking against
the steel plates of the bow ten inches from where my head lay.
The ship pitched abominably, and there was no air. For company I had a strange pair of American youths, each of them ordinary enough, but made unforgettable by the situation that bound
them together. Being sixteen and eighteen respectively and both
husky and able to fend for themselves, they had taken ship as
merchant seamen to South America. Then for adventure they
had gone on a long inland journey, during the course of which
the older of them had met with an accident which necessitated
the amputation of his right arm at the elbow. He had thus become more or less dependent upon the younger, who with the fanaticism of extreme youth devoted himself totally to his friend.
He rolled and lighted his cigarettes for him and even on occasion
helped feed him. During the two-week trip I never saw either of
them alone. The first night they were lying across the dormitory
on two bunks side by side. We talked half the night about Africa
and South America; presently the older boy remarked that they
had found some good marijuana in Maracaibo but had used it
all up. I was not sure whether or not we were talking about the
same substance, but I said uncertainly: "I have some *grifas,* if you
want." Their reaction left no doubt that *grifas* were made with
marijuana. I gave them eight of my *grifas,* and they smoked
themselves to sleep. I refused to smoke any, having decided it was
not for me. The next day the purser assigned me a cabin and
apologized for having forced me to spend the night in steerage. I
got my appetite back on the voyage up from Panama, so that by
the time we arrived in Los Angeles I was feeling like myself.

I spent a month there, staying with Uncle Shirley and his family. The house was high on the side of a mountain, with a vast
view of Los Angeles, the Santa Monica Strait, and Catalina
Island beyond. I had not realized that the United States could
offer such impressive landscapes. The interest lay not in the detail, but in light effects seen at great distances. What created the

beauty, in effect, was the extraordinary clarity of the air. It is strange to think that in the few intervening years the entire area should have been permanently ruined.

I went then to stay a month in San Francisco with cousins of Daddymama's, whose house also had a spectacular view of the city, the bay, and the mountains. There I came down with a severe case of tonsillitis and was confined to bed. Unfortunately for me Aunt Jessie was a Christian Scientist; when my temperature rose, she looked at me accusingly and said: "It's all in the mind, you know." And when after several days I asked for a doctor, she refused to have one called, being particularly proud of the fact that no MD ever had crossed her threshold. At the same time, she had three daughters who secretly sympathized with me, sending me up medicines and goodies via the Swedish housekeeper, so that I was not entirely neglected.

I saw a good deal of Henry Cowell, who was busy teaching in several colleges of the area. He took me out to Palo Alto, where he had a rhythm class at Stanford, and I played the *claves* with the students. In Los Angeles I had written some piano preludes and set to music a letter of Gertrude Stein's; Cowell, who edited *New Music,* decided to publish some of these items, and I was delighted, since no one but I myself had yet printed any of my work.

I told my cousins about the *grifas,* and naturally they wanted to try them. One night we were drinking and driving around the city. We found a dark section of Golden Gate Park, and I brought out the cigarettes. Since it was some time after midnight, we were approached by a police car. The officers made us get out and stand in the road. Sylvia, always referred to as a spitfire, resented this treatment and told them that her father would see to it that they were punished. Doubtless the cannabis had made her more vociferous than usual, for the policeman decided that we were all drunk and proceeded to search the car for liquor. We breathed more easily when they had finished looking, lighted up more *grifas* in their presence, and drove off.

Often during the long hours of sitting and looking out the windows of a North African bus, I had wondered what the same sort of trip would be like in my own country, visiting whatever town I chose and staying a day or two in the more promising ones before moving on. George Turner, whom I had not seen since Tunis, had invited me to visit him at his family's house in Evanston; now I had an opportunity of going all the way to Chicago by Greyhound bus. I stayed over in Reno, Salt Lake City, Cheyenne, and Omaha and arrived in Chicago convinced that the United States was indeed a beautiful country, after all. Thirty-five years ago the symptoms of its forthcoming decline were scarcely noticeable. (There were, however, cranks like my parents who as early as 1920 were indignantly complaining about the air pollution and the general despoiling of the countryside.)

George was very bitter about the Italians in Ethiopia; from Tunis he had managed to get to Addis Ababa and thus felt a special bond with the Ethiopians. The same government had committed the same atrocities in Libya earlier, but the details had not been publicized in any but the Arabic-language press. He took me around to Northwestern to meet Melville Herskovitz, who as a good anthropologist was equally angry with the Italians. The trouble with me was that I could not feel emotion about a place and a people I had not seen; I could merely disapprove on principle.

After a fortnight with George and his family I went on to Baltimore to see Bruce Morrissette, who was then at Johns Hopkins. Through him I met an Austrian named Fuhrman who was suffering from the effects of epidemic encephalitis and spent most of his time in bed. (Years later Gore Vidal and I guided Sir Osbert Sitwell along the streets of New York; he had Parkinson's disease, but his attempts at controlling his movements while he walked immediately put me in mind of Mr. Fuhrman.) Since it seemed to me that any life would be preferable to returning to live with my parents, I listened attentively when Mr. Fuhrman's doctor suggested that I take up residence in the invalid's house in order to read aloud to him for an hour each morning. I told the doctor I would let him know my decision after I had returned to New York.

X

It was decidedly no pleasure to be back at home in the shadow of the unposed question: "What are you going to do now?" I wanted to write music, but the family considered that an avocation rather than a possible profession. I went down to the Village to see Eugene Berman, the Russian Neoromantic painter who had just come to America and lived in a small flat on Washington Square. He suggested we do a ballet together, I providing the score and he the story, costumes, and decor. I have forgotten who we expected to acquire this opus, but I was eager to get to work. Remembering an open grand piano in a corner of Mr. Fuhrman's living room in Baltimore, I decided to write the doctor saying I would take the job reading to his patient, as long as it was understood that I must have the use of the piano. This having been agreed upon, I moved to Baltimore and set to work on the ballet. There was a section in it which Berman had entitled *Promenade Solitaire du Jeune Etranger Qui Ramasse et Contemple des Fragments Antiques.* When Virgil Thomson saw the manuscript, he was amused. It was a description, he said, not only of Berman's paintings, but of Berman himself.

The house in St. Martin's Road was very quiet; it was run by a black couple of miraculous efficiency. I started by reading Michel Vieuchange's *Smara* to Mr. Fuhrman. It was difficult to put across that particular book; I had to sell it to him beforehand in an improvised travelogue, complete with recorded music, photographs, and detailed maps. Since the poor man always lay in bed during reading hours and had to be lifted from it by his valet, he was more or less a captive audience; I felt that the demand for the book had to come from him. It was thus necessary that he be conditioned to request it. That was my theory, at least. At the time this steamrollering seemed perfectly natural. (It now strikes me as totally irrational.)

I went to the Communist Party headquarters in downtown Baltimore and met Bill Browder, the younger brother of the party's Presidential candidate and a hard worker for the cause. I bought party literature and studied the history of the party in each European country. The CPUSA, it seemed to me, could serve only as a harassing instrument; all attempts to give it the air of an American institution were doomed to failure. It was legal and thus absurd; for it to have meaning it would have to be driven underground. I had no faith in any political procedure save conspiracy. Nevertheless, this was the era of the Popular Front and "Communism is twentieth-century Americanism"; one pretended to agree.

In Baltimore I went around to Eutaw Place to see the Misses Etta and Claribel Cone, of whom Gertrude Stein had often spoken. They received me very cordially, and I began to see them regularly. They and their brother occupied two vast apartments, both of them crammed with paintings by practically everyone from Monet onward, although they had specialized in Matisse and claimed to have the most extensive collection of his canvases in existence. I mentioned Berman; they had nothing of his but were interested. I went to New York and spoke to Berman of the possibility of selling them something. He gave me several ink drawings to show them. Those which the Cones did not buy I sold to a curator at the Baltimore Museum. Berman liked having the money, and I was delighted to have served as liaison.

The Friends and Enemies of Modern Music, Inc., a society formed in Hartford, Connecticut, asked Virgil to present a concert of contemporary music at the Wadsworth Athenaeum in that city. He wrote me requesting the score and parts of *Scènes d'Anabase.* At that time, wherever I went I carried with me copies of all my scores, from the *Aria, Chorale and Canonic Rondo* onward. I was sad to miss the concert, inasmuch as I never had heard the piece and longed to satisfy my curiosity about how it sounded, but there was no way of leaving Baltimore.

Since his car was a limousine and the driver was out in front, as it were, Mr. Fuhrman did not think it indelicate of us, he said, to speak in foreign languages while we were on ritual afternoon drives. Sometimes we spoke Spanish, in which he was very much at home; sometimes we talked in French. Occasionally he would go into his native German, but this embarrassed me because there was always at least one word in each sentence with which I was unfamiliar. I have never learned to speak German.

At some point while I was living abroad, Daddypapa had died, leaving Daddymama alone in the big house with only Mary, who was as old as she and much less agile. While I was in Baltimore, a wire arrived announcing Daddymama's death from pneumonia. I went to the funeral in Elmira accompanied by Victor Kraft, who, being a New Yorker of Russian parentage, had not seen the particular facet of American life represented by my family and found everything very surprising. A few months later, when the estate was settled, I received a legacy, small but most welcome, which I salted away in the bank for future use.

For some reason I never was able to fathom, Harry Dunham went to Germany and threw in his lot with the Nazi youth movement under Baldur von Schirach. When he wrote me the news, I vowed to change his mind for him. In the autumn he returned to New York full of enthusiasm. I began my campaign to give his fanaticism a different direction. I was so successful that a few months later he astonished me by showing me his Communist Party book. I had never expected him to go as far as that, even though he used a party name; nevertheless, I was gratified because I knew he would be of great use to the movement. During the year that followed he made the films for Browder's Presidential campaign and paid for sound trucks to show them in likely New York neighborhoods.

However, 1935 was a nadir in my life. No project for travel showed itself on the horizon, nor was there any indication that I should ever be able to earn a livelihood by writing music. Out of desperation I would go down to the headquarters of the League

Against War and Fascism and run their addressograph for them, stamping the addresses on the mailing folders for their publication. Each day I haunted the Worker's Bookshop, studying the titles of the books and periodicals and pamphlets, feeling always that everything was hopelessly foreign and sectarian, that it was all directed at people who could not be influenced because they were already partisans.

John Hammond and Joseph Losey lived on Sullivan Street; I used to go around there and listen to John's jazz records. We had first corresponded when he was a student at Hotchkiss and I was in high school. A few years later I had met him just as he was leaving for the Soviet Union. I thought it very fine that the son of the former ambassador to Spain and the grandson of Mrs. W. K. Vanderbilt should be interested in revolution. John took me up to Harlem to meet a young pianist whom he was helping; his name was Teddy Wilson. John had worked in the defense of the Scottsboro boys; in Huntsville he had found an old "race" record which delighted him. It was by a completely unknown pianist, and he had never come across any other pressings by the same man, although he was still searching. It was his idea to try to locate the pianist if he was still alive and get him to make more recordings. Eventually he unearthed the man, whose name was Meade Lux Lewis. He was washing cars in a Chicago garage. John took him to New York, where he quickly became a great success playing at Café Society on Sheridan Square. His barrelhouse style became known as boogie-woogie and passed into the history of jazz. Joe Losey was busy in the newly formed Federal Theater and was not around Sullivan Street very much.

George Antheil and Böske were in town, living on East Fifty-fifth Street. I enjoyed showing my manuscripts to George and hearing him run through them on the piano. He never hesitated for notes. If he did not hit the right ones, he hit the wrong ones and kept going. One day Harry Dunham told me he was taking me to see Cummings, the poet, on the following afternoon. I saw George the night before and remembered an incident that Aaron had once recounted to me. At a party where George had been playing his music, Cummings had got up and gone into an adjacent bathroom. He had waited for one of the rare pianissimo passages, and then, with the door wide open, he had flushed the toilet. So I told George I was going to see Cummings, and asked him what sort of man he was. "He's a son of a bitch," said George, without elaborating.

Cummings was not a son of a bitch at all. He reminded me of the members of my own family: eccentric, intolerant, and querulous. The great advantage he had over them, apart from his intelligence and talent, was his capacity for enjoying the act of living. He took me to my first burlesque show; it was on the Bowery; we shelled and ate peanuts throughout the performance.

I had often gone to Muriel Draper's teas. They were frantic, and people arrived and departed constantly. The one static element in the midst of the exaggerated animation was Muriel Draper herself, seated high on a gilt throne. Some guests managed to have a brief audience at the foot of the throne; others did not. Eventually we became friends, and she asked me to dinner. At the end of the evening after a long conversation she said to me (partly in jest, I hope): "*What* a devious young man you are!" I felt very much flattered, not knowing the meaning of the adjective. When I got home, I lost no time in looking it up in the dictionary. Then I was mystified. My *Oxford* gave as definition: "remote, sequestered, winding, circuitous, erratic." I can only think she was referring to my manner of relating a story. When I begin to recount an incident, my first intention is to give a bare report of the principal events and nothing more and eventually allow extensions of that material. It must become increasingly obvious to the listener that I am 'withholding information; this can hardly be an endearing characteristic to observe in a friend. In the end I suppose a story told backwards out of uncertainty as to how much need be told could be indistinguishable from a story told backwards out of sheer perversity or in the hope of deceiving.

The Friends and Enemies of Modern Music gave another bash during the summer of 1935, this one taking place in the Hartford house of Chick Austin. Virgil had long been stressing the importance of music as a commodity which must be paid for; a composer who gave away his music was simply a scab, he maintained. This applied even to being cajoled after dinner by one's host or hostess into playing a few excerpts from one's work in progress. Austin agreed with Virgil's point of view; accordingly he hired Aaron, Virgil, George Antheil, and me to perform in Hartford. The occasion had its contretemps for me: somehow in the general drunkenness that followed the breakup of the evening, my suitcase disappeared. I could not very well go back to New York in white tie and tails; Austin had to lend me suit, shirt, tie, and socks in order for me to get out of Hartford.

Another time, and again at Virgil's instigation, Mrs. Murray Crane hired a foursome consisting of Virgil, Aaron, Marc Blitzstein, and me to entertain her guests. A week or so before the occasion we spent an afternoon at her house arranging the program with her. Everything went easily until Marc sang an aria from *The Cradle Will Rock,* which he was just completing. The song's title and repeated punch line was: "There's Something So Damned Low About the Rich." While he delivered it with all the precise venom of which he was capable, Aaron, Virgil, and I stole rapid glances at one another and at Mrs. Crane. Apparently she had discovered the words to be in Aramaic, a language which she did not understand. However, she also let one see that she was following the music with polite interest. When Marc had finished, she leaned forward and said placidly: "Yes, it's fascinating. But I always feel that for a song to be meaningful one must hear the words. I was listening carefully, and I confess I got nothing. But of course there's no reason why you *should* be able to sing. Perhaps you have something purely instrumental?" Marc then played selections from his ballet *Cain,* which Mrs. Crane found suitable. The evening went off smoothly, and we were given our checks before leaving. I felt horribly ashamed at that moment; it seemed a bit like accepting payment for moving one's hostess' chair for her. But Virgil's indoctrination asserted itself: a composer is a professional man, and professionals get paid. I hoped there might be other such musical evenings. It was the Depression, and Mrs. Crane's check seemed extremely generous. But there were no more.

I used to take Berman on long walks along the waterfront and across the East River bridges. He never tired of the skyline. Soon he was making a series of drawings of Manhattan in ruins, as seen from Brooklyn. Both of us had lost the original enthusiasm for our ballet. I had written at least half the score in Baltimore, but I worked very little on it after my return to New York.

Whenever I went to see Harry, I found John Latouche with him. Touche was nomadic and routineless in his life; he ate whatever he found and slept more or less wherever he was when he got sleepy. I, who lived by immutable self-imposed rules, was voluble in my criticism of his carefree behavior, but he seemed to understand that my disapproval came as much from envy as from anything else. Harry took his irregularities as a matter of course and did not complain if he arrived at four in the morning to announce that he was starved. Touche made his living writing song lyrics, although he called himself a poet, and bitterly resented my calling him a lyricist. He collected German and Central European refugees the way someone else might collect tropical fish; he was always eager to add more to his assortment. It was through Touche that I met Vladimir Dukelsky (not a refugee; known on Broadway as Vernon Duke) who gave me a job copying music for him. This was scab work, but at that time the Local 802 stamp was not required to be on each page of orchestral parts; that came later. Vernon's mother, a nice Russian lady, was a great cook and often asked me to lunch. Her cuisine became spectacular at Eastertime.

Henry Cowell was teaching at the New School for Social Research and wanted examples of my North African music to play to his classes. The school had reproducing equipment, although it was not very satisfactory: the copied records were of aluminum and had to be played using prepared thorns as needles. Henry was particularly enthusiastic about the Chleuh collection, and he asked me to make a set of records for Bela Bartok, who was living in Pittsburgh. Later he told me Bartok was incorporating the Chleuh material in a piece. Sure enough, when I heard the Concerto for Orchestra, there was the music, considerably transformed, but still recognizable to me, who was familiar with each note of every piece I had copied for him.

Lincoln Kirstein was running a ballet school on the corner of Fifty-ninth Street and Madison Avenue, with Balanchine in charge. He was thinking of commissioning a ballet from me, but he wanted Balanchine, who was a trained musician, to see some of my music first. I kept taking around old pieces I had written when I was in high school; naturally Balanchine was not impressed. However, the place seemed so chaotic that I was afraid to leave behind any score that I cared about. Eventually Lincoln decided on a subject, and introduced me to Eugene Loring, who was to choreograph the work. Since for Lincoln I was above all a traveler, he thought a ballet based on a sea voyage around the world appropriate. The work was to be called *Yankee Clipper*. I was busy for many months composing the piano score. Indeed, in my ignorance I made the fatal error of writing in such a pianistic idiom that the score was practically incapable of being orchestrated, but I did not find that out until later. It always sounded much better to me on the piano than it did in its orchestral version.

At the same time I was doing scores for a series of several short films made by Rudy Burckhardt, a Swiss photographer whom Edwin Denby had taken to America. In these I was both composer and orchestra: I played piano, sang, whistled, clicked my tongue, and made percussive noises, all as part of the music. Early in 1936 the Federal Music Project presented an all-Bowles concert. In addition to the chamber music, we screened Harry Dunham's film *Venus and Adonis*. Harry had to hold his hand in front of the projector during the nude sequences; the accompanying music together with the blank screen made an effect that was far more suggestive than the images would have been. The audience was an unprecedented mixture of anonymous people attracted by the prospect of a free concert, as well as serious composers and musicians and a few flamboyant members of Café Society. I saw Cecil Beaton and Natalie Paley craning their necks in some back seats. Mother and Daddy were also there; during intermission Daddy muttered: "And this is where our tax money goes now. My God!" Mother took a slightly more sanguine view. "At least they can't ungive the concert now that they've given it. If it were trees they'd been planting, they'd be digging them up again tomorrow."

Most of the works that had been played that night I was hearing for the first time. Above all, it was enlightening to hear them in succession. The much-advertised forum which followed the music consisted of questions written on sheets of paper by members of the audience, read aloud by the chairman and answered by the composer. It was strictly a heckling session. The leftists were against the music on principle. One question read: "Do you take sugar with your tea?" Henry Brant later confessed to having authored that query. Thus the following year when I heard the Philadelphia Orchestra rehearse *Yankee Clipper,* a good many sections of which Henry had orchestrated, I wondered if they sounded the way they did because he had again been in an elfin mood.

Dorothy Norman was a devout follower of Stieglitz, who, angered by the success of the Armory Show and the subsequent notoriety accorded the American expatriates all through the postwar years, had retaliated by forming a group of artists proud of their isolation from European art currents. This hotbed of esthetic chauvinism Stieglitz called An American Place. His wife, Georgia O'Keeffe, a far more forceful person than he, was capable of showing rancor toward those who presumed to disagree with him.

One night at Dorothy Norman's apartment this was made manifest when, unfortunately, the subject of Gertrude Stein was raised. The speed and acrimony with which Stieglitz dismissed both her and her writing astonished and annoyed me, and I counterattacked, despite (or, more likely, because of) several dark hints from Miss O'Keeffe that my behavior was not in order. Poor Dorothy Norman tried to mediate, but by that time the violence of the opinions expressed had caused the ranks to form between the minority which saw nothing shameful in the state of being an expatriate and the majority which considered it a fall from grace. Stieglitz's dogma maintained that an American artist could function only in the United States; therefore, since Gertrude Stein had written nearly all her works in France, she could not be taken seriously. But, of course, he knew better than to say this. What he said was that she was a *poseuse,* an insufferable egotist, enamored of the sound of her own echolalia, and similar things that were equally beside the point. The evening broke up with ill feeling. I was unable to fathom Stieglitz's irrationality and spitefulness at the time, not really knowing the history; much later Maurice Grosser made it all clear to me.

In mid-July Franco invaded Spain; immediately we formed the Committee on Republican Spain and presented a play to raise money for the Madrid government. Kenneth White wrote it, Joseph Losey directed it, I wrote the score, and Earl Robinson was musical director (which is to say that he played piano and organ and conducted the chorus). The title was *Who Fights This Battle?* It was a lively, dramatized documentary on the political situation in Spain. The play's polemic had a staunchly anti-Fascist coloration, as indeed it should have had, in order to get across its point that what was going on was a foreign invasion. Nowadays people speak of the "Spanish Civil War," in which "excesses were committed by both sides," as though defender and aggressor were bound by the same moral strictures. The play raised something under $2,000, which seemed like quite a bit in mid-Depression. The money was sent direct to the minister of education in Madrid.

Virgil Thomson had Alfred Barr's apartment high in the air above Beekman Place for the summer. "I have a job for you," he told me. "First we have to go down to Fourteenth Street." He took me there one evening to meet a young couple named Welles. The husband was in charge of the newly created Project 891 of the Federal Theater and was going to direct Edwin Denby's translation of the Labiche farce, *Un Chapeau de Paille d'Italie,* which Cavalcanti had filmed not too long before. The production needed a great deal of music, and it was Virgil's idea that I should write it. Within ten minutes of our meeting, Orson shocked me by remarking coolly that he saw no hope of there being anything but Fascism in Spain. How right he was! Thirty-six years later he could still say the same thing and be just as right.

Having met Orson, I then had to go around to the Maxine Elliott Theater and meet John Houseman, who saw that my name was entered on the payroll as research worker at a salary of $23.86 a week. Then Virgil and I got to work, he showing me how to prepare a cue sheet, deciding what Bowles material already in existence could be used and what new music I must write and finally indicating much of the actual instrumentation for me to fill in. The job had to be done posthaste, as rehearsals were already in progress. I spent all day every day in the apartment, working frantically among the Arps and Calders. Barr was the curator of the Museum of Modern Art, and his apartment was a bit like an extension of the museum. We got the score ready in time, and *Horse Eats Hat* opened on schedule. Orson directed and played the father, his wife Virginia played his daughter, Joseph Cotten her suitor, and Arlene Frances the suitor's other girlfriend. I enjoyed watching and listening to my music so much that I used to drop by the theater nearly every night for weeks after the show opened. A few months later Orson decided he wanted to do a production of Marlowe's *Doctor Faustus,* using his repertory of magic tricks. Virgil was to have done the score for this, but he had gone back home to Paris (although he was still on the payroll of Project 891) and could not return in time. Thus I got the job and turned out a much more cohesive score than it had been possible to make for *Horse Eats Hat.* When the play was running, Virgil came back to New York. "Well, baby, I see you got your name on the front of the theater all by yourself this time," he said at the opening.

During the winter I met a man named Hacker, who was making a film for the Southern Tenant Farmers' Union and wanted a score. The STFU was in the doghouse politically: it had Trotskyite leadership, or so it was said around New York. Hacker had brought a half dozen or so members of the organization from some remote region of Kentucky; they were strange people who huddled together and whispered. Before I composed the score, they sang for me, and I notated some of the songs to use as leitmotivs. We recorded the singing at the same session as the instrumental music, and I was given a set of records of my own score, which I took along to Mexico with me later. It was militant-sounding music; when the Mexican composers heard it, they remarked approvingly: *"Cómo los Rusos."*

Tonny came from Paris with his wife, Marie-Claire Ivanoff. It was immediately clear that she and I would get on very well together. Tonny was full of complaints about the lack of civilization in the United States; surprisingly enough I often found myself taking issue with him, not so much in defense of the country as in disagreement with his reasons for disparaging it.

One rainy night Touche asked me to meet him in the lobby of the Plaza. When I got there he was with Erika Mann (Thomas Mann's eldest daughter) and an attractive red-haired girl with a pointed nose. We got into a taxi, and Touche gave an address in Harlem. Our destination proved a dimly lighted apartment where guests paid an entrance fee and were given reefers to smoke. Touche was translating Erika Mann's anti-Fascist revue *The Peppermill* for production at the New School for Social Research; they smoked and talked shop. The redhead's name was Jane, and she was not communicative. Several days later I took the Tonnys around to Patchin Place to see Cummings and Marian. Touche was there and had brought Jane. We drank quite a bit and began to talk about Mexico. Soon Tonny announced that he wanted to go there. He was still indignant about the lack of culture in New York; mainly I think he was annoyed because neither he nor Marie-Claire spoke a word of English. I said that if they went, I should go with them. Then Jane announced that she too felt like going to Mexico. She excused herself and went into the next room to telephone. Presently she called out my name. When I went into the room, she handed me the telephone saying that her mother wanted to speak to me. The woman at the other end of the wire asked me my name and suggested I take Jane home after we left the Cummings'. "If my daughter's going to Mexico with you, I think I should meet you first, don't you think?" I agreed and later I went with Jane to the Hotel Meurice, where she lived. I found it hard to believe that Mrs. Auer had accepted this sudden caprice so completely as a matter of course. Yet she seemed to be considering the matter seriously, and asked to meet Marie-Claire and Tonny as well. We made an appointment for dinner during the coming week.

Now that I was about to leave the country, I resigned from the Federal Theater Project. "You'll have a hard time getting back on," they warned me. Berman spoke against my going to Mexico, implying that it was an irresponsible act. His thesis was that when one got any sort of career going, one must never shut it off.

"Je trouve que tu as tort," he said many times. *"Il ne faut jamais cou-per."* For once Mother and Daddy were pleased to see me depart. The idea of my being involved in a thing they loathed as much as they did the Works Progress Administration had disturbed them very much, particularly because everyone had read it in the newspapers. Now they were going to be able to say that I had left the shameful organization.

I went around to a small printer on West Twenty-third Street and gave him three short texts in Spanish to print in vermilion ink on gummed paper. Respectively they called Trotsky the immediate danger, proclaimed that he must not be allowed to remain in Mexico, and asked for his death. The printer's eyebrows went up when he saw my slogans; obviously he understood some Spanish. I said I wanted five thousand of each, six inches by an inch and a half. He hesitated, wanted to know who the work was for. "Just for me," I said. Finally he grunted agreement. "I ought not to do this. This is a union shop, you see. But between you and me the man's a menace. I'll have 'em ready for you Monday."

The fifteen thousand stickers safely packed in my luggage, I set out with the Tonnys and Jane in a Greyhound bus for Baltimore. Tonny had only about $900 in the world. Since he intended to stay several months in Mexico, I felt that he ought to be taking more money, and told him so. His response was: *"Quel sale bour-geois!"* Nevertheless, I was determined that he should not go with so little, because I did not want to have to lend him money. I had an idea that I could sell some of his drawings to the Misses Cone. We stayed three days in Baltimore, and they bought several of them, whereupon I remembered the curator at the museum. She was pleased to invest in some Tonnys too, so that I felt better as we continued on our way southward. When night came, we always got off and took hotel rooms. Generally we spent two nights in each place, so that it took us two weeks to get as far as New Orleans. A week later we arrived in Monterrey and put up in a ramshackle hotel. The first night, I lifted a floorboard in my room and was able, by lying down, to peer into the room below where four Chinese sat talking. This seemed to me an auspicious introduction to Mexico. The next day I went around to the local college and spoke with students about distributing the stickers.

They were all enthusiastic about the idea, and I gave a hundred each to about a dozen students. That evening there was a demonstration. We were invited to take part and clambered into one of the trucks that went slowly through the streets, each manned by a speaker with megaphone demanding further land expropriations. Out of courtesy to us, all four of whom passed as French (and not one of whom was, naturally), they added injurious references to the archfiend Trotsky, who had mistakenly been granted asylum by Cárdenas. It disgusted me to see that they had plastered hundreds of stickers at all angles on the bodies of the trucks, where they served no purpose whatever. Tonny enjoyed the Mexicans' gusto, but was contemptuous of their lack of discipline. "Revolution!" he scoffed. "These people don't even know what the word means."

Beyond Monterrey they were still laying the highway, which often became barely passable. The buses were even more primitive than those of North Africa. Tonny, Marie-Claire, and I were delighted with the hairpin curves, the sheer drops, and the unfamiliar, savage landscape, but Jane had lived a relatively sheltered life in New York and Switzerland and found it all terrifying. For two days going through the mountains she crouched, frightened and sick, on the floor at the back of the bus, unmindful of Tonny's scornful remarks. *"Ecoute, ma petite, tu aurais mieux fait de rester chez ta mère,"* he would tell her, or: *"On a marre de toi et ta frousse,"* or: *"Tu nous emmerdes avec tes histoires de gosse de riches."* The night we arrived in Mexico City Jane jumped out of the bus, seized on some porters, and announced: *"Moi je file pour le Ritz."* I tried to stop her, but Tonny and Marie-Claire thought we should let her go. We three ended up in a cheap hotel on the Calle 16 de Septiembre. The next day we went around to the Ritz and failed to find Jane's name in the register. We discovered her three days later at the Hotel Guardiola in bed, recovering from a flash fever that had struck her the night of her arrival. She said firmly that as soon as she could walk, she was going to the airport and get on a plane for the United States. We chaffed her, gave her enthusiastic accounts of the bullfight we had seen and of the music at Tenampa and the food at Las Cazuelas, and before leaving promised to come by at lunchtime the following day to see if she might be well enough to go out to eat with us. When we called by for her, they told us at the desk that she had taken the plane for San Antonio.

"*Tant mieux,*" said Tonny with bitter satisfaction. He was on edge because he had not managed to get anywhere with her during the trip. I knew he was not going to be able to, because from New York to Monterrey she and I had sat together and engaged in many hours of conversation. She had her own ideas on the subject: she was a virgin and intended to remain in that category until she married.

"If you hadn't been so mean to her she'd have stayed," said Marie-Claire, who was upset by the sudden departure.

"I said so much the better she's gone, didn't I?" he demanded. It was clear that Jane had been a sore point between them for some time.

"*Tu es dégoûtant.*" That was Marie-Claire's way of putting an end to a conversation.

Aaron had given me a note to Silvestre Revueltas, saying I would like both him and his music. I went down beyond the Zocalo to the conservatory where he taught. By coincidence I arrived there during the course of a concert at which he was conducting his *Homenaje a García Lorca*. I was immediately struck by the luminous texture of the orchestral sound. It was music of impeccable style. After the performance I presented my note to him, and was once again impressed, this time more deeply, by the quality of the man himself. He had a truly noble face, one side of it slashed across by a terrible knife scar, with an expression of impossible purity. It was a purity, alas, maintained at the cost of life itself. Revueltas was an incurable dipsomaniac; he spent six months of each year in the gutter. By the time I met him he had arrived almost at the end of the line. He died the following year. The conditions under which he lived, in a distant slum quarter, scarcely left him an alternative to death. Never had I seen such poverty in Europe or North Africa. There were no walls, properly speaking, between one apartment and another. Partitions went up eight feet or so and stopped. The hubbub of voices, radios, dogs, and babies was infernal. It seemed particularly cruel that a composer should have to live in such a place.

It was Revueltas who took me to the *Grupo de los Cuatro*: Ayala, Moncayo, Contreras, and Galindo, all composers in their twenties. They were fun to be with, and all of us together went around the capital for several weeks, having a great time. Then they proposed a concert of my music, to be presented by *El Grupo de los Cuatro*. The programs were printed, and the small *sala* at the Palacio de Bellas Artes rented for the night, but each time rehearsals were called, only a few of the musicians appeared, so that no rehearsals ever took place. Nor, needless to add, did the concert.

Shortly before leaving New York, I had gone to see Miguel Covarrubias, the Mexican painter whose caricatures in *Vanity Fair* had impressed me fifteen years earlier when I was a boy. Covarrubias said he had gone with Diego Rivera to southern Oaxaca, to the Isthmus of Tehuantepec. His descriptions of the place made me resolve to see it myself. The women were the most beautiful in all Mexico, and they bathed naked in the river every morning. There was an oasis, he said, which would remind me of North Africa; he considered it the most exotic and fascinating region in the Western Hemisphere. Whenever we mentioned Tehuantepec to the Mexicans, we found that they agreed with Covarrubias, although none of them had visited the place. It seemed essential that we go to see for ourselves.

The journey to Tehuantepec was arduous, but never boring. First we took the train down to Veracruz; there we waited to get the semiweekly train which ran between Veracruz and the Guatemalan border. We had intended to spend one night at a place called Jesús Carranza. When we arrived there in the evening, we got off the train and walked to the hotel, a desperate-looking construction run by a group of Chinese. Having eaten nothing but fruit since the day before, we set our luggage down in the dining room and ordered large bowls of hot soup. It was very tasty, with pieces of ginger root among the solid morsels floating in the stock. The kerosene lamp shed just enough light to enable us, once we had emptied the bowls of their liquid, to distinguish the corpses of the slugs which lay at the bottom. This was not really surprising, inasmuch as *gusanos de maguey* are considered edible items in Mexico. However, it was sufficient to banish our appetites and startle us into action. We got up from the table and asked to see the rooms upstairs. A balcony ran around the outside of the second story, its railing a single strand of barbed wire. Apparently the rooms were given an annual cleaning. Under each bed lay a great pile of garbage, pushed there so it would not show at first sight. Quickly we went downstairs and paid for our soup, took our valises, and began to run toward the station. We need not have hurried; the train did not move for another hour and a half. We settled into a different third-class coach, ate some avocados, along with pineapples and bananas, bought a bottle of *habanero*, a Mexican rum that cost a peso and a half, and applied ourselves to being comfortable and happy as we rattled along all night through the jungle.

Tehuantepec was unforgettable. Everything Covarrubias had said was accurate (save that he had not told us there were always female guards at the early morning bathing in the river who threw stones at any man or boy approaching within a thousand feet), yet his description had not prepared me for the particular atmosphere of the place. I had imagined it as a more-or-less African landscape dotted with Spanish-looking towns. But the countryside did not remind me of North Africa, nor did the villages, in spite of their Andalusian grilles, ever make me think of Spain. There were indeed oases (the *labores*) of coconut palms towering above the mangos, zapotes, and bananas. A highly spiced hot wind blew incessantly across the countryside, which was not really desert, but an impassable wilderness of bare thorny trees and cacti. To me it was a more forbidding prospect than the Sahara: the vegetation also looked mineral, but the forms it had taken were far more suggestive of hostility than any rock formation ever could be.

We ate our meals at a stall in the market, where the cook would swing the hens by their heads to break their necks. The women in the market had all the money there was in town and did all the work save picking the fruit and caring for the children. Often we looked into a patio and saw a man sitting by a hammock gently rocking it, and in the hammock a baby.

Just before leaving New York I had bought a used accordion for $125. The instrument was inlaid with rhinestones and paste rubies and emeralds—a fancy object with the lush sound characteristic of Italian-made accordions. Evenings when we walked to the park, I would carry it with me; it had a swift success with the townsmen. Very shortly I was Don Pablito. As we went along in the moonlight fifteen or twenty Zapotecans would accompany us.

May Day was about to arrive. We offered them our help in preparing for the parade. I bought all the red cotton bunting in town to make into banners. The slogans they wanted were POR UNA SOCIEDAD SIN CLASES and SALUDAMOS A LOS MÁRTIRES DE CHICAGO (the latter referring to the Haymarket Riots of the 1890's, of which I had never heard until I got to Tehuantepec). I rented a house, and ten of us spent several days there cutting, sewing, and painting banners. I added my own MUERA TROTSKY to be included in the parade, as well as one which read EL COMUNISMO ES LA RELIGIÓN DEL SIGLO VEINTE. It seemed to me to concretize a tendency already extant in the region—that of putting photographs of Marx and Lenin in the votive niches along with *Jesucristo* and *Santa María*. I remarked several times on the custom and got a simple explanation: Marx and Lenin were for the men, the others for the women. During the last few days of April the churches were full of women on ladders, building altarpieces and arches of fruit, flowers, and palm branches. In each church there was to be a festival with dancing and fireworks. When the day came, the parade included about 80 percent of the inhabitants. We marched for miles along dusty roads from village to village. A few old people holding babies waved from the doorways. Practically no one watched the parade in the outlying villages, so it headed back to the main market, where the few *burgueses* were, so that fists could be raised, not in salute but in defiance, at particular individuals watching from their shops or houses.

After May Day a delegation of country people came to the Hotel La Perla. The group consisted of nine men, all of them mute but respectful as only Mexican peasants can play it—all, that is, but the spokesman, who with his hat in his two hands, murmured that everyone was saying we had been sent from the capital to teach and that we could teach them about Communism, and of course everybody wanted to learn how to do Communism, and were we going to open a school for them?

This seemed to me very bad. Tonny laughed and thought it *marrant*; Marie-Claire was overcome with pity for the little men. I was appalled at seeing myself thrown into a false category which implied assuming responsibility. I shrugged and smiled sadly; I could not do anything like that, for it was necessary to have permission to teach, which I did not have. "Then why did they send you?" the spokesman asked.

"We were not sent from the capital," I told him, and he appeared to accept the statement. Nevertheless, he was determined to go away with something. "Tell me just one thing," he said. *"Qué es el comunismo?"*

Since I could not answer the question in a way satisfactory either to him or to me, I brought out some books and pamphlets in Spanish, including one called *El ABC del Comunismo*, but he was not interested. Then I realized that none of them could read and that he was the only one who spoke Spanish. He explained to them in Zapotec what I had said; they shook hands with us and filed out into the street.

We were only a day and a half by train from the Guatemalan border, and we thought that before turning north again, we should look inside. The proximity proved illusory, for when we got to the frontier at Suchiate I was turned back by the Guatemalan authorities for having written the word *ninguna* opposite *Religión* on the application form. Since they were suspicious of me, they said I must get letters from six businessmen of Tapachula. We returned to that godforsaken town where we had just spent a night, all three of us in an ugly mood, passed two days vainly trying to get even one such document, and, finding it impossible (since the pillars of society there were almost all Germans and not at all inclined to be either helpful or friendly), consulted the local headquarters of the Mexican trade unions. The third day they sent a man with us all the way to Suchiate, where we waited and were presented during off hours to an official who not only filled out a new application form for me, but got the Guatemalan authorities to stamp it and engaged a punt to ferry us across the Río Suchiate to Ayutla on the Guatemalan side. Thus we had a rapid three-week glimpse of the decorative little republic before returning to Mexico City.

This time we wanted to live in the country. Tonny had done no work since leaving Paris and felt a productive period coming on. We took pension with an American family who had been living for years in Malinche's palace (built for the Aztec lady by her lover Hernán Cortés, conqueror of Mexico). It was a huge old building with plenty of rooms, and it lay about halfway between Tlalnepantla and Atzcapotzalco. When summer came, I had a wire from Lincoln Kirstein saying that *Yankee Clipper* was to be presented in Philadelphia, and I must get to New York as quickly as I could. This was a dubious triumph: I wanted to hear the Philadelphia Orchestra play my music, and so of course I must go, but the peculiar rustic charm of the life in the place where we were living and the melancholy magnificence of the vast landscape roundabout had already captured me. I had looked forward to a long summer of hearing the roosters crow at Malinche's palace, and now I would not have it.

Tonny had plunged into a period of creative work; he labored with fantastic intensity, seeming scarcely aware that Marie-Claire and I were present. The drawings were of great beauty; he brought the whole series back to New York later in the summer. They were pictures of enormous half-dead tropical trees in whose branches lived whole tribes of naked Indian women and animals. I liked them even better than the Moroccan series, which until then had been my favorite Tonnys.

I left him in his studio with Marie-Claire and went down to Veracruz to take a ship to New York. On the ship I made the acquaintance of a New York woman who was a member of the Communist Party. As we sailed into Havana Harbor I told her about my anti-Trotsky stickers, of which I still had several hundred left in one of my valises. This gave her the idea of taking some of them into Havana under Batista's nose. She mentioned it at first with enthusiasm; then she was silent for a while, and I could see that something bothered her. It came out soon enough. "Individual action," she sighed. "It's forbidden."

"Well, you know best, of course," I told her. No more was said about it until just before we went ashore. Then she sidled up to me and whispered out of the corner of her mouth: "I've decided to do it. Can you get some?" I went to my cabin and returned with a few dozen stickers for her. When I saw her back on the ship, she seemed pleased with her exploit. "They're all on the walls of public buildings," she said proudly, "and don't think it was easy, either."

When I got to New York, I started immediately on the orchestration of *Yankee Clipper*, which had to be done in a few weeks. This was when Kirstein called in Henry Brant to help me. The ballet was a sequence of scenes which alternated between shipboard and ports of call. My idea was to have Henry do the ship scenes (which included the beginning and the end and thus called for tutti passages) while I did the ports of call myself. We followed that method, and came up with the score in time for Alexander Smallens to conduct it between Virgil Thomson's *Filling Station* and Elliott Carter's *Pocahontas*.

Marian Chase and Harry Dunham sometimes talked of getting married. Meanwhile, they spent all their time together, until Harry went to Spain to film the war. Touche had more or less taken Marian over while she awaited his return; thus, it was he who brought her along on the train to Philadelphia. With me I had my mother and Jane Auer. We must have ordered drinks as we rode, for I remember great laughing all the way. That was when Mother decided Jane was wild.

I saw Jane once or twice more that summer and wanted her to come with the Tonnys and me to Glenora, where we went for a month and lived in the woods in one of Uncle Charles' houses. They were still put off by her behavior in Mexico, and so instead of Jane, we had Marian with us. There was a communicating door between her bedroom and mine. Early one morning Marie-Claire burst into the room unannounced and found us together. Although there had never been anything between Marie-Claire and me, this precipitated a fit of hysterics on her part and a series of fights between her and Tonny which went on for several days. When we went back to New York, I shut myself into Edwin Denby's loft on Twenty-first Street. I was writing an opera on a libretto given me by the poet Charles-Henri Ford, erstwhile editor of *blues*. Its subject was the abortive slave rebellion led by Denmark Vesey, who won in a lottery and bought his freedom. Ford was apprehensive when I told him the Juanita Hall Choir was going to present the first act at a concert given under the auspices of *New Masses,* to raise money for that ailing organ. "It's a Stalinist trap!" he exclaimed. Nevertheless, he allowed it to be done, and it was a fine performance.

Vernon Duke had the idea of inaugurating a series of concerts to be called the High-Low Concerts. The purpose was to interest the rich in contemporary music; to do this he proposed to present modern chamber music on the same programs with jazz by well-known exponents of the idiom. At his request I wrote the text of a brochure which he had printed. It read like something out of *Vogue;* this was the tone he thought most likely to succeed. The concerts were given in the ballroom on the St. Regis roof, Serge Obolensky being an old friend of Vernon's. At the one I attended I played drums in the three-movement piece that I had composed in Mexico called *Mediodía,* after which Duke Ellington and his band took over. There were more evenings in the series, but by that time I had left town.

Before that, however, I rented two places in what seemed to me ideal positions. One was at 1 Battery Place, on the corner of Washington Street. It was in an ancient and shabby red brick building. On the first floor there was an Arab café, for at that time Washington Street up as far as Rector was strictly Middle Eastern. From my mansard window on the third floor I looked out on Battery Park and the Aquarium. When I wanted Turkish coffee and honey cakes, I opened my door and clapped my hands twice; soon a waiter appeared from the café below. I filled the oblique-ceilinged room with garish Islamic chromolithographs and kept my accordion there. It was a good room to rest in, sitting at the table copying music. I never slept there or touched the bed because I suspected there might be bedbugs around.

The other place was at 2 Water Street, in Brooklyn on the East River, almost under the Brooklyn Bridge. There I took two rooms and put a piano in. Soon I began to use the place as a general headquarters. It was steam-heated, whereas the loft on Twenty-first Street had no heat. There was room to have general rehearsals of the opera. The members of the Juanita Hall Choir complained of having to go so far from Harlem, and they did not seem to understand why I found the neighborhood so attractive.

When Charles-Henri Ford came to listen, he went to the window, saw the tugboat bobbing at the dock across the street and the seagulls wheeling above it, and said disgustedly: "Paul, you're so *romantic!*"

Jane and I used to spin fancies about how amusing it would be to get married and horrify everyone, above all, our respective families. From fantasy to actuality is often a much shorter distance than one imagines; suddenly we were seriously discussing the possibility. Jane would be twenty-one on Washington's Birthday, and our marriage was performed the day before in a small Dutch Reformed church in the Twenties; no one was present but my parents and her mother, and no one seemed horrified, which made things much easier, if less dramatic. Before we had had time to think about it, we found ourselves en route to Panama aboard a ship called the *Kano Maru.*

XI

After ten days in Panama, during which time Jane saw enough to enable her later to use the place as a locale in *Two Serious Ladies,* our first destination was San José de Costa Rica. To get there we boarded a small craft in Balboa; it had been the private yacht of ex-Kaiser Wilhelm of Germany and was all shining white. From Puntarenas we took a train up to the capital.

San José was one of those towns where earthquakes had been so frequent that the inhabitants had more or less abandoned the concept of architecture. There was a violent tremor one night that got us out of bed and started us running around the room frantically before we had even fully awakened. Still, the provincialism was a relief, and there was practically no traffic in its streets.

We got in touch with people who had a cattle ranch in the province of Guanacaste and accompanied them there. The trip lasted two days. We had to go back down to Puntarenas and take a ferryboat that threaded through the inland lagoons and eventually pushed up a narrow, tortuous river. The vegetation hanging above us as we went inland was exciting, and the crocodiles sunning themselves along the banks not fifty feet away did not even bother to shut their monstrous jaws. We lived on horseback at the ranch: during the nights there was a soft hot wind that carried the sound of an infinite number of screaming insects. At half past five each morning a girl brought us a pitcher of frothing milk, still warm from the cow. We did not ask to be awakened at that hour, but since that was the way things were done there, we fell into step. By nine o'clock the *vaqueros* were waiting at the gate; soon our host would appear and we would go with him and get on our horses. Each day he went out to examine a different region of his immense property. We bought a parrot on the way back to Puntarenas, ingenuously imagining that since it had a chain attached to its leg, it could be left more or less anywhere. It proved us wrong while we were still on the ferry and continued to wreak havoc even after it had destroyed and escaped from its third cage.

We spent a month in Costa Rica, and we sailed from Puerto Limón up to Puerto Barrios. I had not been to Chichicastenango on my introductory trip to Guatemala the previous year and had a great desire to see it, as well as to talk with Father Rossbach, the priest who encouraged the Quichés to continue their sacrifices in the ovens of the cathedral steps, because the ovens had been there before the church was built, and allowed them to bury a wooden Christ six feet deep in the earth behind the altar and dig it up on Easter morning. And so, Holy Week being close, we went to Chichicastenango, and I talked to Father Rossbach about the *Popul Vuh,* which he knew intimately but did not offer to explain. We spent two weeks at the Mayan Inn there and then went down to Antigua, where we had left the parrot in a lemon tree at Señora Espinoza's. (We never got him down again.) Afternoons we would take horses and ride, usually down through the coffee-plantation country, and there we managed to pick up a good collection of old *sutes* (those all-purpose cloths that serve the women as headdresses, infant hammocks, sacks, and towels), impossible to find in any market or shop, simply by buying them from off the heads of the women who wore them as they walked along the roads.

There were Germans everywhere; they all had to go down to Puerto Barrios and board a German ship for the time it took them to vote *Ja* on the referendum Hitler had sent them. But being ardent Nazis, they considered the exhausting trip a privilege rather than a hardship. We rode down from Guatemala City with more than two hundred of them, all with swastikas in their lapels; the ship that served as their polling station was to take us to Europe. At the time the Norddeutscher Lloyd had two ships that regularly made the run between Hamburg and Puerto Barrios, the *Caribia* and the *Cordillera*. We had taken the *Caribia* coming, and we took the *Cordillera* going. More of the same sort of maniacal Germans got on at the Colombian and Venezuelan ports. When we put in at Port of Spain, I bought a lot of calypso records, and we played them on deck softly, with the phonograph between our two deck chairs. The Germans could not bear to hear such music, even pianissimo. They came up to us and gave us a serious lecture on the insidious spread of degenerate forms of music. After that we played the phonograph only in our cabin. Our last American port of call was Barbados; then the ship made straight for Le Havre.

In Central America life had gone smoothly; Jane and I never argued, never grew tired of being together. In Paris she had friends, and I was suspicious of them. It was painful for me to go back to the hotel room at dinnertime and find that she had not yet come in, finally to have dinner alone and rush back to find the room still empty. And Jane was not one to change as a result of my suggestions.

There was a new Popular Front newspaper that year in Paris called *Ce Soir,* for which Henri Cartier-Bresson worked. To boost circulation they were having him photograph thousands of small children in working-class districts of the city. One picture was printed each day; the parents of the winner could then go claim a cash prize. I had known Cartier-Bresson two or three years earlier, having met him at George Antheil's in New York. He was showing George his photographs, and I had never seen anything like them. As he looked for subjects in Harlem and, indeed, lived with a black girl there, we used to go up and have dinner, sometimes at Father Divine's and other times at excellent small restaurants which only he knew about. Now that I was in Paris, I went around to see him. We had lunch, and he took me to meet his Indonesian wife. It was before Munich, and already he was not hopeful about the future. The city was spattered with anti-Jewish and anti-American graffiti.

I called Gertrude Stein and spoke with her for a while. She was packing to leave for Bilignin the next day and could not

spare the time to see us. Stravinsky was conducting an all-Stra-
vinsky program, beginning and ending the evening with the pre-
miere of the *Dunbarton Oaks Concerto*. I had bought tickets in advance; the day of the concert Jane said we were having dinner
with some friends who also were going and would drive us there.
These proved to be Denham Fouts and Brion Gysin. Fouts had
just returned from Tibet. I could not get from him what he had
been doing there, except that he had been practicing archery
and had brought back some huge bows. The arrows were made
with built-in tampons of cotton, to be soaked in ether before use
and then ignited. To demonstrate his prowess with the difficult
bow, he began to shoot from the hotel window down into the evening traffic on the Champs-Élysées. Fortunately there were no
repercussions.

Jane and I had disagreements about her coming in at three
o'clock each morning, but with the result that she was annoyed
with me rather than repentant. (Several years later she recalled
that Henry Miller was one of the people she occasionally saw at
that time; by then I thought it was funny.) After a scene which
was more heated than usual, I took off for St.-Tropez by myself,
but once I got there, I found that I was completely miserable. I
wired and urged Jane to come to Cannes, where I met her.

Soon we took a small house up in Èze-Village, just above the
Grande Corniche. Jane stayed in the kitchen much of the time,
watching a peasant woman prepare and cook our food. It was the
first time the thought had occurred to her that she herself might
learn. This was an excellent beginning to a long and successful
career as a cook. For me it made the difference between good and
poor health.

There were two people in Èze whom we had known previously: Elsie Houston, the Brazilian folk singer, and S. L. M. Barlow, the composer. Barlow was the seigneur of the village and
owned the principal properties. He had turned one of his smaller
houses over to Elsie as a studio, and she spent her time combing
her long Indian-black hair and cooking Brazilian dishes. Unhappily, at the very outset of our stay at Èze, Ernesta, Barlow's wife,
committed the *gaffe* of inviting me to dinner without Jane. This

ground the machinery of friendship to a painful halt. We saw a great deal of Elsie, however, and grew to love her. Since she was a rabid Trotskyist, we kept away from mention of politics.

A few years earlier I had made a song out of a two-line text by Benjamin Péret, the French Surrealist poet. It ran:

If somewhere you come across a woman who mentions Napoléon
   Trois,
Give her a cigar and take her on a trip to Spain.

One day I played and sang it to Elsie. She stared at me after I had finished. "But the words are by my husband, and the woman, *c'est moi!*" Then she told me how, long before she had married Péret, at the beginning of their acquaintanceship, she had talked with him one day at length about Napoleon III. Later he had offered her a cigar, which so delighted her that when he suggested their going to Spain, she had accepted. They were not together now, and I think she regretted it. She consoled herself with a French businessman for whom she felt sorry.

Once again the prospect of a long, unbroken sojourn in a quiet place was shattered. A cable came from Harry Dunham saying that Orson Welles wanted me in New York. He had decided to produce William Gillette's ancient farce *Too Much Johnson* at the Mercury Theater, Harry was already shooting the accompanying film sequences, and I was needed immediately to provide the score.

We had been traveling heavy, with huge wardrobe trunks, and between us eighteen large valises. It was difficult to move around with all this, although not nearly so difficult as it would be today with only half as many pieces.

We took another German ship, the *Europa,* to get to New York. Once arrived, we went to the Chelsea Hotel. Friedrich Kiesler, the Austrian architect who had designed the Space House I had visited in Berlin back in 1931, offered me his studio in the penthouse of 56 Seventh Avenue, and so each day I went there and worked on *Too Much Johnson.* When I had finished the score, I took it to Orson, but he had decided to present *Danton's Death* first. (*Too Much Johnson* had a tryout in Stony Creek, Connecticut, the following summer. Joseph Cotten was magnificent, but the production, minus Harry's amusing film sequences in early Keystone style, was lackluster.) I made a small suite of some of the numbers and called it *Music for a Farce.*

We were now very poor, having spent what was left of our wedding money, after the Central American honeymoon, in getting settled in our house at Èze. The fact that we had then given it all up and returned to America on the strength of a promise which failed to materialize rankled considerably with me. I felt that I should have had some compensation for my work and my trouble, something more than the $100 I was given. But there was nothing to do about it.

I found a cheap place for us to live, in a strange old house on the corner of Seventh Avenue and Eighteenth Street, run by an elderly woman named Saunders. She divided her time between building fireplaces and bookshelves for her lodgers and drinking wine with odd characters from the neighborhood. Lady, as she was known to everyone, was what might be called an alcohol addict. She smiled and sometimes borrowed a dollar or two if the rent money was not forthcoming when it should have been. Even when a particularly hot fire in our fireplace ignited the floor, so that the fire department had to be called to extinguish it, she laughed and set to work rebuilding it hersef. This labor was not finished for such a long time, and the bitter winds that blew in over that side of the room became so unbearable that we accepted the kind offer of a friend to spend the coldest months with him in his apartment.

In some way I met Mrs. MacFarlane, a director of the Federal Music Project; she thought it would be an excellent idea to create a status for composers as such on the project, giving them specific assignments to write music for use by WPA instrumental and vocal groups. If she could get composers onto the payroll as composers and not camouflaged as something else, she assured me I would be the first to be signed up. The catch was that in order to be eligible for the project one had to be on relief. This had not been the case when I had worked on the Federal Theater Project.

I tried to find out how to go about getting on relief. People advised me to inquire at the nearest relief agency, but I had a better idea. I went to Communist Party headquarters and told them of my problem. Then I asked them how to solve it. The man I spoke to was direct and matter-of-fact. First I must establish residence in a very cheap room, preferably in a slum quarter. Then I must go to the nearest Workers' Alliance hall and declare myself an unemployed. They would try to push my case and get an investigator to come around soon. Also, they would do their best to see that it was a sympathetic individual who came, but that could not be guaranteed. The hard part about getting on relief was the waiting for your case to come up.

I still had the room on Water Street in Brooklyn, and that seemed an ideal place to install myself and wait for the investigator to arrive, for I had to be there in person when he came. I thanked the official and followed his instructions.

The investigator came sooner than I had dared hope and was more than sympathetic. She was an intelligent and attractive girl named Kaminsky, very much interested in culture. I explained that I was in the midst of writing an opera and played her some of the second act of *Denmark Vesey,* which I was working on there. I told her how I had given up my home in France and come to New York to work for the Mercury Theater, only to be let down and left stranded. She was indignant and thought I had a case against the theater, but I insisted I was not thinking of lawsuits— only of getting on relief. She said she would do everything she could to help me and hoped to be able to bring me my card on Friday. I suggested that she come to dinner Friday night at John Becker's at Sutton Place, where Jane and I were actually living. The guests, the champagne, and the works of art pleased Miss Kaminsky very much. She did have my relief card ready for me, and she went home at two in the morning as happy as I was.

At last I was on relief; I went once a week to Brooklyn, where my relief board was situated, and brought back suitcasesful of sugar, butter, prunes, and flour. The idea of getting something for nothing is always exciting (even though it was that poisonous concept, according to Daddy, which had started the country on its sharp downward course). And I began to collect $23.86 once again each week, this time not as a "research worker" but as a composer.

I thought this the right moment to get into the Communist Party and told Harry, who was glad I wanted to join. Touche was already in but for some reason would not admit it; I discovered the fact later. Jane and I were assigned to a new members' class for seven weeks. When I was asked under what name I wanted to join, I said: "How do you prefer it?"

The man looked at me. "Oh, we'd rather you used your real name, of course."

"Fine." So we went in as Paul and Jane Bowles. Then we were sent to a deadly class in Marxism-Leninism at the Workers' School. "I don't know what I'm reading," Jane complained when she studied our textbook. I knew what I was reading, but that made it worse. We tried to compensate for our lack of devotion to Marxism-Leninism by seeing every Russian film that came to New York.

The Group Theater was still functioning. Robert Lewis was going to direct William Saroyan's *My Heart's in the Highlands* and wanted me to write the score. He gave me Clifford Odets' apartment for six weeks, Odets being on the Coast, and there were no interruptions at all. I sat at his Hammond organ and did the work.

That spring we saw a lot of Bill Saroyan. His way of seeing life around him reminded me of Cartier-Bresson's, save that it was less objective, more whimsical. Still, if the stance did not prove too exacting to hold, it was a poetic and bold position he took, and I admired the fact that his writing had an immediately recognizable style. Latouche moved into the penthouse on the roof of our handmade house on Eighteenth Street. Christopher Isherwood came by to see me on his way from London to Los Angeles, where he has remained ever since.

Marian and Harry had decided to get married. The ceremony took place at St. Thomas', with Virgil at the organ playing the two wedding marches he had written for the occasion and had marked respectively "In" and "Out." Almost immediately Harry had to leave on another filming exploit, much farther this time—

to China, to stay with Mao Tse-tung and Agnes Smedley at Sian.

With the money I got for *My Heart's in the Highlands* I went to the south end of Staten Island and paid five months' rent on a farmhouse I particularly liked. We moved out there, where we had a constant flow of guests. Colin McPhee was back from his eight-year stay in Bali and would spend several days at a time with us, cooking his fine Indonesian meals. I knew that Lenny Bernstein had an allergy to cats, and so I hid Baby Mildred, our Siamese, far out in the sheds behind the kitchen when he came to spend the weekend; but of course the allergy knew she was there, scenting her presence, so that he sneezed all one night and declined to spend another.

Once a week I had to go into the city to sign in and collect my check. I was given certain definite assignments, such as writing a piece for eight clarinets (they had such a group somewhere in the Bronx), some first-grade piano music for students, or choral pieces for large adult groups. This took very little of my time, so that I was relatively free to do my own work.

The World's Fair was holding forth at Flushing Meadows. Something of mine was being played there at a concert given by the Music Project, and I met some of the musicians for lunch beforehand. Being all either CP members or sympathizers, they were a very gloomy lot: the news of the Ribbentrop-Molotov Pact had just broken that morning. Said one of them bitterly: "Well, where do we go from here?" I replied that we went straight ahead as though nothing had happened, because we would see it later as a Soviet ploy to crush the Nazis, and I argued that to falter in one's convictions at this point merely because of a detail like the pact would be proof that one's faith in the Soviet government had never been profound. Some of them agreed, hesitantly; the others continued to look sad.

Gertrude Stein was publishing a series of articles called "What is Money?" in the *Saturday Evening Post,* in which she took the point of view of an arch-Republican. Roosevelt was destroying both the economic and the moral fabric of the country, by changing the meaning of money and by prescribing predigested, formulated ideas for the young so they would not have to think for themselves. I wrote her that I thought he was an excellent President who had saved the United States from collapse when it was in trouble and that, besides, there were a lot of young men who needed predigested ideas because their systems could not take raw ones. She did not reply, but she paraphrased my letter in a later piece, to exemplify her earlier allegations.

Suddenly I received a letter from Mary Oliver, who had helped me so generously my first year in Paris. Jock had died the previous year, and she was in the United States with her German maid. She wanted to visit me for an unstipulated length of time and had enough money for "beer and champagne" if I had enough for food. I suspected that her arrival would bring trouble, but I could scarcely do otherwise than tell her to come whenever she felt like it.

First she called from the Waldorf Towers, saying that we must join her for dinner and the night, given the remoteness of the farm. I agreed, still feeling that none of it boded any good. When we arrived, she was looking very smart in a Schiaparelli tweed suit. During the evening she told us that she had recently lent $50,000 to an actress named Ruth Chatterton with the understanding that the sum would be returned to her by a certain date. The date had come and gone, and Miss Chatterton had not been able to fulfill the terms of the agreement. As a result, Mary had had no money at all until a lawyer had managed to attach a percentage of the actress' weekly earnings. That minimal sum at the moment kept Mary alive. Shortly she would collect the money for some jewelry she had sold; until then she would have to be very frugal. I explained that my sole means of support was the $23.86 I got each week and expressed doubt that all four of us could live on it. "Of course we can!" Mary cried. "Food is fantastically cheap in this country. And you have your relief food, too. It'll be easy, because I shall pay for all the liquor."

The maid was plump and almost sinister in her surliness. Clearly she regarded Mary as an idiot. After a few weeks of living with us, she made an unexplained visit to Chicago. We learned later that she had been working for the German government—a simple spy.

The quantity of alcohol consumed at the farmhouse increased by the week. Mary would call the nearest liquor store, which was several miles away, and get the manager to promise to drive out with some bottles after he closed. Once there, he would begin to drink and would stay on interminably. Then she would find a pretext for not paying him. When I left the establishment, she owed him more than $200. I kept urging Jane to leave with me (for there was no way of getting Mary to do anything quickly), but Jane said she was enjoying herself and saw no reason to cut the enjoyment short in such an arbitrary fashion. If she did not come with me, I warned, I would not answer for bills that came after my departure. But Jane intended to leave the farm on Woodrow Road when she got ready and not before; she advised me to relax. I suddenly had become a teetotaler, from long watching of what happens to people when they drink too much. Also, abstention naturally gave an edge to the voicing of my complaints. But from the drinker's point of view there is nothing so unpleasant as having a nagging ex-drinker at his side. Eventually I implemented my threats and moved into the city. Soon afterward I received a bill, forwarded by Jane, for $180 from the telephone company, together with a list of Mary's latest long-distance calls. She was always saying: "Katusha's in Dublin. Let's call her and cheer her up!" Or she would tell the operator: "I say. I want to call London collect. Why not? That's ridiculous!" Then she would give the number and make the call. Mary had been generous with me, and she was a friend, and although I worried about what might happen, I could not bring myself to speak to her. I wrote to the telephone company saying that I was on relief and could not pay the bill.

There was a room on Columbia Heights in Brooklyn with a superb view of lower Manhattan and the harbor. I took it, hired a piano, and went on working. When I made a trip out to the farmhouse to see what was going on, I found that Mary had got hold of a capable Austrian woman, who had taken over the household and was managing it perfectly. She was going to get her husband to move the trunks and luggage to New York to West Thirteenth Street, where Mary already had rented an apartment, and there she would go on keeping house for them. This all sounded quite insane, but I said nothing. Jane came several times to spend the night with me in Brooklyn but claimed she did not want to live there, and anyway Mary was ill, and she had grown very fond of her and felt that Mary needed her to help her land on her feet. "You'll ruin your health," I declared. "Nobody can drink that much."

The apartment Mary had taken was an unfurnished basement with a garden in the back. She still had no money, but people did not seem to believe it; she began running up large bills at Esposito's, a meat and grocery store on Sixth Avenue around the corner. She had orchids and masses of cut flowers delivered each day from the florist. Then she went to Wanamaker's and asked to see the manager. To introduce herself she showed him her British passport, and he noted that she lived in Surrey, which led them from one place to another, until Mary, being an astute listener as well as an engaging talker, discovered that the man had a passionate interest in Lawrence of Arabia. She then recalled remarks Lawrence had made to her during the many dinners he had eaten at her house, after having ridden down on his motorcycle. And she recounted arguments between him and H. G. Wells and told him small scandalous details about his life. When she asked to open an account, he complied immediately, and when she warned him that she was going to furnish an entire apartment, he assured her that it was quite all right and that she must buy whatever she wanted. Then they chatted another twenty minutes about Lawrence while the Austrian housekeeper sat outside in the waiting room. When Mary came out with her card, she went downstairs and bought two electric fountains, many white rugs, a white enamel baby grand piano, couches, cushions, china, cutlery, and linens. The apartment was attractive and was kept in order by the Austrian woman. Almost immediately Mary took to her bed. She had laid in a big supply of gin and many cases of Broadcast Hash, which I remember as being the cheapest canned food one could get, at nine cents a can. Wanamaker's did not sell food.

Mary would lie in bed and drink. Then she would practice what she called subjective levitation. "I'm leaving my body," she would call out, whether anyone could hear her or not. She said the ceiling was troublesome; she had never been able to get through it and was constantly being pushed up against it. Maria

Ouspenskaya, the old actress, used to come and sit with her during these practice flights. About this time Mary began to say she was the illegitimate daughter of Gurdjieff. Perhaps she was; she looked like him. Certainly she did not seem like the offspring of the bluff, Blimpish British major who had been presented to me as her father.

Mary's friends were Café Society people who thought she was very brave, living as she did. They tried to get her uptown with them, but she would not budge. The pinnacle of her season was the arrival for dinner of Otto of Hapsburg and his wife, pretenders to the throne. The Austrian woman, on being presented to them in the kitchen, knelt for an instant before him as she curtsied and murmured: *"Herr Österreich."*

That winter I went several times to see Auden, who lived only a block or so from me in Brooklyn Heights. I was considerably in awe of him. His learning and the strange way in which he expressed himself when he spoke combined to make me always unsure of the meaning of his words. But that in itself was a pleasant, if losing, game.

There was a night when Kirk and Constance Askew, who ran the only regular salon in New York worthy of the name, invited Jane and me to dine with Salvador and Gala Dali. It was very formal and so dark in the candlelighted room that when the butler set the salad bowl down near Dali before tossing the salad, Dali gazed over the twilit surface of the top lettuce leaves and said that he was reminded of Switzerland. Then he told a story about a small girl lost in a blizzard in the Alps. When she was more dead than alive, a fine St. Bernard arrived with a keg of brandy around his neck. The dog then attacked her and ate her. *"C'est beau,"* he added, looking at the salad bowl as though the story were still glowing there in the air above it.

Gala had adopted fantasy for the evening. No matter what the general conversation was about, she brilliantly brought it back to the *idée fixe* she had chosen, which was that I must buy a large aviary and shut her into it and then come and scatter food to her and whistle at her. *"Je veux être votre perroquet,"* she told me, fixing me with her startlingly shrewd eyes.

One weekend, between Friday and Monday, Bill Saroyan

wrote a play called *The Time of Your Life*. Eddie Dowling directed it, and it was a success. Soon Bill came up with another, *Love's Old Sweet Song*, which the Theatre Guild acquired and gave to Dowling to direct. Both Theresa Helburn and Lawrence Langner were offended by Dowling's cavalier treatment of the script. I was called in to do the score. One day after rehearsing a scene all afternoon, Dowling exclaimed: "We gotta get a bop in this thing. Bill, why don't you go out for a beer and rewrite it? We'll rehearse the kids in the meantime." Langner was beside himself. "This is not a vaudeville turn!" he cried. Then he began to walk up and down in the dark at the back of the auditorium, seizing me fiercely at one point and propelling me along with him. "We creative artists must stick together," he whispered. Saroyan, however, was quite willing to rewrite and continued to do so even after the play had opened in its pre-Broadway tour. Walter Huston, who played the lead, did not seem to mind having to learn new lines, sometimes whole new scenes, each day. It was a hard show to tour because there were a dozen small children in the cast, and their mothers were always around, constantly complaining of the lack of heat in the dressing rooms.

Oliver Smith, who had been twelve the summer we had spent together at Aunt Mary's, was now twenty-two. He had a special talent, I thought, for stage design. He came to Philadelphia at my suggestion while Jane and I were there for the *Love's Old Sweet Song* tryout. I wanted Saroyan to see his sketches. He showed them in our hotel room, and Bill was so impressed that he asked Oliver to design his next play, *Hello Out There*. Oliver's family were not at all in favor of what he was doing, and thus, when he needed $1,000 to go to Hollywood, where the entrance examinations for the Stage Designers' Union were held that year, they refused to give him anything. He went to Aunt Mary, who sold some jewelry and made it possible for him to get to California, take the examination, be accepted (along with one other, Salvador Dali), and return to New York to get to work on the sets for Saroyan.

Teddy Griffis was the daughter of Stanton Griffis, the financial wizard who owned Madison Square Garden and derived his income from Standard Oil and Paramount Pictures. We had been seeing her with Touche now for a year or two, she had spent a weekend with us on Staten Island, and we had visited her at her house in New Canaan, so that it was very good news when Touche told us they were getting married. In the meantime Touche had achieved great notoriety with his song "A Ballad for Americans." He had asked me to write the music for his long lyric, and I had been embarrassed by the subject matter; there were too many concessions to popular taste. Touche then went to Earl Robinson, the Communist Party's unofficial composer, who set it in just the right idiom for it to be immensely popular. Touche used to twit me about my refusal. "Wouldn't you like to have written 'A Ballad for Americans'? I came to you and asked you, you son of a bitch, and you wouldn't." I pointed out to him that my music would have made it an entirely different song, which would have had no popular success. This did not please him either, for to him it implied that the music had a preponderant part in the song's creation.

About this time my relief case came up for review. I had hoped to keep from the board the fact of my father's existence, but they got wind of it finally and sent an investigator to his house. The man they sent was black; he was asked to use the service entrance rather than the front door, where he originally presented himself. His report read: "Not in present need," and I was swiftly dropped from the relief rolls and thus from the Federal Music Project. "Damned good thing, too," said Daddy.

Almost simultaneously the Department of Agriculture asked me to write music for a film being made by the Soil Erosion Service about the Rio Grande Valley. The appointment and the ensuing checks were signed by Henry Wallace, which enabled my father to fulminate some more against the government. "My God, what is this nation coming to?" he ranted. Besides, from a purely ethical viewpoint, according to him, a member of the Communist Party should not under any conditions be receiving government funds. He found it impossible to understand how I could bring myself to accept what I must consider tainted money. Nor could I admit to him or anyone else that my interest in "the movement" was limited to what I thought of as its harassing and disrupting potential. The party was well organized and could cause a lot of trouble; this seemed sufficient reason to support it. To reinforce my belief in the rightness of my attitude, I went to meetings backed by the German-American Bund which were held in the Innisfail Ballroom on Third Avenue. There were always a dozen or more policemen standing along the wall near the doorway in the back of the hall. Each meeting featured a minute or so during which the public, to the rhythm of feet pounding the floor, chanted: "Kill Jews. Kill Jews. Kill Jews." One night as I was leaving early, a policeman at the door said to me: "You ought to stick around. These people've *got* something." Following instructions from the CPUSA, Harry actually joined the Bund and worked with its members. I did not like to think of what would happen to him if they discovered the deceit.

Jane was not eager to accompany me to New Mexico and stay while I worked on the film there, but she agreed to come along if she could bring a friend named Bob Faulkner, who lived in Patchin Place and worked at the *New Yorker*. I was so eager to get away from New York that I did not much care who came along with us. I knew Bob was a heavy drinker, just as I knew that was the reason why Jane wanted his presence. She had finally told me that my "view of life" depressed her so deeply that when she was with me, everything seemed hopeless. The result was, she said, that she could be with me alone only for short periods, and then she had to escape the overwhelming gloom I created. (Much later she confided that she was frightened of being alone with me, particularly away from New York.) In Bob, who liked to laugh more or less continuously, she hoped to find a counterbalance to me. For my part, I imagined that I could control events and see to it that she did not drink too much.

I had asked several years earlier for a Guggenheim Fellowship to record music in Africa and had been refused. Recently I had applied once more, giving the same project. This time they had called me to the office and told me to fill out the forms again, specifying a project in "creative music"; not being able to think of anything else, I had stated that I proposed to write an opera. From the attitude of the director, I suspected that this time I stood a better chance of being awarded a fellowship. I had talked with Bill Saroyan about the possibility of his providing a libretto for me, and although he claimed never to have been even once to the opera, he said he would send me something when I got to Albuquerque.

As we sped southwestward on the Santa Fe from Chicago, and I saw the sky growing cleaner and brighter, I felt that life was opening up once again and taking on meaning, an ill-defined sensation which inexplicably comes upon me when I move toward unfamiliar regions. I had every intention, once the film was finished, of continuing to Mexico and remaining there as long as possible.

Albuquerque in 1940 was a pleasant little town, of just the right size. We found an apartment a mile or so to the north in Old Albuquerque, a suburb where there was a colony of New Mexico lovers, very regular citizens hoping to become bohemian by dint of living close to the "real people"—that is, the Indians and the Spanish. These well-intentioned men and women were our neighbors; they were friendly, gregarious, the sort of people who read Thomas Wolfe and left opened jugs of wine on the table. I must have bothered them with my never-ending pounding on the piano, but they did not complain.

The man making the film was Richard Boke; he and his wife, Sally, were a civilized couple, graceful and well groomed as only the consciously bourgeois can be. They lived in the country, in a large adobe house, which was considered a luxury. It was a luxury with drawbacks, I soon realized, when one morning Sally called me into the nursery to show me a black widow on the sheet of the baby's crib.

There was a bar not far from where we lived, where Bob's martini once had been spiked with a drowned black widow. To that bar there came regularly a character we knew as Desert Rose, whose capacity for liquor was phenomenal. One evening she invited us to her house for drinks. She had a small son and an enormous collie dog which felt itself to be very much one of the family. The conversation shifted to the war in Europe and the likelihood of our getting embroiled in it. Desert Rose, whose sentiments were always of the best Made-in-America variety, suddenly tossed patriotism out of the window, declaring passionately: "I can tell you I didn't raise *my* dog to be cannon fodder."

She did not even notice our laughter but forged ahead in her denunciation of war.

I was for keeping the Bokes away from our apartment, but Jane felt that courtesy demanded we invite them, since she and I had so often been their guests. I suspect, too, that the idea of having them see Bob living there with us intrigued her. It was one of those setups that appealed to her dramatic imagination. And so, typically, she invited Desert Rose, too, for the same hour. The effect on the Bokes was interesting to watch. At first they took for granted, because she had a certain flair, that she was an eccentric drunk from their own milieu, but they did not remain under this impression for more than a minute or so, I should imagine. When they understood that they had a primitive in front of them, they were disconcerted. I glared at Jane for having called into existence this uncomfortable situation. I had asked her: "Who is Bob supposed to be?" "We're brother and sister," she had said, and this is how he had been presented. What with the nervousness caused by Desert Rose's presence, for she continued to talk, both Jane and Bob forgot their roles, and each began to refer respectively to "My mother" and "*my* mother." The Bokes looked confused, but again not for long, even when Bob tried to make it all into fantasy, saying, "*My* mother's on tour with Barnum and Bailey. She's got two heads." As all nightmares do, the scene eventually came to an end.

What made Albuquerque feasible was the open country roundabout. I had only to go out to the river, walk north, and there was nothing but the complex sinewy pattern of rocks, sand, driftwood, and pebbles. Then I could walk for miles in undisturbed silence, carrying the scene sequence and a stopwatch, planning the score.

The Mexican elections were coming up. With the fate of Spain at the hands of General Franco still fresh in everyone's mind, liberals feared that General Almazán, an avowed Fascist, might possibly win. Civil war would then be inevitable, the border would as a matter of course be shut, and my chances of getting to Mexico City would be reduced to zero. The more I read about the situation, the harder I worked to finish the score for *Roots in the Soil* and get across the Río Bravo into Ciudad Juárez before the trouble began. The Department of Agriculture people thought I should visit the Jemez Mountains where several tens of thousands of pure Spanish peasants still lived. It was beautiful high, rugged country; sometimes I could have thought myself in some poor remote hamlet of the Sierra Nevada in Andalusia. Under any other circumstances I should have been fascinated by this ethnic enclave. The government people offered to fly me up and down the Rio Grande Valley, so I could get "the feel of it," but as I never liked flying enough to do it unless it was necessary, I declined, and they took me on some tours by automobile.

Just before I completed the score, Saroyan's libretto arrived. It was called *Opera, Opera!*, and it was not a libretto any more than Gertrude Stein's text for *Four Saints in Three Acts* was a libretto; it needed a Maurice Grosser to provide one for it. I was at a loss how to proceed, but I took it along with me when we left for Mexico, in order to study it.

We spent a week in Zacatecas. Now that we were across the border I was in no hurry to get anywhere. Still, we had promised Peggy and Louis Reille to be in Mexico City by mid-July, and so we continued on our way over the lilting roadbed of the Mexican Railways. We got to the capital in time for the trouble, and were in the Alameda on election morning, hiding behind the stone benches like everyone else, as the cars and trucks roared past, spraying bullets indiscriminately. The shooting went on all day, and there were the sounds of heavy explosions from time to time. Ávila Camacho won the day, luckily for everyone. We forgot about General Almazán's Fascist threat and began to look for a place to live. Remembering Malinche's palace, I wanted to find something similar and even more remote, if possible.

I found it at Jajalpa, an old hacienda 10,000 feet up, on the road to Toluca. It was a huge place with many rooms around a great courtyard. The mountaintops were on all sides, and the volcano of Toluca was there in all its detail, across a wide valley. I used to sit in an abandoned upstairs room and look at it. The vastness of the landscape had a paralyzing effect on me, and I remembered Thomas Mann's observation that being in the presence of a great natural spectacle impedes the desire to create.

Jajalpa was so isolated that it was impossible to keep a staff of servants functioning. Someone was always leaving, and we often went into the capital to see if an agency could get us an immediate replacement whom we could take back with us in a taxi. It was a melancholy place; the fact that it was so beautiful made the melancholy more insidious, more corrosive. The maidservants insisted that evil spirits wandered around at night in the rooms. They would come from their quarters long after we had gone to bed, knock rapidly on the door, and whisper: *"Señor! Señora! Hay pasos, pues."* This was how they announced the fact that they were going to spend the night in our room with us, in the corner on the floor. If there were footsteps, then etiquette demanded that we allow them to sleep with us. This did not happen every night, nor was it all the servants, but it happened regularly with certain of them. Each master bedroom was provided with a loaded rifle, standing by the head of the bed. We thought of the old firearms purely as part of the somewhat comic decoration, but the servants took them with complete seriousness.

I went down to party headquarters in the capital and offered my services. They wanted to know where I lived. When I told them, they decided to run Sunday bus excursions to Jajalpa for tourists who wanted to visit a real, old-fashioned hacienda. This happened on only two Sundays. The sightseers were largely American, although there were a few Europeans among them. They looked at the livestock (we had eighty-five cows and hundreds of sheep) and the chapel and the immense courtyard, and wished they were back in Mexico City. But they had to have lunch first, for they had paid the agency for that before starting out. Jane was stoical about the situation. It gave the Mexican party a little extra money, more, certainly, than we could have given them.

Slowly I became aware of a constant feeling of repletion and incipient nausea. I found it impossible to eat; the thought of food made me shudder. I realized that the altitude was interfering with my digestion and decided to get out quickly. I went down to the capital. Lou and Peggy Reille were there with Esteban Francés, the Spanish painter, and were about to drive down to Acapulco. I went with them; they had rented Bill Spratling's beach house there, a fine long house on top of the cliffs, shaped like a bent dumbbell whose rod was a huge terrace connecting the two parts of living quarters. Spending the whole day in the sea for a fortnight helped me a great deal; my appetite returned with a vengeance. A wire from Jane announced that she and Bob were arriving and asked me to find a house immediately. Lou was an old Mexican hand who later married Dolores del Rio; he found a house with a patio 150 feet long, shaded by avocado and lemon trees. There was a wide covered *corredor* between the rooms and the garden, strung with hammocks.

Jane and Bob arrived with two dwarfish, popeyed Indians they had found in Toluca, a youth and a girl, who under the guidance of an older local woman in the kitchen would constitute our staff. They told a strange tale about the owner of the hacienda, the grand lady we had visited at her ostentatious house in the city when we had signed the lease. She had prepared a typed list several pages long of objects which she said were missing from the hacienda. It included furniture, farm tools, and pigeons, among other things. They could do nothing but stare at the list. Bob singled out one item, a *zarape* valued at an unheard-of-figure— enough to buy twenty *zarapes*—and called her attention to the price she was asking for its replacement. It was not the *zarape* that was valuable, she explained; it was the bullet hole in it that made it valuable. Her brother had been wearing it the day he was shot and killed. They got the bill down by $100 before they paid. I was indignant, but since I had left Jane to do the boring work of getting things out of the hacienda, I could say nothing.

The two Indians soon began to weep as they worked. They wanted their mothers, they explained, as though it were natural for people eighteen or twenty years old to need maternal protection. They could not sleep at night because their mothers were so far away. We tried to get them to bathe in the sea at Los Hornos, but they would not even walk onto the sand. At the end of their month they had to be put onto the bus and sent back home. They did not understand Acapulco at all.

The house lent itself to the collecting of birds and animals. One merely let them loose in the jungle of the garden, and they enjoyed themselves. This was not true of the two coatimundis;

they insisted upon being with people. One of them would sleep only on Jane's head, wrapped in her hair. If she slept late, so did the coatimundi. I learned not to try to remove it; its resistance was expressed in two phases, the first of which consisted of covering its eyes tightly with its two paws and chattering rapidly, and the second of suddenly sinking its terrible little teeth into my hand.

One morning when we were getting ready to leave for a day at the beach, someone arrived at the door and asked to see me. It was a round-faced, sunburned young man in a big floppy sombrero and a striped sailor sweater, who said his name was Tennessee Williams, that he was a playwright, and that Lawrence Langner of the Theatre Guild had told him to look me up. I asked him to come in and installed him in a hammock, explaining that we had to hurry to the beach with friends. I brought him books and magazines and rum and Coke, and told him to ask the servants for sandwiches if he got hungry. Then we left. Seven hours later we got back to the house and found our visitor lying contentedly in his hammock reading. We saw him again each day until he left.

Presently Jane drove up to Taxco for a weekend with some Americans. She stayed on a few extra days, and then sent me a telegram saying that she had taken a house there. I was annoyed, because Taxco was the one town in Mexico where I did not want to live. I had spent a week there with Tonny and Marie-Claire three years earlier, and the carefully nurtured bohemian atmosphere depressed me. The place had been adopted by foreigners, and as a result, it attracted too many visitors.

We moved up to Taxco; it was more comfortable, and Jane seemed much happier, but after Acapulco I found the still mountain air oppressive. I was sorry, although not desperately so, to be suddenly called back to New York by the Theatre Guild. Helen Hayes and Maurice Evans were signed to play Viola and Malvolio in *Twelfth Night*. The production needed a score.

The pattern of events was familiar, but this time Jane would wait for me. I would write the score and come back within six weeks, and we would resume our life at Casa Hall. Air travel was pleasant in those days: I had my own cabin with a bed in it, and under sheet and blankets I slept during most of the flight.

After the anarchy of *Love's Old Sweet Song*, *Twelfth Night* was clean and relatively easy to do, although it required a good amount of work on my part, inasmuch as I had chosen an idiom meant to sound like antique and intricate chamber music. We toured New Haven and Boston and had scarcely opened in New York when I was called in by Theresa Helburn and given *Liberty Jones*, whose script Philip Barry had just finished writing. I could see that this was going to be practically a musical extravaganza and would require an enormous amount of work, so I wired Jane and told her to come, since I had no idea of how long the job would take.

Now that Germany had invaded the Soviet Union, my attitude vis-à-vis the Communist Party had undergone a transformation. It seemed certain that the United States would get involved in the war sooner or later. If we were going to be partners of the Russians, I must get out of the party. I went around to the offices of Section 20 on Columbus Circle and expressed my desire to resign. The man who listened smiled wearily. "Comrade," he said, "don't you know you can't resign from the party? You can only be expelled."

"Well, then, expel me," I said.

He said it was an involved process, and one that could not be initiated by one individual. As if he thought the news might mitigate my chagrin, he added that it had already been decided to expel Jane, but that my name would be retained on the party roster.

"*You* may consider me a member, but I'll pay no more dues and go to no more meetings, and as far as I'm concerned, I'm out," I told him. "That's up to you," he said calmly. Then he went on to say that the section had had disturbing reports about me from Mexico—from Acapulco specifically—which caused them to doubt my sincerity as a member. I was merely living there, having a good time, their informant had told them. "I was on vacation," I said angrily, trying to think who could have been watching me in Acapulco. "There's no vacation from the class struggle; you know that, comrade," he said.

"So? Can't you see I'm not fit material for the party?" I demanded. Again he merely smiled. "It suits us to keep you in the party," he said; that was his final comment. I left the office puzzled but relieved.

XII

Jane came from Mexico, still working on her novel. We spent the whole winter in New York, I trying to supply music for my various commitments. *Twelfth Night* had scarcely opened on Broadway when the Theatre Guild came up with a far more ambitious project for me. Philip Barry had just finished the script of *Liberty Jones,* which was to be a political extravaganza with music. I remember that there were a hundred and fifty-eight musical cues in the score and that there was music going on during most of the evening. It was a big, hard job for me, but we eventually got to Philadelphia with the show to try it out at the Forrest Theater. At the party after the performance on opening night Jane was introduced to the guests as "Paul's delightful little Mexican bride," and so she tried to act the part, accent and all.

Leonard Bernstein was there in Philadelphia at the Curtis Institute, and we were seeing him every day. A ballet company in New York asked me to orchestrate two old scores for them quickly. I asked Lenny if he had the time to do the work, and he said he did. Only then did I accept the offer. He amused himself with the instrumentation, particularly in the work by Pugni, which he arranged in the most perverse and unlikely fashion, giving to the brass those passages which lent themselves to strings. It was not at all what the ballet company wanted, he told me subsequently, and with glee (since only my name appeared on the scores); they had to have both ballets reorchestrated.

After *Liberty Jones* had opened in New York, I wrote some music for Lillian Hellman's *Watch on the Rhine.* Then Lincoln Kirstein had an idea not only for a ballet he thought I should write, but also for a house where I could live while I wrote it. Lincoln had made it possible for George Davis, who at that time was fiction editor of *Harper's Bazaar,* to sign a lease on an old brownstone house on Middagh Street in Brooklyn Heights. The purpose of his gesture was to provide reasonably priced living quarters for a group of people working in the arts. Gypsy Rose Lee had taken up residence in the house while writing a mystery called *The G-String Murders* (which George Davis always claimed he wrote), and having finished the book, she had moved out. Jane and I occupied the two empty rooms.

To me the house was a model of *Gemütlichkeit.* It was furnished with what are now called antiques: examples of nineteenth-century American Ugly which George had picked up on Third Avenue and on Brooklyn's Fulton Street and combined with capricious perversity to make a comic facsimile of his grandmother's house in Michigan. It was well heated, and it was quiet, save when Benjamin Britten was working in the first-floor parlor, where he had installed a big black Steinway. George lived on the first floor, Oliver Smith, Jane and I on the second, Britten, Auden and Peter Pears, the British tenor, on the third, and Thomas Mann's younger son Golo lived in the attic. Later, when we moved out, Carson McCullers took our rooms and Richard Wright moved in with his wife and child. It was an experiment, and I think a successful one, in communal living. It worked largely because Auden ran it; he was exceptionally adept at getting the necessary money out of us when it was due. We had a good cook and an impossible maid (except that I doubt that any maid could ever have kept that house completely clean and neat), and we ate steaming meals that were served regularly and punctually in the dim, street-floor dining room, with Auden sitting at the head of the table. He would preface a meal by announcing: "We've got a roast and two veg, salad and savory, and there will be no political discussion." He had enough of the don about him to keep us all in order; quite rightly he would not tolerate argument or bickering during mealtime. He exercised a peculiar fascination over Jane, who offered to do his typing for him; astonishingly enough, he accepted, and she had to get up every morning at six o'clock and go downstairs to meet him in the dining room, where they would work for three hours or so before breakfast, calling out from time to time for more coffee from the kitchen.

In the cellar behind the furnace there was a small room where I put an upright piano, and in here I worked all day and half the night, writing *Pastorela* for the American Ballet Caravan. The esthetic of the ballet was based on the pre-Christmas *posadas* as celebrated by the Indians of Mexico; vocal sequences using the actual words and melodies were interspersed throughout the score. I did not hear it until six years later; by that time I had forgotten it to such an extent that I had the impression it was by someone else and was able to enjoy it.

At that time Dali did occasional illustrations for *Harper's Bazaar*; once they had been reproduced, George would bring them home and have them framed. One of these pictures was a fine pencil sketch of Harpo Marx playing a harp strung with barbed wire, while in the desert background some giraffes burned spectacularly. George had left the picture on his windowsill and gone out, and a rainstorm had come up. When he returned to the house, he found his Dali drenched and stained, just where he had left it, and the window still wide open. He rushed to Susie, the maid, and began to recriminate with her, pointing at the picture and repeating: "How could you, Susie? It's ruined! Ruined!" Susie was used to this sort of thing, but she sympathized and shook her head. "Yes, Mr. Davis, you right," she said. "It sure is too bad, and it was such a beautiful picture of your mother, too."

A stray cat which had been hit by a car lived in our kitchen; it had a terrible open gash on its side. We thought regular food and a warm place to sleep might hasten the healing, so we allowed it to stay there, "underfoot," as the maids said. At a late party one night several of us were standing in the kitchen making coffee. Dali wandered down, saw the cat, and grew pale. Seeing that I had noticed his reaction, he confided: *"Je déteste les chats, et surtout avec des plaies."* This would not have been an endearing remark, even if made to an ailurophobe, and I must have looked at him with much the same expression on my face that the sight of the cat had brought to his.

My suspicion that a Guggenheim Fellowship might come my way proved correct. Along with the money from the other commissions and weekly royalties arriving from *Watch on the Rhine* and *Twelfth Night,* I felt that there was no point in staying longer in New York, and so once more Jane and I turned southward. We sailed to Veracruz and went on to Fortín for a few days. As everyone who has been there recalls, the entire valley reeks with the perfume of gardenias. The surface of the swimming pool at the Hotel Ruiz Galindo was strewn freshly each morning with hundreds of the flowers, which gave me the idea of buying enough gardenias to cover our bed. We got them at intervals throughout the day rather than all at once, so as not to be seen lugging a great quantity of them past the reception desk. When we had what seemed a sufficient amount of the blossoms, we dumped them all onto the sheeted surface of the bed, undressed, and lay on top of them. I have a hyperactive olfactory nerve, so the experience was unforgettable.

We went up to Mexico City to spend a week. Lou Reille was there; I met him in the Ritz Bar one morning with Leopold Stokowski, who then and there gave me my first mescal, and, I should add, made me take the *gusanos* with it. I had often watched the ground-up slugs being mixed with salt on the side of the hand of a drinker about to down a glass of mescal, and I had just as often refused to participate in the ritual. Now, since it was Stokowski proffering it, I felt obliged to disregard my finicky distaste. What with the salt and lime juice paste and the jolt of the kerosene-flavored liquor, there might just as well have been no powdered worms there: I could not distinguish any taste at all.

In New York at a party one night Katharine Hepburn had told me that her younger brother Richard would send me a play he was finishing and to be on the lookout for it. When I got to Taxco, it was waiting for me at the house, together with a letter from Hepburn asking if I could provide music for the lyrics interspersed throughout the text. We corresponded a bit and arranged the fee. Then I was ready to start. This meant that I had to find a piano, an item even scarcer in Taxco than it had been in Tangier. Inasmuch as harmony rather than melody was the pivotal element in my musical thinking, I was unable to compose without having access to a keyboard instrument. I can hear clearly only up to five simultaneous tones on my mental keyboard; after that I falter.

A Russian woman named Tamara generously offered me the use of her piano, and I got to work. The actual composition went very well, but the many more hours I had to spend orchestrating and copying were not easy, principally because I wanted absolute privacy for that, and it was not available at home. Jane and Bob were there (he still shared the house and had lived in it alone all winter). They both liked an atmosphere of people and drinks.

I resolved to find a little house far from everything, where I could work every day in strict silence. Since no inhabited region can be silent, my search for a place had to be carried out on horseback; it was the only way I could get far enough away from the town. After several long rides I found what I was looking for. It was about an hour from home, near the top of a cliff overlooking an abyss where, from far below, there rose the faint roar of a waterfall. The small red adobe hut with one room and a palm-thatch-covered veranda stood under the avocado trees and faced the nothingness to the south.

Each afternoon when everyone else was at siesta, I got astride the little rented horse and rode down to my hut to work for three hours. In the room I had a table and a chair. For the veranda I had a wide string hammock I had bought in Tehuantepec. When I was tired of orchestrating *Love Like Wildfire,* I would throw myself across the hammock and hang there in space for five minutes, hearing only the far-off hollow sound of the invisible waterfall. To the best of my knowledge the play was never produced and the music never performed.

Matta (Echaurren), the Chilean Surrealist painter, whom we had known in New York, now had a house in Taxco. With the aid of Pajarito, his wife, he demonstrated a method of work he had evolved; he called it *la peinture métaphysique* because at the beginning of each canvas the process was largely aleatory. Pajarito would blindfold him, give him a brush, let him choose a color and get some of it onto the brush, then steer him to a blank white canvas that he would eventually manage to touch with the brush, making a small spot. He would repeat the action with as many other brushes and colors as he chose, and then starting from these random focal points whose colors had already been arbitrarily imposed, he took off the blindfold and began to weave connecting patterns between them. The finished paintings were mysterious and vaguely incandescent. Matta himself was always amusing. He talked steadily; sometimes he sounded like an excited parrot, particularly when he laughed.

After Bob Faulkner and I had words over what I considered his late hours and accompanying noise, he moved to his own house. Jane seemed constantly to be enlarging her circle of acquaintances. There were constant parties where everyone drank far too much, and there was an American woman named Helvetia Perkins whom we saw every day. She had a station wagon and would take us to market down in Iguala, where along with the fruit and vegetables we always bought great quantities of pottery. Mornings Jane sat out on the terrace working on *Two Serious Ladies*. I still had my little hut overlooking the valley, but I seldom went down to it. Instead, I made expeditions upward into the mountains above Taxco.

Soon Oliver Smith was among us with his mother and stepfather, Ivan Bernkoff. They had with them a young Mexican painter, Antonio Álvarez. He was very proud of being totally Indian; as a child he had been bathed in a tub of bull's blood. We all went down to Acapulco to live again at Spratling's beach house. The food was wonderful, and the sun, the surf, and the wind made it even better. Everyone else returned to Taxco after three weeks or so, but I stayed on, living in a tent on the grounds of the Hotel Costa Verde at Caleta. One afternoon I saw an Indian in the plaza with an ocelot cub on a chain. Those days I bought animals and birds, and an ocelot was something I had not yet experienced. It was an exquisite little animal with huge sapphire eyes and big fistlike paws. I bought it and took it back to the tent, where it seemed happy. At night I would lie on my back, and it would pace up and down interminably on top of me, going down to my legs and coming back up, always rubbing its jowl against my chin as it turned, faithful to its own imposed rhythm, to go the other way once more. As long as it paced, it purred, with a sound like a rumbling motor. I thought it would be a fine mascot for the house in Taxco. Since I intended to go up on the bus, I had a spacious cage made, put the ocelot into it, and carried it to the bus terminal two hours before the vehicle was due to leave, so they could not claim there was not enough room for it on top of the bus. When I arrived at departure time, I looked up and saw that everything up there had been covered over with the tarpaulin. I expostulated with the driver, the ticket seller, the mechanic, the porters; it was too late to unpack, they said. The bus was about to leave. "The animal will die!" I cried. "Maybe not," they said.

Quickly I climbed to the top of the bus and pulled the tarpaulin from the luggage. Then in a transport of anger I began to heave everything down into the plaza: boxes, crates, trunks, and bags, objects which under normal circumstances I probably could not even have lifted. The cage was at the very bottom of everything. I seized it and carried it with me down the ladder, and then I hired a taxi to take me and my ocelot to Taxco. When we got up into the mountains, the odor of the night air coming in through the window excited the animal; it stood on its hind legs and sniffed. I expected it to make a sudden leap, so from then on, we drove with the windows nearly shut.

Back in Taxco I did not feel well. I took enterovioform and kept living my life, although I could not eat, and when I did manage to, often felt worse afterward. Some people from *Life* magazine got wind of the ocelot and sent a letter asking if they might make a film and photographs. I agreed, but the morning they arrived I felt so low that I could not watch the routine they had devised. This consisted of letting a white pigeon loose on the terrace (its legs were tied together, so that it walked with difficulty) and letting the ocelot stalk it. At this point, naturally they began to film and snap. The denouement of the filmed episode was the delayed killing and eating of the pigeon. But the end of the story came on the following day, when, weaker and sicker than I can remember ever feeling before or since, I had to watch Adalberto, the Indian houseboy, come triumphantly into my room holding up a dripping spotted pelt. *"Aquí está su gato!"* he chanted, a wide grin on his face. "The bones of the bird cut through his tripes."

It was a bad period. I was so sick that I have no memory of the trip up to the capital or of the first few days I spent in the British Hospital. I had a very heavy case of jaundice and became deep orange, with egg-yolk eyes. The hatred of Taxco which I had conceived during the days I lay ill there was so intense that I told Jane to get rid of the furnishings and the house. We lived that autumn in an apartment house in the capital. I thought it time to get to work on my Guggenheim project. I had finally decided to write the opera using García Lorca's *Así Que Pasen Cinco Años,* rather than Saroyan's libretto. I hired a piano and began. It was not long before I went back into jaundice, save that this time they called it *derrames biliares* and sent me down to a quiet sanatorium in the country outside Cuernavaca. There for a while I was given nothing but unsalted boiled rice. After each feeding, a nurse put a burning poultice over my liver and wrapped me round with a long cummerbund. After two weeks I could walk about. Living in the hospital, I found a place to work in Amatitlán nearby where an American lady had a good piano. Each afternoon I rented a bicycle and rode over to add a bit to the score of the opera. One afternoon I finished work early and pedaled back to Cuernavaca via the center of town, to relax for a while in a café on the square. As I sat there, I heard a sudden cascade of incredible news items come out of the radio. San Francisco and Los Angeles had been bombed, and Hawaii was in the hands of the Japanese. I immediately cycled down to Jack Creek's house where Jane was staying; they had heard the story, too, but they were busy playing badminton and were not particularly interested. The next day *El Nacional,* the government paper, had the same news we had heard on the radio. Later, after the fact of Pearl Harbor had been firmly established, the parts about the Californian bombardments and the Japanese occupation were retracted. (The editor had been in California that day, which explained everything.)

While I was still in the sanatorium, Jane brought me the completed manuscript of *Two Serious Ladies.* I already had heard her read sections of it aloud the year before in New York, when she had had a small room on West Eleventh Street where she went each day to write. Sometimes she would invite a few intimate friends for drinks and read from the novel. A good many people were partially acquainted with the book. No one, however, had read it from beginning to end when she gave it to me. I doubt that I told her how much I admired it, but perhaps I did. I hope so, as I know I found great fault with it for its orthography, grammar, and rhetoric. "You can't let anyone see such an abject manuscript!" I shouted. She was very calm about it. "If there's a publisher, he'll take care of those things," she assured me. "They don't publish a book because it has perfect spelling, Gloompot."

When I left Dr. Würzburger's sanatorium, he suggested I give up living in the capital for a while, where the altitude made proper functioning of the liver more difficult. We were briefly in Mexico City, and then, together with Helvetia Perkins and Antonio Álvarez, we left for Tehuantepec.

It was exactly the same as it had been in 1937, save that more small boys were playing baseball. They still shouted to one another in Zapotec; occasionally there was a cry of *Faúl!*

We stayed for perhaps six weeks in Tehuantepec. There were fiestas nearly every night, most of them within walking distance of the hotel. Tehuantepec was not so much a town as it was a region, an agglomeration of small villages clustered around a central market. Since there was no traffic in the place, and the streets were of sand, a blessed silence reigned in the evening air when you stepped outside into the street, a stillness which made it possible to listen for drums. Even though they might be in one of the more remote villages, you could hear them, and start in their direction. The *bailes* were uniform: a thatch-covered pavilion with rows of carbide lamps flaring, the marimba and drums at one end, chairs around the sides, all full of young men watching the girls and women dance together. Eventually some of the men danced, but only if the women asked them. This unaccountable passivity on the part of the Zapotecan males fits nicely with my observation that for them the ultimate sexual thrill is sucking a woman's breast. The jokes, the ditties, the conversation among the men when they sat in the park and talked—

all made it clear that given a nipple to suck on, they would not demand more.

One day someone took Antonio and me across the river on the railroad trestle to Santa María, to show us the farm where cats were raised to be sold as food. Until I saw it I discounted its existence, but there were the rows of cages, each one just big enough for a monstrously fat, unmoving cat to hunch in. From then on I suspected the authenticity of rabbit meat each time it was served at the Hotel la Perla. It was impossible to tell, even by the patches of black and white fur in the pot, which species of animal one was eating.

At Ixtepec one day I saw an old Indian with a drum I coveted. At first he would not hear of parting with it, for he played it on the platform of the station while the trains stopped, and collected coins afterward from the passengers. The boy who was with him blew on a *chirimia* and did the actual begging. After some drinks that night, the old man let Antonio have it for eleven pesos. I took the drum back to Mexico City and put it into the baggage room of the Hotel Carlton, where the manager, a pleasant German named Oskar Schwab, had allowed Jane and me to store a large number of crates and boxes.

It was a bad year for my health. Once again my liver failed, and I had to return to Cuernavaca to the sanatorium. When I came around from that, it was discovered that the tumor which had been removed from my jaw in 1923 had grown in again, larger than ever. And so that needed to be pried out. The operation took so long that the dentist had to send to Sanborn's for another pound of ether when he was halfway through. The results of his handiwork were dramatic: my face and neck swelled to fantastic proportions. The dentist, coming to call on me in the hospital the next day, brought two dozen very long-stemmed American Beauty roses, so that in case I had died, he explained to the nurses, they would be able to use them around the casket. He had made an error and cut into the submaxillary gland. After two weeks I left the hospital, but my jaw has never been the same since then.

Jane suddenly decided she wanted to go back to the States. She had an opportunity to drive up with Helvetia Perkins in the station wagon, and it seemed an easy way of dealing with all the things that were piled in the *bodega* at the Hotel Carlton. I went up to Guadalajara to rest. The rhythm of the city was slow; the altitude was less. It was a place of church bells and horse-driven carriages; I had the impression of living during the first decade of the century. Yet Ajijic, where I spent a few weeks later at Don Pablo Heuer's on the dubious shore of Lake Chapala, while much more primitive, was contemporary in feeling. I visited Lawrence's depressing little house in Chapala, with its stuffy rooms and its back-street atmosphere. During this time I read, and, for discipline's sake, only in Spanish. Thus I became acquainted with all the poems and plays of García Lorca, the two novels of Adolfo Bioy Casares, the memoirs of Rafael Alberti, the accounts of early colonial days in Mexico by Bartolomé de Las Casas and Padre Sahagún. And for the first time I came to know the stories of Borges. It was gratifying to open this door and discover a whole world behind it—a literature I delighted in and to which I felt almost as close as I did to that of the French.

Suddenly I realized that I had no desire to stay alone in Mexico. Aunt Mary had just died, and Holden Hall, which she had left to my father and Uncle Charles, was empty. My idea was to hurry back and occupy it, and I wrote to Jane suggesting that she make the arrangements so that we could move in as soon as possible (or, better, that she move in herself first, before I got there). What actually happened was that we lived in it as a quartet— the same foursome that had gone to Tehuantepec. For some time Antonio had wanted to kill himself; accordingly he had swallowed a bottle of Nembutal capsules—an overdose. When I got back to the capital, he was partially paralyzed and in the hospital. His mentor, a poet named José Ferrel, whose translation into Spanish of Rimbaud had just appeared, thought he should have treatment in New York. Since he was soon able to walk, I agreed to take him with me, remembering that Latouche had a miracle-working doctor, to be used only in desperate cases.

I still had many things in the *bodega* at the Carlton, and I asked for everything to be taken up to my room, in order to repack. There was no Ixtepec drum, although Jane had told me she was going to leave it behind. After everyone had searched for it, and to no avail, I sent off a wire to Jane at Holden Hall, which read: PLEASE WIRE WHEREABOUTS OF DRUM STOP SCHWAB CLAIMS NOT IN BODEGA.

Ever since our first prenuptial trip to Mexico, when I had expounded at length to her on the subject, Jane had harbored what many would consider an excessive fear of the police. My wire, instead of being delivered to Holden Hall, went into the hands of the FBI, that had reasons of its own for believing it a coded message. On a sweltering afternoon it sent two sober-faced men in business suits to Holden Hall. They identified themselves and were shown into the library, where Jane was sitting. Then they opened their attaché cases, took out papers, and began to shuffle them. Helvetia meanwhile had met the maid, and the maid had told her who was in the house. When she heard that, she flew up the back stairway to her room, locked the door, and busied herself making a fire in the fireplace. But in that windless August air the smoke, instead of curling up the flue, curled downward and began to fill the fireplace of the room below, which was the library. The two men looked at each other, and one of them said: "It's a rather hot day for a fire. Isn't it?" Jane shrugged. "They're testing the furnace," she said.

One man got up and began to look at the books that lined the walls. "Some very interesting old books here."

"They belonged to my husband's aunt."

Then she said they both turned toward her. "Yes. We want to talk to you about him." And they began a rapid-fire interrogation, asking Jane to confirm dates and places and names, reaching back farther and farther into the past, until she was unable to remember. They interpreted this as a refusal to answer, but let it pass and went on collecting more information. "And where were you in March, 1938?" "Panama." Finally they came to a dead stop, allowed an expressive silence to intervene, and said: "Mrs. Bowles, you move around a lot, don't you?"

Jane sighed. "We certainly do," she said.

They became very intent. "Mrs. Bowles, *why* does your husband travel so much?"

Jane shrugged once more and said: "*I* don't know. He's nervous, I guess."

Finally they got around to the telegram, holding it out to her and saying: "This wire is from your husband in Mexico City. Can you tell us what it means?"

Jane's explanation did not satisfy them at all, even when she added that the drum was safe in the Hotel Chelsea in New York. They wanted to know why I worried so about a drum, they were most interested in Schwab, and they asked if Jane herself had been to Bodega, and if she could describe the route taken in order to get there. But when she explained the word *bodega,* they went back to Schwab. From the wire they jumped to a telephone call Latouche had made to Jane a week earlier, a conversation of which they appeared to have a script. "Do you remember what you talked about?" they wanted to know. Jane didn't, except that Latouche had given her a lengthy account of a lunch he had just had with Eleanor Roosevelt and had added that the rest of the government ought to be chloroformed. (He had been denied a passport and was very eager to get to the Congo.) However, Jane did not have to face all that, inasmuch as they pressed on: "Who is Friedrich von Winewitz, Mrs. Bowles?" This was a joke among the three of us; since Latouche's mother was Jewish, he pretended to believe that mine was, too, and his derisory name for me when he was in that mood was Friedrich von Winewitz.

After the two men had left, Helvetia came downstairs. The reason for her panic was that she had some letters from an acquaintance who had just received a very long prison term for accepting $75,000 from the Japanese in order to do propaganda work in the United States. Obviously she had been unaware of the man's commitments until the news had broken in the press; nevertheless, the idea of being found in possession of a stack of letters signed by him terrified her. When she had burned them all, she decided to cover her traces by continuing to burn other inoffensive papers, just in case they came in and caught her in *flagrante delicto.*

This grotesque confrontation in my absence had its counterpart after I arrived in Watkins Glen. Antonio took long walks through the gorges and on the hills roundabout. Wherever he went, people hidden behind the curtains of farmhouse windows rose and went to their telephones. Then they called the police to say that a suspicious-looking Japanese man had just walked by. Even I was arrested twice, once at gunpoint, and held for questioning until Uncle Charles could be telephoned at Glenora. He had to come to Watkins Glen and identify me before they would release me. It was the summer of 1942; there were air-raid sirens and blackouts. Xenophobia reached such a pitch that in public we dared speak only in English, which meant that we had to whisper occasionally in Spanish to Antonio.

I was trying to finish composing *The Wind Remains*. The music room at Holden Hall was cool, spacious and private. I could not have asked for better working conditions. Sometimes, of course, the family would arrive *en masse*. Mary, the Irish cook we had brought from New York, being a secret tippler, was flexible and would obey the most arcane culinary orders, with the result that we ate extremely well. Mother and Daddy would sometimes bring bourbon and gin, but never wine, which held more interest for gourmet-minded Jane and Helvetia. The fact that most of the conversation in the house was about food Antonio found quite incomprehensible. His palate had been so atrophied by the *chile* in Mexican food (which he ate as *picante* as possible) that all American food was tasteless and nearly indistinguishable to him.

Antonio went to New York and began undergoing treatment by Max Jacobson. His back, shoulder, and arm were mottled with a great purplish-leaden stain, and the arm was all but paralyzed. During his treatment he lived in Latouche's house in Turtle Bay. Betty Parsons, whom we had known earlier in Taxco, had just opened a small gallery and gave an exhibit of his paintings. He sold several and went back to Mexico cured and with a little money. Not much later I heard from Ferrel that he had gone to Acapulco with friends to spend two or three weeks and one morning had announced to them that he was going off by himself for a day to explore the lagoons beyond Pie de la Cuesta. He did not return to Acapulco that day or any other. Several searches were inaugurated but gave no results other than the fact that although people everywhere in the lagoon villages remembered seeing him, they all had the same reply: he had been on his way through, going somewhere else. Two years later Ferrel wrote me again. He had just spent two weeks in the lagoons looking for some trace, but without success.

Helvetia wanted to hunt for a small property of a hundred or two acres in which to invest; she proposed a motor trip through Vermont and New Hampshire. The maple leaves would be "turning," it would be beautiful. I begged off, wanting to get back to New York and continue work. She and Jane set out; I returned to the city and took a room at the Hotel Chelsea, where I set to work orchestrating the opera. The Marquise de Casa Fuerte, organizer of the musical society La Sérénade in Paris, had the hope of being able to launch a similar series of concerts in New York later in the season, and wanted the opera ready for production. She too was interested in food, having recently arrived from Europe where it was scarce; later in the season she and Jane took turns preparing meals with what one could get at Washington Market, and we managed to continue eating well.

Marcel Duchamp had been living in Kiesler's auxiliary penthouse. Sometimes he and I would have lunch together at a Spanish restaurant on Fourteenth Street. He was a gentle and quiet man and, I thought, supremely intelligent. Soon he moved into a loft, leaving the penthouse empty. Kiesler offered it to me at a price I could afford. There was a small terrace with a good view of downtown New York and the harbor. I moved a piano into the penthouse, which otherwise was completely furnished, and went on working, spending my leisure hours with Jane and Helvetia at Waverly Place, where they had an apartment.

Peggy Guggenheim had returned to New York from Europe, taken a house on Beekman Place, and filled it with Surrealist paintings. Soon Max Ernst joined her, and they were married. Peggy's next idea was to build an art gallery which would be like no other art gallery. She commissioned Kiesler to do it; he created one that remains in the mind of everyone who visited it. Unfortunately it did not live very long, for when Peggy left for Venice, she had it dismantled and destroyed. *Art of This Century* was a success; Peggy charged an admission fee and often sat the whole day at the table by the entrance door, selling a book which bore the same name as the gallery and collecting ticket money from the visitors. There was no need for her to do this; any one of her employees could have done it for her. But in that case, she explained, she would not have had the thrill of being handed money all day long.

I had been writing musical criticism in *Modern Music* for several years. Virgil Thomson thought I ought to join the staff of the *Herald Tribune*, where he was the music critic, and write a daily article for them. The idea was interesting, but I was worried by the time element. Forty-five minutes, which on the average was about the length of time available for turning out a piece, did not seem very much in which to organize and write a literate critical report. Virgil assured me that this was something one worried about only for the first night or two. I took the job, and found that he was right, even though I did suffer two or three bad headaches during the first week of the routine. I was vain enough to enjoy having a regularly appearing by-line; at this point I have forgotten why I thought it necessary for my name to be constantly in print. I certainly believed that if the public got to know the name, regardless of whether there were any particular concept associated with it, the name would remain. Very likely I had other equally superstitious theories. Also I felt called upon to justify spending so much of my time doing secondary work rather than writing music, since upon self-examination the only reason I could find why I was doing it was that it augmented my monthly income. Only after a year, when I no longer felt any tension connected with the activity, did I come to enjoy the *Herald Tribune* routine. Then I began to propagandize for a regular jazz column in the Sunday edition and was allowed to institute it. This opened the door to folk music as well, inasmuch as it was my contention that every category of recorded music (except strictly commercial popular) ought to be covered. Soon records began to arrive almost daily; there was not enough time to listen to them all. Crooked black pillars of unjacketed 78 rpm's rose from the floor and grew constantly higher.

I was well aware that New York was the most extraordinary city of them all and, from a distance or from the air, a surprisingly beautiful one. Now I discovered that even from the inside it was often breathtaking. Since I was covering concerts every night of the week—sometimes in the afternoon as well—and used most of what hours were left for writing music, I felt the need of getting outdoors now and then. My solution was to buy a light British bicycle and pedal around the streets of Manhattan. I started my jaunts for exercise and continued them for the sheer delight they gave me. The streets and avenues were empty of traffic, and at night the city was blacked out. If there was a moon, any ride through lower Manhattan became a trip out of a dream. Silence and darkness in the gorges, and moonlight reflected from the cliffs shining far above. I developed a variety of circuits adapted to the length of time I could devote to pedaling. One night when I was riding along, I saw Brion Gysin, and stopped to talk. He was now well into the fourth of his consecutive nationalities; he said he was organizing a local for the union in a shipbuilding plant in New Jersey. Shortly afterward he went into the Army.

Selective Service called me to report for examination. Very early one morning I had to be at an armory on the East Side. Women had set up little counters and were handing out rather good doughnuts and coffee. Then a large parade of us straggled up Fourth Avenue to Park, and on to the Grand Central Palace. It seemed grotesque to have to walk into the psychiatrist's office stark naked and sit before him while he put his questions and cocked his head to one side. "How do you feel about the Army? Think you're going to like it?" I said I was worried about one thing: I doubted that I'd be able to sleep. I explained that I was a composer and lived day and night trying to escape noise, to such an extent that I wore wax stoppers in my ears to reduce its volume. The doctor looked at me with a suddenly aroused interest. He reached out quietly and pulled a pair of scissors toward him across the surface of the desk—out of my reach, I noted. Then he said something very strange, with an inflection which made him sound as though he were reasoning with a small child: "No one's going to hurt you." I did not reply. I thought of saying: "I know," or "Aren't they?" But he had got started on a whole train of thought that interested him, and he went ahead questioning me, finally getting me to admit that I felt hostility toward him. Cheered by this confession, he went on from there. In the end he wrote: *Not Acceptable. Psychoneurotic Personality.* I went back to the penthouse, had a whiskey, and continued my work.

During that winter we began spending an occasional weekend with Samuel Barber and Gian-Carlo Menotti at Mount Kisco. They were fine hosts; being unlike one another, they always managed to be entertaining ones. Gian-Carlo was interested in *coups de théâtre*, appearance and deception; Sam was a romantic (albeit in his music often a *déjà-romantique*). Talullah Bankhead, who lived not far away, used to come over for drinks; she was very proud of her ability to do high kicks and one evening managed to knock a large painting off the wall.

Xenia and John Cage had an apartment at Fifty-ninth Street and Madison Avenue. We used to eat together, they, Jane, and I, the meals being prepared sometimes by Xenia, sometimes by Jane. Xenia was a wild Alaskan blonde, part Russian and part Eskimo, who looked like a hungry wolf with slanting greenish eyes. She often laughed, which was fortunate, since, when things did not go well she could be terrifying. John was very lovable. I came to that decision when I saw him roll on the floor in an ecstasy of delight as he listened to a recording of his own music. It was not the fact that he rolled, which concerned only him, but that he felt no embarrassment whatever for having done so—it was the naturalness of his behavior which made me like him.

Yvonne de Casa Fuerte had raised the money for the *Sérénade* concerts, to be given at the Museum of Modern Art. The evening scheduling my one-act opera *The Wind Remains* was dedicated to Federico García Lorca. Oliver Smith designed one of his best sets. I gave Lenny Bernstein the score, as he had agreed to direct the orchestra. Merce Cunningham choreographed the opera and danced the part of the clown. The musicians had to perform under considerable difficulties, crouching in the concavities of Oliver's set. Lenny conducted standing against the back wall of the auditorium, wholly invisible to the audience. He did more than anyone else could have done with my music. The trouble with the opera was that its text was an excerpt from a Surrealist play. It meant nothing and went nowhere; nor was it an opera, but rather a zarzuela with solo songs, spoken dialogue, instrumental sections, dances and choruses. There was a party after the performance. One of the cast was asked to leave when he tried to send a large pineapple through Tchelitchew's portrait of the hostess.

Two Serious Ladies, which Knopf had accepted while we had been living at Holden Hall, was now published. I had always admired Borzoi books for their physical presentation; unhappily, wartime restrictions made Jane's novel an undistinguished item that might have come from any publisher. Her reviews depressed her; for the most part they dismissed the novel as either inept or meaningless.

Lawrence Vail had taken a large, pleasant place beside a small lake in Connecticut. There was an empty house on the adjacent property. Peggy Guggenheim, who at one time had been married to Vail, was still a good friend and mentioned the possibility of renting the place next to his for the summer season. He advised her not even to consider it: all the landowners with lake frontage had agreed not to rent or sell to Jews. Peggy called and asked me if I would mind leasing the place in my name and then "inviting" her to spend the summer. I said that I was not good at deception, but that I would do it. I had to go downtown to an office high above Broadway and talk with a jovial man who took my check and made out a three-month lease in my name. Jane and I went with Peggy and Kenneth MacPherson one weekend. Sybille Bedford and friends were staying in the other house, and we all ate a jolly, enormous, endless meal. When the season was over, Peggy gave me the keys, and I returned them to the office on Lower Broadway.

Peggy and Kenneth had bought two identical, contiguous houses in the East Fifties. Each of them built a very large room on the top floor for entertaining. When they gave joint parties, they opened some large double doors they had installed between the two rooms and made one room of them. On the lower floors the two houses were entirely separate. So that people would not be bored waiting for the elevator in her foyer, Peggy asked Jackson Pollock to paint gigantic murals to cover the walls of the room. We returned to her house after lunch one afternoon and came upon Pollock, standing among cans of paint, straddling one of the panels, looking down at it intently. "Such a wonderful man," she murmured after we had got into the lift.

Peggy wanted to issue a series of albums of contemporary art-music, to be called *Art of This Century Recordings*. She decided to start with my music. A well-known French flautist was in New York, and through Virgil I got him to agree to learn my Flute Sonata. It had been finished for eleven years and was completely unknown. Peggy induced Max Ernst to provide a jacket design, and we were ready to go into production. Soon the albums were being sold on the table at the gallery entrance.

I took my vacation in October and went to pick up Jane in Vermont. We had never been to Canada and were curious about what lay across the border. We got on a train for Montreal. As we read and looked out of the windows, Jane did not seem unduly nervous; only after some time had passed did I realize she was ordering one whiskey after another. By then it was too late to undo the mischief. In Montreal we got off the train and onto an escalator that took us up into the main waiting room of the station. As we reached the end of the escalator, Jane lost consciousness. People helped me lay her out on a bench and found a cab for me. At the hotel she came around, but with no idea of what had happened.

Although Montreal was dull, Quebec still looked French, and the language was unlike anything we had ever heard. In the hotel they referred to an English-speaking film as a *vu aïngla*. It delighted me to think that so foreign a place existed so close to New York, and one which, moreover, could be reached merely by stepping onto a train. Absurdly, when I returned to New York the city seemed a little less sinister and virulent, because I knew that Quebec was nearby.

Eleanor Roosevelt's intercession on Latouche's behalf meant that he had been granted a passport and had gone to the Congo, where he had spent a year traveling and preparing a script for a documentary film on the colony. Suddenly he was back in New York with André Cauvin, the Belgian cameraman who had made the film. He got Cauvin and me together for talks, and I agreed to compose a score. The film was being produced by the Belgian government in exile, and there was a good supply of money available. I had second thoughts whether it was logical, or even ethical, for me to associate myself with a vehicle of colonialist propaganda, for there was no suggestion in the film that the Congolese might ever be granted their independence; they were happy as they were, working with (for) the Belgians, and the Congo was a great, mysterious, beautiful country pulsing with life. The End. Still, when Paul Robeson told me he was going to read Latouche's commentary, I felt better about it.

Cauvin went back to the Congo and began to send me large air parcels full of records of native music. I tried to write some sequences which would sound like the music of the Pygmies, in which each man plays only one note, but plays it as part of a regularly recurring rhythmic pattern. At first this made for conducting difficulties when we came to record; in the end, however, it sounded right. When the film was completed, the Belgians gave a private showing in the projection room of the Museum of Modern Art. I took my mother and father; we went with Paul Robeson to his apartment for drinks afterward. They both admired him unreservedly. "But *why* does he have to live with a white woman?"

Oliver Smith wanted me to meet the Marqués de Cuevas, who suddenly had access to a vast sum of money and intended to found a ballet company. I went to several parties at the Marqués' house, and found him an eccentric in the grand tradition, opera cape and all. He had a beautiful Dali miniature painted on ivory, with a frame of heavy gold. When he showed it to me he confided that he would like to see a ballet done by Dali and me; he thought we would make a good pair. The idea interested me, largely because it struck me as odd that he should see points of similarity between us. He did not believe any of what he was saying, but it was only later that I became aware of that. Several times I went to his house to lunch. He would prepare the food himself, and afterward I would play to him, either on the piano or recordings of my music. He seemed to be slowly narrowing his focus; finally he told me he had hit on a subject, and he knew just how he wanted the music to sound. His choice was a poem of Verlaine: *Dans un vieux parc solitaire et glacé.* . . . Dali was alerted in Europe, and began to send sketches, of which the *marqués* showed me only those which had to do with the backdrop. This was a Böcklinesque garden scene with tall cypresses, gloomy and vaporous.

"*Eso es!*" The *marqués* cried, pounding the drawing feverishly, for, as he himself said, he was a passionate man. "It will be like this, your music, sweet and ghostly, time forever lost. This is the soul of our ballet."

Having signed my contract, I composed the music and orchestrated it. Then I flew down to Mexico for a month, wanting to visit Manzanillo, which I did not know. I thought the best way to get there would be to go to Guadalajara and get myself a plane. When I saw the tiny Panini Company's craft at the airport, I regretted my decision. Apart from the pilot there was room for only two passengers. A man kept pushing the propeller around in order to start the motor; finally he was successful, but then masses of thick yellow oil sprayed out all over the isinglass windshield. When that was cleaned up, we took off, flying over Colima Volcano straight to the Pacific coast. At Manzanillo the sierra rises directly behind the narrow coastal plain where we were to land. The pilot spiraled down, only to see that the airfield was full of horses galloping back and forth. There being nothing else to do, we came down among them and safely.

I found a good hotel just north of Manzanillo on the beach of Santiago de Colima and settled in there. The proprietor had an old open truck which I thought would be ideal for driving through the jungle.

One day I persuaded him to take me and his brother as far as the road went. We walked on from there, following a path of sorts through the dense vegetation. Suddenly at my feet lay a superb python, immobile, and with both extremities hidden by leaves. I stood still, and they saw it. The proprietor uttered a groan of revulsion, raised his rifle, and shot several times. When we were carrying it back to the truck, we met a very old Indian with a tiny white beard. He looked at the snake and said: "It was a sin to kill it." I felt somewhat the same way and was curious to know what reason the old man had. He had gone on his way. The proprietor spoke of a superstition among the locals that serpents ought not to be killed. Certainly this one was loath to die.

While we were driving down to the hotel, it twisted itself under the partially open floorboard at my feet. By then we had agreed that the skin was to be mine, since it was I who had nearly stepped on it. Thus it was already in my charge, and I felt stupid when we got back to the hotel and were unable to detach it from whatever it had seized onto in the bowels of the truck. We left it for a while; later we pulled it out easily. The next day the proprietor began to cure the skin for me. Two or three days later I interrupted the process in order to fly up to Uruapan. "It's almost cured," he told me. "Keep it in the sun and it will dry." In Uruapan I followed his advice and spread the skin out between two chairs on my terrace.

I went to spend a night sitting on cooling lava, looking over at Paricutín, the volcano which had been born the year before and already had built itself up more than 3,000 feet from the valley floor. The fire shot out all night every ten seconds with a magnificent roar, a sound deeper and viscerally more exciting than any sound I have ever heard. Hundreds of dust-covered refugees moved along the roads between the ruined areas and Uruapan. Everything lay beneath a blanket of fine gray ash.

The next morning I awoke to find a terrible odor in the air. As I lay there in bed sniffing, I also became aware of a peculiar, unending metallic sound coming from the terrace. I got up and stepped outside. The skin was thick with hundreds of murderous-looking black and yellow wasps, and the stench it gave off was unbelievable. I went in, shut the door, and did not venture onto the terrace again before I left for Guadalajara. I bought a half dozen snakeskin belts, some wallets, and some bedroom slippers; to make up for the things I had been hoping to get from my snake.

Some of the flights around Mexico that summer were hair-raising. Many of the villages where the planes would make landings to pick up passengers and poultry had no airstrip at all. The pilot skimmed over the tops of the trees on the hills and settled down into pastureland where the passengers waited in the open country, huddled with their bundles. Once in the plane, all the women immediately crouched on the floor, entirely covered by their *rebozos*, praying. Their supplications were audible and disturbing. The men merely crossed themselves and looked out the window. Often I found myself forming a resolution—to wit: never to get on another plane if I managed to get off the one I was sitting in at the moment.

The *calandrias* still waited in line around the plaza in Guadalajara, each with its two thin horses. I liked to hire one in the afternoon and go out to Tequila, where there was a ramshackle hotel that served an edible dinner. Sometimes I dismissed the carriage and spent the night, taking a taxi back to Guadalajara at dawn.

When I returned to New York, I resumed reviewing concerts at the *Herald Tribune* and attended orchestra rehearsals of my ballet *Colloque Sentimental*. It was going to sound just as I had hoped it would. Because of my reviewing, I could not watch the dance rehearsals, but I did manage to get to the dress rehearsal. My heart sank as I saw the stage and what was happening on it. Eglevsky and Marie-Jeanne came on sporting underarm hair, great hanks of it that reached to the floor. There were men with yard-long beards riding bicycles at random across the stage, and there was a large mechanical tortoise encrusted with colored lights (Dali's little Huysmans joke) that moved unpredictably this way and that, several times almost causing upsets among the performers. I sat looking incredulously at the chaos onstage. The *marqués* had assured me repeatedly that this ballet would have none of the usual Dali capers; it was to be the essence of Verlaine, nothing more. I had been royally duped. Not by Dali, for whom music was something you turned on at the beginning of the evening and turned off at the end, rather like the heating in the auditorium. He was sitting directly in front of me with Gala, watching the rehearsal. All at once he swung around and said: *"Vous auriez dû être ici hier soir. Merde, c'était beau! J'ai pleuré."* I wanted to reply: *"Ce soir c'est mon tour."* Instead, I smiled vacuously and said: *"Vraiment?"*

Opening night the audience was sophisticated and bellicose. No sooner had the curtain risen on *Colloque Sentimental* than the hisses began. As the ballet progressed, there were almost constant catcalls, boos, shouts, and whistles. I was desperate, because my music might as well not have been being played, for all it was heard. At the party afterward, Dali was gleeful; he considered the noisy reception a triumph. "Americans are learning," he said.

My work at the *Herald Tribune* prevented me from going back to other performances. I saw the ballet once again somewhat later, when conditions were quieter: the sounds of protest had become simple giggles. It was, however, no more convincing as a spectacle than it had been before.

Suddenly Tennessee Williams turned up again, sporting a mustache and in the company of Margo Jones and Donald Windham. He had with him the script of a new play which he left with me. I read it and liked it. For a play aiming at a Broadway production at that time it was somewhat experimental, envisaging as it did the use of projected color slides to serve as comments on, or asides to, the dialogue and action. The next time I saw Tennessee, the production was set, and what with the drawing up of contracts and my habitual refusal to write anything until I had stuffed an advance into the bank, I found myself with three days in which to compose and orchestrate the score. There were no difficulties. In December we went to Chicago to try out the play at the Auditorium. The projections had been deleted from the script; what came through was a poetic and, I thought, moving play, made magic by the presence of Laurette Taylor. *The Glass Menagerie* was a success before it came to New York, and after the Broadway opening, Tennessee was suddenly a famous man. His mother made a visit to New York. I remember sitting at a table with her in a hotel lobby while several people interviewed him simultaneously.

I was having a difficult time with my hearing; there were crickets, church bells and flutters in my ears, and the high register of soprano or a flute was painfully distorted on its way to my consciousness. One doctor assured me that my tonsils were bad; the infected drainage from them caused an inflamed eustachian tube. This was purely a theory, and a quite incorrect one, as I discovered after the tonsillectomy. I spent ten days in Harkness Pavillion recuperating. The time was longer than it should have been, because the incisions opened on the fifth day and began to bleed. From my room with its snowy view of the Hudson Oliver

Photo by Brion Gysin.

Outside an abandoned brothel in Morocco, 1951.

My parents in California, 1957.

At work on *The Spider's House,* Taprobane, 1957.

Photo by Hugh Gibbs.

At the Villa Muniriya, Tangier, Summer, 1961. I stand at the left; then come Allen Ginsberg, William Burroughs, Gregory Corso and Michael Fortman.

Photo by Allen Ginsberg.

Looking at the eastern end of the Djemaa el Fna, Marrakech, 1961.

At Merkala Beach, Tangier, 1962.

Paul Bowles and James Pu

Photo by Carl Van Vec

A village in Tafraout, Morocco.

Photo by Paul Bowles.

Jane visiting Marrakech, 1963.

Greeting the neighbors who lived next door to the house at Amrah, 1967.

Photo by Terence Spencer.

Photo by Terence Spencer.

With Mohammed Mrabet, at the time of the publication of his novel *Love with a Few Mairs*. The Café del Hafa, Tangier, 1967.

A dinner party on the Mountain, Tangier, 1967. Left to right: John Hopkins, the Bowleses, Marguerite McBey, Joseph McPhillips.

Photo by Terence Spencer.

Jane in Tangier, 1968.

Smith took me to the Biltmore Hotel, where I continued to convalesce for a week or so. One afternoon there, lying in bed looking through a pile of magazines, I came across an article in Cyril Connolly's review *Horizon* describing Sartre's most recent play *Huis Clos,* which had just been given a production in London as *Vicious Circle.* The argument intrigued me. When Oliver came in, I gave him a summary of what I had just read, and he reacted immediately. Further discussion increased his interest. His idea then became to find Sartre and get the American rights to the play. Since Sartre was in the United States at that moment, this seemed a possibility. From the government, under whose aegis he was touring the country, Oliver got all the dates and places of his itinerary. He began to send wires to cities in Texas, and then to New Orleans, from where the first reply came. A meeting was arranged at the Statler Hotel in Washington. Oliver and I took the train down and had a long lunch with Sartre. While we ate, he went through the script in detail, I providing a running translation for Oliver, whose eagerness to acquire the property was visibly growing. The contract was signed over coffee, and we returned to New York with our mission accomplished. Two days later Theresa Helburn and Lawrence Langner went around to the Statler to get the rights to the play for the Theatre Guild; they were incredulous and indignant to find them already gone.

Oliver's idea was to put me to work on the translation and produce the play himself, getting European actors for it. Once we had the rights, the element of haste was greatly reduced; I did not start on the translation until months later. What preoccupied us then was getting settled in new living quarters. The era of Middagh Street's comforting facsimile of family life was a part of the distant past, misted with nostalgia. Oliver, Jane, and I often sat evoking it wistfully. Oliver, who had a stronger belief than we did in the importance of a good place to live, took steps to transform fantasy into reality. He got hold of the top three stories of a large old house on West Tenth Street, had the landlord pull out some walls and remove the plaster from others, leaving only the brick surface, and induced Jane and me, as well as Helvetia, to join in the venture. Helvetia signed the lease for the second floor, he for the third, and I for the top. My front studio thus had a high painter's skylight. I went out and got a used Steinway for $1,000, and set it under the skylight; their slants were at the same angle. The piano was the first prop to go onstage in the setting up of the new scene, whose action took place at 28 West Tenth Street.

XIII

Until I had left the penthouse behind, I was not aware that I had had enough of living twenty-four stories above the ground. It was a pleasure now to come home, shut the street door behind me, and immediately feel the carpeted quiet in the house, broken only by certain faintly creaking steps, as I went up the stairs. A new era began once we got our respective floors completely furnished. Work and sleep were private, while eating and entertaining were largely communal. The cook was stationed on Oliver's floor, the middle of the three, but since each floor had its kitchen, she was able to serve meals on any one of them.

It was a confused and somewhat disorderly period, yet it was a productive one for both of us. During it I wrote a great deal of music, including the scores for seven shows, and Jane wrote her play *In the Summer House*. And it was then that I suddenly found my way back into writing fiction, a territory I had considered forever shut to me.

My almost constant companion during the whole two and a half years was Peggy Glanville-Hicks. We were composers with much the same musical tastes, so that it was not surprising that we should enjoy being together. Her husband, Stanley Bate, a British composer in a very different tradition, had a brutal streak in him; when he was drunk, which he was regularly, he expressed himself by beating Peggy and tossing her around the apartment. Once I found a trail of blood leading from the sidewalk into the building and up the stairs straight to their door; when I spoke of it to Peggy, she said: "Stanley beat me night before last. He always does. Didn't you know?" I said I had heard something to the effect but had no idea it was that bad. "Oh, yes," she sighed.

Peggy was a staunch admirer of certain of my musical works and made impeccable copies of many of the unpublished ones in her clear musical calligraphy, thus preserving items which might otherwise have disappeared, as do most manuscripts of which there is only one copy extant.

One day Jane received an abnormally fat, legal-sized envelope. There were eight sheets of paper in it, written in longhand, and they were signed by Anais Nin. I helped decipher the handwriting. It was a compendium of all the faults Miss Nin had been able to find with *Two Serious Ladies*. I was indignant, since neither of us knew the sender save by name, but Jane laughed. Not long afterward we went shopping on Eighth Street during a snowstorm. At the head of Macdougal Street a small woman suddenly bore down upon us and drew Jane aside. They talked together for forty minutes while I stood holding packages and shifted my feet in the deepening snow. It was Anais Nin, going over the points she had made in her letter. When at last we were walking again, I cried in exasperation: "But what did she *want*, for God's sake?" Jane said: "Oh, nothing much. She just wanted me to know what a terrible writer I am."

When Sartre came to New York, Jane met him at a party a day or so before he came around to Tenth Street for lunch, with his Portuguese friend Dolores Ehrenreich. As I took his overcoat from his shoulders, I heard Jane remark that they had met at a house on Washington Square. Sartre shrugged and said: *"Ah, peut-être. J'ai oublié."* But then Jane insisted: *"Moi pas,"* which I found so gauche that I burst out laughing. Sartre, an exceedingly unlaughing man, noticed nothing and began to talk. My laughter, however, had made Jane see her little remark in the context in which I had seen it; she looked once again at Sartre and ran out of the room in order not to explode with laughter there. He was famous and eccentric-looking, and we were nervous; what Jane and I both understood implicitly was that once having seen his face, she could never forget it.

After lunch while I reclined on the couch in the studio, he strode up and down for hours telling me about Jean Genet. At times he trembled with the intensity of his emotion. My admiration for Sartre was already full-blown, because I had read *Le Mur* and *La Nausée*; I decided to read some Genet. The books were not available in New York, but Gian-Carlo Menotti let me see his Swiss edition of *Le Miracle de la Rose*. Not having met anything like it, I could think of it only as pornography and thus automatically removed it from the realm of serious consideration. It would not let itself be dismissed in this fashion, of course. Three years later I reread the book; now that the pornographic glow had faded, the tragedy became apparent, and I reclassified Genet.

For several years Charles-Henri Ford had been editing *View*. It began in newspaper form, but gradually grew in format until it was a fairly thick—and very slick—art and literary publication. About this time I joined the board of editors. At first I wrote jazz criticism, and then I started to make translations of material I thought would interest Ford. He published my English versions of Jorge Luis Borges and Ramon Sender, of Francis Ponge and André Pieyre de Mandiargues, of parts of Chirico's *Hebdomeros* and the Quiché *Popul Vuh*. In the spring of 1945 I edited an issue of *View* comprising texts of my own, translations, and photographs I had taken in Central and South America. For no perceptible reason Parker Tyler thought it necessary to rewrite my preface; in doing so, he made it mean exactly the opposite of what I had said. He was apologetic, but the damage was done; doubtless no one noticed the difference.

I had been reading some ethnographic books with texts from the Arapesh or from the Tarahumara given in word-for-word translation. Little by little the desire came to me to invent my own myths, adopting the point of view of the primitive·mind. The only way I could devise for simulating that state was the old Surrealist method of abandoning conscious control and writing whatever words came from the pen. First, animal legends resulted from the experiments and then tales of animals disguised as "basic human" beings. One rainy Sunday I awoke late, put a thermos of coffee by my bedside, and began to write another of these myths. No one disturbed me, and I wrote on until I had finished it. I read it over, called it "The Scorpion," and decided that it could be shown to others. When *View* published it, I received compliments and went on inventing myths. The subject matter of the myths soon turned from "primitive" to contemporary, but the objectives and behavior of the protagonists remained the same as in the beast legends. It was through this unexpected little gate that I crept back into the land of fiction writing. Long ago I had decided that the world was too complex for me ever to be able to write fiction; since I failed to understand life, I would not be able to find points of reference which the hypothetical reader might have in common with me. When *Partisan Review* accepted "A Distant Episode," even though I had already sold two or three other tales to *Harper's Bazaar,* I was triumphant: it meant that I would be able to go on writing fiction.

After the hot weather arrived, Oliver decided that he wanted to visit Central America and asked me to go along. I got permission from the *Herald Tribune* to extend my vacation by a month. Jane had insisted on going to Vermont, where she said she felt at home. Oliver and I got on a plane for Havana and spent a week or so at the Nacional. Another plane took us to Varadero, whose white beach proved my undoing. I was careful to stay in the water during the entire time I was on the beach, in order to avoid getting burned. But I had not taken into account the mirrorlike reflection of the coral sand in that clear water. I spent two days in bed at the Nacional, lying on my belly. Twice a day the doctor came and dressed my back. When I was well, we went to Santiago to see Oriente Province, where Oliver conceived a strong desire to take a sloop across to Port-au-Prince, so much so that we spent a day finding and talking with the Haitian consul. Luckily, considering the state of the tiny boat we would have gone in, he gave up the idea, and we went back to Havana instead. Then we flew on to El Salvador, which was at that time, for the tourist at least, a delightful little tropical Switzerland. Ilopango Airport was like landing on the lip of a pitcher. The carcasses of the planes that had not made it were there, draped over the big trees just below us. The day we left the country we noticed a certain air of feverishness among the Salvadorans as we sat waiting for our flight announcement. Once we were in the air, the craft

headed due south. Since we were supposed to be going to Guatemala, I immediately began to worry. "Relax," said Oliver com-
fortably. "They know where they're going." We soon came to the
Pacific and saw the line of the shore recede behind us. On and on
we went, with nothing beneath us but the flat sea glittering in the
afternoon sun. The woman across the aisle had turned pale and
was sitting very straight. "Can't you see this isn't the way?" I
kept asking Oliver. When we had been out of sight of land for
fifteen minutes or more, the plane began to fly in a wide circle.
Slowly we banked and went around and around, until I was certain the pilot had gone mad. People rang for the stewardess, but
she did not come. They looked at one another and then quickly
looked away. Eventually the plane righted itself and set off toward the northwest. A while later the stewardess appeared from
the pilot's cabin and began to talk animatedly to a passenger in
the front. It took a long time for the news to creep back to us.
There had been a rebellion in El Salvador that afternoon, and
our pilot had been trying to spot the wreckage of a plane shot
down at sea by loyal elements of the army. That was the story as
it reached us, but who knows who shot down whom?

In Guatemala we traveled by car across the mountains to the
Alta Verapaz, that strange region with the lush landscapes that
make one think of the improbable pictures on certain kitchen
calendars. Then we went downward by car and by an absurd little railroad train that wound through the jungle to a riverboat
that bore us along between mudbanks covered with crocodiles,
out into Lake Izabal, and finally down the river into the Gulf of
Honduras. The mosquitoes were bad at Quiriguá when we went
to examine the stelae. Oliver had bought a good many pre-Co-
lombian figures. They were all taken away from him, however,
when we got to the airport to fly back to Havana.

Wifredo Lam was Cuba's foremost painter, and Oliver wanted
very much to meet him and see his studio. Since Lam had
painted the cover for the issue of *View* I had just edited, I telephoned him and introduced myself. Lam was an extraordinary
man of combined Chinese and African origin, thin as a pencil,
and looking at least twenty years younger than he actually was.

In his youth he had lived in Paris, where he lives now; I have not seen him since that year, but occasionally I get a greeting from him by word of mouth from a mutual friend.

I went to see the Cuban writer Lydia Cabrera, another *View* contributor, who, when I mentioned my desire to see some part of an African religious ritual, arranged for our presence at such a ceremony in Guanabacoa a few days later. She took us there in a gold-glassed Rolls brougham, scarcely a suitable vehicle in which to visit one of the most desperately poor quarters of Havana. The atmosphere that afternoon was vaguely familiar to me: it was rather like waiting in a Moroccan house for one's host to arrive. We sat for several hours in a small room looking out into an empty patio—empty, that is, save for a primitive altar at whose feet someone had placed an object with a face, a kind of fruit with cowrie shells pushed into it. When it got late, they brought in a goat, but it was clear that they were hoping we would leave so they could get to the business at hand. None of us wanted to watch the goat being sacrificed, and so we said good-bye.

I had been growing increasingly impatient with the frequency of disagreeable situations met in the course of traveling by air. Aside from the consideration of the time "saved" thereby, I can conceive of no valid reason for using a plane if there is some other way of getting to the place one is going. Between Havana and Miami we found ourselves in a very rough storm; several times the plane plummeted downward like an elevator whose cables have been cut. I made my customary vow to remain henceforth on the ground, a vow not so easily kept in an age when most people are willing to sacrifice their physical well-being for an abstraction like speed. My feeling is that humanity invented the concepts of time and speed in order to reinforce its basic delusion that the experience of life can be considered from a quantitative viewpoint.

Back in New York I read the headlines about Hiroshima and Nagasaki, felt bitter about being a national of a country with a government of so little moral intelligence, and began to wonder how many years it would be before the United States was subjected to the same kind of treatment at the hands of Asians. Per-

haps it is with this in mind that we have been busy ever since re-
ducing the number of that particular people.

Schuyler Watts, who had directed the dramatic action in *The
Wind Remains,* had now translated Giraudoux's *Ondine* and, although he had no producer in view, came to me to commission a
score for it. I took on the work, and rented a Hammond Novachord, somewhat bigger than a Hammond organ. The principal
difference between the two instruments was the presence in the
Novachord of a sostenuto which caused tones to continue to be
heard after the finger left the key. This made it possible to create
all kinds of watery sounds which, combined with other instruments, would give character to the score. The composition of the
music took several months; meanwhile, the Theatre Guild asked
me to write the music for Franz Werfel's *Jacobowsky and the Colonel.*
The score was to be full of nostalgia for prewar Paris. That all
went very smoothly, and I returned to *Ondine*; I completed it, but
the project never came to fruition.

There were not enough hours in each day to do all the work I
had to do. When the end of the year came, I resigned from my
post on the *Herald Tribune,* agreeing to continue writing regular
articles for the Sunday edition.

I worked on the translation of *Huis Clos,* wrote a score for and
went on the road with a play by Arthur Koestler, *Twilight Bar,*
which might have lived had it been properly directed and cast,
but which died, alas, in Baltimore. Soon I took on a play called
The Dancer, a melodramatized version of episodes in Nijinsky's
life. This was a really difficult task. The script required that the
music at times slip out of its function as background music and
take on the quality of concert music. These moments occurred
when Nijinsky, played by Anton Dolin, began compulsively to
dance. It was a new kind of problem to solve musically, and for
this reason working on it was a pleasure. The show was a flop,
nonetheless.

I was called in more or less at the same time to furnish music
for a play called *Land's End.* The only thing I recall about the
production is that it ran no time at all, indeed was dead before
the week was up.

That summer Jane and I lived in Southampton with John Uihlein. It was a large quiet house in front of the beach, so that we slept with the sound of breaking surf in our ears. Only in such serenity could I have found the theme I was looking for with which to open my Concerto. It came one morning after I had drawn a bath and shut the water off. The taps continued to drip, and the theme was in the succession of drops of water as they fell into the tub.

Somehow Richard Hepburn had got in touch with me again and suggested that I spend a weekend at Fenwick, on the Sound in Connecticut, where his parents had a house facing the water. It was here that I had my first contact with the nascent permissive society. There were several small children in the house. They were allowed to do as they pleased and at all times. At mealtimes anarchy and disruption were expected and, of course, proved inevitable. The more civilized the family, the more stoical its members become in the face of bedlam, I reflected. It made me uneasy to realize that I reacted so violently against the atmosphere of chaos created by the children, and I wondered if it was because I had none of my own. Katharine had none either, yet she seemed not to mind the racket. But of course, they were her nieces and nephews, and besides, she could escape it all by going off with her father in a boat for the day; the others stayed at home and coped.

In autumn we returned to town, where I continued to work on the Concerto for Two Pianos, Winds and Percussion, which Gold and Fizdale had commissioned from me. José Ferrer began to come around, bringing with him another Ferrer, young, thin and blond, whom he called Mel. Mel did not talk much, but Joe made up for his silences. He was planning a production of *Cyrano de Bergerac,* and he knew exactly what each scene was going to be like. After we had discussed the show for a fortnight or so, I started work on the score, using as one of the instruments a Novachord, since I still had the rented one in the studio. It was a carefully planned show and a good one, Joe directing and playing the lead role. It was also a great hit, and that was a pleasant change from the succession of failures with which I had been associated that year.

At this point someone came up with a fine job for me: I was to spend two years in South America, going from capital to capital cataloguing all the music in each national archive. This was a part of our good neighbor policy of the era. When the telephone call came from Washington, supposedly to confirm the appointment, an anonymous voice announced that the project was "out of the question" for me and that no more need be said. I understood that this was an unstated reference to my past political ties and let the matter drop.

John Huston came from the West Coast to direct the translation of *Huis Clos*. Oliver, who was producing the play in collaboration with Herman Levine, had seen *The Maltese Falcon* recently and was convinced that Huston was the man in whose hands he wanted to place the property. Since there were only three players in the cast, he thought it would be possible to use French actors in the parts; accordingly he hired Claude Dauphin and Annabella and looked around for another actress to play the role of Estelle. Somehow he hit on Ruth Ford for this part, and the show was cast. His idea of using Kiesler to design the set was a sound one, but the imported actors were always a problem. I gave Annabella daily lessons in English pronunciation; after a few weeks she arrived at a point where it was possible to understand what she was saying, but only if one concentrated. Dauphin was better, but even he occasionally went off the track, so that the words came out sounding as if they had been put through a scrambler. Sandwiched between the two overpowering French accents, Ruth Ford's all-too-recognizable Southern belle intonations were even more shocking in their bitchiness. I was worried about this, but opening night proved me wrong: the audience liked Ford. It was only subsequently that I discovered that she had performed partially under hypnosis. This was one of Huston's tricks. During World War II he had used hypnosis as psychiatric therapy to help cases of combat fatigue. The documentary film he made on five such case histories, *Let There Be Light*, was extraordinarily moving, but the Army forbade its distribution, so it was buried. This particular facet of John's personality intrigued me, and I kept talking about it with him, until finally he began to include hypnosis sessions in the rehearsals. What I found fascinating in these experiments was the way in which they revealed the extreme malleability of the human psyche. One afternoon Tyrone Power came to watch. John put on a good show for him. He had already got both Annabella and Ruth Ford to the point of being able to induce trance in them merely by snapping his fingers close to their faces. Annabella was wearing a shirt with the sleeves rolled up. John snapped his fingers and reached out with his arms to keep her steady on her feet. He brought out a metal pencil and lit a cigarette. Then he said to her: "This is going to tickle you. I'm going to touch you with the end of my pencil." He pushed his cigarette into the flesh of her upper arm hard enough to extinguish it. Annabella giggled and rubbed her arm a bit. Then John said: "Now I'm going to touch you with my cigarette." He gently pressed the pencil against her other arm, and she gave a cry of pain. When he had returned her to herself, he had us examine her arms: there was no mark on the one where he had put out his cigarette, but where he had touched her with the end of the pencil there was a very visible red spot.

This set me wondering. There seemed nothing extraordinary about the false burn, but the fact that the skin of the other arm had withstood the contact of fire and remained unscathed was much more difficult to understand and led inevitably to the question of degree. Up to what point can the flesh remain impervious?

I suggested that Oliver give a dinner party and have John demonstrate his prowess later in the evening. This worked so well that he had Ruth Ford back in Fulton, Kentucky, at the age of eight, remembering a near accident to an aged black man on the railroad track. On several occasions during the course of the evening John tried his power both with Jane and with me, but inevitably he began to say sternly: "You're resisting me." And although we were both eager to have the experience (or, according to him, imagined we were, when in actuality we feared it), neither of us was able to achieve it. John maintained that had our acceptance of the idea been total, the thing would have proved easy. Very likely he was right; in my mind hypnosis involves a dubious action: the absolute relinquishing of power to another. It seems only natural that the psychic organism should furnish automatic protection against such possibilities.

There were difficulties connected with *Huis Clos*. John wanted to particularize the references made to his past life by the male character upon his arrival in hell; by substituting political for metaphysical motivations he hoped to enliven the argument for the American public, which he considered generally incapable of appreciating the play's existentialist basis. I was against any changes being made in the script, but my secondary status in the venture was made clear to me at a succession of meetings called for the purpose of making a series of just such textual alterations with an eye to "Americanizing" the material. At one of these, John's father (then usually referred to in the press as "veteran actor Walter Huston") came up with a well-intentioned but fatal suggestion, which was to divide the play into two acts and separate them by an intermission. I objected that during the entr'acte we would lose most of the momentum which had been building until then; there could be no intervals in the hell Sartre had created. But my voice was lost in the hubbub of highball clinking and free advice. Then John decided that for the play to make sense to New Yorkers the hero must be a collaborationist. Once that door had been opened, anything could sneak in, and many things did. In this fashion the deeper meaning of the play was obscured. Sartre got wind of what was afoot and sent me a cable of protest from Paris. John's opinion, however, was that Sartre was surrounded by busybodies who hoped to sabotage the American production. He believed that he was clarifying the play rather than weakening it. Very likely the drama was made more immediately interesting to a great portion of the New York public by being presented in this way, but since it was done by injecting political concepts into a primarily philosophical argument, it seemed not only unethical but self-defeating. However, I had agreed to "adapt" *Huis Clos* to the satisfaction of the producers. Since Huston had consented to take on the show only if he received a high percentage of the gross, he was thus master of the entire undertaking. The intermission was definitively incorporated into the production, and dress rehearsals included a suggestion of hellfire and fumes upstage center when the door of the hell-cell opened, a dramatic addition, but one of which Sartre would very likely have taken a dim view. What a blessing, I thought, that he was not in New York! Although, had he been there, he might have found a way to protect his work from the ideological distortions that besieged it. These were not numerous or striking, but even one of them could conceivably suffice to deform a *pièce à thèse* as tightly woven as *Huis Clos*. The blame for these small mutilations devolved upon me; it was officially my adaptation, and my name was signed to it.

The finding of a title was a lengthy process. John, Oliver, and I had drawn up lists with hundreds of plausible titles raked from the Bible, Dante, Milton, Poe, and Eliot, but none seemed to have the conciseness of *Huis Clos*. Finally, as we were about to choose one of the less offensive literary titles, the subway gave me the right words, rude but effective. When you try to get out of the subway by inadvertently using an "in" turnstile, you are given a physical jolt; simultaneously you see in front of your eyes the printed words NO EXIT. I thought about it as a title; apart from its sound and appearance, which I liked, it had an applicability to the play as a whole which I thought valid. I tried it on John Huston 'and got a positive reaction. We decided that would be the play's title. Stuart Gilbert was preparing a literary translation of the play for Knopf, my rights being limited to the performing script. I should have expected them to invent their own title, but they used mine. Not only that: Blanche Knopf and Justin O'Brien came to rehearsals and sat in the back making copious notes as they watched. This did not bother either John or Oliver.

As rehearsals progressed, I grew nervous. Each short scene was worked and reworked meticulously to a state of perfection, only to be abandoned for the next short scene, which was treated with the same degree of detail and intensity until it too was perfect. If we had been filming, so that the separate scenes could have been frozen and fixed while they were in all their excellence, we would have had a masterpiece. But the actors, being human, found it impossible to remember the plethora of details they had learned in rehearsal, and in a run-through one was aware of definite breaks between the scenes, as though each new scene were being shot from a slightly different camera angle. With so much against the production, it is surprising that it ran as long as it did and that it received the Drama Critics' Award for the best foreign play of the year.

In 1940 after the opening of *Twelfth Night* at the Schubert in New Haven, Thornton Wilder had taken the trouble of going into the basement of the theater to look for me. When he found me, he complimented me warmly on the score. Now, at the opening of *No Exit*, he took quite as many pains to come and let me know how unsatisfactory he considered my adaptation to be. He was right; it was an undistinguished translation. But he went further and gave me counsel. "You stick to your music and you'll be better off," he told me.

In her several years of cooking Jane had become an expert in the preparation of certain festive dishes, one of which was *canard à l'orange*. This information leaked to Annabella; Jane found herself delegated by Oliver to provide the dish for a dinner party. Like most specialists, she felt that her reputation was at stake and applied herself to her work with great intensity all afternoon, seeking frequent aid from the bottle of scotch she had on the sink beside her. At dinnertime Annabella and Claude Dauphin arrived with others and were given drinks. Jane stayed on in the kitchen. Eventually Oliver thought it was time to eat, and went out to tell the cook, who said that the ducks were ready and that Mrs. Bowles had gone to bed. We ate dinner to sounds of praise: *"Ah, mais ce canard est divin!" "Superbe!" "Exquis!"* But Jane did not hear them.

It was the same winter that I went to a dinner party where I found myself the only man at a table of many women. Among them I remember with certainty only three: Esther Strachey Arthur, Elsa Schiaparelli, and Janet Flanner. I was not supposed to be there at all, having been included only at Jane's insistence. It was a very good dinner, and it lasted for a long time, what with the wines and the conversation. Suddenly one of the ladies, adopting her most jovial manner, said: "Now, little Mrs. Bowles, suppose you give us *your* ideas on the world situation." Jane put down her napkin and murmured: "Excuse me a moment." Then she left the room. We waited for her to come back, but there was no sign of her. After a while I went to see what was wrong. I found her asleep; she had gone into another room and curled up on the divan. "What else could I do?" she demanded when I ridiculed her later.

Latouche and Duke Ellington, perhaps inspired by the success of *Cabin in the Sky* (which Latouche and Vernon Duke had done seven years earlier and which also combined a black cast with the subject of poverty), had written a musical which they called *Beggars' Holiday,* and we went up to Hartford to see the opening. After the show we found ourselves in a bar. Latouche was there, sitting with Libby Holman. We talked a long time with her. Subsequently we often went with him to spend weekends in her big house in the middle of the woods. She was great fun to be with and had a private glamor all her own. And life in her house was wonderful.

I now took on a job translating the Giraudoux play *La Folle de Chaillot* for two young producers who had obtained the property. They wanted the finished adaptation within six weeks; this seemed to require a complete break in routine and the adopting of a new, intensive schedule. Accordingly, I flew down to Jamaica in order to concentrate on the work at hand. Montego Bay was already beginning to attract tourists. After two or three days there I moved to Ocho Rios, where I spent most of the time. The hotel was empty save for one or two other people. I got the work done on schedule and returned to New York. The night of my arrival I saw my ballet *Pastorela* for the first time and was favorably impressed. The same program presented Stravinsky's animal cantata *Le Renard,* with magnificent costumes by Esteban Francés.

Another play, *On Whitman Avenue,* needed a short score, and I provided it. Then, sent by Latouche, a filmmaker from Germany, Hans Richter, got in touch with me. I remembered having seen a film of his twenty years earlier at the Fifth Avenue Playhouse, and mentioned it to him; I think it surprised him. Richter was now finishing a picture in collaboration with Max Ernst, Marcel Duchamp, Man Ray, and Calder. He was in need of several separate scores, and he came to John Cage, David Diamond, and me in order to get them. I had already written a score for a short film on the collages of Ernst's *Une Semaine de Bonté*; Ernst himself chose the same basic material for his section of this new film, *Desire*. The most germinal of his works, *Une Semaine de Bonté*, was a series of volumes of collages, each volume devoted to aspects of a different element. *Desire* was suggested by certain pictures in the book bearing the title *L'Eau*. I left specific sequences free for Max to treat as cadenzas, where he used the score going backward, with choral screams and whisperings—not at all standard procedure in 1947. The other film, by Calder, was given over wholly to mobiles whirling and floating and was called *Ballet*.

At one point Oliver, who had just become a director of the Ballet Theatre, thought that Jerry Robbins and I ought to collaborate on a ballet. Jerry was elaborating one in his mind; it was to be called *Interplay*. He would come down to Tenth Street in the afternoons and talk about it. He worked in a very different way from the choreographers with whom I had previously collaborated. To me everything he said had the air of being supremely subjective, almost to the point of being hermetic. For Jerry it was somehow connected with the psychoanalysis he was undergoing at the time. We never managed to get anything decided during our discussions, and finally we gave up the project. Later Morton Gould wrote the score.

From various points of view this period on Tenth Street might have been considered a full and productive, and thus satisfying, existence. It is true that I "produced" during those years, but in such a way that I always seemed to find myself doing what someone else wanted done. I furnished music which would embellish or interpret the ideas of others; this is taken for granted, of course, in the writing of functional music. The obvious remedy was to seek refuge in the writing of one's own music. I did; the works were two commissions from Gold and Fizdale. It was great fun composing them and, of course, even more listening to them when they were played. But when I had finished them, I did not go on working on my own music. On the contrary, I accepted more theatrical commissions and consequently never attained the state of freedom I sought. To my way of thinking I was only marking time. The malign effects of writing too much *Gebrauchs-*

musik gradually became apparent during the spring. I was made aware of a slowly increasing desire to step outside the dance in which inadvertently I had become involved. I would go on taking part in it for an indefinite period unless I cut the thread that held me. Happily, daydreaming on the subject of escape was not given the opportunity of growing into an *idée fixe;* the decision was made for me.

One balmy night in May, asleep in my quiet bedroom, I had a dream. There was nothing extraordinary about that; I always dreamed, and sometimes I awoke and wrote the dreams down immediately without even turning on the light. This dream was distinctive because although short and with no anecdotal content beyond that of a changing succession of streets, after I awoke, it had left its essence with me in a state of enameled precision: a residue of ineffable sweetness and calm. In the late afternoon sunlight I walked slowly through complex and tunneled streets. As I reviewed it, lying there, sorry to have left the place behind, I realized with a jolt that the magic city really existed. It was Tangier. My heart accelerated, and memories of other courtyards and stairways flooded in, still fresh from sixteen years before. For the Tangier in which I had wandered had been the Tangier of 1931.

The town was still present the following morning, fresh and invigorating to recall, and vivid memory of it persisted day after day, along with the inexplicable sensation of serene happiness which, being of the dream's very essence, inevitably accompanied it. It did not take me long to come to the conclusion that Tangier must be the place I wanted to be more than anywhere else. I began to consider the possibility of spending the summer there.

About this time I had the idea of putting all my stories together and showing them around to likely people, in the hope of eventually getting them published in a volume. Dial Press asked me to visit their offices, not, of course, to tell me that they were going to bring out such a book, but to advise me that no publisher would buy a collection of short stories by someone who had not previously published a novel. According to them, an agent was essential; they offered to telephone then and there to make an appointment with one for me. The agent in question was

Helen Strauss of the William Morris Agency. A week or ten days after she and I had had lunch together, at which point I had given her my stories, she called me to say that Doubleday had offered an advance on a novel. Once I had signed the contract I began to make plans for my trip to Tangier. North Africa had long since acquired a legendary aura for me; the fact that I now had decided to go back there made the place more actual and revived hundreds of small forgotten scenes which welled up into my consciousness of their own accord. I got on a Fifth Avenue bus one day to go uptown. By the time we had arrived at Madison Square I knew what would be in the novel and what I would call it. Before the First World War there had been a popular song called "Down Among the Sheltering Palms"; a record of it was at the Boat House in Glenora, and upon my arrival there each summer from the age of four onward, I had sought it out and played it before any of the others. It was not the banal melody which fascinated me, but the strange word "sheltering." What did the palm trees shelter people from, and how sure could they be of such protection? "Oh, Honey, wait for me/Out where the sun goes down about eight. . . ."

The book was going to take place in the Sahara, where there was only the sky, and so it would be *The Sheltering Sky*. This time at least I did not have to lie awake nights searching for the right title. In essence the tale would be similar to "A Distant Episode," the short story I had just published in *Partisan Review,* and it would write itself, I felt certain, once I had established the characters and spilled them out onto the North African scene. By the time I got up into midtown I had made all the most important decisions about the novel. Then I resolved to give it no more thought until I started the actual writing.

Gordon Sager had just published a novel about our days in Taxco, called *Run Sheep Run.* He was disappointed in the reviews and longed to go somewhere far away and get on with another book. Thus it was that when I decided to sail for Casablanca on the SS *Ferncape,* Gordon also took passage, thinking that he might work in Morocco or, failing that, continue to Italy. The morning of the day we were to leave, Gordon came to Tenth Street early, several hours before we needed to be aboard. In view of the amount of luggage I was taking along, I called the Cadillac rental agency and asked for a car to drive us to South Brooklyn. We had lunch, and I began to collect my things. Soon I realized that my passport was seriously missing. It had been lying on a bookcase shelf earlier that morning. Now it was nowhere to be seen. We searched feverishly; the car was due to arrive in a half hour. Gordon was for going through all my valises; he thought it likely that at some point I had unthinkingly slipped it inside one of them. We continued to look for it everywhere. Just before the car came, I unearthed it, buried beneath a neat pile of Jane's underwear in the back of a bureau drawer. It was a mystery; Jane earnestly claimed to know nothing about it. Yet no one else had come into the apartment. We looked at her accusingly. She laughed. "You *know* I don't want you to go," she said. "So I must have."

I merely left the apartment, as though I were going away for the weekend (a very poor idea, as things turned out) and with far too much luggage boarded the ship. The stateroom was big, and the sea was calm all the way across. During the voyage I wrote a long story about a hedonist; it had been vaguely trying to get born for six months, ever since my visit to Jamaica. I finished it the day before we got to Casablanca and called it "Pages from Cold Point." Then we landed, and Morocco took over.

XIV

After the humid summer air of the Atlantic that we had been breathing aboard the *Ferncape,* the dry, scented winds of inland Morocco were exhilarating. I lived in a state of perpetual excitement. It was hot, and we walked for miles every day, in all the quarters of Fez. It was more than enough just to be present in the landscape, smelling the fig trees, the cedar wood and the mint beds, and hearing the murmur of the fast-running water. Fez was still in its golden age; it seemed scarcely to have changed since I had last seen it long before the war. Traffic sounds were limited to the jingling of bells on the horses that drew the carriages back and forth between Bab Bou Jeloud and the Mellah. Outside the walls at Bab el Hadid, where my room looked across the valley of the Oued el Zitoun, there were shady paths where the wind rattled the high canebrake. The food was good, and I began to write my novel.

Gordon found Fez overwhelming and thus depressing, and went on to Marrakech to join a friend. After he left I met a highly implausible couple, a mother and son whose behavior was strange enough to interest me. In an unlikely series of coincidences spread over a period of two or three months, we found ourselves meeting in hotel lobbies, first in Fez, then up in Tangier, after that in Algeciras, and finally in Córdoba, after which they went on their way. By this time they were firmly implanted in the narrative of my book as subsidiary characters. Their inclusion now seems unfortunate, not because I used them, but because they turned out to be caricatures. I had already chosen my method regarding the selection of descriptive detail. The structure and character of the landscape would be supplied by imagination (that is, by memory). I would reinforce each such scene with details reported from life during the day of writing, regardless of whether the resulting juxtaposition was apposite or not. I never knew what I was going to write on the following day because I had not yet lived through the day.

After the disappearance in Córdoba of the mother and son, I went up to Ronda to stay in one of my favorite hotels of the prewar days, the Victoria, on its precipice high above the surrounding mountains and valleys. Here I worked intensively; the silent nights and the sweet mountain air provided energy.

Back in Tangier I lived first in one hotel and then in another, until finally I found El Farhar on the Mountain, directly opposite the place where Aaron Copland and I had lived. Here I was able to have a small two-room cottage with a fireplace and an exceptionally beautiful view. I bought an Amazon parrot that giggled and was once more made aware of the great difference that exists between an empty room and one with a parrot in it. I wrote Jane and told her that Morocco was still all that it had been and that she must come as soon as possible.

The novel moved ahead; I reached the scene of my hero's death by typhoid. The Moroccans were constantly talking about *majoun,* which might otherwise be described as cannabis jam. Often I had accepted a pipe of kif when it was passed to me, but since I had never inhaled the smoke, I had not received the effect and still thought of kif as a bad-tasting sort of tobacco. Thus the idea of *majoun* interested me, particularly after listening to certain vivid accounts of the wonders seen under its influence. I got the address of a house in the Calle Ibn Khaldoun where you could go and knock on the door and hand in your money and a few minutes later would be given a small package. It all worked as it was supposed to; for ten pesetas I bought a big bar of it. It was the cheapest kind and therefore tasted like very old and dusty fudge from which all flavor had long since departed. However, this in no way diminished its power. I returned to the cottage on the cliff and then climbed much farther up the mountain to lie in the sun atop a slab of rock high above the strait, sometimes lifting my head to look across at the distant line of the sierra in Spain. The effect came upon me suddenly, and I lay absolutely still, feeling myself being lifted, rising to meet the sun. For a long time I did not open my eyes. Then I felt that I had risen so far above the rock that I was afraid to open them. In another hour my mind was behaving in a fashion I should never have imagined possible. I wanted to get off the boulders, down the mountainside, and back home as fast as I could. When I returned to the Farhar, the sun was low. I could see its pink light fading on the villas that edged the cliffs across the valley. There were cypresses outside the cottage; they stood unprotected, high above the sea, directly in the blast of the *cherqi*, which roared through them with a sound louder than that of the waves against the rocks. I lighted a fire in the fireplace, gave a piece of banana to the parrot, and made a pot of tea. Then in the fading twilight I lay on my bed and stared into the fireplace at the flames. For a long time I did not move. Among many things, I was trying to imagine the death of my protagonist. Later that night I noted a good many details, and the next day wrote out much of the scene. Very consciously I had always avoided writing about death because I saw it as a difficult subject to treat with anything approaching the proper style; it seemed reasonable, therefore, to hand the job over to the subconscious. It is certain that the *majoun* provided a solution totally unlike whatever I should have found without it.

Tangier was windblown and blue. I wandered for days in the upper Medina and the Casbah until I knew every street and alley. Soon I began to ask about seeing empty houses. They were all absurdly cheap, the dozen or so I examined, ranging from $2,000 for big ones with covered courtyards down to $250 for a two-room Spanish-style cottage with orchard. I wired Oliver Smith inquiring if he wanted to share in the buying of a Tangier house. He agreed, and I chose one with what I considered the finest view of all, near the Place Amrah. Getting possession of the keys to the house was easy, but the legalization of the deed took the better part of the next two years to accomplish. Since I thought it unwise to make additions and install plumbing until the title was clear, it was not until 1950 that it was possible to move into it. But at least I had made the purchase now and could go off happy to Fez.

There I made inquiries about *majoun* and was directed to a barbershop behind the Zaouia of Moulay Idriss where there were always four or five tins of it in a drawer along with the clippers. I felt that I had come upon a fantastic secret: to change worlds, I had only to spread a bit of jam on a biscuit and eat it. I began a series of experiments with the still-unfamiliar substance in order to determine my own set of optimum conditions regarding the quantity to be ingested, the time of day for the dose, the accompanying diet, and the general physical and psychological ambiances most conducive to pleasure during the experience. Large quantities of hot tea were essential. Twilight was the best hour for taking the dose; the effect came on slowly after an hour and a half or even two hours had passed, preferably at the moment of sitting down to dinner. A clear soup followed by a small steak and salad seemed to interfere the least with the *majoun*'s swift circulation. It was imperative to be unmitigatedly content with all the facets of existence beforehand. The most minimal preoccupation, the merest speck of cloud on the emotional horizon, had a way of italicizing itself during the alteration of consciousness and assuming gigantic proportions, thus completely ruining the inner journey. It is a delicate operation, the taking of *majoun*. Since its success or failure can be measured only in purely subjective terms, it is also a supremely egotistical pastime. Above all, there must be no interruptions, no surprises; everything must come about according to the timetable furnished by the substance itself.

Several months earlier, during the summer, I had come to know M. Abdessalem Ktiri, an unusually pleasant Fassi gentleman with a great number of sons and daughters. At M. Ktiri's I now met several young men, all natives of Fez, who in another decade would be occupying top posts in the Moroccan government. At the moment they were attending the College Moulay Idriss. I also met Ahmed Yacoubi, the future painter. M. Ktiri's enormous house lent itself to long and rather formal lunch and dinner parties which were always a delight. During the years that I frequented the place I ate in at least eight different rooms and courtyards. Within the house the family lived like nomads, continually shifting the furniture from one region to another and always finding the present situation the most agreeable. Yet they never traveled. Once M. Ktiri announced apologetically that the house was in great disorder because his wife had just gone away for two weeks. She was visiting at her sister's near Bab Fteuh, at the other end of the Medina. What with the packing and the difficulty of transporting her and all her luggage so far away (a distance of at least two miles) the family had not been able to restore order to the house. In the end Madame Ktiri stayed almost a month and returned from her trip completely exhausted.

The arrival of winter in Fez set me thinking of the Sahara, where even though it might be cold, at least the sky would be clear. The parrot had a stout brass cage which I wound with two woolen cummerbunds for warmth; without these the bird undoubtedly would have died. I took the train to Oujda and spent several days there gathering information.

Between Oujda and Colomb-Béchar the old narrow-gauge railway passed over the high plateaus. The morning I boarded the train a blizzard was in progress; all day long the snow sifted up from underneath into the rickety wooden coach where I sat, the only first-class passenger on the train. At one stop I explored the other class, separated from my lone coach by a string of freight cars. The coaches were labeled *IVe Classe* and had benches running their length; in one of them a group of Moroccans had built a blazing fire on the floor and were crouching around it, warming their hands. Naturally the floor began to burn, and it was not long before the train stopped so that the conductor and the fireman could extinguish the flames, which they did with a great deal of shouting at the natives. The train had left at half past six in the morning. At half past nine in the evening it pulled into Colomb-Béchar. Halfway, during a long halt in a frozen village deep in snow, a French employee on the line had told me that the Algerian customs men carried out their inspection aboard the train upon arrival. When we finally rattled to a stop at the terminal station, I stayed in my seat, still sitting on my feet for warmth, and merely looked out into the darkness. A few figures in burnouses moved in the distance, some of them carrying lanterns. No one came to examine either my passport or my luggage, and so after a while I handed all my valises out the window to a man who offered to be a porter. By the time I had carried the parrot out to the platform there were seven such porters; each seized a bag and balanced it on his head, and we set off through the dark, skirting vast puddles where the snow had fallen and melted during the day.

In the course of the week the weather cleared, and I continued by produce truck to Taghit, probably the most intensely poetic spot I had ever seen. The tiny hotel atop the rocks was run in conjunction with the military fort nearby. There was a solitary old servant who did everything; fortunately he had only one other guest besides me, an elderly Swiss lady who taught school in Zurich and spent her winters in the Sahara. She and I got on perfectly and took long walks together in the valley to the south. What made Taghit so special was its situation, overlooking on one side the rocky hammada with its incised, meandering river valley bristling with palm trees, and on the other side the very high *erg* of orange-gold sand, its base only a five-minute walk from the hotel.

On a short trip like this, limited to six or seven weeks, I could do no more than reconnoiter, with an eye to later and more leisurely visits. I wanted to go as far south as possible on the Route de Gao, knowing that at some point I should be stopped, and would have to turn north again. I went on to Béni-Abbès, still confused by many with Sidi-bel-Abbès, the erstwhile French Foreign Legion headquarters. Although there was no Legion post anywhere in this area, the Saharan forts looked like the sets for every film ever made about the *Légion Étrangère*. The fort dominated the countryside, with the recently constructed part of the town nestling at its feet. The high dunes were never very far away (although nowhere so dramatically close as at Taghit). In the opposite direction and lower down would be the stain of green that was the oasis. The mud villages were invisible from a distance; I would come upon them suddenly as I roamed through the palm groves, sometimes having to go through the long dark tunnels of their streets in order to continue my walk. In Béni-

Abbès there was a kind of belvedere across from the hotel, below the fort but looking out onto many miles of desert. On this spot the French had built an open pavilion for public worship. At sunset a great crowd of turbanned men always gathered here, each carrying his prayer mat; they salaamed in unison facing the empty hammada.

Timimoun was Sudanese in aspect and thus spectacular. I thought the Hôtel Transatlantique a work of art and decided to settle in for a while. The food was sketchy, but I had my first camel steak there. It was an even better night when they served gazelle. Each morning I lay in bed studying the African designs incised in the mud walls of my room and continued to write the novel.

In every Saharan town I made a point of going to pay my respects to both the military and the religious, those two institutions necessary for the installation and maintenance of a colonial regime. French commanding officers lived extremely well; often they were pleased to have an extra head at dinner. The captain here was a good raconteur. After a meal one evening he told a tale which particularly struck my imagination. The previous year three Moslem merchants had been murdered on their way south across the desert. The killer had appropriated their caravan and gone on with it to the murdered men's destination, where their colleagues had recognized the merchandise. They reported their suspicions to the French military authorities, who surprisingly enough gave them carte blanche in the matter. Accordingly, they carried the man far out into the desert and buried him up to his neck in the sand; then they left him to die. The vaguely disturbing story remained with me, flopping around in my head, but it was a year before it was ready to be written.

I continued to Adrar. To have gone on to Reggan would have required a special permit and the posting of a rather high bond, not returnable for some time. After a week I started north again, this time by plane. There were only the pilot and I. Strapped into the co-pilot's seat at his side, I was obliged to pretend enjoyment when he engaged in a mock dive-bombing of the populace in the marketplace and missed the Adrar minaret by only a few feet. Since we were flying blind, we had to land when the sun went down. Early the next morning we were aloft again. We reached Algiers that day. At the Hotel St.-Georges there was a message from Jane saying that she had arrived in Tangier and was waiting for me.

To compensate for my four years of familiarity with Morocco, Jane had spent the autumn in Paris attending the École de Langues Orientales, with the result that on her arrival in Tangier she already had a basic understanding of Arabic word formation and grammar. To augment this, immediately after getting here, she had decided to continue her study under a Moroccan tutor. Even though she had gone to Marrakech during this period, her powers of absorption were so considerable that by the time we were reunited, less than two months after she had arrived in Morocco, she was able to speak as well as I. But because my vocabulary was larger and I was more fluent, she imagined that I was more proficient than she. A confusing thing about Moghrebi Arabic is the fact that it changes with the region; thus the word used in Tangier is often not the word used in Fez (and much less Marrakech). Jane soon opted for the Tangier dialect, whereas I felt more at home with the vocabulary and pronunciation of Fez. She would ridicule me each time I opened my mouth to use it. This little game went on between us for many years, until eventually I capitulated and learned how to use the Tangier speech, absurd though I considered it. We had the same divergencies in our appreciation of Morocco itself. She loved the hybrid, seedy quality of Tangier (for the city was heavily flavored with Spanish detail, even the Medina, where several thousand Spaniards lived side by side with the Moroccans). I preferred the medieval formality of Fez, even in its state of decay. My taste for Fez was a touristic one, but Tangier fascinated Jane because that was where she had Moslem friends to whose houses she could go. She loved to be with Moroccans, principally, she claimed, because of their sense of humor. Like Jews, they spent their lives with their families, distrusting, ridiculing, and reviling one another, and yet managed to laugh together betweentimes.

For the first few years in Morocco our lives were nomadic. Scarcely a week passed that we did not change location. We traveled back and forth between Tangier and Fez, between Rabat and Marrakech, getting our joint reaction to cities, inhabitants, and restaurants. (I had my personal preferences, which did not inevitably coincide with the joint reaction by any means.) Morocco can still be a very disturbing country to explore for the first time. I had told Jane about the cults whose rituals I had witnessed in the early days, but apparently my descriptions were not sufficiently vivid to prepare her for the shock she got at the very beginning of her stay when she visited Moulay Brahim. With her friend Jody she had arrived in Tangier before me, while I was still deep in the Sahara. The two went south to Marrakech. At that time the Mamounia was still an excellent hotel. Happily the weather was clear; from their balcony they could see the Atlas snow glistening. Then someone suggested Moulay Brahim. It was in the mountains—that much they understood—but from their informant they got the impression that they would be going to a country fair. There would be music and dancing. They asked the hotel to put them up a picnic lunch, packed some wine and whiskey into a hired car along with the food, and instructed the driver to go to the *amara* of Moulay Brahim. One of the things no one had told them was that an *amara* is a gathering of pilgrims on a spot in some way connected with a specific local saint, often the site of his tomb. Another thing was that this particular *amara* took place a good deal higher up than any vehicle could travel. The car had to stay down in the valley, the driver explained, and he would stay with it. The two ladies could climb all the way up there if they wanted, but he was going to remain with his car.

It was a really steep climb, Jane said, through scrub forest and around huge boulders. After a half hour they began to hear sounds up ahead and assumed that they were about to arrive at the fair. A minute later some thirty men were suddenly running full tilt down the mountain toward them, their eyes staring like marbles, their mouths wide, screaming, their faces and garments red and wet with blood. "Oh, my Gawd!" said Jody. Jane said nothing at all, merely stood waiting for the onslaught. The men ran by, still screaming, and disappeared down the mountainside. After resting for a while on a rock beside the path, the picnickers decided to start back to the car rather than continue upward. The men were Aissaoua who had just gone through the ceremony of eating a live bull; in their altered psychic state they probably did not even see the two Nazarene women cowering there among the boulders.

Poor Jane also had a traumatic experience the first and only time she tried eating *majoun*. It was in the Palais Jamai in Fez. Ahmed Yacoubi's mother, a magnificent cook, had prepared a batch of the stuff in candy form for us that day, and Ahmed brought it around during the evening after dinner. I was the only European present who had had any experience with the substance. Accordingly I issued repeated warnings to Jane, Jody, and Edwin Denby on the importance of eating only a small amount at first and then waiting until the effects had been produced before trying more. We drank tea, which I made several times, and played the phonograph while we watched Ahmed draw pictures on the hotel stationery. "You should go into the Ville Nouvelle tomorrow and get him some decent paper and India ink," Jane told me. At one point I heard her remark: "Ah, this stuff is nothing." I turned and saw her finishing off a further large piece of *majoun*. "It has no effect," she explained. I was angry. "But I told you, the effect is delayed. Now you've taken too much."

She was contemptuous. The evening wore on. Jane got sleepy, and I began to be convinced that she was right. I went into my room and slept. The next morning she was in a highly emotional state. She had not yet been able to fall asleep, she claimed, and her night had been ten nights long and totally horrible. First she had begun to worry that something was happening to me; then as the drug came on more powerfully, she had become convinced that I was about to steal in and murder her. Finally she had noticed her hands and had not understood what they were. When she saw her fingers move, she became paralyzed with terror. Illogically enough, from that day on she remained an implacable enemy of all forms of cannabis. The fact that her experience had been due solely to an overdose seemed to her beside the point. "Anything that can do awful things like that is dangerous," she contended.

In the spring we returned to Fez and stayed at the Belvedere. I was completing *The Sheltering Sky,* and Jane was deep into her

novella *Camp Cataract*. At the break of day we would have breakfast in bed in Jane's room. Then I would go into my own room,
leaving the door open so that we could communicate if we
wanted. At one point she had a terrible time with a bridge she
was trying to build over a gorge. She would call out: "Bupple!
What's a cantilever, exactly?" or "Can you say a bridge has but-
tresses?" I, immersed in the writing of my final chapters, would
answer anything that occurred to me, without coming out of my
voluntary state of obsession. She would be quiet for a while, and
then call out again. The rushing of the stream directly beneath
our windows covered all but the most penetrating sounds; com-
munications had to be fairly important to make it worthwhile
shouting them. After three or four mornings I became aware that
something was wrong: she was still at the bridge. I got up and
went into her room. We talked for a while about the problem,
and I confessed my mystification. "Why do you have to *construct*
the damned thing?" I demanded. "Why can't you just say it was
there and let it go at that?" She shook her head. "If I don't know
how it was built, I can't see it."

This struck me as incredible. It never had occurred to me that
such considerations could enter into the act of writing. Perhaps
for the first time I had an inkling of what Jane meant when she
remarked, as she often did, that writing was "so *hard*."

About this time Libby Holman asked her sixteen-year-old son
Christopher Reynolds what he would like to do during the summer vacation. His answer: "I want to go to Africa with Paul
Bowles and have my tongue cut out." Libby arrived with him in
July, a month or so after Oliver Smith had come. We made a fine
long trip through the mountains and the desert. With her Mexican ordeal of a decade earlier still fresh in her mind, Jane insisted on staying behind in Tangier. We had said that we were
going to cross the High Atlas, and that was all she needed to
hear.

The heat was often painful, and we spent our days jealously
watching one another take sips of whatever liquid happened to
be in the car. It was the month of Ramadan, so the driver could
not touch water until sunset. At that moment, wherever we happened to be, in the middle of a mud village or at the edge of a

precipice, he would bring the car to a halt and pull out his thermos of water and one hard-boiled egg. After a few minutes of respectful silence on our parts while he refreshed himself, he would
start up again, and we could resume our chatter.

Libby had recently read García Lorca's play *Yerma*. She
thought it would make a good singing and acting vehicle for her
and suggested that I try writing a score. We discussed it walking
in oases, lying on the beach, driving through the infernal landscapes of the Anti-Atlas, and in a score of hotel rooms throughout
Morocco. I decided that if I were to do it, I should have to make
my own translation first, and she agreed to that.

When the others had left and Jane and I were back in Fez, I
received a wire from Tennessee asking me if I could return to
New York to provide a score for *Summer and Smoke,* scheduled for
the autumn. I had finished *The Sheltering Sky* and sent it off to
Doubleday. So I decided to accept the work. Leaving Jane at the
Hôtel Villa de France in Tangier, I took passage for New York.
Libby generously gave me her town house on Sixty-first Street to
live in, a gesture which for me made all the difference between a
pleasurable sojourn and a grim one.

While I was writing the score, Gore Vidal would come by
nearly every day at lunchtime, and we would go out to eat. Gore
had just played a practical joke on Tennessee and Truman Capote which he recounted to me in dialect, as it were. He had
called Tennessee on the telephone and, being a stupendous
mimic, had made himself into Truman for the occasion. Then,
complete with snigger, he induced Tennessee to make uncomplimentary remarks about Gore's writing. They gossiped awhile
and hung up. A few days later Gore saw Tennessee and during
their conversation made oblique but unmistakable allusions to
some of Tennessee's remarks made over the wire. To Tennessee it
seemed quite obvious that Truman had run to Gore and maliciously repeated the telephone conversation. As a result, he was
angry with Truman, which had been the object of the ploy.

There were no hitches in the production of *Summer and Smoke.*
We went on tour to Buffalo, Cleveland, and Detroit. For no apparent reason Gypsy Rose Lee came along with us. Each morning after breakfast I went to Tennessee's room, and we would

talk about the previous night's performance. Marlon Brando was trying to persuade him to lend his name to some worthy liberal organization's list of sponsors. Tennessee was a bit doubtful, only because his agent, Audrey Wood, had begged him not to align himself with any group which was even remotely political. Brando would telephone from New York, and I would answer and speak with him about the play, finally saying that Tennessee was in the bath and would call him later.

In early December Tennessee, Frank Merlo, and I boarded the *Saturnia* to go to Tangier. It was a particularly stormy month; the wind blew harder than usual and uprooted the eucalyptuses, and violent rains washed out the roads and bridges in the International Zone. Tennessee had brought a convertible with him. We stayed in Tangier only long enough to decide to go to Spain, which Jane thought would be fun. Málaga was rainy, too. We stayed at the old Miramar, where we sat in our enormous chilly rooms watching the rain over the Mediterranean. We came back to Tangier, where if possible the weather was wetter and wilder. Four days before Christmas we set out, minus Jane, for Fez. At Aqbaa el Khamra, the border of the Spanish Zone, there was a customs shack where two unkempt Spanish soldiers acted as *aduaneros*. We had a great amount of luggage packed into the car, all of which had to be brought in, opened, and examined beneath the uncertain flare of a carbide lamp. Since we were the only ones crossing the border, the soldiers took their time looking over our belongings, and above all Tennessee's. They must have assumed that none of us understood Spanish, for they began to appraise the objects, adding phrases like "That's for me," or "That wouldn't be bad," as they piled them on top of a big table suspiciously far from the counter where we were standing. "He's got three razors," said one, laying two of them on the table. "All those clothes for one man?" exclaimed the other. Deliberately they held up three suits on hangers and examined them as though they were on sale in a clothing store. "What are they doing?" demanded Tennessee. "Tell them I'm going straight through their zone, not even stopping." It was clear that these two were going to give us trouble no matter what we told them. I kept silent and watched the game continue. When they set Tennessee's typewriter on the table in the dark corner, he exploded. Seconded by Frank, he insisted that the two soldiers pack everything into the valises, and we drove back to Tangier, frustrated and indignant.

The next morning Tennessee telephoned to the American legation and complained at length of the treatment accorded us at Aqbaa el Khamra. The officials promised to call the Spanish consulate and inquire into the matter. Three days later we started out again. This time, even before they unhooked the chain that stretched across the road, they began to shout *"Diplomáticos!"* We sailed through without even having to show our passports. Not much later, when we got to the border of the French Zone, we had cause to regret our rapid passage through Aqbaa el Khamra, since the police looked in our passports for entry stamps and found none. We were thus in the country illegally and had to wait several hours while they tried to put through a call to the International Zone to check on our identities. Then we learned that we should have applied for gasoline coupons back at Aqbaa el Khamra. (Motor fuel was still in short supply as a result of the war.) From then on the trip was difficult: we went through the driving rain on futile side trips in search of individuals said to be willing to sell their extra coupons. Sliding mud and rocks were slowly covering parts of the road, and Tennessee began to complain volubly of "vibrations," a symptom he produced that year whenever things were not going smoothly. We got to Fez a little before midnight, just in time for the Christmas Eve *reveillon,* complete with *bûche de Noël,* at the Palais Jamai.

That winter Jane and I went to the Sahara for a month or so. She was wholly taken with it. "It's the least sinister place on earth," she said. In Taghit she wrote a story, "A Stick of Green Candy," and I typed it for her. When we stayed in Béni-Abbès there were two Swedish women living at the hotel; one had as a lover the French schoolteacher of the region; the other had nobody and was unhappy about it. Jane suggested that she look for a native, but the idea terrified her, and so she spent her time wandering up and down the main street of the village staring straight ahead.

In the spring I went to Paris. Gold and Fizdale were going to play my concerto at a Salle Pleyel recital, and I wanted to hear it again. The French instrumentalists found it too difficult for their undeveloped rhythmical sense, but they got through it. Aaron Copland was in Paris, and I saw him for the first time in many years. I remember Ned Rorem rushing here and there, always in a mist of alcohol, and a long conversation with James Baldwin one night in a bar on the Boulevard St.-Germain. There was also a day when Gore and I sat in the downstairs bar at the Pont-Royal, examining the literary habitués of the place. Sartre walked past our table on his way out and bowed as he mumbled: *"Bonjour."* I had been so certain that he would refuse to recognize me that when he spoke I was frozen and merely stared at him.

Truman Capote was back in Paris then, and as usual, Gore was pulling out all the stops in order to annoy him. When Truman announced that he was spending the summer in Tangier, Gore secretly decided to get there before him and continue his game. I went first; Gore arrived a few days later. "Come to the dock with me," he told me the afternoon Truman was to land. "Watch his face when he catches sight of me." As the ferry pulled in, Truman leaned out over the railing, grinning widely and waving a very long silk scarf. When he saw Gore standing beside me, he did a little comic-strip routine. His face fell like a soufflé placed in the ice compartment, and he disappeared entirely below the level of the railing for several seconds. When he had assumed a standing position again, he was no longer grinning or waving. Gore stayed around Tangier only long enough to make Truman believe he was going to spend the whole summer, and then he quietly left.

David Herbert, second son of the Earl of Pembroke, settled in Tangier a good many years ago and has been its unofficial social arbiter ever since. Throughout the years he has made vigorous efforts to persuade his friends to become property owners here; as a corollary he has gently discouraged those who did not seem good Tangier material. In the summer of 1949 he had not yet moved into his house at Jemaa el Mokra on the Mountain and was sharing the Guinness house on the Marshan with Cecil Beaton. Tangier was not really to Truman's taste, but he stuck it out all summer at the Farhar with Jane and me because of Cecil's presence. There were some very good parties that summer, including an unforgettable one given by the Comtesse de la Faille, in which she cleared out the ballroom, leaving only the Aubussons on the walls, and then covered the floor with straw for the snake charmers and acrobats. The Moroccans built a fire in the middle of the room and made themselves completely at home. Another party held on the beach at the Caves of Hercules, with one grotto previously decorated by Cecil, served only champagne and hashish. Truman, who claimed to be afraid of scorpions, had to be carried by a group of Moroccans down the face of the cliff in order to get there. An Andaluz orchestra was partially visible, surrounded by rocks and lanterns; the guests lay in the moonlight among cushions on the sand, went swimming, and sat around a big fire. The summer proved the apogee of postwar prosperity in the International Zone. Immediately afterward the cracks in the façade began to appear, and they constantly grew wider, until the entire edifice collapsed in the riots of 1952.

When Cecil Beaton left at the end of the summer, David Herbert asked Jane and me to move in with him and share the expenses. During that period Jane came down with measles and I went each day to watch the rebuilding of the little house in the Medina. *The Sheltering Sky* was published in London, and since the press was extremely good, John Lehmann thought I should be there in person. Doubleday had refused the book, writing me that they had contracted for a novel and I had produced something else. They did not specify what I had given them, but they unhesitatingly rejected it. I then sent it to James Laughlin, at the other end of the publishing spectrum, hoping that he might add it to his New Directions list, which he did.

David Herbert invited us to go with him to England and stay at Wilton. This was a privilege, to be able to see the great house from the inside, as it were. From there I wanted to go somewhere in the tropics. Perhaps as a result of just having finished reading Michaux's *Un Barbare en Asie,* I felt a special desire to go to Asia. This seemed as good a time as any. We could go to England, and when I left for the East, Jane would cross over to Paris for the winter.

Jane and I slipped down to Fez for a last look before we left

Morocco. There we found Ahmed Yacoubi making large drawings of country festivals. He still did not know that there were such people as artists; nor had he ever seen a painting. Yet he had made enormous stylistic progress during the year, merely working by himself in his father's house in the Medina.

One day we went to M. Ktiri's for lunch. He had told us beforehand that his uncle was to be present and that we would find him interesting. The uncle was a very noble-looking old gentleman with a full white beard who took snuff and told jokes. After lunch, during a lull, he suddenly rose and walked over to an ancient piano that stood in a corner. He sat down on the bench, waited for complete silence, and began. Not exactly to play, for he did not even attempt that; he merely pounded with his two hands as hard as he could and sometimes with his forearm. For almost eleven minutes he hit the piano. I could not see that anyone besides Jane and me thought it even faintly funny, but the two of us avoided each other's eyes. When the venerable pianist had stopped, he turned to his audience and explained the piece he had just played by saying complacently: "Manchester." He had been in the industrial city as a young man at the turn of the century and assumed that his improvisation was a valid and comprehensible description of it.

Somewhere, not long before we were to leave Tangier, David bought a Pekingese puppy for Jane. It was a very active little animal, and she called it Manchester. We persuaded Jane's erstwhile Arabic teacher, Said Kouch, to keep the parrot for us while we were away, and then the three of us, David, Jane, and I, plus Manchester in his traveling case, boarded the old Paquet liner *Koutoubia* for Marseilles. David's Jaguar was down in the hold. From Marseilles we set out on a *tournée gastronomique* up the Rhône Valley. This included of course the Pyramide in Vienne and a tiny place in Meursault where there were only six items available, all equally superb and equally damaging to anyone like me who suffered from colonial liver. I was not surprised by the three days I spent in bed at Lyons with an attack. Jane and David would go out and try one great Lyonnais restaurant after another, and then return to the hotel to sit in my room going over each bout of gorging. The concept of eating was in itself repulsive; the lingering descriptions and discussion of the food's texture constituted a kind of torture.

Since the quarantine laws of the United Kingdom made it impossible to take Manchester into England, David suggested that Jane look for a kennel in Paris where she could leave him while she was gone. Instead, she presented the puppy to Truman, and he took Manchester to New York with him.

David lived on the estate at Wilton, but in a small house known as the Park School. The big house, where his father, the Earl of Pembroke, lived, had been Field Marshal Montgomery's headquarters during the War. While the military were there, dry rot had somehow set in and had damaged the Van Dyck ceiling and murals in the ballroom; they were in process of repair at the time. The work cost a fortune, only 90,000 pounds of which the British government would furnish as compensation.

I had a literary host in the person of my publisher, John Lehmann, who generously allowed me to stay at his house in Egerton Crescent whenever I went up to London. He saw to it that I met everyone I wanted to meet. I let it be known that I was looking for ship passage to either Siam or Ceylon and would take whichever turned up first. Both Lady Sybil Colfax and Cyril Connolly got busy on the matter. Suddenly I was about to leave for Colombo. I had rather hoped it would turn out to be Ceylon, in any case, because of David's scrapbooks, which I had just seen at Wilton. There was almost an entire album devoted to a ravishing little island where he had stayed with his parents in the mid-thirties. Taprobane lay just offshore in the Bay of Weligama at Ceylon's extreme southern tip. I had studied the photographs of the lush vegetation and noted the geographical details in my mind, with the intention of going to see it myself, should the first passage prove to be one to Ceylon.

Toward the end of our stay at Wilton Lady Juliet Duff invited us to dinner. Somerset Maugham was there, a bit petulant. I have never seen a man with smaller feet. He himself remarked about them rather proudly and sat with one leg over the other, the better to display them. He intended to go later that winter to Morocco; it was a foregone conclusion that I should prepare him an itinerary. I mapped out a five-week tour for him to follow, there on the floor of Lady Juliet's drawing room.

The ship I was to take, a Polish freighter called the *General Walter*, left from Antwerp. I went across the Channel to that gray town three or four days early, after getting my yellow-fever inoculation in London. The streets were wet with fog; it was like being in a Simenon novel. To escape, I telephoned André Cauvin, the filmmaker who had produced *Congo*. As I had expected, he invited me up to Brussels for the weekend. I had a lot of good food at the Cauvins' and then hurried back to Antwerp to make certain that the ship did not sail without me (for as on all cargo ships the captain was in doubt about the day of departure). The afternoon we set sail I bought a copy of *Time* and found a review of *The Sheltering Sky* in it, along with a snapshot taken by Edwin Denby. They were grudgingly laudatory; I was surprised most of all by their calling it "supersexy."

As far as I could discover there were aboard only three other passengers: two nuns and a priest. At dinnertime, after we had lifted anchor and were moving painfully seaward through the fog, a very small Asian in a dark business suit came quickly into the dining room and anxiously inquired if there was any rice to be had. The steward was not in a mood to humor him, but at length he admitted that rice could be cooked. The little man went back to his cabin; we did not see him again for several days.

There was a language complication at the table. As an alternate to Flemish the two nuns spoke some French, while the priest spoke a kind of English. The ship was a sordid old tub; a quick inspection left no doubt about that. On it the spy Gerhardt Eisler had escaped to safety behind the Iron Curtain.

Chains clanked all night against the metal wall beside my pillow. Even with pills I could not sleep. The ship pitched and rolled like a camel; it was infuriating to think that I was committed to it for the next twenty-four days and nights. By six in the morning the two nuns and the priest were up celebrating early mass in the dining room. At breakfast, in the middle of a difficult conversation in our three languages, the padre suddenly cried: "Now moose I womit!" and rushed out of the room.

The sea remained rough until we were off the Portuguese coast. The night we sailed through the Strait of Gibraltar, I stood on deck staring longingly into the dark on the southern side of the ship. A rush of nostalgia for Tangier had seized me. I went inside and got into my berth. Then I began to write something which I hoped might prove the nucleus of a novel about Tangier. The first scene was on the cliffs opposite the point we were passing at that moment. Dyar stands at the edge of the cliff and looks out at the freighters going by in the strait. From that scene the book grew in both directions—backward as cause and forward as effect. By the time we had reached Suez I had made decisions about form and drawn diagrams clarifying motivations and was well into *Let It Come Down*.

Strange little things happened aboard the *General Walter*. The first morning after breakfast I went into my cabin and found the Polish steward reading my copy of *Time*. He had placed it open in the top drawer of the bureau; as I entered, he pushed the drawer shut with his knee and began to sweep. I offered to lend him the magazine, but that only embarrassed him. He frowned and shook his head. In the Mediterranean, off Cartagena, we hit a dramatic storm in which, during a twenty-four-hour period, we not only made no progress, but actually ended a few kilometers behind the point where we had been on the preceding day. The same cape was there to the west, and the same lighthouse. The sailors had not been very thoroughly indoctrinated with Marxism. They blamed the storm on the presence aboard of the priest. It was a well-known fact, several of them told me, that a priest on a boat often caused shipwreck.

On Christmas Day the sun was hot over the Red Sea where we sailed. The captain chipped paint all day on the fo'c's'le deck, because he was not a party member; the man who made the decisions aboard was a mechanic. In the wretched town of Djibouti at a sidewalk café, surrounded by carrion crows, the unhappy captain drank beer and told me his troubles. It was hard to be a captain, he complained, unless you had command of the ship. Understandably he did not relish the humiliation, in front of his crew, of being singled out to do hard labor all during Christmas Day.

In Djibouti, besides the ubiquitous crows, there was a Place Arthur Rimbaud. I photographed the wall into which the blue and white enamel street sign was incorporated. The sun was hot, and there were flies everywhere. The European town stood on a low hill which at times caught a feeble breeze from the gulf; Africans were restricted to the "native quarter," in a fetid swamp behind the hill.

We sailed east. The anchor chains had not pounded since Port Saïd. The little Indian who had ordered the rice finally joined us at table and announced very clearly his disapproval of Christian missionaries. Conversation became almost impossible; save for occasional words in Flemish the priest and the two nuns were silent. The most comfortable place for me was in bed, and once there, the only thing to do was work.

I had the illusion of being about to add another country, another culture, to my total experience, and the further illusion that to do so would in itself be of value. My curiosity about alien cultures was avid and obsessive. I had a placid belief that it was good for me to live in the midst of people whose motives I did not understand; this unreasoned conviction was clearly an attempt to legitimize my curiosity. I tried to get as many pages written as I could before arriving, in order not to be sidetracked by the initial contact with an unknown land.

XV

I have forgotten what I imagined Ceylon would be like—an intensification, I suppose, of all the hermetic mystery of Morocco, plus the specific characteristics of the locale: elephants, Buddhist temples, and tropical forests. Whatever my preconceptions may have been, they proved to be wide of the mark and were swiftly obliterated by the experience of landing in Colombo. Ceylon was not a super Morocco; it was simply a very different place and one that quickly proved to agree with my health. I was constantly exhilarated by the light, the climate, and the vegetation; this euphoria kept me walking most of the day. I developed an appetite and ate great quantities of rice and curry at the Mount Lavinia Hotel, where I had settled. It was on the beach about eight miles south of the fort in Colombo; the only sound I heard from my bed was the crash of waves.

During my first week in Colombo I had dinner with the queen mother of Sarawak; at that time she lived in Hong Kong and was making a brief visit to Ceylon. Her life on the island of Borneo had been an extraordinary one. I hoped to hear how it felt to hold in one's hands the fate of a million people. But all her anecdotes had to do in one way or another with the undying love her subjects had expressed for her, and not at all with her feelings about them. In a Colombo bookshop that week I also met an Anglican minister, intelligent and affable, who invited me to his house. My untrained eyes saw no visible racial differences between the Reverend Keunemann and his wife; nevertheless, his marriage had estranged him from his mother for several years, and they were just beginning to see each other again. "My husband's family are Burghers," explained Mrs. Keunemann. It was simple: under the British occupation Burghers lost caste by consorting with Sinhalese. The term "burgher" was employed to designate a Sinhalese with an admixture of European blood (generally Dutch, Portuguese, or French). Since the Burghers composed only a tiny fraction of the population, it was clear that with British control of the country now removed, Burgher society had not long to survive. I was curious about the Reverend Keunemann's mother. Having divorced his father, she had married an English tea planter and was living on a remote plantation up-country. This sounded like the kind of place I wanted to visit. From the interest I showed in the subject my host guessed what I hoped for. The following week Mr. and Mrs. Trimmer invited me up to Maldeniya Estate.

The site was one of great natural beauty, high in the forested hills and overlooking a river valley. Mr. and Mrs. Trimmer were exactly the kind of people I wanted to see. They had both been born in Ceylon, between them spoke Sinhalese and Tamil, and had an inexhaustible supply of information and anecdotes about the country. I stayed with them two weeks, and then, after promising to return, I resumed my traveling. On a trip to the south coast I caught only a glimpse through the palms of the little island where David Herbert had stayed. Then the train rounded a bend and I lost it.

Not long after I got to Ceylon, I received a series of letters from Gore Vidal, some of them forwarded from Tangier and some from London. To understand them I had to read them in the order of their writing. He had suddenly decided to pass the winter in Ceylon with me, he said, and accordingly had purchased his passage to Colombo on an American President liner. The morning of departure he arrived early at the dock, in plenty of time to catch the ship, which was to sail at noon. When he saw no ship alongside, he was startled. It did not take him long to discover that somehow he had miscalculated, that instead of being Thursday, it was Friday, and that his ship had sailed at noon the previous day. He took his luggage back home and did not go to Ceylon.

Late in the winter I crossed over to South India, going first up to Madura. The hotel accommodations were all upstairs over the railway station, to enable the guest, I was told, to look out of his window onto the platform below and make certain that his train had not yet come in. Whenever a train did arrive, it stayed a very long time and made a great amount of noise. The profusion of people everywhere in the landscape was both exciting, because to my eyes it looked vaguely festive, and disturbing, because I knew so well that the mere existence of each person was a threat to all the others. South India was a place to which one could not remain indifferent. My reactions oscillated continuously between strong delight and equally strong disgust. Perhaps if I had not seen the temple at Madura when I did, the needle might have stuck at the point of repulsion and stayed there, but for some reason the temple helped the chaos, noise, and filth fall into place, so that afterward I noticed them less. One could hardly stay even a few hours within its precincts and not find the world a little changed upon coming out again into the street.

The temple at Madura was like nothing I had ever seen before. Max Ernst, given carte blanche, might have invented some of the inner courts with their colossal painted god figures. At the entrance to one such sanctuary where I glimpsed, behind the rising columns of incense, a forty-foot-high pink elephant seated on a mammoth throne, I was pushed violently back by a guard wearing nothing but a long beard and a yellow loincloth. He pointed behind him and cried fiercely: "God! God!" Then he pushed me again, no more gently, and indicated the direction from which I had just come. "God-*dess!* God-*dess!*" he advised. I gathered that it was tolerated for a barbarian to gaze at an image of Parvati, but not at one of Ganpati.

If there were a capturable music of the spheres, I think it would sound like the music I found in a distant and relatively unfrequented corridor in the temple. I stood in the dimness listening for a long time; this music provided the ambience of eternity suitable to a place of worship with far greater success than the music we are accustomed to hearing in European cathedrals.

The central court owed more to Dali than to Ernst. There was a vast rectangular basin with steps leading down into froth-laden water. The court was floodlighted with a glaring and lethal green glow, so that the water and its scum shone green, and the bearded naked men immersed in it were also wholly green. Between this court and the entrance there was a covered market with stalls where they sold everything from kitchenware to images carved in sandalwood of Krishna and Saraswathi, of which I bought several before returning to the Railway Rest House. There during dinner the keeper enthused about the temple's five gopurams, which appear on the horizon long before anything else as you approach the city. Each tall tower is totally covered with countless thousands of sculpted images; according to the keeper, there are more than fifty thousand avatars represented on each gopuram. I have always had a particular fondness for Churrigueresque and Manolina detail in architecture; the over-populated gopurams of the Dravidian temples seemed their prototype.

Traveling by train in South India was a new experience. The compartment reached all the way across the car, and its only doors gave onto the tracks. There was no corridor to walk in. Each compartment had its own lavatory and shower. Surprisingly, the plumbing worked; this was fortunate because the daytime temperature stayed well over a hundred in the shade, and air conditioning was still unknown. Food was provided by Spencer's, a catering service whose men came aboard with trays of very good curry and side dishes, set up a table in the passenger's compartment, and jumped off the train as it started up. An hour or so later, at the next station, more Spencer's men came on, presented the check, and removed the trays and dishes. Then the passenger lay back on his cushions and sweated.

I went to Trivandrum for a few days. There was a fine zoological park not far from the hotel, and the temple was inhabited by scores of great bats which sallied forth just at twilight and staggered for a moment above the dark ghat before disappearing over the city. But in Trivandrum I encountered a form of hostility no less chilling for being subtle. The technique was simple: it consisted in pretending that the person against whom it was directed did not exist. One afternoon I went out with a dozen letters in my hand to look for the post office. I walked through the city stopping pedestrians, saying: "The post office, please? Which way?" and waving my letters. No one stopped; no one answered; no one looked at me longer than it took to gaze into my eyes and then through them into infinity. Eventually I found a small bookstore where an Englishman sat behind a desk. I inquired about the post office and mentioned the inscrutable behavior of the townspeople. "Or do they all understand nothing but Malayalam?" I suggested. He smiled. "They understood you perfectly, I assure you."

When I got to Cape Comorin, I decided to settle in for a while and work intensively on *Let It Come Down*. There was a big, airy hotel overlooking the sea, and I was its only guest. The food was not ideal, and there was no electricity. I worked naked by the hot light of oil lamps. Finally the heat became more than I could enjoy, and I thought of returning to Ceylon.

I had to go to Tuticorin in order to catch the boat to Colombo; there were two departures a week. Of all the cities I have examined, Tuticorin is the foulest. I lived in the one room available to travelers over the railway station. Where I should have slept those three nights if the room had been occupied by someone else, I have never tried to imagine. The air stank of human excrement, inside and outside the station. Curious about the all-pervasive odor, I mentioned it to the station keeper, who lived downstairs somewhere behind the restaurant. It was inevitable when the breeze was from the sea, he said. The hundred thousand people living in the city had no sewerage system, so they very carefully used the beach. In fact, he added, no one went near the beach for any other reason.

The boat down to Colombo was a floating extension of Tuticorin. The walls of the cabin seethed with big shiny cockroaches, and the fiery breath of the engine room belched through the doorway from across the corridor. The decks were crowded with seasick goats. Being tied together in groups, they were powerless to remain upright as the ship rolled. For fifteen days after arriving back in Ceylon I reported each morning to a district medical officer to be checked for cholera.

I moved around Ceylon for a while and stayed several weeks in Kandy at Queen's Hotel, working constantly, sometimes on the score for *Yerma,* sometimes on a short story, and sometimes, but not often, on the novel in progress. Later I joined Mr. and Mrs. Trimmer in Bandarawela and spent a few days motoring with them through the highlands; after that they took me back to Maldeniya Estate with them.

I was delighted to be living again in the rhythm of the Trimmer household. There was an old upright piano in one of the bungalow's rooms, where I spent my afternoons writing *Yerma.* About four o'clock each day, as the rain clouds covered the sky, I would sit down to work. The pitch of each string in the old instrument was merely a token pitch; a B-flat could sound like an A, and it had no great importance. The action was fairly normal, at least until one afternoon when I sat down to work, pushed the keys, and found them strangely blocked. I assumed that the rain had brought about a sudden further disintegration of the mechanism, and attacked fortissimo. Then I sprang away from the piano, knocking over the bench. A large snake was rising vertically out of the piano's open top, its black tongue flickering in my direction. As if it were being lifted by an invisible rope, it continued to go straight up, until it had wrapped itself around a beam of the ceiling. Then it hoisted the remainder of its body out of the piano and went on up into that spacious portion of the house that lay between the ceiling and the roof. In my world, to have a ten-foot serpent come out of the piano and disappear into the ceiling was an extraordinary event, but my hosts were only mildly surprised. "I wonder why he came down into the piano," mused Mrs. Trimmer. "The roof may be leaking," her husband said. "I'll have Siringam take a look at it."

They took much more seriously the fact that it was now the leech season and warned me against stepping off the veranda in the late afternoon. At the hour when the rain ceased and the sun's first hot rays hit the steaming lawn, the leeches came out of the ground, glistening and black, thousands of them (they were only about an inch long) bending and stretching their bodies as they moved forward and waving their triangular snouts in the direction of whatever was there for them to attack. I stood out there one day and watched them become aware of my presence and start in my direction. It was like a scene out of science-fiction, as if the earth itself were sending out countless tiny black tubes, each with the sole aim of filling itself with my blood. Another day I let one bury its jaws in my ankle. I felt nothing as it made the incision. After a while I pressed the end of my cigarette against its body until it let go. The little triangular wound bled freely and left a mark which is visible now, after more than twenty years.

I took a P. & O. liner to London. John Lehmann met me at Tilbury, and I stayed again for a few days as a guest at his house. Then I went on to Paris to join Jane at the Hôtel de l'Université. Carson McCullers was also staying there. She had a front room which, although it was large, got all the traffic sounds from the street below. Some mornings we would take our breakfast trays up to Carson's room and talk with her while we ate. Eudora Welty was staying at the hotel during part of the time. She lived in joyous expectation of letters from the United States, principally in order to follow the adventures of Li'l Abner. Enclosed in each letter she received from home were all the strips that had been cut from the newspapers since the preceding letter. Never having heard of Li'l Abner, I found her preoccupation with him the height of eccentricity.

I saw Brion Gysin. He had just passed a year in Bordeaux doing research on his Fulbright project and now seemed to be at loose ends. I suggested Tangier for a while, and he decided in favor of it. The house in the Medina was finished at last and equipped to be lived in. Jane was not ready to leave Paris. She was working well in the hotel and thus was happy there. I took the train down through Madrid to Algeciras and crossed over to Tangier. About a week later Brion arrived.

The house was pocket-sized but with several stories. Brion lived on the second floor, and I on the fourth, in the tower which I had built on top of the original structure. Each of us could go in and out without coming near the other's quarters. As a cook we got the butler who had worked for David Herbert the year before. He had been employed by Barbara Hutton earlier and still went to her house occasionally; it was just around the corner. Sometimes as we were finishing lunch, he would come and stand in the doorway to the patio, holding a towel in his hand and tell us unlikely stories about her.

Libby Holman wired that she was driving down from England and wanted me to meet her in Málaga. I went over, and for a full month she and I traveled around Andalusia, coming to rest finally in Tangier. We talked incessantly about *Yerma;* when we could get to a piano, as we did in Seville and Granada, we worked together on some of the finished songs. The night before she was to leave Morocco for New York, news came that Christopher, her son, had died in an attempt to scale Mount Whitney.

Brion and I went to Fez. We did not know it then, but we were living through the last two or three months of the old, easygoing, openly colonial life in Morocco. (That winter the French encouraged the Glaoui to send his troops to Rabat and threaten the sultan, and thus a period of tension set in. Instead of subsiding, the nervousness steadily mounted, until the removal of the monarch by force set off the terrorist war against the French.)

Eventually we continued to Marrakech. Later in the autumn when we returned to Tangier, Brion stayed again in the house, but this time by himself. I did not want to have to cope with the problems that I knew winter would bring to the little house, and so I went to try out a new hotel that had just opened at the far end of the Marshan. The winter was abominable; by Christmastime it had already rained more than the usual amount for the entire wet season.

A woman arrived from Paris with a letter from Truman Capote. Her name was Nada Patcevitch, and she intended to write an article on the Sahara for *Vogue.* Not only that; she looked like someone from the pages of that magazine. She came several times to dinner at the Hôtel Villa Mimosa to discuss the itinerary; at length she proposed that I accompany her. I was immersed in the routine of writing *Let It Come Down.* The book was proceeding much more slowly than I had anticipated, what with all the interruptions, and my first reaction to the invitation was negative.

The rains went on. Madame Patcevitch, worried about the condition of the roads and fearful of not being able to get through to the desert if she waited too long, remarked that we could be escaping the bad weather if only we were in the south. When the rain ran down my bedroom wall, covered the entire floor, and continued out under the door into the corridor, my thoughts changed their course, and the prospect of a bit of Sahara sun became definitely attractive. I agreed to go with her.

The trip was doomed from the beginning. In Fez, no sooner had she got settled in her hotel room than the toilet bowl in her bathroom began to spew out its contents over the floor. She changed rooms; when she touched the tap in her washbasin, it came off, and the water shot out of the wall straight across the room. She had to be given a third room.

It rained, on and on. Along the highway going eastward, we found great quantities of mud partially covering the road. When we got to Oujda, we learned that the trail south was blocked by snow. The car had to be shipped by train to Colomb-Béchar. We too took the train and got there several days before the car. This did not matter too much, for Nada Patcevitch had contracted a very bad case of bronchitis on her first day in Colomb-Béchar. This was because she had chosen to sleep in the hotel's annex across the street from the main building. The roof of the annex was of recent construction and let the rain through. When I went to see her in the morning, her bed was entirely wet, and she was in a state which I found alarming. Luckily she had strong recuperative powers.

At last one day the car arrived, and we managed to get it cleared through the Algerian customs. Although Nada still had a hacking cough and a fever, she insisted on driving south to Igli, where the only Europeans were a young French lieutenant and his wife. They agreed to let us spend the night in the house, although they apologized for having no place to put Nada but the kitchen table. She felt too ill to care one way or the other. I was given a straw mattress outside in the sheep shed. The roof was half gone; the hard, bright moonlight shone in and awoke me. I lay awake listening to the sheep snuffling. In the morning we found Nada on the table, but with her head inside the oven. The warmth, she said, had helped her, and she felt better.

In Taghit her luck did not change. One night I awoke to hear her moaning and scratching at my window. It took me a long time to wake up; then I found her in a heap out on the terrace. She had been partially asphyxiated by a charcoal burner which she had innocently left in the room when she went to bed. At three in the morning I had to go to the fort and fetch the captain, who had charge of the only medical supplies in the region. He was highly displeased at being awakened; there was nothing he could do in any case, he told me. However, he went with me to her room. "People like you ought not to come to the Sahara," he told her impatiently. This was the opening shot of a feud between them which lasted until we left. When we got back to Colomb-Béchar, she went to the military headquarters and complained about him.

Back in Tangier I remarked to Brion that the trip had made me long to have my own car, so that I could go where I pleased and leave when I felt like leaving. "Well, buy one," Brion said. "You can afford it." This shocked me. I had never thought of myself as a possible car owner. Nor had it occurred to me that money was something that could be spent. Automatically I always had hoarded it, spending as little as possible. Brion's suggestion was like the voice of Satan. I began to look at cars, and within two weeks I had bought a new Jaguar convertible.

When the English proprietress of the Hôtel Villa Mimosa saw the automobile, she immediately announced that I must hire a driver. I assured her that there was no chance of that, because I had no intention of taking on the expense of a driver's salary. One morning when I returned from town, the *botones* opened the hotel door for me in a state of excitement, crying: "Your chauffeur is here!" A young man stood stiffly at the foot of the stairs. The English lady bustled forward and explained that she had taken it upon herself to ask the cook to send his grand-nephew for me to try out as a driver. He had worked for an American she knew, and she considered him efficient. "Put your heels together," she admonished him. "And say *señor*. Haven't you got a better jacket than that?" The young man said he would return later in the day with a different jacket. "You'll have to have a uniform made for him," she told me. In this way I found myself, to my initial annoyance and eventual pleasure, responsible for both a car and a chauffeur. Brion proposed that we take a trip to break in the Jaguar.

First we went only to Fez and Marrakech, but then we set out for more recondite places, to which there were only trails. Before leaving Marrakech, I ran into Abdelkader, whom I had taken to Paris twenty years before. He had managed to salt away enough money to buy a small olive grove and a house on the road to Benguérir, and there he lived, bicycling into Marrakech only when he needed to buy provisions. He asked about Harry; when I told him he had been killed in the war, he said: *"Le pauvre. Il n'a pas eu de chance."*

The Jaguar suffered on her maiden trip: she traveled many hundreds of miles of rocky trails through the south of Morocco, forded rivers, had to be dragged out of quicksand when we got across the border into the Algerian Sahara, and eventually met a two-day sandstorm where we could make almost no progress because the water in the radiator boiled as soon as we had gone a mile. Our desert trip lasted three or four months; I continued to work on the novel wherever we went. Temsamany was perhaps not the ideal driver for those parts. The contempt he felt at the sight of such backward people (for how could they be otherwise, he reasoned, living in such a benighted land?) let itself be seen on all occasions. Perhaps because of his military-looking uniform and shiny boots and puttees, they made no objection to being patronized.

While we were in Fez, where we stayed a few weeks on our way back to Tangier, I heard from Jane. She wanted now to get out of Paris and suggested that I drive as far as the French border to pick her up. Leaving Brion in Tangier, I invited Ahmed Yacoubi to go along with me. Our trip through Spain was marked by bursts of excitement each time pigs appeared in the landscape. Temsamany would stop the car, and both he and Ahmed would stand up, shouting and waving their arms wildly. The Spanish peasants were mystified and somewhat fearful. They still had unhappy memories of Moors as pillagers and rapists in the Franco invasion and were not inclined to feel sympathy toward us.

We nearly had trouble at the cathedral in Córdoba. As we entered, both Temsamany and Ahmed washed their faces, rinsed their mouths, and gargled with the holy water in a fount by the door. Then they squared off and began to spit it at one another. I hurried them out of the building before the sacristan, who had witnessed the shenanigans from the other end of the cathedral, could get to us.

As everyone knows, Franco's elite guard is composed of several hundred Riffians, all of whom lived, in 1951 at least, in the village of El Pardo. Franco's residence is not easily approachable; there are guards on horseback here and there whose business it is to keep everyone far from the palace. When we careened into the village, Temsamany hailed the soldiers in Riffian, calling them brother and blessing them. The top of the convertible was only half open, so that I was hidden in the back. The guards saw only Temsamany in uniform and visored cap, and Ahmed wearing a white turban and djellaba, and they let us go right up to the palace before someone saw me and stopped us. Then they were apologetic, and as a consolation they insisted that we go with them for couscous. There was mint tea and plenty of kif. We drove back down to Madrid in a beatific state. I thought the two Moroccans should see the Bosches at the Prado. After that when anyone asked Ahmed to name his favorite painter, he would answer: "Bosch." We watched from the back of Burgos cathedral during mass. Ahmed liked the music; Temsamany found both music and ceremony wholly without interest. Then we went up to Santillana del Mar to see the caves of Altamira. The paintings of the animals were beautiful, but it was unsettling to reflect that they had been executed some eighteen thousand years earlier.

Jane was in fine form and seemed delighted to be out of Paris at last. We spent a few days in San Sebastián, and then headed southward in leisurely fashion. Each time I took the wheel to relieve Temsamany, Jane would complain that I was driving too fast. The complaints would continue until Temsamany sat once again in the driver's seat. I believed this was because she had no confidence in my driving. She claimed that it was only the fact that she always knew just what I was thinking and thus felt almost as if she herself were doing the driving, so that it was impossible for her to relax. When we came to Úbeda, we fell in love with the town and the dry, wheat-covered hills around it. Three weeks went by before the four of us checked out of the Parador del Condestable Davalos and drove on to Granada.

In Tangier Jane and I lived together in the house for the first time. She established an early-morning market routine which never varied. While I still slept, Temsamany would arrive and go with her on foot down through the Medina to the Grand Socco to buy the day's food. I would get up, make coffee, and take it back to bed with me, to work until about noon. I still had a good way to go before the novel would be done. My idea was to go up to Xauen to write the last few chapters, and I did this. The town was a place of great beauty, and the silence in the hotel room at night was broken only by distant sounds of cockcrow from across the valley. I made great progress in Xauen and began to feel happier about the novel. It was now two years since I had started writing it. Irving Thalberg, Jr., arrived and spent three days in Xauen with me. I think he knew how fortunate he was to have happened to be present in a café during a Jilala ritual. A mountain Jilali came in, sat beside us, and soon went into a trance. As he danced, he slashed himself, covered his face with the blood, and licked it from his arms and fingers. It was tremendously impressive, the more so for having been done without a word being spoken.

Jane would come up to Xauen for a weekend now and then. She was constantly getting messages from Ruth Gordon and Garson Kanin, who seemed to be about to put on *In the Summer House*. Soon she had to go to New York. That production fell through, but there were two others during the season: one by Jasper Deeter of the Hedgerow Theater, and the other at Ann Arbor with Miriam Hopkins in the lead role. Before she left Tangier I went down from Xauen to stay with her and finished *Let It Come Down* there in the house.

I spent the month of December in Tetuán at the Dersa Hôtel. Ahmed Yacoubi was there painting, and Robert Rauschenberg was living just down the street. There was a night distinct from the others when Ahmed served a platter of very powerful *majoun* to Bob and a friend of his without explaining to them what the substance was. Finding it tasty, they spread large quantities of it on their crackers and cookies and washed it down with hot tea. Since they were both totally inexperienced in the use of cannabis, they had no way of understanding what was happening to them. They were in a very strange state when they left the Dersa. Later in the evening we went around to the Hôtel Bilbao to see how they were. We climbed up the dark stairway and stood for a moment outside Rauschenberg's room. Through the door came the sound of groaning. We decided that since he was already embarked on an unhappy journey, our arrival could only make it worse, and so we went quietly down the stairs and out into the street.

One day in Gibraltar I saw a poster in the window of a shipping office advertising first-class passage to Bombay for eight pounds. The explanation was that the ship was the *Batory* of the Polish Ocean Lines. I had not thought of going to India that winter, but suddenly it seemed a good idea and an economical one—almost cheaper than to stay in Morocco. I would drop Ahmed Yacoubi, from the Medina of Fez, into the middle of India and see what happened.

He enjoyed the sea voyage, and so did I. The food and service were astonishingly good. Down in tourist class there was a troupe of thirty dancers, all of them American blacks, who came up onto the sun deck each morning and rehearsed in their bathing suits. They had marijuana from New York with them; soon they were offering it to the captain. Without being explicit, he let it be seen that he disapproved of all such degenerate bourgeois customs, although he seemed somewhat taken aback that it should be members of a victimized class who were sporting such vices.

Having no previous experience of India to prepare him for the reality of India, Ahmed was more shocked than I by the sight of the ubiquitous refugees who slept, ate, and defecated in Bombay's streets. To him the Hindus seemed totally insane creatures, not even of this planet; the Indian Moslems, knowing no Arabic save the *chehade,* the brief profession of faith which they often recited for him to prove their adherence to Islam, were scarcely more acceptable. India must have struck him as a malign, hostile place. More than once in the dead of night I heard him, crying out in his sleep from the adjoining room: *"Fi el khaouf!"* ("I'm afraid!")

I liked the hotel in Aurangabad, and so we settled there for a while. The English manageress was a Christian Scientist and gave me some copies of the *Monitor.* She also mentioned that a countryman of mine, a Mr. Monahan, was due to arrive at the hotel within the next few days. Perhaps I knew him? I said I did not. "He's very famous," she insisted. "A famous violinist." I told her that I had never heard of him, adding that since I had been out of America for several years, he might have become famous since my departure. "No, no. He's been ever so famous for years," she said.

A few days later Mr. Monahan did arrive and with Mrs. Monahan took the suite next to mine. It was not long before he began to practice. Ahmed straightway pulled out his Moroccan *lirah,* or cane flute such as shepherds carry, and footled with it. The practicing stopped; there were muffled murmurs of surprise and incomprehension in the neighboring room. Each time the violin started up, Ahmed shrilled on the *lirah.* Presently Mr. Monahan retired into a further room and shut the door, to continue his work unmolested. I hoped to avoid having to come face to face with him on the veranda. During siesta time that afternoon somewhere in the hotel a woman began to call: "Yehudi! Yehudi!" At that point I realized who Mr. Monahan was. "Do you hear what that woman is calling her husband?" demanded Ahmed. "He ought to knock her down." In Morocco when a mule or a donkey refuses to move, he gets the word *"yehudi"* screamed at him. I thought of this, and in order not to call forth some awful scene, I did not explain to Ahmed that Yehudi was actually the man's name. Later in New York when I saw Menuhin again, I asked him if he remembered the flute in the hotel at Aurangabad, and he did.

I wanted to see the caves of Ellora while I was in the region. We rode out through the wild dusty country in a rattletrap taxi and found only one other occupant in the Rest House, an Englishman named Codrington. Professor Codrington had been living at Ellora for many weeks and knew the temples and caves extremely well. The first night after dinner we sat on the veranda in the dark. For Ahmed's benefit the professor was evoking the great antiquity of the temples, and he stressed the idea that over thousands of years literally millions of pilgrims had visited the shrines. Ahmed wanted to know who these millions of people had been and what religion they had followed. When he heard that they all had been either Buddhists or Hindus, he seemed relieved. "If that many Moslems had died, there'd be no more room in paradise by now," he explained in perfect seriousness. Professor Codrington did not dispute this.

When I got back to Bombay, there were ten copies of *Let It Come Down* waiting for me at the American consulate. Since we had well over a thousand pounds of luggage between us, a few more books made no difference. The train compartments were still spacious, but the showers now gave no water, and often there were no meals to be had en route. We ate biscuits and fruit.

We found the troupe of dancers from the *Batory* at the Hotel Connemara in Madras; they had got hold of some extremely strong *ganja* which they generously shared with us. We went to an orthodox Hindu wedding in Bangalore where we sat on the floor for hours and chewed areca nuts. It was not unlike a similar occasion in Morocco, and Ahmed gave the first signs of feeling at ease among Indians. We traveled slowly back across India to the Arabian Sea and down the coast. Perhaps a month later we were in Cochin, where a good hotel functioned on Wellington Island in the middle of the harbor. Both Europeans and Indians came here to spend their holidays around the swimming pool. This was where Ahmed sat each day as he drew and painted. Inevitably he attracted a great many onlookers and was soon selling pictures to those who cared to buy. A mother and daughter from Bombay showed consistent interest in his work until one day he drew a flock of birds. "Most attractive," they said. "What is the title?" When he told them the picture was called "The Tower of Silence," they froze and then walked away without another word. A Hindu lady explained later that they were Parsees and had found the title offensive, referring as it did to the celebrated construction on Malabar Hill where the Parsee dead are traditionally devoured by vultures.

It was not a good year to be in India if one attached any importance to eating. There was a rice shortage, and Nehru had decreed it illegal for restaurants and hotels to serve rice in any form, reasoning that those who ate in such establishments could afford to order other items instead, whereas the poor had access to nothing else. Curry with fried potatoes, however, is unsatisfactory. One day while we were staying on Wellington Island, we got into a dinghy and had ourselves rowed out to an Indian freighter anchored in the harbor. The ship's cook was very kind and gave us a five-pound sack of rice, which we carried in triumph back to the chef at the hotel, asking him to prepare some of it for the curry at dinnertime. He was adamant in his refusal: no rice could be served in the dining room. Nevertheless, he consented to cook it for us if we would eat in our rooms. From then on, wherever we went, we did exactly that, carrying our own rice with us.

Another day we returned to the port and went aboard a Japanese ship, in quest of more rice. Before giving it to us, they led us belowdecks to a corridor where the body of one of the seamen lay, surrounded by candles and small bowls of food. The boy had been crushed by a crane. "He die," they repeated, grinning widely. Ahmed found their facial contortions very upsetting, and wondered later if perhaps they had not killed him themselves.

One of the peculiarities of Cochin was the presence in the area of a large Jewish colony, divided among the towns forming the complex. (Ernakulam had the largest community, consisting of about six thousand souls.) The Jews were indistinguishable from the other Tamils among whom they lived. We met one at the port; he was carrying a magazine called *Zion,* and offered to show us the synagogues. As we walked through the streets of the Jewish quarter, Ahmed, no doubt remembering the Mellah of Fez, said accusingly to our cicerone: "You not real Jew." The man was indignant. "On the contrary!" he cried. "We are the *only* real Jews. Direct descendants of King Solomon!" I thought it wiser not to translate this last bit for Ahmed. King Solomon is one of the top Moslem prophets, and Jews have no right to claim him as theirs.

The synagogues were modest structures, with old Dutch tiles covering the floors and walls. Instead of being a scroll the Torah was incised on a series of thin brass plates, which were turned on the lectern like pages. Ahmed's theory about the Jews of the Malabar Coast, expressed to me subsequently, was that they were so ignorant they imagined Judaism to be a step up from Hinduism and had adopted it to improve their social position.

In Cochin I read of the riots in Tangier and the resulting flight of gold to Montevideo a few days later. Clearly this would be a mortal blow to the carefree Tangier I knew. Among the press notices on *Let It Come Down* was the one from the *New York Times Book Review*; this time they had given me the whole first page, although the critic was not certain he approved of the book. The possibility occurred to me that the riots might have transformed *Let It Come Down* from a book about contemporary life into a document dealing with a bygone era, but this did not prove to be the case. Even now, twenty years later, the popular image of Tangier has not altered much. People still arrive expecting the old atmosphere of excess and prodigality which prevailed in the forties; sometimes they even claim to have found it.

When Jane left for New York, she took all of Ahmed's larger works with her. Betty Parsons scheduled an exhibit at her gallery on Fifty-seventh Street, but then I received a letter from her. Unfortunately, I started reading it to Ahmed in Moghrebi translation before I saw its message. Then it was too late to stop. In brief, a Frenchman named Jean Dubuffet had gone to the gallery, and Betty had taken him into a back room and shown him Ahmed's pictures. M. Dubuffet (who was by then a famous painter but at one time had taught art to Moroccan children) told Betty that someone had hoaxed her. The drawings were not by a Moroccan at all, he said, but by a European artist hiding his identity behind a fictitious name. Having great respect for Dubuffet as a painter, Betty was baffled and uneasy, and was writing me for more details. In those days little sympathy existed between the French and the Moroccans, and Ahmed's francophobia was abnormally acute. He wanted to fly to New York immediately and instigate a lawsuit against Dubuffet. During the trial he would make a drawing before the eyes of everyone, so that there would be no possible doubt who had created the others. We compromised on a letter to Betty which would be displayed at the exhibit. After several days of vituperation, he drafted a long anti-French tirade which I mailed to Betty, special delivery, urgent and airmail, from the Wellington Island post office.

We took a boat through the inland waterways, down to Alleppey and Trivandrum, and then visited Madura. I enjoyed seeing the temple again. At the end of these thousands of miles of snaking back and forth across India we were suddenly arrested and thrown into a "screening" camp run by the Ceylon government at Mandapam on Indian soil. It is a sobering experience to be locked into a compound with twenty thousand other people, many of whom have languished there for several years, and to have no inkling of what will happen. The uncertainty went on for only forty-eight hours, after which we were released. We continued to Dhanushkodi and caught the ship to Ceylon. In retrospect, however, the hours passed in the camp do not seem a part of time at all; they are a static and permanent thing, outside time's flow.

Mr. and Mrs. Trimmer had left Maldeniya and gone to the lowlands in the south, to a place called Gintota, where they were expecting us. What with the two weeks of daily appearances for cholera checking that had to be made before the district medical officer, I thought we should stay in a place where the visits would be easy. We chose Anuradhapura. The walk from the hotel to the doctor's office, shaded by giant trees, took only five minutes.

The Trimmers had a very fine bungalow at Gintota. We would stay a week, travel for two, and return for another week. We visited innumerable Buddhist and Hindu temples; at the mosques, I waited outside while Ahmed prayed. In the vihara of the Hikkaduwa temple we met a man who told us about the island of Dodanduwa, a heavily forested hill rising out of a lagoon, where eight Buddhist monks had founded a sanctuary. Each day they went out in a boat across the water to the villages with begging bowls. They brought back rice and fruit and vegetables—never money, which they were not allowed to possess or handle. We decided to go and visit the place. An outboard motorboat took us across to the island. We landed on a well-shaded shore and told the boatmen to return in two hours. They started

off, after calling back to us one small admonition: "Mind the co-
bras!" The path, however, was wide and clean-swept; no cobra
could have lurked unseen within striking distance of its center.
Presently we came upon a yellow-robed monk raking leaves, and
he took us on a tour of the island, saying that it was better for us
to be accompanied, since the snakes recognized the monks and
never had attacked anyone in their presence.

I went down to Weligama with the express purpose of crossing
over to the little island of Taprobane. The pictures in David
Herbert's scrapbook still remained in my mind. A savage-looking
man whose mouth was a red gash from chewing betel met me at
the gate at the end of the jetty and, after muttering a few unintel-
ligible phrases and pocketing two rupees, unlocked the gate. An
octagonal house stood on an eminence in the center of this tiny
paradise, surrounded by garden, then by forest, and finally by
the breakers rolling in from the Indian Ocean. The owner, an
up-country rubber planter and racehorse breeder named Jinadasa, occasionally passed a weekend there and was not interested
in selling. However, I asked Mr. Trimmer to watch the situation
and, if any change occurred, to notify me immediately. The
island had been bought and sold three or four times since the
death of the Comte de Mauny-Talvande. None of the purchasers, however, including Mr. Jinadasa, had acquired the place
with the intention of living in it. I interpreted this as being in my
favor, since the fact that it was generally regarded as a pleasure
dome rather than a dwelling made the possibility of a sudden
sale seem more likely.

To get back to Europe before the monsoons broke, we took the
Tai Yang, a Norwegian freighter on its way from Rangoon to
Oslo. On board was Mercia, a beautiful Eurasian girl of Irish-
Malaysian stock, who was carrying a shipment of several dozen
assorted reptiles and quadrupeds to Switzerland for the zoo at
Basel. Her prize captive was an eleven-year-old female rhinoceros named Joy, quartered in a carefully constructed bamboo
stockade on the fo'c's'le deck. The girl had an agreement with
the Norwegian deckhands according to which they were to feed
and wash the animal regularly. The cook would boil up a huge
caldron of oatmeal for her each morning, and I would often go

down and watch her have breakfast. One of the sailors would climb inside, and another would hand him the pail of gruel to give her. Oatmeal cascaded from each side of her mouth as she ate, and she switched her tail happily.

The monsoons began before we were halfway across the Arabian Sea, and the unfortunate rhinoceros had to stand there for a week while the waves crashed over her at each roll of the ship. Mercia worried that the salt water would damage her hide and begged the sailors to go and hose her down with fresh water. It was useless work, they said, and they refused.

One morning it was discovered that at least a dozen of the big lizards had somehow got out of their pen in the fo'c's'le head. They led the sailors a crazy chase that lasted several hours. Mercia was indignant; she considered it sabotage. The sailors were annoyed because it was hot work looking for lizards, even five-foot ones, in such cramped quarters. When we got to the middle of the Red Sea, the Norwegians suddenly announced that they were having nothing further to do with the care and feeding of Joy. Mercia went up to see the crotchety old captain. He declared that from the start he had been against the idea of taking a rhinoceros on board, adding hastily that since she had paid the fare for it, he was duty-bound to deliver it at the dock in Genoa. At the same time, he told her, the arrangements she had made with members of the crew did not concern him in any way, nor did it interest him whether Joy ate or starved. Mercia came back from her interview on the bridge furious and dejected. It was then that Ahmed said he would feed Joy her oatmeal every morning and hose her down afterward. He did this until we got to Haifa; after that the Norwegians thought better of their little mutiny and took over once more.

At Genoa we were met at the dock by Albert Rothschild, who drove us up to his house on the shore of Lago di Orta to spend two or three weeks. Brion Gysin was there painting, and Albert's brother Hans Richter, who had made *Dreams That Money Can Buy* and was shooting another film which he described as a game of chess. One sequence was to be called *The Middle Game*; he wanted Ahmed and me to play in it, and I said we would. From Orta we went down to Venice to stay with Peggy Guggenheim in the Palazzo Venier dei Leoni.

The first morning after breakfast Peggy sent a servant to say that she was on the terrace. I went up first and found her sunbathing in the nude. "Do you mind?" she said. At that moment Ahmed appeared in the doorway. His face froze. For him the situation was wholly without precedent. "We'd better go down, hadn't we?" he muttered.

"Oh, is he embarrassed?" Peggy cried. "Tell him to come on out. In a minute I'll put on my bathrobe." Ahmed was still talking out of the corner of his mouth. "He doesn't think it's right for women to sit naked in front of strange men," I told her, translating and censoring the gist of his remarks.

"How strange. You mean they don't do that where he comes from? I'm sure they do. Tell us, Ahmed."

At Peggy's request Ahmed took over the kitchen on several occasions to prepare Moroccan meals; the work sent the entire kitchen staff rushing in various directions to fetch herbs and spices on the other side of the Grand Canal. Peggy was going to play in the Richter film; after that she intended to go to India to meet a maharajah. I asked her which one, but she would not tell, saying instead: "Any maharajah. It doesn't matter."

We continued later to Madrid, to arrange an exhibit of Ahmed's drawings at the Galería Clan. They sold very well. Ahmed went out with some of the proceeds and bought a boxed collection of more than a hundred Klee drawings, which he put under his pillow at night in order to absorb their content more completely than he could have done through his eyes. His larger works were all in New York, where Betty Parsons had decided to show them in spite of Dubuffet's warning.

While I was in Madrid a telegram came from Mr. Trimmer, saying that if I acted swiftly I could buy the island of Taprobane. Without hesitation I went out of the Palace Hotel and hurried to the post office to cable New York to wire the money to Ceylon.

Now that I owned the island, I wanted to go and see what it was like to sleep there. In any given place, the decisive criterion of its viability for living purposes is the quality of my sleep. But for the moment there was no question of going to Ceylon. *In the Summer House,* Jane's play, was about to have another production, this time on Broadway, and I was needed in New York to write the score. Because its ships left directly from Tangier rather than from across the strait, I decided to try the Jugoslav line. It proved an unsatisfactory way of crossing the Atlantic. Hans Richter was now in New York and would soon be ready to shoot his film sequence with Ahmed and me.

I wrote the score for *In the Summer House* and, leaving Ahmed with Libby, went with Jane to Washington, where we rehearsed and tried out the play. Both Judith Anderson and Mildred Dunnock were brilliant, but the direction was chaotic, and the script itself had a few equivocal spots which needed clarification. We spent New Year's Eve in New York with Judith. Since both Oliver Smith and Roger Stevens thought the director must be changed, when we reached Boston José Quintero was called upon to take over; with some difficulty he managed to pull the production together. Overnight Jane tightened the play and wrote a new scene for Mildred Dunnock. I was astonished to see the work complete the following morning, and triumphant when I saw how beautifully it played.

Libby was instrumental in arranging a series of exhibits for Ahmed in eastern American cities ranging from New York to Cleveland. Jane and I stayed on at Libby's after the play came into New York, principally at the house in Connecticut. In the spring Hans Richter came and filmed the sequences for what he now called *Eight by Eight.* At this point Arthur Gold and Robert Fizdale were given the money to commission a work to be presented at their next concert. They asked James Schuyler to invent a text, and me to make a cantata out of it for four female voices, two pianos, and percussion. *Yerma* was still only half-finished, and I had not worked on it in a very long time. Writing a new score might banish the guilt I felt at not returning to struggle with *Yerma.* I left Jane and Ahmed at Libby's, hurried back to Tangier, and rented a piano.

XVI

I passed the spring in Tangier, setting Schuyler's text
and traveling around Morocco, visiting religious festivals in the
country. I never had bothered to get a driver's license, but during
a fortnight's stay in Xauen I got into the habit of taking long
drives up into the western Rif by myself in the Jaguar. Incredibly, I was never stopped by the police.

A telegram in the early summer from Tennessee Williams
started me off, still in the Jaguar, for Rome. Temsamany and I
took turns driving through Spain and France. Ahmed, who had
just returned from New York, sat in the back playing the *lirah*
and singing, as far as Barcelona, where, having been refused a
visa which would enable him to go through France, he emplaned
directly for Rome. The reason for the journey was that Tennessee
had arranged for me to write the dialogue for a film which Luc-
chino Visconti wanted to make. Its action was to take place during the Austro-Italian War of the mid-nineteenth century.

Visconti was a man of great charm and suavity. When I had
been on salary for six weeks and had finished my work, he told
me that he was not satisfied with the love scenes. In a week Tennessee, who he originally had hoped would write the dialogue,
had given him exactly what he wanted. We shared the credits on
the film, which eventually was called *Senso*.

I had agreed to write an article for *Holiday* on Istanbul. This
was the moment to go and do it. Booking passage with the De-
nizyollari line, I sailed to Istanbul, returning the next month to

Naples, where Temsamany was waiting for me at the dock with the car.

As we drove up, open-topped, from Naples to Rome, Temsamany did something that Riffians are wont to do: he began to sniff the air with great thoroughness. Slowly his expression shifted from casual to determined. The car slowed down, and we pulled off the road and stopped near a group of farmers. Temsamany got out and sauntered over to them. There was a brief conversation, and I heard him crying: *"Grazie! Grazie!"* Then he picked up an armful of dry stalks, great piles of which were being stacked there in the field, and brought them to put in the rear seat. He made several trips, so that the car was stuffed with the stalks. Then we continued to Rome, going straight to the Via Firenze, Temsamany remaining mysterious about his stalks until he had the entire load of them in the apartment. At this point he announced that he was going to make the best *majoun* that Rome had ever seen. The fields had been sown with hemp for several miles along the road, he said, and the peasants had been generous and told him he might take all he wanted. For him that was the important thing: the kif had been free. The fact that it was not smoking-quality hemp did not matter, because it would be excellent for *majoun*. And so it was. I moved that week out to Monte Parioli and gave a party which featured Temsamany's concoction. It had a fine flavor and a powerful effect. Lillian Hellman and Stella Adler were there, and Stella's daughter Ellen, who held her *majoun* like an habituée.

Tennessee wanted to drive to Tangier. We started off from Rome in the two identical Jaguars, spending a few nights at Portofino, where Truman Capote had an apartment at the top of a house on the waterfront. I was in a hurry to see what Morocco would be like now that the terrorists had started their campaign against the French; behind my curiosity lurked the fear that the country would cease to be inhabitable for foreigners under the new circumstances.

My fears seemed well grounded; there was now an element of distinct unfriendliness abroad in the streets of Tangier. I had the impression that everyone was waiting for a signal to be given, and that when it came, all hell would break loose.

As the trouble increased, the French became more difficult and querulous. They were specifically anti-American in their behavior, because they believed the arms that the Moroccans used against them came from the American bases. There were demonstrations by Moroccans in the streets of Tangier nearly every day; the shopkeepers were kept busy rolling the steel shutters of their shopfronts down and up as the sound of the mob came and went. Tennessee found the atmosphere oppressive and did not remain long in Morocco.

I had let my typhoid shots lapse, being convinced that I would not catch the disease again. This was a bit of foolishness on my part, for I suddenly found myself in bed with paratyphoid. Three weeks of lying in a cold room at the Hotel Massilia saw me through the fever. Temsamany brought in stoves, and they at least helped to make the place less damp. Jane, having returned from the United States, was installed in another room on the same story of the hotel. There she had two maids sleeping on the floor; they helped her prepare my food, using charcoal burners for fire, which they kept hidden in the closet so that the hotel management would not learn of their existence.

During my convalescence a tall thin man came to see me, brought by a Tangier acquaintance. His name was William Burroughs, and he had just written a book entitled *Junkie* and sold it directly to a paperback company; this was the first time I had heard of anyone doing such a thing. There was something about the contract that bothered him. If I remember correctly, he had good reason to be dissatisfied with its terms. His manner was subdued to the point of making his presence in the room seem tentative. I recalled having seen him before from time to time, walking in the street, not looking to right or left. We continued to cross each other's path, and now we nodded.

I wanted to see Fez in a time of political unrest. On the way we had to draw up alongside the road and wait while French tanks and armored cars rolled by. There were tanks stationed outside the walls at Bab Fteuh when we got there. A startling change had come over the city. Each day the newspapers published lists of the previous day's atrocities. No one knew where the next dead body would be found or whose body it would prove to be. The faces of passersby in the street showed only fear, suspicion, and hostility.

Later in the spring I returned to Tangier to meet Peggy Guggenheim, who had arrived from Venice with two Italian men carrying guitars. She stayed only two weeks, but we had some good meals together, and Jane and I made her promise to visit us at Taprobane the following winter. Then she and her friends went to Spain.

For the summer I found a house at the edge of the cliff at Sidi Bouknadel and began to rent it on a monthly basis. I was ready to write another novel and wanted to use the place as a studio. The house had been built, strangely enough, over a spring, so that the rooms on the ground floor had water trickling down the walls. I painted and arranged the second floor; the work proved a good way of generating the energy necessary for starting the book. Fez was on my mind. What would it be like to see one's city, the only city one knows, falling to pieces from day to day before one's eyes?

Each night I set the alarm for daybreak. When the bell awoke me, I would reach out and take the thermos of coffee I had prepared just before going to bed. The sound of the ocean striking the cliffs came in through the window at the head of my bed. I lay still and wrote. At noon I had finished for the day.

When autumn came, I moved to a house inside the walls of the Casbah; it was higher up, and drier too. M. Ktiri came to visit me there one afternoon. He had just arrived from Fez and was still in an emotional state. The previous morning when he had opened the door of his house to go out into the street, he had stumbled over the body of a man who had been murdered during the night. "But who does this?" I demanded. *"Les terroristes,"* he said, his lips trembling. Since he had always been in the habit of showing the documents that proved the close ties that had existed between his father and the French military commanders in Fez, he had cause to be more than a little uneasy about the turn events were taking.

That December I booked passage for Jane, Ahmed Yacoubi and me on the *Orsova,* bound for Ceylon. Another exhibit of Ahmed's paintings had been arranged by a gallery in Colombo.

Temsamany wanted very much to come along with us. Jane suggested he go as far as Gibraltar and see if there were a tourist-class accommodation to be had. He did, and there was, and so we started out as a quartet, with Temsamany somewhere down in the ship's entrails. There he drank beer with Australian girls and experienced for the first time the excitement of being on wholly equal terms with Europeans. A new light shone in his eyes when the boat trip was over. Perhaps he was slightly less deferential in his manner toward us, but he entered with zest into the business of helping us get settled in Ceylon.

Jane's first reaction to Colombo was that it was hot—hotter than Panama, she said, by which she meant too hot for her comfort. She liked the mosquito nets hanging from high above the beds and the big ceiling fans, and as we began to be invited to eat at the houses of friends, she began to show interest in the food. When we got to Weligama and she saw the island of Taprobane there in front of her, a mere tuft of rain forest rising out of the sea, she groaned. We waded across and climbed onto the jetty. A newspaper photographer from the *Times of Ceylon* snapped our pictures as we did so. Then we came to the gate, and she looked up the long series of stairways through the unfamiliar vegetation, toward the invisible house. "It's a Poe story," she said, shrugging. "I can see why you'd like it." I had prepared her for the nightly invasion of bats (flying foxes, they call them), but she had not expected so many, she said, or that they would have a three-foot wingspread and such big teeth. Once it was dark you could no longer see them unless you pointed a flashlight out into the trees. This was a regular and compulsive action on the part of us all when we first moved into the house. Each one of us had his own flashlight, which he used going from room to room. There was no electric power on the island, and the house had only one bright oil lamp, which was generally in the center room where the problem was to protect it from the sea wind that always blew through the place. But since the central room's ceiling was thirty feet high, there were many shadows even there. The rest of the rooms were dimly illumined by the wavering flames of inefficient old oil lamps and candles.

Once we got the right cook, life became pleasant. We went to fetch Peggy Guggenheim at the railway station of Weligama in a rattling bullock cart. She was rapturous about the island and could not really understand why Jane hated it. Jane agreed that it was beautiful but claimed this did not help. The day after Peggy arrived at Taprobane, a fat, legal-sized envelope was delivered to her, sent by the government in Colombo. It contained a set of tax forms which she was to fill out in triplicate, declaring her global income. Peggy did not wait; we went to Galle to consult a lawyer. The man calmed her and advised her to disregard the letter.

Jane was fascinated, not by the Ceylonese, whose living pattern was too foreign to be much more than an abstraction, but by the Burghers, because they were staid members of the Dutch Reformed Church, spoke an archaic English, and were touching in the way that only a group about to disappear can be. Mrs. Trimmer had relatives in Galle, and they entertained us in their house. It was strangely evocative of Central America: the straight-backed chairs were in rows along the walls of the *corredor,* and the patio was crowded to excess with the same profusion of large-leafed plants.

Ahmed spent his time painting and swimming. Nights he and Temsamany would join the gardener, the cook, and his assistant on the rocks along the west side of the island, catching lobsters for the next day's curry. Temsamany got on well with the local Moslems and sometimes attended prayers at the mosque with them, although he thought them ill educated in religious etiquette. Ahmed said they were ridiculous and impossible to talk to, and so he did not cultivate their friendship.

Peggy wanted to visit Yala, the wildlife preserve in the southwestern corner of the country. We hired a station wagon; the driver was a pleasant Buddhist and on the second day asked if we might stop briefly at Tissamaharana, where there was a great tank—an artificial lake—full of sacred carp to which he wanted to make a small sacrifice. We were glad of the chance to get down and walk along the edge of the lake in the shade of the huge trees. The driver, Temsamany, and Ahmed went in the other direction. Suddenly the morning calm was shattered by a huge splash behind us. When I turned, I saw what had happened. I ran back. Temsamany was grinning triumphantly, pointing to the surface of the water, where several large fish floated on their sides. The driver had been scattering broken wafers to the carp; they were all there, eating, when the blow fell. "I got eight with one rock!" shouted Temsamany. The driver's face was convulsed with horror and disbelief; Ahmed snickered in the background. He was an old Ceylon hand. The driver, although he remained courteous, never smiled again and even looked askance at all of us for the remaining days of the trip.

We spent a day at Kataragama, on an island in a jungle river, one of the strangest places in all Ceylon. It looked like an abandoned miniature world's fair built around a long central village green. All the religions of Ceylon are represented there, each by a decayed booth. There was even one marked "YMCA." At the far end from the fallen tree trunk which served as bridge across to the island, there was a small but imposing Hindu temple, and this was where the action was taking place. Pilgrims were busy, preparing tubs of sticky pink rice, to be left in dishes and on squares of banana leaf as offerings. The temple was circular, and custom demanded a particular form of worship which consisted of traveling its entire circumference, outside its walls, by rolling over and over on the earth while chanting the prescribed prayers. The presence of hundreds of capuchin monkeys on the scene complicated it tremendously. The animals were everywhere at once, scooping up the rice and scattering it absently over the pilgrims as they cavorted. The sight of all these human bodies flopping about in rice that was such a bright pink was more than Temsamany could bear, and he walked away to wait for us at some distance from the temple. "It disgusted me," he explained, when we rejoined him.

We never arrived at the wildlife preserve. Only a few miles from the lodge where trackers are assigned to the visitors, we found ourselves in a flood that was swiftly inundating the whole open plain. The driver managed to turn the car without getting bogged down, and we fled in the direction from which we had just come.

Peggy had arrived in Asia with two purposes in mind: one was to meet a maharajah, and the other was to acquire some Lhasa terriers. During lunch one day at Taprobane she almost achieved the first objective. Benedict, our red-toothed gardener, came up to say that a large party of Indians had arrived at the gate down on the jetty and were asking to be shown around the island. I told him we were not expecting visitors. He went down and delivered the message, but with such force (so he said later) that one of the ladies fell to the ground as a result. This caused a small uproar, it seems, with the women screaming and the men talking very fast. Benedict, being on home ground, was not disturbed by the commotion. He merely shouted at them once again to get off the island. Then he shut and padlocked the gate and went to his quarters down in the side of the cliff. Later he remembered the card one of the gentlemen had given him at the very beginning of the confrontation. He brought it up and handed it to me. It was the calling card of HRH the Maharajah of Bhorot. Ten days after Peggy left, she wrote me from India, where she was staying with a far more prestigious potentate, the Maharajah of Mysore. From there she went north and got her dogs.

I had established a strict routine that never varied: at six each morning I had early tea, put on a sarong and walked around the island, watched the sun rise from the south point, and then set to work writing *The Spider's House*. When it was all finished, I boxed it and addressed it to Random House. While I was trying to mail it at the Weligama post office, word got quickly around the immediate neighborhood that the American was about to pay more than 400 rupees ($80) for the stamps to go on a parcel of papers. The small post office began to fill up with onlookers who had no other reason to be in there save to watch the stamps being affixed to the parcel. It was the high denominations of the stamps that fascinated them. It seemed like a lot of money to me, too, but the postal clerk showed me the regulations and rates, printed in Sinhalese, and I had to assume that I was not being overcharged. My principal concern was whether or not Random House was ever going to receive the packet. I had already lost too much outgoing mail in Ceylon not to expect the worst. However, this time it got through safely.

Jane complained regularly about the heat. Finally she came to me and said that she and Temsamany had been talking together and had decided that they both wanted more than anything to return to Tangier. I objected that it was too early in the season; the weather there would still be bad. "But it won't be hot," Jane said, and so she and Temsamany booked passage to Gibraltar.

After this I met Arthur C. Clarke, the English writer, then living in the suburbs of Colombo. Clarke was a very quiet man who enjoyed skin diving. He had thought of examining Weligama Bay. I told him to drive down, which he did several times with assistants and equipment. They would arrive and promptly disappear beneath the water off the south end of the island. A few years later in New York I bought a book Clarke had written, called *The Reefs of Taprobane.*

One day I read in the paper that the P. & O. liner *Chusan* would be making a round-trip voyage from Colombo to Japan. I suspected that if I got rid of the cook and his assistant, as well as the lavatory coolie, retaining only the gardener and maid, who formed the permanent staff, it would not cost much more to spend the six weeks on a ship than at Taprobane. I felt that I might not have another chance to see such places as Singapore, Hong Kong, and Kyoto.

The voyage was uneventful. On the *Chusan* Ahmed met a woman who arranged an exhibit for him in Hong Kong. The showing took place during the two weeks we were in Japan, and he picked up the paintings that had not been sold on our return to Hong Kong. The place I really liked was the island of Penang, off the west coast of Malaysia. I determined to return one day and stay longer.

When I got back to Taprobane, the house was depressingly empty without Jane in it. Monsoon time would be arriving shortly, in any case. I said good-bye to Benedict and Lili, who clasped their hands in the traditional prayerful attitude of Buddhists; this was surprising in them because they were both Roman Catholics. But then, I never succeeded in understanding their thought processes.

We stopped at Cairo on the way back to Tangier, to see the National Museum and Gizeh. There my camel saddle slipped, my foot caught in the device that served as a stirrup, and I was dragged headdown by one leg as the camel ambled on. The point of the anecdote is that the dragoman was not allowed to come to my aid until after the police had questioned him and noted his name and license number. Then he came running to stop the camel.

Tangier was more turbulent than ever that summer. Men were installing iron bars outside entrance doors all over the city. At the beginning of the trouble it had been strictly forbidden to shout publicly for the return of Mohammed V; however, with fifty thousand people demonstrating every day, up and down the city, there was not very much the few policemen here could not do other than exercise restraint. There were several potential riots each day, but they seldom ended in violence. When the police did throw tear-gas bombs, these exploded with a roar that was audible all over the city, and the shrapnel wounded dozens. But no deaths due to the hostilities between France and Morocco were reported in Tangier.

During the summer I got a letter from a publisher in Zurich inquiring whether I should be interested in seeing a collection of exceptional photographs of Africa, with an eye to making a book out of them. I replied that I should like to see the pictures. They were indeed very fine. Some were identified on the back by a place-name; others were not. Peter Häberlin, the young Swiss who had taken them, had just died in an accident in the Andes, and there was no way of getting any further documentation on the itinerary he had followed in Africa, for he had made no notes. It was an interesting job of sleuthing for me; I enjoyed discovering his route and put the book together in the form of a journey across the Sahara and the Sudan. *Yallah* came out first in German; then McDowell and Obolensky published it in New York.

With anti-European feeling increasing in Tangier, our house in Amrah (a strictly Moslem neighborhood with the notable exception of Barbara Hutton's block) was no longer feasible. It seems sensible to stay far from hornets when they are in an irritable mood. Jane and I took two apartments on the top floor of a tall new apartment house on the outskirts of Tangier. We had enormous terraces and splendid views over the city, the sea, and the mountains. Not long after we were installed, Jane left to visit Oliver Smith in Beverly Hills.

One very stormy night in the winter Christopher Isherwood came to see me. It was my first glimpse of him since before the war. I noticed that his speech had become very American. Ahmed gave him some *majoun* that sent him out into the gale in a state of disorientation. He wrote me later from Italy describing the (largely subjective) difficulties he encountered before managing to reach the Hôtel Minzah.

Francis Bacon was a regular visitor to the apartment that season. I had long admired his paintings, and when I finally knew him, I extended the admiration to him as well. He was a man about to burst from internal pressures. Even with the articulate description he gave me of his method of work, I was unable to imagine for myself exactly what happened as he painted. Later he allowed Ahmed to visit him at his studio up in the Casbah and watch him paint. He consented to do this because Ahmed had been having great difficulty learning how to manage oils; for months he had been trying to invent a viable technique. Another problem was that there were no artist's materials to be had in Tangier. Francis went to London and brought back a good quantity of Winsor and Newton colors.

When Bill Burroughs came around (for we finally had come to know each other), we would discuss everything but writing. I introduced him to Brion Gysin because I thought they would get on well together. I was right: eventually they became inseparable. Kerouac arrived in Tangier to visit Bill, but I did not see him, having gone across to Portugal with Michael Fordyce. Michael had an Aston-Martin and habitually drove at breakneck speed through the Tangier streets; he was impatient with Temsamany's normal pace and would have liked to take over the driving, but there was no question of Temsamany's ceding him the wheel.

While I was in Lisbon, I received a letter from Mother saying that she and Daddy would be arriving in Morocco the following month. I got back to Tangier in time to prepare for them, and Jane wired that her return from California was imminent. When she came, it was with several others, including Tennessee and John Goodwin, who already had visited Morocco on several occasions and was not very fond of it.

Although Tangier was still a reasonably attractive town at that time, and not the vast slum which it has since become, it nevertheless was not the sort of place I should have expected my parents to enjoy. But thanks to Temsamany's constant attentions, they were enthusiastic about it. They smoked kif when it was offered to them (although naturally they preferred whiskey) and in general made a point of enjoying all the little, specifically Moroccan details of life which visitors ordinarily either overlook or criticize. There was a place called the American Club, which they immediately joined. When I was not showing them the countryside, they passed their time sitting by the swimming pool there at the club. Daddy was then seventy-eight. It was in Xauen, with its steep streets and smooth, slippery paving stones, that I first noticed his difficulty in walking. After a few painful sorties, we kept close to the hotel. But it was Mother who had the fall; toward the end of the summer she stumbled in the darkness into a ditch and broke her ankle and thus returned to New York on crutches.

A man whom we did not know arrived from America and called on us, identifying himself at the door as Dr. Weiss. He had read Jane's novel *Two Serious Ladies* and had disliked it intensely. After he left Tangier, he sent two gifts. One was a black opera cape from Casa Seseña in Madrid, and the other was a book, *Nectar in a Sieve*, by Kamala Markandara. A note was clipped onto the end-paper which read: "This is my idea of a good novel." The author's photograph on the back of the jacket showed a strikingly beautiful Indian girl. Jane thought the cape ridiculous and did not read the novel. I began it, found it engrossing, and finished it.

I had moved a piano into the apartment and was spending most of my time composing and orchestrating *Yerma*. Since the *romería* is the trans-strait version of the *amara* in Morocco, I had gathered many musical ideas at the various pilgrimage spots I visited in the hills around Tangier during the years that I had been writing the work.

Generally I was busy doing an article for *Holiday*. I found these pieces difficult to write, in spite of the magazine's ideal editorial attitude. It was merely that they took form very gradually; only after the passage of a certain amount of time would the outline become perceptible to me.

I told Jane that I thought of selling Taprobane, since she disliked it so heartily. "But you like it," she said. A remark Peggy Guggenheim had made in all innocence during her visit had remained with me. "I think it's wonderful that you have this place," she had said, "but of course you can't afford it." I had just about decided in any case that considering what I had to spend each year in wages, maintenance, and repairs, I was not getting my money's worth, and no one can afford that. There was no question of selling the property, however, until I got permission from the Finance Control in Colombo to convert the proceeds of the sale from rupees into dollars. I decided to set out for Ceylon as soon as I could.

Suddenly the world became complex. There was war in Egypt, the canal was blocked, and ships en route to Asia no longer called at Gibraltar. This meant having to go to London by railway and trusting to luck to find a vessel about to sail around Africa bound for Colombo. I started out, once again accompanied by Ahmed. He always made himself so extremely useful on journeys that I no longer considered going alone and taking care of everything by myself.

We had been in London only a week or ten days when I discovered a ship of the British-India Steam Navigation Company called the *Chakdara,* about to sail for Ceylon. I should have been willing to take almost anything that would have got me away from the depressing London weather, and I was delighted to be aboard. The ship's cook and stewards were Goanese; there were only eight other passengers.

Our first meal aboard was served as we moved down the Thames. The passengers assembled in the dining room and were assigned their places at the table. Beside me sat an Asian girl whom I was certain I had met before somewhere. Thus I was not too surprised when in the middle of lunch she turned and asked me if by any chance I was the author of *The Sheltering Sky*. All at once I realized where it was that I had seen her face: on the jacket of her novel *Nectar in a Sieve*. Her name came to me intact, and I managed to startle her when in turn I asked her if she were not Kamala Markandara.

Except for Kamala, Ahmed, and me, each one of us a different kind of foreigner, the passengers were British. They were also the sort of people who appear to feel that being together at a meal calls for continuous laughter. Since their merriment was clearly due to the lack of ease they felt in one another's company, there was no inducement to share in it. This and the fact that no one of us played bridge served to isolate us from what they called "ship's routine." In Cape Town we learned firsthand about apartheid. We had to use separate entrances to the main post office, because Kamala counted as nonwhite. We were unable to have tea or coffee together, save eventually in the basement of a restaurant, where they set us up a table near the laundry. Ronald Segal, the editor of the antigovernment magazine *Africa South*, piloted us around the city during the few days we spent there. Cape Town reminded me of New York in the thirties; it burgeoned with clandestine meetings and benefit parties given in the houses of liberals for the relief of local political martyrs.

During the five-week sea voyage I wrote a piece for *Holiday* and a short story, "The Frozen Fields," which I sent off to *Harper's Bazaar* the day I arrived in Colombo. After a month or so at Taprobane, I spent five weeks in Colombo, going each sweltering morning to the government buildings in the fort, in order to arrange nine separate documents which were essential if I expected to get my dollars out of Ceylon. When all this paper work was done and the papers were piled in the vault of a lawyer's office, I turned my attention to the wildlife preserve at Yala, where the flood had turned us back two years earlier. This trip proved successful, in that we got into the precinct. We went with Hugh Gibb, who had just been making a documentary film in North Borneo. We were able to photograph elephants on three different occasions—even (from well over a mile away and with the wind in our favor) a rogue, pacing back and forth on a wide plain, thinking his private, criminal thoughts. The rogue's impulses become destructive from the moment he is excluded by the herd, but being powerless to vent them upon his own kind, he attacks people, telegraph poles, signboards, and passing automobiles.

I left Ceylon feeling that I had done everything possible to get my money out of the country in the event I sold the island. The ship this time had the unlikely name of *Issipingo*; it went only as far as Mombasa and took nine days to get there.

While Ahmed and I were up in Nairobi, I heard from Michael Fordyce, who was in Zanzibar with his wife and children, living, so he claimed, in a house full of bats. I agreed to meet them in Zanzibar in another three weeks. At that time I was doing an occasional piece for the *Nation,* and I thought I ought to move around as much as I could while I was in East Africa. My principal objective in Nairobi was to interview Tom Mboya. Ronald Segal of Cape Town had given me a note to him. (Segal himself had a dramatic and well-publicized escape from South Africa shortly afterward, in which he and a friend swam the Limpopo River to safety in Rhodesia, with the police shooting after them.)

Mboya was an impressive man, full of charm but absolutely firm with everyone. He made it possible for me to visit various trade-union headquarters and thus get myself invited to the dwellings of some of the delegates. The blacks lived in closed compounds with military guards at the entrances. Mau Mau memories were still fresh, and the iron bars at doors and windows in buildings where whites lived had not been removed. At the hotel each morning I had to unlock the grille myself and let in the Kikuyu who cleaned the room. In Ceylon Ira Morris had given me a letter to a friend of his, but when I inquired about the man, I learned that he was in the Athi River Detention Camp, and had been there for several years.

The animal preserve near Nairobi was like a vast circus being given for one's sole benefit. I had the recurring impression that it had all been rehearsed, that the cheetahs had been trained to stalk the zebras while I watched, and the lions to lie unconcernedly in the grass for me to photograph. Ahmed was impressed. "It's better to be an animal in Kenya than a man," he said to our tracker, who, being a black, did not reply.

I remember waiting for what seemed an interminable stretch of time in Mombasa, while it grew hotter and hotter, until the first monsoons hit. Then the rain poured down and filled the streets. There was no certainty that we were going to be able to get a cabin on the ship. In the end we did, and it sailed for Zanzibar. We did not see the Fordyces, but we were taken in hand by a group of revolutionary Moslem students who showed us the city, led us to their headquarters where they gave us literature, and saw to it that we ate well during the days we stayed there.

The ship edged slowly down the coast of Africa, stopping every day or so at a different port. The Fordyces were aboard. During the two days at Cape Town I visited the offices of *Drum*, run by Cape Coloreds for Africans. (Later in London I had lunch with Tom Hopkinson, who was about to leave for Cape Town to become an editor of the magazine.) At the end of a month we disembarked at Las Palmas, Gran Canaria. As I left the ship, I was handed a telegram. It was signed by Gordon Sager, and it said that Jane had suffered a slight stroke several weeks earlier and was recuperating. In my innocence I failed to recognize this message as the first statement of a theme which would become the principal leitmotiv of our lives. I did not know it, but the good years were over.

XVII

It was a blustery April in Tangier. Jane was staying with a friend in a drafty old house high on the cliffs above the strait. She did not look ill, and she seemed in good spirits, in spite of having been left with a strange sort of aphasia which regularly caused her to use the antonym of the word she meant to use. Everyone found this amusing—merely one more charming eccentricity of Jane's, to be added to the rest. She recounted what she considered a funny story, of how someone had telephoned and asked to speak with me. Told that I was somewhere in East Africa, the man had introduced himself by saying: "This is Allen Ginsberg, the Bop poet." "The *what* poet?" It took some time for Jane to understand the word, but when she had got it, she merely said: "I see."

"Then," said Jane, "this complete madman asked me if I believed in God. 'Do you believe in God, Jane?' I told him: 'I'm certainly not going to discuss it on the telephone.' But he's still here, if you want to see him. At Bill Burroughs'."

It was not long before I did meet the Bop poet; he was with Peter Orlovsky and Allen Ansen, staying at the Villa Muniriya, collecting the typed pages of a work in progress by Burroughs which had been lying on the floor of Bill's basement room these many months. Often I had looked down at the chaos of sheets of yellow paper being trampled underfoot, thinking that he must like to have them there, otherwise he would have picked them up. Now these three had arrived in Tangier with the express purpose of picking them up for him. I liked Ginsberg for being honest and dedicated, but Jane found him insensitive because he mentioned William Carlos Williams' recent stroke and its unfortunate results upon his ability to work. Since Jane's vision had been largely destroyed by the cerebral hemorrhage, she worried that bad effects might appear later. It seemed essential that she see a neurologist quickly, to discover whether she had an operable lesion or not.

We went to London and saw several doctors. One of them told her: "My dear Mrs. Bowles, go back to your pots and pans and try to cope." It was August, but August masquerading as November with a continuous cold drizzle. I bought winter clothing and took Jane to Oxford, to Radcliffe Infirmary for the necessary tests. The lesion had been miscroscopic; surgery was impossible. We returned to Tangier, with Jane in an extremely tense and anxious state. And now as a result of undue pressure on the cortex of the brain, she began to suffer from epileptoid convulsions. We remained only two weeks in Tangier and went swiftly back to England, where Jane entered a hospital in the country somewhere in the Midlands.

That autumn, in the course of a London epidemic, I caught Asian flu. During the nine days I spent in bed, I ran a high fever which prompted me to write a story about the effects of an imaginary South American drink, the *cumbiamba*. It was called "Tapiama" and was something of an experiment for me, being the only fever-directed piece I had written. On the tenth day, when the story was finished and typed in duplicate, my thermometer showed ninety-eight and six-tenths. I got up, dressed, and went to Harrod's. A few hours later I was delirious. The next morning they plumped me onto a stretcher and removed me to a hospital. Pleurisy set in, and I spent a bad two weeks in a ward with fifty other pneumonia cases, too sick to notice the oxygen tanks being wheeled in or to watch those who had not been saved by them being wheeled out. In the end Sonia Orwell came and rescued me by reserving a room at the Hôpital Français in Shaftesbury Avenue and taking me there in a cab.

Here the good food hastened my recuperation. Angus Wilson came one day with a big pile of books for me, and at the end of another two weeks I was well enough to leave. It had been agreed that Jane and I would stay at Sonia's when I came out of the hospital, and so I moved into her house in Percy Street while I waited. I had brought with me to England a manila envelope full of short stories which had not yet been published in book form in the United Kingdom. It seemed the right moment to look for a publisher. Sonia had helped edit Cyril Connolly's *Horizon* before her marriage to George Orwell and had many friends. She made an appointment for me with an editor at Hamish Hamilton, gave me a letter to him, and told me how to get to the office. Through inattentiveness I went, not to Hamilton, but to Heinemann. I discovered my error only after I had shown my letter of introduction to a secretary on the ground floor. The secretary alerted someone on the second floor, and I was asked to go up. When I came back down, the book belonged to Heinemann. Then Sonia had to call Hamish Hamilton and explain.

I finally brought Jane from the hospital, and we had a short holiday at Sonia's before sailing for Morocco. Jane's former anxious state was temporarily in abeyance, but she continued to have convulsions, including one on the ship the first day out of London. We stayed only two months in Tangier, and then, partially because the police were making wholesale arrests of certain European residents, deporting some and packing the rest off to jail, we decided to get out of Morocco and not return until the new regime had attained its balance.

Jane had heard there were good doctors in Lisbon. We flew there. Lisbon was rainy and dark and full of cold winds; we spent our time sitting and shivering in the strange little pastry-shop bars of which there were so many. At one point we boarded an ancient vessel of the Royal Mail Line on its way to Buenos Aires and disembarked at Funchal in Madeira. We had a month or so there and might have stayed longer despite the constant rain, for we liked it. But Jane's passport had expired, and the nearest place to attend to it was the American embassy in Lisbon. There we were told that a new passport could be issued to Jane only with the approval of the Federal Bureau of Investigation. We waited nearly three weeks for a reply, and when it came, it was negative. Jane was then informed that she must leave immediately for the United States. As a document she had only the paper which the embassy had given her in exchange for her passport. After Tennessee and I had come to a telegraphic understanding that he would meet her at the airport in New York, I put Jane on a TWA plane, and off she flew. A few weeks later Libby Holman wrote me that her lawyer had managed to get her a new passport. These were a few more notches in the rope of absurdities which trailed after both of us as a result of our adherence to the CPUSA back in 1938 and 1939.

I stayed in Portugal all that spring. Maurice Grosser arrived to paint, and we drove down to Albufeira, a tourist-free fishing port, where we took a house with the intention of passing the summer in it. But astonishingly Libby was able to reach me by telephone, to ask me to return to New York for a production of *Yerma*. Having just paid the rent on the house the previous day, we abandoned it with some regret. Maurice drove me to Lisbon, not wanting to stay in the house alone. I gave him the keys to my flat in Tangier. Thus he spent the summer in Morocco rather than in Portugal. Very reluctantly I went to New York.

On the telephone Libby had told me that an aria was needed quickly for Rose Bampton, who was going to play what until then had been a minor role. During most of the week it took to cross the Atlantic, I spent my time searching for and translating a suitable text by García Lorca, which I found in the *Romancero Gitano*.

The play had been in rehearsal for some weeks before I arrived on the scene. Shortly after I got to New York, I ran into Carl Van Vechten in the street. We agreed to meet the following day. During lunch Carl asked me if there was anyone I wanted to meet. "Meet?" I repeated. "How do you mean?" "I mean is there anyone you don't know that you'd like to know?" In Lisbon I had just read and been impressed by a collection of short stories called *Color of Darkness* which James Laughlin had sent me. I pronounced the name of the author, James Purdy. "Come Wednesday evening at seven," Carl said. I went, and Purdy was there, a reticent and unassuming man whom I immediately liked. Carl took photographs all during the evening. I did not see him again before he died.

A plane was chartered to take the cast of *Yerma* to Denver.

The director, Angna Enters, preferred to travel by train, as did I, and so we went overland together. The orchestra in Denver was lamentable. We then went to Ithaca, where the instrumentalists were better without being as good as I should have liked. As always, there was not enough time devoted to orchestra rehearsals. Almost as soon as they heard the musicians start to read their parts, the dancers and actors began to run through their routines onstage. Lack of organization in the production was offset by personal devotion to Libby on the part of the cast, but the project was clearly not slated for success.

Jane's mother was at the opening in Ithaca; we spoke of finding the right rest home where Jane could recuperate for a few weeks. Jane herself was wholeheartedly against the project; on the other hand, she was growing increasingly troubled by the persistent nature of her aphasia. At the Lenox Hill Hospital she was given a daily reading lesson, which she found useless. Her mother eventually decided on New York Hospital, and there Jane spent the following three months. As if to distract me while I waited for her, José Ferrer asked me to Hollywood to write the score of *Edwin Booth*. I had to fly, but at least on the plane I was given a real bed with sheets and blankets. (There was one other such bed on the plane; Harry Belafonte had it.)

During that month in Hollywood I realized to what extent life in the United States had changed. The behavior of people bore little resemblance to what I remembered as American behavior. I felt that I was in the middle of a truly exotic culture, and perhaps one of the strangest of all time. A large convertible pulled up to the curb as I walked along the street, and the youths inside called to me. "Hey, man! Got a dollar for gas?" I said: "No. Sorry." They looked at me as if I had been a basket case and drove on. One day the air was yellow and unbreathable. The papers carried headlines about a new phenomenon, which they called smog. Old jazz tunes from the twenties were being played with *danzón* and *bolero* rhythms. Decidedly civilization had turned and begun to devour its own body. One night I sat at a desk for forty-five minutes talking with Oscar Levant; the following night I watched our encounter on television during a Chinese meal at the Gershwins' house. It was both horrible and fascinating. I believed it implicitly when I was told again and again, both seriously and in jest, that Los Angeles was the City of the Future. There seemed no doubt about it.

Back in New York I went one day with Gore Vidal to Chandler Cowles', where I saw Auden for the first time in nearly twenty years. I was unable to guess whether he had forgotten the circumstances of our last encounter, when he had stormed out of the house in Middagh Street in a rage. Jack Kerouac was among the guests. Gore and I went with him to an apartment in the Village. During the evening Jack grew expansive on beer. As we went out he handed me a paperback copy of *The Subterraneans,* in which he had written: "To Paul—a man completely devoid of bullshit." Later, when Jane came out of the hospital and saw the book and its inscription, she said: "But are they all going through a Céline period, or what?"

Jane and I had scarcely got ourselves settled back in Tangier when a telegram came from Cheryl Crawford, who was producing Tennessee's new play, *Sweet Bird of Youth,* and wanted music for it. I agreed to have the score complete and be in New York within six weeks. Then I went through the old Tangier routine of looking for an out-of-the-way dwelling of some sort in which to put a piano. This time I found a small apartment on the roof of a building in the middle of the European quarter. I rented the usual shrill Erard at the local piano store and set to work. Most of the score was finished before I got onto the ship; the rest of it I wrote at the piano in the *Saturnia*'s ballroom at night after everyone had gone to sleep.

Sweet Bird of Youth was already in an advanced state of rehearsal when I arrived in Philadelphia. Kazan wanted only a few extra cues written for certain of Paul Newman's scenes. We then recorded the score. I had always objected to the idea of either recording or amplifying theater music; I wanted the sound made by musicians in the flesh. But this time I had decided to experiment and had written the score with possible microphones in mind. The New York opening was blessedly free of the usual problems with dynamics which are inevitable if one uses live musicians.

The Beat writers, in particular Burroughs, Ginsberg, Corso,

and Kerouac, were receiving enormous publicity at that moment. In New York I stayed on Sixty-first Street with Libby, who recently had become friendly with three high-ranking officials from the Soviet consulate around the corner. She suggested a dinner to bring the Russians and the Beats together. The evening began pleasantly enough, with caviar and vodka and a humidor full of marijuana cigarettes on the table in front of the fireplace. (These items were not announced as such and were discovered with glee by Peter Orlovsky, whom Allen had brought with him.) Allen then offered the open box to the Russians, explaining clearly what it contained. Although all three of the officials were equally formidable, one of them seemed to have been delegated to make the decisions for all. The spokesman took a cigarette and slipped it into his pocket, saying he would smoke it later. Then he frowned and asked if it were not true that marijuana was illegal. Allen tried earnestly to make him understand that precisely for this reason it was necessary to smoke it and to encourage others to do likewise. When the man had fully grasped that idea, his face assumed a set mask of disapproval. Beginning about then, the Soviet diplomats showed a distinct tendency to huddle close to one another.

At dinner the three Russians sat on one side of the table. Allen, Gregory, and Peter sat opposite them, with Libby and me at the ends. Presently Gregory remarked in passing that Khrushchev was an idiot. "Why do you say that?" the spokesman said quickly. "We don't say Eisenhower is an idiot." Then Allen cried: "You should, because he is. They're both idiots. Why shouldn't we say it if it's true?"

Without answering, the three Russians rose quietly and went out of the room, while Libby's expression turned slowly from crestfallen to apprehensive. In a minute or two they returned, apparently having reached a decision on the course of action they were going to follow under these unprecedentedly trying circumstances. From then on the spokesman addressed himself exclusively to Libby, in an attempt to keep the conversation from falling into the hands of the poets. In the music room after dinner the three stood drinking coffee while Allen explored the extreme limits of their tolerance, first by explicit verbal suggestions which could only be taken as sexual, and then by actually touching them. Suddenly they left, looking extremely uncomfortable. It was not many months later that the spokesman and one of the others were expelled from the United States as undesirables.

Peggy Glanville-Hicks was still campaigning to help me get a Rockefeller grant for recording Moroccan music. I had applied twenty-five years earlier to the Guggenheim Foundation for a fellowship to carry out the same project, but without success. No one had been interested in discovering what music might exist in this part of the world. This time there was enough interest to make the grant possible. I went to Washington to see the people in the Music Division of the Library of Congress (for whatever material I got for the Rockefeller Foundation was destined to go into the archives there) and learned how to use and care for the big Ampex they were going to send me via the American Embassy in Rabat.

Then I took the creaking old *Conte Biancamano* and sailed for Lisbon. From there I went to Madeira for a while because I was doing a piece on the island for *Holiday*. When I had left New York, Tennessee had been with Kenneth Tynan in Havana; when I got to Tangier, there he stood with Jane on the dock waving while the ferry pulled in. Jane seemed well, even though she was still medicating herself very heavily. I spent a month with her before it was time to set out for Rabat to get the necessary documents from the Moroccans. Their reluctance to cooperate made the project difficult to set in motion. They were loath to give me any sort of blanket credential that I might use in dealing with local authorities. The trouble was that at that moment there was no official attitude toward Moroccan culture in general. Each man had his own ideas, but no one felt qualified to make a definite statement.

After the return to the throne of Mohammed V, the musicians of Morocco, taken under the wing of a governmental department called *Jeunesses et Sports,* were commissioned to invent new songs to celebrate the country's independence. They responded with hundreds of works in dozens of genres and in several languages. It was easy for them, since they used traditional melodies and merely made up new words which fitted them. There was ample material to be recorded in all parts of the land.

Christopher Wanklyn, a Canadian who had lived for five years in Tangier, agreed to go with me on a preliminary field trip which would take about six weeks. If all went well, he would stay with me throughout the project. There was a Djibli in Tangier named Mohammed Larbi Jilali, who had gone on a British expedition across the Sahara and the Sudan. A book had appeared subsequent to the journey, in which Mohammed Larbi figured. I asked him to come along. Christopher spoke good Moghrebi, but he was a Nazarene. It is always better to have a Moslem with one, no matter where one goes in Morocco.

After two weeks of stasis I hit on a solution to my problem. I wrote a short To Whom It May Concern text explaining the project, stating that the United States government was assisting in it, and asking whatever assistance might be necessary from the local administrators. I found a sympathetic governmental functionary willing to have the text retyped on official paper and sign and stamp it. I had my photograph stapled to the improvised document. All this was worked out with the help of repeated visits to the embassy for advice. It was a neat and fairly impressive document when it was completed, and I clipped it into my passport.

In high spirits we set out on our trip through mountains and desert. It was summer; we knew that it would not rain and that there would be many nights with fires and drums under the stars. We did not know that we would find relatively few places where we could record. The music was there, but for a variety of reasons it was often impossible to capture.

We would arrive in a town known to be the center of a region rich in music and present our documents to the super-caid of the district. If he proved friendly, we could count on his cooperation, and would find living quarters. Usually only after we were installed could we start inquiries concerning the electrical facilities of the place. The Ampex functioned only with 110-volt AC and had no batteries. Often we discovered that either the current or the voltage was wrong for us, so that we had to continue the following day without recording anything. In Tamanar the only generator supplying what we needed belonged to an irascible Frenchman who would not even discuss allowing us to use it. We had to go back to Essaouira and wait three days for the musicians to be shipped to us from Tamanar by truck. Sometimes we encountered such disapproval from the official when we presented our papers that the best course was simply to leave the province. These men seemed to consider us part of a conspiracy to present Morocco as a backward nation, a land of savages. It was they themselves who used the expression *une musique de sauvages;* feeling as they did about it, they could be expected to consider it their patriotic duty to see to it that the shameful sounds made by their countrymen did not reach alien ears. The only exception they made was that of Andaluz music, and I suspect that this was only because the texts are in classical Arabic. Wherever that attitude manifested itself, we left the region quickly and went on to another.

Mohammed Larbi abandoned us during the third field trip and hurried back to Tangier to see his wife; apparently she was tired of being left alone for such long stretches of time. But Christopher stayed on with me to the end, and after that for several years he and I continued to make trips into the remote south, carrying more manageable equipment (which had since been put on the market), to record some of the music that we had not been able to get with the Ampex. Eventually Folkways produced a collection of his tapes. But although the Library of Congress has been intending since 1959 to issue an LP of some of my material, an insufficient budget has thus far kept the music in the archives.

Jane and I spent most of the following year in Tangier, watching the city become progressively de-Europeanized. In spite of having come under Rabat's direct political control at the time of the sultan's return, Tangier had been allowed to retain its charter until April, 1960. This delay gave local Europeans time to bring their businesses to an end and leave the country without undue losses. When the charter expired, Tangier's finances would be subject to the same controls as in any other Moroccan town. There was a great deal of uninformed speculation and needless anxiety among the European residents as to their future.

Most of us agreed that eventually we would be forced to leave; the arguments occurred over the amount of time we had left.

When *The Sheltering Sky* was first published, I heard in a roundabout way that Barbara Hutton had found it objectionable and would not "have it in the house." This seemed an odd reaction from a woman who had been five times married and who was about to become the bride of Porfirio Rubirosa. When I met her, I understood. She liked everything around her to show an element of the unreal in it, and she took great pains to transform reality into a continuous fantasy which seemed to her sufficiently *féerique* to be taken seriously. One summer when she gave a ball, she brought thirty Reguibat camel drivers with their racing camels from the Sahara, a good thousand miles distant, merely to form a *garde d'honneur* through which the guests would pass at the entrance of the house. The animals and men stayed encamped in the Place Sidi Hosni for many days after the party, apparently in no hurry to get back to the desert.

That year I was working on articles, but only in the daytime. At night, after Jane and the maids had gone to bed, I enjoyed myself writing stories about Moroccans. The pleasure consisted in inventing a new problem and finding a way to solve it. The problem I set myself was not unlike the one described by Raymond Roussel in *Comment j'ai écrit certains de mes livres*. Let us say that I started with four disparate fragments—anecdotes, quotations, or simple clauses deprived of context—gleaned from separate sources and involving, if anything, entirely different sets of characters. The task was to invent a connecting narrative tissue which would make all four of the original elements equally supportive of the resulting construction. It seemed to me that the subject of kif smoking, wholly apart from the desirable limiting of possibilities it implied, would provide an effective cement with which to put together the various fragments. By using kif-inspired motivations, the arbitrary could be made to seem natural, the diverse elements could be fused, and several people would automatically become one. I did four of these tales, and then there seemed to be no more material. Lawrence Ferlinghetti, who was here in Tangier briefly while I was busy writing them, published them at City Lights under the title *A Hundred Camels in the Court-*

yard. He had designed a cover for the book, but I wanted very much to have a photograph rather than a drawing on the package. I took a series of pictures of kif pipes with a variety of backgrounds and sent them off to him immediately, hoping he might be persuaded to make a change. His reply: "Photos socco." (A pun on my address: Tanger Socco.) He used one showing a pipe from Marrakech, a naboula from Tetuán, and a palm mat from Rissani.

About a mile down the hill from where I live there is a small beach with high cliffs at each end, known as Merkala. That year I often walked in the afternoon down through the village of Ain Hayani to the shore, where I would pace from one end of the deserted strip of sand to the other, taking the sun and sea air for an hour before starting back home. There was a café-restaurant overlooking the beach, but the Moroccan who owned it had boarded it up. A guard lived there; sometimes at twilight I would see his pot of coals glowing outside the entrance. One day the guard called to me, thus beginning an acquaintanceship which ultimately added a whole new dimension to my writing experience. The guard had recently come out of jail and, being of an introspective nature, considered himself something of a social pariah. Doubtless this was a reason why he was content to have a job which isolated him month after month on that lonely strip of shoreline. A few anecdotes he told about his life impressed me deeply, not with their unusual content, but because of the way in which he recounted them. His rhetorical sense was extraordinary; he knew exactly which nuances and details to include in order to make a tale complete and convincing.

In the spring Christopher Wanklyn and I had rented a house together in Marrakech and given it a few basic Moroccan objects of furnishing. It was a fairly spacious loft over the souks in the Medina, but it had been divided into six or seven rooms. There was a large flat terrace where it was pleasant to spread big reed mats and pillows and lie looking up at the stars. The venture began as a mutual caprice, but quickly Christopher decided that he liked living there better than in Tangier, and so it became his house.

When summer came, Bill Burroughs announced that Allen

Ginsberg and Gregory Corso would be arriving presently in Tangier. The afternoon they came there was a long reunion in the little garden of the Villa Muniriya, celebrated with multiple picture taking. Then, the Muniriya being too dear, they went down the street to another still smaller hotel called the Armor and found a very poetic garret apartment overlooking the harbor.

Timothy Leary came to Tangier. He was still teaching at Harvard, and while he was here, he got Bill Burroughs to agree to stay with him in Cambridge later and assist him in his experimentation there. I met him at Ahmed Yacoubi's studio among the masks and narghilehs. When he left he gave me a bottle of psyllocybin capsules made by Sandoz, which I never got around to trying. Subsequently Bill went to Massachusetts. His sojourn at the Leary house did not last more than a month. Soon he was back in Tangier, remarking that Leary was the most "unscientific" man he'd ever known.

During the year or two when Bill had lived in Paris in what was referred to as The Beat Hotel at 9 rue Gît-le-Coeur (which was where Brion Gysin also lived), he had come to believe unequivocally in Brion's recommendation that prose be chopped up and rearranged in aleatory fashion. Between them they devised various methods to use in accomplishing this. One of Bill's favorite procedures was to tape his own voice reading at random from magazines, newspapers, and books; he would run the tape back and forth, cutting in with new material wherever it happened to stop and continuing until all phrases were "cut up." One night he came and gave me a demonstration, using the reading matter available in the room. At the end, when he played back, the tape still sounded like the prose of William Burroughs and nobody else. (Once when I expressed doubts about the advisability of using the cut-up method in fiction, he replied that "in the hands of a master" it became a viable technique.)

When he returned from his stint with Tim Leary, he took an apartment on the roof of the erstwhile Tangier Stock Exchange, which since independence has functioned as the Lottery Headquarters. The walls were almost completely of glass, but the place had a certain amount of privacy since there were no equally tall buildings nearby. Here Bill developed his personal writing procedures. All around the walls he installed wide shelves at a convenient height for writing in a standing position. On these he spread his collection of scrapbooks, crowded with clippings, letters, photographs, passages written in longhand, and postcards, and these formed the material for his writing. He would go from one scrapbook to another, taking a phrase here and a sentence there, which he used either verbatim or after subjecting it to one of his chopping procedures.

About this time I had a communication from a magazine called *Second Coming,* asking for a manuscript. It occurred to me that I might take one of the anecdotes told me by Larbi, the guard at Merkala, and translate it for them. I asked Larbi to record his recollections of jail. When the piece was translated into English, I sent it off to *Second Coming.* Very promptly a check arrived in payment for it. I think Larbi had not really believed it possible that anyone would pay him for such "work," but when he held the money in his hands, he wanted very much to continue recording. And I, seeing the quality of the product, agreed that we should go on. He then went back to his early childhood and recounted a section of that, which *Evergreen Review* printed. Soon we were working almost every day. On the basis of the sections they had seen, Grove Press contracted to publish a book. At some point Richard Seaver had the idea of presenting the volume as a novel rather than as nonfiction, so that it would be eligible for a prize offered each year by an international group of publishers, of which Grove was a member. In the voting Larbi's book was defeated by Jorge Semprun's *Le Long Voyage.* However, when it was published, it sold well in several languages and went quickly into paperback editions in both America and the United Kingdom, with the result that Larbi made enough money from it to look for a bride.

Allen Ginsberg wanted to see Marrakech. He and I went down one day by train, arriving in the evening. When we got to the Djemaa el Fna, I realized from the unusual commotion there that something was amiss. During the day the entire southern section of the souks had gone up in flames, destroying between four and five hundred bazaars. We went to the house and stood on the terrace watching them carry the damaged goods from the shops out into the street. In the air there was still the stench of burning wool. Thus Allen did not manage to see Marrakech while it was beautiful, having missed it by one day. When the destroyed quarter was reconstructed, European building materials were used, which gave it the contemporary effect so admired by Moroccans. They are always happy if something ancient can be made to look as though it had been built yesterday.

Tennessee appeared for a few weeks after I returned to Tangier. He and Jane could be found every day at Sun Beach in an atmosphere of deck chairs, towels, highballs, and cold cuts. But Jane's health suffered reverses. She was obliged to undergo two surgical interventions within the space of a few months, the second being for a hernia which had developed as a result of the first. She became excessively thin and was plagued by insomnia. Our combined worlds orbited around the subject of her poor health. Each week she seemed to have a new symptom to add to the old ones; the horizon of her illness was slowly widening. It took me a long time to realize that my life had undergone a tremendous change. The act of living had been enjoyable; at some point when I was not paying attention, it had turned into a different sort of experience, to whose grimness I had grown so accustomed that I now took it for granted.

One evening an Englishman named Peter Owen called on me, with his wife. They were looking, they said, for a manuscript to publish. The only item I could invent was a volume of travel essays. Owen was enthusiastic and agreed to do the book, including photographs I had taken in the Sahara and in Morocco and Ceylon which could serve as illustrations. The articles had been printed in magazines, but I rewrote them and added an account of music hunting in the Rif. At the same time that I sent the collection to Owen, I posted a copy to Random House, enclosing a different selection of photographs. The two editions of *Their Heads Are Green* appeared in New York and London more or less at the same time.

The dry season in Morocco is so beautiful that I am always loath to spend it in an apartment in the town. I want to get out where I can hear the cicadas and the wind in the trees. In 1962 there was still a dearth of tenants in Tangier. It was possible to go out at any time and rent a house for the summer. Each year when the month of May came around, I began to look for the ideal place to spend the next few months. That year I found a run-down house on the Old Mountain, at some distance from the road, sharing the top of a knoll with some ancient cypress trees. Some rooms were empty, others filled with old pieces of furniture that had not been moved for decades. It was a good place to go on a summer's day and lie listening to the birds and crickets. The rooms were spacious; I spread out reed matting and piled cushions along the walls. It was not meant to be a place in which to sleep. We took picnic lunches there, these becoming more elaborate when it was realized by the maids that the old house had a kitchen with a stove that worked. Moroccan women love being part of a picnic, particularly if it involves making a fire and doing some sort of cooking. A sandwich picnic strikes them as a very tame undertaking, explained only by Christian laziness.

A letter from Tennessee asked me to find him a house within walking distance of the beach and rent it for three months in his name. He came, but he was in no state to remain. Soon he went off to Spoleto, to try out his current play *The Milk Train Doesn't Stop Here Any More*. Later he returned here for another short stay, this one being overshadowed and eventually truncated by a bitter feud he had with his landlord concerning the electricity bill. He paid it finally and then packed up and left for New York.

Although Jane's mother had visited her in Tangier on more than one occasion, from time to time she campaigned vigorously for Jane to reciprocate by visiting her. My own parents likewise made constant allusions to an American trip I was assumed to be about to make. Influenced by all this propaganda, we consulted shipping schedules and then booked passage. In early September we went to Spain for a few days to stay with an acquaintance of Jane's, and then we sailed for New York.

My parents looked smaller than I had remembered them. They were very happy, particularly with the great number of birds in the region. In the early morning the birdcalls were extraordinary; lying there in bed, I might have thought myself back in Ceylon, rather than in Florida.

The crisis over Russian missiles in Cuba reached its peak during the two weeks I spent with them. "We'll be the first to be hit," Mother said grimly. And then she repeated what she often said when general conditions were bad. "All I can say is, I feel terribly sorry for the young people growing up today. What chance have they got? They're beaten before they start."

I had grown used to thinking of my parents as an inexhaustible and more or less permanent archive of information and anecdotes about their early days, family tradition, and New England folklore. Now I found that they no longer recalled many of these things. It was saddening and unsettling to think that I had become the sole repository of memories that at one time we had shared. I left somewhat sobered by my stay with them, making promises to return as soon as I was able—perhaps even the following year.

I put Jane on a ship to Gibraltar because I expected to be busy and I thought it would be bad for her to be left to her own devices in New York. Tennessee had asked me to write music for *The Milk Train Doesn't Stop Here Any More*, now that it had been tried out in Spoleto. Virgil Thomson was not in New York, and had arranged for me to stay in his flat in the Hotel Chelsea, where I composed most of the score. It was surprising to run into Arthur C. Clarke in the elevator there; the last time I had seen him he had been wearing skin-diving gear on the jetty at Taprobane. He had a room on the floor above me, and gave me all the news of Ceylon. *Milk Train* opened in New Haven and went on to Boston before coming into New York, but since the score had been taped beforehand, there was no need for me to go farther than New Haven.

I had no reason to stay any longer in New York, and so I bought passage on the first ship going toward Tangier. I got back to Morocco to find calamitous floods everywhere. The weather was bad on both sides of the Atlantic that winter. Mother wrote that freezing temperatures had ruined her garden in Florida, killing even the big trees.

In the autumn a series of border battles between Morocco and Algeria occurred, in a dispute which has yet to be settled. The entire country was euphoric when a group of unarmed peasants in the village of Ain Chouater captured four Egyptian military officials in a helicopter and turned them over to the government. Because of the incident, Egyptian music was withdrawn from the radio programs of Morocco, which I thought a wonderful idea, since Egypt's *kitsch* had been flooding the country for a very long time. Unfortunately the Moroccans were ready for the situation: they merely redoubled their efforts to improve their own commerical product. But since their only concept of popular music was Egyptian popular music, they manufactured imitation Egyptian *kitsch,* and this was even more objectionable than the authentic variety. Much later, when the ban was lifted, it was, incredibly enough, with a certain relief that I once more heard the real thing, with Abd el Wahab and Om Kalsoum and Farid el Atrache performing it as it should be performed.

The so-called war was taking place in the extreme east and south of Morocco. We wanted very much to spend some time in the south. (Most Tangier residents regularly feel the necessity of going to the desert; the sudden dryness of the air is a great tonic.) Christopher Wanklyn drove Jane and me to Tafraout, where we were able to record an *ahouache,* but not the jackals that came yelping down from the heights of the Anti-Atlas each night. It would have made a fine recording. About half past one they would arrive, some thirty strong, trotting down the valley past the hotel on their way to the marketplace, where they engaged in noisy battle with the local dogs. There was no way of recording their nightly visits, for the generator was always shut off at half past ten.

After two weeks Jane wanted to get back to Tangier. We returned first to Marrakech, coming down out of the High Atlas one cold night when our principal preoccupation was having a hot meal. We went to Christopher's and found that Boujemaa, prepared for our arrival, had dinner cooking on the stove. Soon he came in, eager to talk, and told us that President Kennedy was dead. Knowing Boujemaa, I suspected that this was one of his complex jokes, particularly when he specified that the death was due to bullet wounds. This sounded too Moroccan to be anything but an invention. Boujemaa (also known as He of the Assembly) was inclined to prophesy, and he did so that night. With personal bitterness, as though Jane and I had had a hand in the assassination, he warned that as a result of having killed Kennedy Americans would watch the United States disintegrate and change its character until they would wish that they were citizens of any country in the world rather than their own. "But why?" we insisted. "Because they will want to go on living," he said. "And in the United States there will be only death." These words did not delight us, but we nodded and said: *"Ikoun. Yimkin."* Since then, whenever he has seen us, Boujemaa has reminded us of the evening. "And my words about your land. Are they true?"

During the winter I began to work on a novel whose writing I intended to make a purely pleasurable pastime. I tried to recapture the state of mind which had produced the thrillers I had read to the seventh grade in primary school, to discover what result that point of departure might give now. The ploy worked: I got caught up in the elaboration of the tale fairly quickly and knew I was going to finish the book. Spring burst upon the landscape. I wanted to be far from any people, removed from all their sounds, and free to wander in the open country as I wrote.

I found the right house, at the edge of a cliff overlooking the sea, 400 feet above the waves. The property included twenty-five acres of forest land. For six months I strolled along the paths with a notebook, writing as I went. Jane would arrive at noon with the maids, who got to work in the kitchen and prepared lunch. Often at night Brion Gysin came, bringing his two cooks, Salah and Targuisti, with him. Then we would have a Moroccan feast: *harira, qotbaine,* and *tajine.* There were not many visitors that summer. Susan Sontag put in a brief appearance. Tennessee came, but he was feeling so low that not even Tangier could touch him, and he left again before two weeks had passed. Once more Larbi was with me as houseboy. He was growing increasingly nervous about the possible official reactions to the French edition of his book, which Gallimard was publishing shortly. His anxiety, continually expressed, communicated itself to me, and I too began to think it would be better if he were out of the way. I got him a visa for the United States; he left with Bill Burroughs on the *Independence,* and has never returned to Morocco. In mid-November when I moved back into Tangier I had finished *Up Above the World.*

In the spring Jane and I went to the United States. At one

point I stayed with John Goodwin in Santa Fe. Twenty-five years had passed since I had last seen the town, but the changes were still only in degree and had not yet become qualitative. The rest of the country now seemed far ahead in the race toward destruction; Santa Fe was the least objectionable city in the United States. I went to Florida. My father's mobility had been severely reduced. He found it hard to get about, even with a cane. I took him walking every day. He had made arrangements to be cremated, he said. I asked him why he spoke of it, and he let the subject drop.

When we got back to Tangier in June, I began to think seriously about an offer from Little, Brown to write a portrait of Cairo as a volume in a projected series of books on cities. The prospect of going to live in Cairo for a year was not seductive, and the more seriously I thought about the idea, the less enthusiasm I felt. I sent off a series of letters suggesting some cities which would be easier to live in, such as Marrakech, Hong Kong, and Lisbon. But for various reasons, none of these was acceptable. Still I could not bring myself to agree to Cairo. As a last hope, and one of whose absurdity I was aware, I suggested Bangkok, where I had never been and about which I knew nothing. When Harry Sions answered: Fine, I was both delighted and taken aback. I had not expected agreement, and was not ready to face making a decision. There was no question of leaving Jane in Morocco by herself in her present highly nervous state. We worked out a schedule, however: she and I would go the following summer to New York. There I would put her on a train for Florida and proceed via ship to Thailand. To my way of thinking, planes are strictly for businessmen; those who enjoy travel manage to find some other means of transportation.

Jane's novel *Two Serious Ladies* finally had been republished, after being unobtainable for more than twenty years. Peter Owen's London edition had met with considerable critical success, and the book had since been published in five other languages. Now Owen asked for a collection of her stories. Jane, as always highly ambivalent about the desirability of being published at all, announced with satisfaction that she had no copies of the stories. But I had kept copies hidden away for just such a contingency. Then she claimed that there were not enough of them to make a volume. I scratched around and unearthed the tear sheets of an old *Mademoiselle* article which she had done many years before, insisting that she rewrite it, making it fiction. In the end the material filled a small book, and the book was published under the title *Plain Pleasures.*

Daily life in Tangier then, while it did not provide the solitude and unlimited leisure needed for fiction writing, left me enough work periods of short duration so that I could busy myself with translating. I had been working during the winter on an English version of a book-length story which I had taped in Moghrebi Arabic, this one an invention by Mohammed Mrabet.

It was May. The year was moving along into summer, and I was about to set out alone to live in Bangkok. I waited to feel the spark of pleasure which I thought should accompany the prospect, but it did not appear.

XVIII

In the nine years during which I had had a headquarters at the Inmueble Itesa I had grown fond of the place. There was no particular reason to like it, save that it was visually neutral, and the bedrooms had a wide view of the leafier quarters of Tangier, with thousands of houses in the distance and a strip of sea. But I also liked the nights. Sometimes there were the cries of nearby frogs and owls, and sometimes there were only crickets and the sporadic distant barking of dogs. The early-morning call to prayer from a series of distant mosques reached me in my bed an hour before dawn, when everything is at its quietest. From my windows I could make fine recordings of wedding drums and rhaitas in the village of Ain Hayani below.

After years of patient training Jane had made excellent cooks out of both Cherifa and Aicha. Although she could not work in the kitchen as she had before, we continued to have magnificent dinners. At times during this period Jane's only pleasure was that of eating; such excursions into gourmandise were always followed by sudden self-imposed fasting. Then she would grow excessively thin very quickly, and her friends would insist that she start again to eat. I realized that I should miss our evening meals by the fireplace and the hour of stretching out on the cushions afterward. Now that the time to leave approached, it was suddenly clear that all these things were of great importance to me, and that no matter what sort of life I found for myself in Bangkok, I would be very sad to have left Tangier.

A telegram arrived in June, saying that Mother had suffered a heart attack and was in a coma. She never recovered consciousness. The following week I received word that Daddy also had died. Jane and I already had a cabin booked on the *Independence* for the first of July. There was no need to change it.

For some reason the death of my parents diminished my unwillingness to leave Tangier; very likely the shock made itself felt by leaving me in a state of indifference. I can only deduce that I felt profoundly guilty for having excised them from my life.

Having used the Wilhelmsen Line once before and been favorably impressed, I booked passage on the *Tarantel*, scheduled to leave New York in July. Farrar, Straus and Giroux were about to publish a volume containing Jane's complete works, with an introduction by Truman Capote. On our arrival in New York they took Jane over completely, arranging her social schedule and even seeing that she got her train reservations for Florida.

The last day before I was to board the *Tarantel* I paid a visit to my editor at Simon and Schuster, who loaded me down with books for my journey. Fortunately the ship turned out to be a good one, for I had to spend more than seven weeks on it, including two- and three-day stopovers at Los Angeles, San Francisco, and Hong Kong, as well as an unappreciated eight-day wait in Manila harbor during a typhoon.

Bangkok was not the verdant and hushed city of canals and temples I had expected. The place had lost so much of its original Thai flavor that what little was left seemed perverse and absurd in the midst of so much determined Westernizing. Foreign residents were in agreement that it had been feasible as a place to live in until the arrival of the American GI. Then it had broken down. By the time I reached it in the autumn of 1966 it was hopelessly overpopulated and its thoroughfares were choked with motorized traffic. Everywhere the waterways were being filled in; those that were left had become putrid and noisome, so that the process was having to be carried ahead with increasing rapidity. My initial reaction to the city was one of severe disappointment.

I had received a letter from Jane in Hong Kong, but in Bangkok I got nothing at all. I continued to write her at her mother's address. She had begged me for months to take her along with me. I had steadfastly refused, knowing that the climate was not for her and that having her with me would create a situation in which work would become difficult. I assumed that now she was in a sulky mood and was punishing me for having gone off by myself. Suddenly a letter came from her, posted in Tangier. She had felt an urge to return and had shortened her stay in the United States by several months. However, now that she was there, she said, she could not understand why she had made the decision. She had got herself into precisely the situation that we had so carefully planned to avoid. No more letters came from her. I continued to write each week, keeping her informed about my life and trying to persuade her to reply. Eventually I began to send letters to friends in Tangier, to inquire where she was. The answers were definite enough as to her presence there, but very vague about why she was not communicating with me.

Most of Bangkok looked like the back streets of the nethermost Bronx relocated in a Florida swamp. Getting from one side of the city to the other was not an easy task. The complications and the danger involved in crossing a street, the length of time it took to find a taxi, the great distances within the city, which made it impossible to go on foot, the heavy heat and the motor fumes in the air—all these were cogent reasons for going out as seldom as possible. I stayed in my hotel room reading, writing and recording Thai music from the radio. Surprisingly enough, there was a good deal of traditional Thai music being broadcast every day.

Oliver Evans, whom I had first met in Tangier, was in Bangkok, teaching at Chulalongkorn University. When I arrived he already had made firm friendships with several Buddhist monks, and together we went to visit them at their wats. I understood why Oliver enjoyed their company. Despite the serious language barrier—for Oliver was just starting Thai lessons and I knew not a word, and the monks' English was very limited—they provided our only possibility for intelligent conversation in Bangkok. The ceremony involved in being with them in their wat quarters demanded the same patience it takes to visit a bourgeois Moroccan family at home. As with the Moroccans, their reckonings of time were made in units of much longer duration than ours. One never does anything for an hour or two; one does it for half the day or perhaps the entire day. The monks sat on the floor with their shaved scalps and eyebrows, pulling their yellow robes around their legs, smiling because they could not understand why I left in order to get to the embassy for my mail before it shut. "You wish to go?" they would ask, surprised. "No, but I must." Then they would smile more widely, to show civility in the face of what to them was clearly a falsehood.

I went with Oliver and a group of the monks on a pilgrimage to Ayudhaya, and in return they took us on a really extraordinary journey by boat through the mangrove forests south of Bangkok to a shrine named Oparit, lost in the jungle.

When I had got to a certain point in my structuring of the book, I changed my headquarters to Chiengmai, a city which still had trees to give shade to its streets and innumerable temples, both ruined and in use. At that time, in contrast with Bangkok's several hundred massage parlors, Chiengmai had only two; these were dependent for their patronage upon the few American GI's who came on rest and recreation trips from the war in Vietnam. The massage parlors were first on the list of attractions chanted by the rickshaw men waiting in line in the garden whenever I went out of the hotel. After that came opium, of which there were tons stored in warehouses all over the city. (It is estimated that 75 percent of the world's commercial raw opium passes through Chiengmai.)

I had a stereo tape recorder with me, which I consistently set up outside temples where chanting or music was in progress. In addition there was a musical phenomenon in Chiengmai very similar to one which had existed in Fez forty years ago when I first arrived there. This was a tradition according to which the members of the leisure class took it upon themselves to perpetuate an ancient musical form. In Fez friends got together after dinner and performed a *misane* of Andaluz music; in Chiengmai they formed little orchestras and sat in their houses, in a circle on the floor, playing the music which dated from the time seven centuries ago when their city was the capital of the Thais. Naturally I made a point of trying to tape whatever of such music I could get. We had no language in common, but they were hospitable and cooperative, and I was able to make many good recordings. I liked the Thais; they seemed pragmatic and intelligent and, although quick to take offense, most expert at hiding their feelings. I did not particularly like living in Thailand, however. The principal reason was that the authorities steadfastly refused to grant me a visa of more than fifteen days' duration. Never being certain of more than a two-week sojourn ahead made me uneasy. Several times in Chiengmai I had to hire a car and be driven northward toward the Burmese border, to an immigration office near Ban Chiang Dao, where I showed my passport and got a new stamp put in it.

At Christmastime I had a letter from Joseph McPhillips in Tangier asking me to transform my short story "The Garden" into a play for him. I replied: I'm in the middle of my book on Bangkok and can't even consider it. Then I began to imagine how I might have built the play if I had had the time to do it. This was a dangerous train of thought; soon after embarking on it, I wrote another letter to Joe in which I started out by musing on the impossibility of conceiving such a play and ended by sketching a first scene. In this way I soon found myself writing the play. I posted Joe one or two letters each day, and they constituted the so-called script. Surprisingly, they all found their way safely from Chiengmai to Tangier.

A letter from Jane's doctor in Tangier informed me that Jane was suffering from intestinal adhesions. She also suggested that my presence was needed. Since I was still gathering documentation necessary for the writing of the book, I wanted to stay on in Thailand for as long as the authorities would allow me, but it was not going to be possible.

I took the overnight train down to Bangkok to pay for my passage westward. It was a Danish ship, the *Simba*, bound for Singapore, Port Swettenham, Penang, and Genoa.

It was good to be sailing down the Gulf of Siam in the breeze, leaving behind the smog and squalor of Bangkok. I suspected that I had failed in my project, that I would not be able to finish the book with the incomplete documentation I had, but if that turned out to be true, there was no help for it.

The ship stayed only one day in Penang. The island did not seem to have changed much in the twelve years that had elapsed since I had seen it, save that Waterfall Gardens, George Town's fine public park, was not in the same verdant state in which the British had left it. I got to Tangier in March, hoping that Jane was merely in a surly mood because I had refused to take her along with me. The trouble was far more serious, however. She was in a deep depression which made both sleeping and eating next to impossible. The doctor's opinion was that she needed to be hospitalized, but on the chance that my presence might possibly cause some change, we decided to wait a month or so and see if any improvement appeared. After six weeks had passed, I reluctantly agreed to go to Spain and look for a hospital that would accept her as a patient. I found a clinic in Málaga, and after arranging with the mother superior and the doctor in charge, I went back to Tangier to get Jane. She did not agree about needing hospitalization, but she went anyway, I suppose out of desperation. Each time I visited her she begged to return to Tangier. I did not bring her back, however, until early August.

Two days after we arrived in Tangier a photographer and a writer from *Life* magazine came to do a story on us. For a week and a half they stayed with us like our shadows—in the house, in the street, at the beach, and at whatever social engagements we had made. At one party given by John Hopkins, there was a group of Jilala musicians to entertain the guests. To Europeans, the music of the Jilala is Moroccan folk music being played on long, low-pitched transversal flutes and large flat hand drums. To a member of the cult, however, it is a sequence of explicit choreographic instructions, all of which are designed to bring about a state of trance, or possession. Thus it was that Mohammed Mrabet, whom John had innocently invited to the dinner party, began to dance along with other guests. But being a Jilali, his participation soon passed from casual to compulsive, and before long he was in a deep trance. The musicians, far from being disposed to interfere, were delighted to have found an adept among the guests. Still the rest of us had not noticed what was going on at the far end of the terrace. Suddenly there was a crash, and an explosion of burning embers showered over the dancers. I stood up. Mrabet had a long curved knife in his hand. John also saw him, and he and three other men tackled him. In the melee on the floor among the glowing coals, John managed to get his knee dislocated and spent the next week in bed. As for Mrabet, the psychic shock of being interrupted in his ritual was such that it took him about an hour to recover consciousness and begin once more to function. It is doubtful that he would have returned to his normal state without the aid of the musicians, who consistently played the necessary music for him until he was awake and able to speak. It seemed unthinkable that anyone should have dared to interfere with a Moslem in the state of trance. I remembered what had happened to Temsamany's grandmother, who had begun to walk in her sleep across the countryside toward the distant sound of Jilala music. When it stopped, she had fallen where she stood and lain there all night. And when they found her, although she had been lying over an anthill and was covered with ant stings, she was still asleep and could not be wakened. The family had to find the same group of musicians and take them to the house to play. It was only after a specific program had been gone through that the old lady recovered consciousness. The evening of the party, after Mrabet was himself, Jane thought that the experience might have unfitted him for driving us home. But he merely said what all people say who have just returned from a trance state: "My body has no weight. I feel wonderful." The *Life* people were surprised to learn that what they had just been prevented from seeing, the ceremony of self-laceration, was the normal concomitant, and indeed the sole purpose, of the music they had been hearing all evening.

I had been working hard in the hope of being able to write the Bangkok book with the material I had already noted and written. Finally, rather than allow myself to get into a state of unhappiness over it, I wrote to Little, Brown saying I would not be able to provide them with the manuscript. One day shortly after this Alec Waugh was at my house for drinks. In the course of our conversation we reached the subject of the abandoned book, and I asked him why he didn't take on the assignment. The idea appealed to him. As a result, he too went off to Thailand to write a book for Little, Brown, the difference being that his was completed and published.

Mrabet's first book *Love with a Few Hairs* had appeared in both New York and London, where BBC produced it on television. He was encouraged by this to record a second, a longer novel called *The Lemon*. I worked at its translation all the following winter and spring. Jane's health did not remain strong. In January I went with her back to the hospital in Málaga, and there she stayed until summer. Meanwhile, Mrabet recorded a series of stories which I translated when I had the leisure, and Lawrence Ferlinghetti published the collection at City Lights under the title *M'hashish*.

During the sixties several colleges in different parts of the United States had written me, offering one-year visiting professorships. With my past sins recorded and on file, it seemed a useless thing to consider, even if I had been interested. And indeed, at one point when I had written in answer to a wire from a college in Florida, because the place was not too far from where my parents lived, and it would have given them great pleasure to have me there, the college had quickly written back that it was not going to be possible, after all. When Oliver Evans suggested such a stint at San Fernando Valley State College, to begin in the autumn of 1968, even though it was tempting—since Jane's doctor said she would be hospitalized for a good many months more—it seemed scarcely worthwhile considering. Nevertheless, for some unexplained reason they agreed to have me there and to allow me to decide at the end of one semester whether I wanted to stay on for another.

And so I went off to California and taught Advanced Narrative Writing and the Modern European Novel. The sojourn was not too different from what I had imagined it would be, save that the people were better and the circumstances of their lives far worse. Too many elements of the long-burgeoning nightmare were now reaching full bloom in the vicinity of Los Angeles. When the four months were up, I hurried back home to Tangier, stopping in Florida to sell the house and everything in it but the silver.

I brought Jane back from Spain, in considerably worse health than the last time I had seen her, and installed her in the lower apartment with a nurse and a maid. But Jane was used to living in a hospital, and she needed the kind of care she was accustomed to getting there. The doctors had warned me that my experiment was doomed to failure; I tried it anyway. When she got alarmingly thin, I took her back to Spain. There in the familiar atmosphere of the hospital she quickly put on weight.

I did not choose to live in Tangier permanently; it happened. My visit was meant to be of short duration; after that I would move on, and keep moving onward indefinitely. I grew lazy and put off departure. Then a day came when I realized with a shock that not only did the world have many more people in it than it had had only a short time before, but also that the hotels were less good, travel less comfortable, and places in general much less beautiful. After that when I went somewhere else I immediately longed to be back in Tangier. Thus if I am here now, it is only because I was still here when I realized to what an extent the world had worsened, and that I no longer wanted to travel. In defense of the city I can say that so far it has been touched by fewer of the negative aspects of contemporary civilization than most cities of its size. More important than that, I relish the idea that in the night, all around me in my sleep, sorcery is burrowing its invisible tunnels in every direction, from thousands of senders to thousands of unsuspecting recipients. Spells are being cast, poison is running its course; souls are being dispossessed of parasitic pseudo-consciousnesses that lurk in the unguarded recesses of the mind.

There is drumming out there most nights. It never awakens me; I hear the drums and incorporate them into my dream, like the nightly cries of the muezzins. Even if in the dream I am in New York, the first *Allah akbar!* effaces the backdrop and carries whatever comes next to North Africa, and the dream goes on.

Now, since I started to write this book, I stay in Tangier for months on end, choosing from among the vast number of fragments of memories unearthed those which can serve my purpose. The fragments are being used to reconstruct, piece by piece, a sequential skeleton, taking care not to force in any part that does not fit. As I see it, this precaution implies making the effort to reserve judgment and the resolve to give a minimum importance to personal attitudes. Writing an autobiography is an ungratifying occupation at best. It is a sort of journalism, in which the report, rather than being an eyewitness account of the event, is instead only a memory of the last time it was recalled. Borges illustrates the situation with the story of his father's attempt to show him the untrustworthiness of memory; he lays a coin on the table and calls it the image itself. He puts a coin on top of the first one and calls that the first memory of the image. The next coin is the memory of that memory, and so on. Since this state of affairs is axiomatic, it follows that writing an autobiography is not the kind of work one would expect most writers to enjoy doing. And it is clear that telling what happened does not necessarily make a good story. In my tale, for instance, there are no dramatic victories because there was no struggle. I hung on and waited. It seems to me that this must be what most people do; the occasions when there is the possibility of doing more than that are becoming rare indeed.

The Moroccans claim that full participation in life demands the regular contemplation of death. I agree without reserve. Unfortunately I am unable to conceive of my own death without setting it in the far more terrible *mise en scène* of old age. There I am without teeth, unable to move, wholly dependent upon someone whom I pay to take care of me and who at any moment may go out of the room and never return. Of course this is not at all what the Moroccans mean by the contemplation of death; they would consider my imaginings a particularly contemptible form of fear. One culture's therapy is another culture's torture.

" 'Good-bye,' says the dying man to the mirror they hold in front of him. 'We won't be seeing each other any more.' " When I quoted Valéry's epigram in *The Sheltering Sky*, it seemed a poignant bit of fantasy. Now, because I no longer imagine myself as an onlooker at the scene, but instead as the principal protagonist, it strikes me as repugnant. To make it right, the dying man would have to add two words to his little farewell, and they are: "Thank God!"

INDEX

INDEX

Wilkes, Sylvia Astor, 57, 58
Williams, Colonel Charles, 170, 171, 174, 175, 177, 178
Williams, Tennessee, 229, 256, 288, 289, 290, 321, 322, 323, 332, 351, 352, 353, 355
Williams, William Carlos, 104, 338
Wilson, Angus, 338
Windham, Donald, 256
Winewisser, August, 11, 12, 13, 15, 25
Winewisser, Mrs. August "Gramma", 11, 12, 13, 15, 26
Winewisser, Emma, 12, 31, 32, 40, 59, 61, 168
Winewisser, Fanny, 12
Winewisser, Margery, 56

Winewisser, Rena (Mrs. Claude Bowles), 9, 10, 12, 15, 16, 18, 20, 22, 24, 25, 26, 27, 332, 358
Winewisser, Ulla, 11, 12, 30
"Without Stopping," 97
Wood, Audrey, 289
Wright, Richard, 233

Yacoubi, Ahmed, 280, 286, 293, 308, 309, 310, 311, 312, 313, 314, 315, 318, 319, 320, 324, 326, 327, 329, 331, 333
Yallah, 330
Yankee Clipper, 192, 193, 204, 205
Yerma, 303, 305, 320, 332, 340